THE FIGHTING SPIRIT

LOU HOLTZ

with **JOHN HEISLER**

THE FIGHTING SPIRIT

A CHAMPIONSHIP SEASON AT

NOTRE DAME

POCKET BOOKS

New York   London   Toronto   Sydney   Tokyo

POCKET BOOKS, a division of Simon & Schuster Inc
1230 Avenue of the Americas, New York, NY 10020

ISBN: 0-671-67673-3

First Pocket Books hardcover printing September 1989

10 9 8 7 6 5 4 3 2 1

To the Notre Dame family—
past, present, and future

ACKNOWLEDGMENTS

The idea for this book didn't come as an afterthought just because Notre Dame won the national championship in 1988. It was conceived in March 1988, when I was approached about the chances of chronicling a year in the life of the football coach at Notre Dame. I was hesitant to do so and only agreed to after consulting the administration of Notre Dame. This book couldn't have come to fruition without the help and encouragement of so many people:

To the Holtz family—Beth, Luanne, Skip, Kevin, and Liz. Being coach of the national champs is not nearly as satisfying as being husband and father.

To Father Ted Hesburgh and Father Ned Joyce, for never compromising the spiritual, academic, and athletic values of Notre Dame. The commitment to excellence in academics and athletics is rarely found in one university. Without their belief in me, I wouldn't be at Notre Dame.

To Gene Corrigan, for his belief in me and for his support. He laid the groundwork for this past season.

To Father Ed "Monk" Malloy and Father Bill Beauchamp. They gave me advice, they answered my questions, they let me do what I was hired to do—coach.

To Dick Rosenthal, for his friendship, his counseling, his professionalism. Only Notre Dame could replace a great athletic director like Gene Corrigan with another great one like Dick. He is as talented an individual as I have known and a great person to work with.

ACKNOWLEDGMENTS

To all our assistant coaches. May they someday have the privilege of working with a group of assistants as talented, cooperative, and productive as they have been.

To George Kelly, Jan Blazi, and the secretaries. Without them there would be no book.

To the Notre Dame fans, for their undying support. Without their belief, Notre Dame wouldn't be the same.

To the '88 players. You wanted to win, and you did. I believe your attitude would have enabled you to succeed regardless of who coached you.

To Mike Kovaleski, Steve Beuerlein, Byron Spruell, Chuck Lanza, Tim Brown, and the rest of the seniors from the '86 and '87 teams. You started the building process by your attitude and performance.

To Jack Romanos and Irwyn Applebaum at Pocket Books, for their constant, enthusiastic support.

To Paul McCarthy, for his patience, prodding, and professionalism in editing this work.

CONTENTS

CONTENTS

FOREWORD

In the summer of 1977 I was standing at the registration table of the Gerry Ford Invitational Golf Tournament in Vail, Colorado. A man in line behind me tapped me on the shoulder and said, "Hi, I'm Lou Holtz." Ten years later our lives were to become more entwined.

Rev. E. William Beauchamp, Notre Dame's executive vice president, suggested I talk to Lou Holtz when I was discussing the possibilities of becoming the athletic director at Notre Dame. After a thirty-year career in banking, and never having been involved in athletic administration, I told Lou I was concerned about my lack of experience. He said, "You ought to take the job, we'll have a heck of a lot of fun." As always, he made good on his promise . . . in spades.

Lou Holtz is first and foremost a teacher. He is a man of principle and has lived his life in complete harmony with his values. Never have a person's ideals meshed so completely with an institution's philosophy than have Holtz's and Notre Dame's. He is the consummate Notre Dame man.

Notre Dame's 1988 football success was forecast in two events. The first of these occurred after the Cotton Bowl loss to Texas A&M. I sat alone with Lou in the coaches' room at the Cotton Bowl. Lou, who is a great competitor and hates to lose, sat for a few moments in silence. Then he expressed regrets about the Cotton Bowl loss. It was a one-sentence comment. Although feeling low, he talked for the next half-hour about what our team would need to do to get better next year. The process started the very next morning with individual meetings with each of the assistant coaches. Lou had the discipline to realize nothing could be said or done to change the Cotton Bowl score. He recognized the future demanded the best of his experience, energy, and coaching genius. He would give Notre Dame players nothing less than the best that was in him.

Lou has been amazingly accurate in assessing our team's strengths and weaknesses in his annual report, and this offered the second forecast for the '88 season. He commented, "You can't win on the road unless you play great defense. The national syndications have predicted we had a good recruiting year. We will have to wait to see if that is true. We believe if a young man does not have a good personality, he will not do well at Notre Dame, and, further, he must want to come here. If we get this kind of athlete, we'll have overachievers, and without our share of overachievers, we can't win at Notre Dame. Players will have to switch positions, we will have to stay healthy and take advantage of breaks. The schedule is exceptionally difficult, but we can't do anything about that. We are going to have to have an outstanding team to compete in light of this schedule and will just have to play one game at a time. If we get better as the season progresses, we'll have a chance."

Ten games later we were undefeated, ranked number one, and about to play USC. We were still the underdogs. The writers favored USC at home and probably rightly so. The morning of the game, at 6:00 A.M., I visited with Lou. He was very peaceful and said, "I don't know who will win, but I am confident we will play very well today." It proved to be another accurate call.

Our coaches felt the highest-ranked opponent we could hope to play in a post-season bowl game would be West Virginia. They were a team that had everything. If we received and accepted a Fiesta Bowl bid, we would have a chance to climb yet another mountain.

During the week preceding the game, we began to wonder if we had bitten off more than we should have. We'd come so far against so many tough teams; could we do it again? Lou sensed this doubt, and the day before the game, he called the team together after a brief workout at Sun Devil Stadium in Tempe. He encouraged our players to get a good night's sleep and to do their best. Almost as an afterthought, he said, "One more thing. After we win tomorrow, tradition has it that you will have to carry me off the field. We need to practice that."

Lou is a very humble man, and the comment seemed out of character. When no one moved, he said, "I'm serious," and then suggested that he had a better idea. He assigned underclassmen to carry the seniors off the field because "these overachievers brought us to the party." Lou Holtz didn't want to play a game with anyone having doubts about the outcome. After practice no one did.

FOREWORD

This is a book about a winning experience. Winning at Notre Dame is not a braggodocian exercise. We don't want to win so we can say we're better than you. If that's all there is to it, we would soon determine that we paid too high a price for a hollow thrill. Winning at Notre Dame is an educational experience and starts when a group of young people adopt a common goal, make a total commitment with their coaches, pay the price of rigorous training, and find a way to win. This is why the winning spirit endures at the university and losing is tolerable and can be accepted with honor.

This is why Lou Holtz is the Notre Dame coach.

Enjoy the book.

Dick Rosenthal
Athletic Director
University of Notre Dame
June 1989

THE FIGHTING SPIRIT

1

THE COTTON BOWL LOSS:
AN END AND A BEGINNING

As I walked off the field at the 1988 Cotton Bowl in Dallas, the biting, bitter wind matched the taste in my mouth.

I caught a brief glimpse of the scoreboard as I headed for the tunnel. It read 35–10 in favor of Texas A&M. I couldn't imagine a more disappointing loss in a bowl game.

We had been 8–1 at one point in 1987, but losing our last three games ruined the entire year. Even after eighteen years as a head coach, I do not handle losing well. I absolutely *hate* to lose, and I couldn't remember when I had felt worse.

During my years as head coach at the University of Arkansas, we won a portion of the Southwest Conference championship in 1979. But because of the way the conference determines who goes to the Cotton Bowl, we never had the opportunity to come to Dallas. I've taken football teams to virtually every major bowl, including the Rose Bowl when I was an assistant at Ohio State. The Cotton Bowl was the only one left. Consequently, I had really looked forward to the Cotton Bowl on a personal level.

We had hoped for a happy homecoming for Tim Brown, our Heisman Trophy winner, who was from Dallas. We got off to a 10–0 lead and had a chance to extend it. But an interception in the end zone turned things around, and our defense had trouble stopping them after that. We came out throwing the ball fairly well, but we never really did get our ground game established, and that always seemed to be a bad sign for our team. This final loss was a discouraging way to end the year.

I didn't know what to say to the team. There wasn't much. I told the

1

players they needed to handle success and adversity the same way. All they could do was ask themselves the question, "What are we going to do now?" I thanked the seniors and sent the team on its way.

That night was a long one, as they always are when I'm replaying a loss in my mind. The only thing that got me through the night was a quotation from the Bible, "This too shall pass." The sun did rise the next morning as my wife predicted and we got up early, said goodbye to various friends and relatives who had come to Dallas to watch the game—including my uncle, Lou Tychonievich. Then we flew straight to Japan, where I was going to coach the following weekend in the Japan Bowl all-star game. I wasn't very excited about the Japan Bowl after what had happened to us in Dallas. At least I didn't have to be concerned about the time the trip would take, because the national coaches convention was going on and there was a moratorium on recruiting. So I didn't feel I was jeopardizing the University of Notre Dame's chances of winning in the future.

I'd had a chance to visit with Dick Rosenthal, our athletic director at Notre Dame, just prior to leaving for Japan. We decided we would get together when I got back and decide what we had to do to move the program forward.

The eighteen-hour flight was long and tedious, but I spent most of the time analyzing where we had gone wrong the last three games. I thought I had a good feeling for what our problems were, but I didn't want to make rash decisions.

We had lost our last three games on the road. If you're ever going to be successful on the road, you've got to be outstanding on defense. We certainly didn't qualify in that respect after giving up 21 points to Penn State, 24 to Miami, and 35 to Texas A&M. When you take your equipment, you'd better pack your defense, your discipline, and your kicking game, or you aren't going to have a chance to win on the road.

As I went over each of the athletes on our football team, I asked three questions about them: One, could I trust them? Two, were they committed to excellence? Three, did they care about their teammates and the future of Notre Dame? I tried to make sure our coaches could answer yes to these three questions when they asked them about every member of our team. It was also imperative that our players felt they could trust our coaches, know our coaches were committed to excellence and cared about the players. When things go wrong, there's always a tendency to point a finger at everybody else. I felt the first person I had to look at was myself, and I had to think about some of the changes I needed to make.

I've always been very involved in coaching, and I enjoy it thoroughly. Losing makes me work all the harder to keep from losing the next time.

There were a lot of good things about our football program, and I did not want to overlook them. Over the season we made progress in a lot of areas, but there still were some things we needed to improve. Quickness was one area we talked about from the very beginning. That's an area you don't change overnight, because recruiting plays a key part in it.

The quickest way to improve team speed is to take a committed athlete whose speed is marginal at one position and move him to a position where his speed can be an asset. For example, Andy Heck's speed is marginal at tight end, but it's much greater at tackle. We accomplished the same thing by moving Frank Stams from fullback to defensive end. Both those players finished their careers as all-Americans in 1988.

Another area that was improving, but wasn't there yet was our complete commitment to excellence at Notre Dame.

Ironically, I was head coach of one team in the Japan Bowl, and Jackie Sherrill of Texas A&M was head coach of the other, just as we had been in Dallas the week before. Galen Hall of Florida and Vince Dooley of Georgia also worked with me. I brought my wife Beth and three of our children—Liz, who's a freshman at Notre Dame; Kevin, who'll be a senior finishing up at Notre Dame next fall; and Skip, who's a graduate assistant at Florida State. I felt it would be a good opportunity for us to spend a little bit of time together as a family, because you sure don't get it during the season.

Being around the Japan Bowl was a great experience for Skip, who wants to coach. When he first approached me with the idea of being a coach, I said, "Have you told your mother yet?" He said, "No." Then I said, "Please make sure she's unarmed when you do. Because she is apt to shoot you. We didn't send you to Notre Dame to be a coach but it's your life to spend as you desire."

We lost the all-star game, which was disappointing. Although when it comes down to it, the results don't mean much. I'll never forget when I was at North Carolina State, coaching in one of the post-season all-star games when John McKay of USC was the opposing coach. We lost the game, and I took it hard. John came up to me at a party after the game and said, "Lou, you're going back to your alums and I'm going back to mine. They're all going to ask the same question—'Coach, where have you been the last week or so? I haven't seen you around.'" In other words, not many people remember who won an all-star game.

But I couldn't forget the Cotton Bowl. That was a loss that couldn't be dismissed so easily.

By the time I got back to South Bend we were just two days away from the start of classes for the second semester. I spent a lot of time preparing for our first squad meeting on January 18.

Pat Eilers, senior flanker

We had a meeting at four o'clock on the first day of classes in January, once we were back in school after the Cotton Bowl. Coach Holtz gave us a big speech on how our new mission was to strive for perfection, that we would accept nothing less, and that Notre Dame deserved nothing less than perfection. That was after we had lost to Penn State, Miami, and Texas A&M. We kind of fell apart at the end of the season.

I think that set the tone for the entire road to the national champion-ship, because we worked our butts off that winter during conditioning. Those six weeks were probably the most challenging winter-conditioning period we've ever had. Then we worked our butts off during spring ball, and almost everybody stayed here and kept working during the summer. But when I think about the whole season, I think that meeting was the start of it, the first chapter.

What I've learned from Coach Holtz is that you compete against yourself. You don't compete against other teams, necessarily. You're out there competing against yourself. Make what you're competing against be perfection and try to be the best you can, instead of just going out and trying to beat another team. Just go out and play your game and do what you can to the best of your ability. Then everything will take care of itself. When you play above yourself and try to do more than you're capable of doing, that's when you start losing, when you slide. I think if there's anything I learned from Coach Holtz this season, that would be it.

He referred back to that meeting, too. He would talk about it after practice—"Remember how we said in January that our goal was going to be perfection? I'm still not going to accept anything less." I remember another thing he did in that meeting. He said, "Who in here wants to be great? If you want to be great, stand up." The entire room stood up. So for the remainder of the year, he would bring that up. He would say, "You guys told me you wanted to be great. I'm only doing what you guys wanted to do." It's something we joke about if we're out there working hard in practice or in the weight room, if you're tired from a test and you still have to lift. You say, "Well, you wanted to be great, so . . ." We kind of get on each other about that.

Coach Holtz has a way of doing things like that to make us more self-motivated, instead of him trying to motivate us.

We explained to the squad that what was over was over. But, once

4

again, the big question remains: What are we going to do now? Are we going to sit around and wallow in self-pity? Are we going to say, "Well, we came close." Or are we going to reach down a little further?

Maybe we wouldn't be a particularly talented football team in 1988, at least on paper. But we certainly had enough talent to win.

The '88 squad would be an exceptionally young one, and we would have to replace Tim Brown's leadership and that of our captains, Chuck Lanza and Byron Spruell, as well as the veteran offensive line. We would not have a very strong senior class, as far as numbers or talent. But if they were great leaders, they could be part of one of the most important senior classes at Notre Dame in a long time.

We talked about where we wanted to go, and more importantly, how we were going to get there. I told the players, "The progress you make during the winter program and spring practice will decide the role you play in the fall. We might have to play freshmen in the fall, but if we do, it will be because the upperclassmen don't take advantage of the opportunity afforded them in spring practice."

We didn't try to be emotional. We didn't try to get them all fired up. We didn't try to make it seem like we were really going to come back. We just put it to them that it was a question of which direction they were going to take. We weren't worried about their bouncing back, because young people always seem to bounce back a lot higher and stronger than older people do. I'm certainly starting to fall in the latter classification, as far as bouncing back is concerned. We knew if the football players didn't respond to a basic challenge like that, then we would have to look for some other people.

But we were pleased with the attitude our players developed as the weeks went by. Scott Raridon, our strength and conditioning coordinator, ran as fine a winter program as I've seen, to make our athletes improve themselves between the bowl game and spring practice. In our winter program we work in the weight room for three days and then the other two days a week, we do agility drills in shorts at six different stations. The drills only take an hour, but they're very demanding. You can tell a lot about a team during the winter program. The players can go through the motions or they can really make an effort to get better.

If they have a strong desire to be outstanding players and be part of a great team, they're going to do two things. One, they're going to provide great leadership and put peer pressure on each other to work exceptionally hard. Two, they'll demand that a great effort be made by each and every individual to get better.

I told them, "Effort is a great yardstick, because so many times you can't see yourself getting quicker from one day to the next. But if you have a great commitment, you'll approach everything in the best manner possible."

Flash Gordon, senior defensive end

When Coach Holtz first arrived at Notre Dame, Coach Faust had just given his last speech to the team. Coach Holtz walked in, and everyone was pretty much slumped in his seat, not really paying much attention. When he walked up to the stage, the first thing he said was "I want everybody sitting up straight. I want everybody listening and looking me straight in the eye."

Right then and there everybody knew Coach Holtz meant business. That respect started to build every week because he demanded so much. He wanted to command respect and earn that respect from his individual players. He did that, and that's the most important thing he has done with this team—just getting it to be more disciplined and to have more respect toward coaches and toward each other.

After a month on the road recruiting, I met with our team again on February 10 to update them. Even though we were six weeks from the start of spring practice, we wanted this meeting to set the tone. Recruiting was finished, and now all our attention was focused on getting this team prepared for 1988.

I felt so strongly about what I said in the meeting and wanted the squad to retain a greater percentage of it than normal that I sent them a letter which summarized my comments.

Here's what I told them:

"Three weeks ago, when I set up this meeting, I knew we would have a lot to talk about, and I really looked forward to this meeting.

"First of all, I want to congratulate you on your success in the winter program and in the weight room. The things I hear are outstanding, and when I have been there, I have been impressed. Unfortunately, not everybody falls into this category. However, the overwhelming majority of you do, and for that I congratulate you on your commitment to greatness.

"There are going to be some changes, but I can assure you they are going to be positive changes. I want you to pay attention to this—we are going to practice strict loyalty to one another. We are going to be loyal to the University of Notre Dame, the administration, coaches, and team-mates. We are not going to make a negative comment about anybody on this football team, unless it is said in my office.

6

"We are not going to criticize another player. If I hear a guy make a negative comment during the course of a football game, you're going to the locker room. We cannot be a good, close-knit football team without showing respect and concern for one another. This loyalty will extend to coaches as well. You aren't going to complain and moan about them; you aren't going to talk among yourselves. By the same token, the coaches aren't going to say a negative thing about you. The coaches aren't going to deride you, ridicule you, or question your courage. The coaches will show you how to become the best football players possible. They will tell you what you are doing wrong and in what areas you need to improve. If you have a problem with someone, get it straight. Remember, if you can't say something good about somebody, then don't say anything. This is a good philosophy to practice the rest of your life.

"I don't know if any of you saw this television program on the educational channel, but the topic was 'Why do men die for their country?' They examined the Marines, the French Foreign Legion, and the British Commandos.

"The first conclusion they arrived at was that discipline is very important. Why does the military conduct their close-order drill, although it carries no military significance whatsoever? Because it stresses discipline.

"The second reason was the history of the regiment. They talked about its great tradition. They highlighted the successes of the regiment, particularly those accomplished against overwhelming odds.

"However, the most important reason why men died for their country was their love for their fellow man. They interviewed a soldier who related a most revealing story. He was wounded in combat and was convalescing in a hospital when he discovered that his fellow soldiers were going on a dangerous mission. He escaped from the hospital and went with them. Then, while participating in this mission, he was wounded once again. When they interviewed him, he said, 'You work with people and you live with them, and you soon realize that your survival depends on one another.' Whether it be a military battle or Notre Dame football, we can only enjoy success when we realize that we must be able to count on one another.

"It is important that I express my thoughts about this university—which you may or may not agree with. This school was founded by Father Sorin in 1842. It was founded as a tribute to Our Lady on the Dome. I believe the overwhelming majority of our football team believes in Jesus Christ. We may have some whose religious beliefs are such that they do

7

not recognize Jesus Christ. That's fine, also. I don't wish to change anybody's religion or philosophy. This school was built as a tribute to the Blessed Virgin, the mother of Jesus Christ. I firmly believe that if you really look at this school, you realize it has been blessed. The people who attend this school are blessed. Father Sorin said it best in 1842 when he said, 'I've raised Our Lady aloft so that men will know without asking, why we have succeeded here. All they have to do is look high on the Golden Dome and they'll find the answer.' When we do what is right, we bring glory and honor to Notre Dame. When we win in football, we help this university. Spend some time at the Grotto, and you'll discover that this school is special. There is a special mystique about it. You are special for being here as a student at Notre Dame.

"There will be no drinking during the season. We had this rule last year. There may have been violations, but rest assured that if they occur this year, we will find out. Our coaches will frequent the favorite hangouts. If you can't control yourself or exercise self-discipline, you aren't going to be successful, anyway.

"Concerning the length of our practices—I checked with Ara Parseghian and many other coaches who have enjoyed success. One thing they all had in common was that they practiced two and a half hours a day and met one hour a day. This was a typical day for Notre Dame when Ara coached: At three-thirty P.M. they were on the field. They practiced until six P.M. They arrived at the training table at six-thirty P.M. At seven-thirty P.M. they had an hour meeting every day. This meant they spent approximately four hours on football daily.

"Most schools, including Arkansas, Michigan, and most of our opponents, meet during lunch. After lunch, they go to class. At Arkansas, we would meet for an hour starting at two-thirty P.M. We would practice from three-thirty to six. At six-thirty we would eat, then meet again from seven-thirty to eight. At eight P.M. we had study hall until ten-thirty. In fairness to you, we do not meet at night, so you can fulfill your primary purpose for attending college, and that is to get an education. However, the minimum amount of practice time we need is two hours, plus kicking game. We must have an additional half-hour each day in meetings.

"Some people have complained that we practice too long. There is no other way to be successful. Your social life must be nonexistent during the season. In addition, our practices must be more productive and our retention greater. We cannot waste any time on the field, and we must insist upon improvement. I don't believe we made the improvement as a football team last year that we have to make this year.

"We need to improve the courtesy we extend to people. I think it is beneficial to look people in the eye and give them a firm handshake. Use the words 'Yes, sir—no, sir—yes, ma'am—no, ma'am.'

"I don't know if anything is more important than self-discipline. We have scientists who go into space and scientists who go to the depth of the oceans. It's ironic that we can conquer space and we can conquer the oceans but many times we can't conquer ourselves. Until we learn to have self-discipline, we cannot control our own destiny. Self-discipline is the greatest asset an individual can possess. I think perseverance will be an important part of our success this year. We must overcome all adversity. The only reason for a person to exist is to be the best he can be. If you don't have the desire to be the best that you can be in every single phase of your life, you need to check your values. This attitude will develop perseverance. You shouldn't do the things that simply give you physical pleasure. When you do things for the sole enjoyment of self-satisfaction, you'll forget about it in two days and want to do it over again.

"There are millions of people who live and die with Notre Dame football. There are an awful lot of Catholics and non-Catholics, Irishmen and non-Irishmen, successful and less-fortunate people, who follow the University of Notre Dame—and you should feel a sense of obligation to them. They follow Notre Dame football because it is synonymous with success.

"I really look forward to this season and working with you. We are going to be positive, and we are going to have fun in what we do. I want you to pay close attention to what I say because I don't want any misunderstandings about how I feel.

"I'm here to win football games for the University of Notre Dame. Not some of our games, and not most of our games; I'm here to win all of our games. Every doggone one of them. We aren't here to come close. We are here to win every single football game we ever play at the University of Notre Dame from this point forward.

"I want you to be the best, the very best, in all areas of your life. I want you to be the best student you can be. I want you to be the best person you can be. I want you to be the best football player you can be. The only reason a person should exist is to be the best he can. To play at Notre Dame is to seek perfection. I'm basically a perfectionist. I've heard all the reasons why you can't reach perfection. I want to tell you something. We are either going to reach it or we're going to come so close that the average person won't know the difference. To strive for perfection means you've got to be totally dedicated. It can't be an occasional thing—it's got

9

to be a total dedication in everything you do. If you don't have total dedication to perfection in your life, then I believe your attitude toward life is flawed.

"Perfection at Notre Dame will not only be demanded, it will be expected. I don't ever expect to lose another football game as long as I'm at Notre Dame, and I sure don't expect to lose one this year. I expect to see a perfect football team, because that's going to be the criteria we use to evaluate it. A loss is absolutely disastrous. You cannot give me one reason in the world why we should ever lose a game at Notre Dame—not a one. There is no reason. You can tell me about the schedule, but I don't want to hear it. There is no reason we should ever lose another football game at Notre Dame, and we aren't going to. Less than perfection is a personal embarrassment to me, to you, and to this university. For us to ever represent the University of Notre Dame with less than perfection is totally inconsistent with our goals, our objectives, and our beliefs.

"We're going to write another chapter in Notre Dame football history. We're going to seek perfection in football in the same manner as this university seeks perfection in every facet of the school. The Notre Dame football team is going to set a trend for this university as well as for the entire athletic department. The football team is not only going to be the best team at Notre Dame, it's going to be the best team in the entire country. We cannot achieve perfection if we do not have disciplined workouts, and this can only happen if people are totally committed.

"We are not asking for perfection—we are going to demand it. Please don't expect us to lower our standards to satisfy people who are looking for mediocrity, because this won't happen. Mistakes are a thing of the past. We are going to expect perfection, and we are going to get it.

"The last thing I wish to say to you is this: This is our football team—yours, mine, and Notre Dame's. This football team will be positive. The coaching staff will be positive. We will not be Pollyannas and whistle in the dark. We know what perfection is. We know what we have to do to achieve it, and we are going to achieve our goals.

"I want to tell you what our football team is going to be. It is going to be tough. It is going to be physical. It is going to be relentless. It is going to be a fourth-quarter team, and it's going to be one that performs best when it faces adversity. We will look adversity in the eye and we will turn it into success. There isn't going to be another football team in the country that's going to excel in all phases of the game as this football team is going to do.

"I'm sure that we have some people in this room right now who are glad to hear this and say, 'We want to be the best. We want to strive for perfection. Tell us what we have to do, because we're willing to pay the price.' On the other hand, there may be some people in this room who will say we can't do it. I don't care who questions our ability to succeed as long as they aren't members of this team.

"Congratulations once again on the fine start you have made in the winter program. That is our first step toward perfection."

2

THE COACHING STAFF: PUTTING THE PIECES TOGETHER

I'VE used the line so many times, but it still rings true:

"The Bible says Peter died leaning on his staff. The same will be said of me someday—he died leaning on his staff."

It's impossible to overestimate the value of an outstanding coaching staff, especially in this day when coaching overall is so competitive. It's always been that way, but there's so much more sophistication now than when I first got into the profession.

One thing that hasn't changed is the importance of having great chemistry within your coaching staff. It's kind of like doing a crossword puzzle. If you're missing just one word, it's not going to work. It's the same way in this business. If you have one missing link in your staff, it can keep things from falling together the way you want them to.

Thanks to all my different stops in coaching, I have a good feel for what's involved in putting together a staff. It's more than hiring people you know and are comfortable with. Hiring nice guys doesn't guarantee success. It's also more than hiring people who know football on a technical basis. The best X-and-O guy can be useless if he can't communicate with the players and get them to learn what he knows. Somewhere is that middle ground where you combine personality and football knowledge with dedication and commitment and a tremendous desire to be successful. This combination is difficult to obtain, but we must achieve this objective or we will not succeed. I personally feel that our players at Notre Dame have every right to receive the best coaching in the country. They have the best teachers, best tutors, best dorm rectors, and the coaching they receive must be the best.

One of my first full-time coaching jobs was in 1964 and '65 at the University of Connecticut. Rick Forzano, who coached me at Kent State and went on to be head coach at Navy and with the Detroit Lions, was the head coach. I still have as much respect for him as anyone I've ever met in coaching. He put together an excellent group of young coaches that included Sam Rutigliano, who went on to become head coach of the Cleveland Browns; Dave Adolph, the Browns' defensive coordinator; Dan Sekanovich, now one of Don Shula's assistants with the Miami Dolphins.

It was the same way at Ohio State when we won the national championship in 1968 under Woody Hayes. Besides me, the other assistants included Bill Mallory, now the head coach at Indiana; Earle Bruce, who was head coach at Iowa State before going back to Ohio State as head coach; Lou McCullough, who became athletic director at Iowa State; Hugh Hindman, who became athletic director at Ohio State; George Chaump, who joined the Tampa Bay Buccaneers staff and now is head coach at Marshall; and Rudy Hubbard, who became head coach at Florida A&M. While I was there, Dave McClain, who later died while head coach at Wisconsin, joined the staff.

At Notre Dame, after losing the last three games of the '87 season, there were a lot of things about our chemistry we didn't like. Any head coach has to expect changes in the staff on a routine basis. Coaches are going to come and go in all kinds of situations, even at a place like Notre Dame, and you've constantly got to have some replacement people in mind for when those times come.

Making the right decisions in those circumstances is critical to your team, and yet no one appreciates enough how important those assistants are. But when you're part of a successful situation, you learn how much it counts.

One individual I knew was going to make a decision was Joe Yonto, our defensive line coach. He had been a member of the staff at Notre Dame since 1964, when Ara Parseghian took over—and there's no one I came to appreciate more, not just as a football coach, but as a gentleman and as a great representative of Notre Dame. Down through the years Joe probably has been as popular as any assistant coach Notre Dame has had, and he's been here through the regimes of Ara, Dan Devine, Gerry Faust, and now ours.

Joe has coached so many outstanding defensive linemen at Notre Dame, it would take a week to list them all—starting with Alan Page, Mike McCoy, Steve Niehaus, Ross Browner, and so many others. But, at the age of sixty-two, a chance to get into administration and work with Dick Rosenthal was something Joe had to think about. Joe made the decision to go that way before January was over, but we really didn't want to do anything until recruiting was finished.

I received a phone call the Monday before the February 10 national signing date from Marion Campbell, the head coach of the Atlanta Falcons. He wanted permission to talk to Foge Fazio about a position on his staff—something that didn't particularly surprise me.

Foge had had a number of opportunities after leaving Pittsburgh, and one of the choices he had to make was whether to stay in college football or move into the professional ranks. Frankly, I think we'd been awfully fortunate to be able to hire him. He helped me tremendously as far as taking over the defense, and I think his experience as a head coach added to the credibility of what we were trying to do—especially with the players. I knew Foge wouldn't stay at Notre Dame forever, but I think it was a good move for everyone involved for him to join us in 1986, no matter how long he stayed.

So, Campbell's call was no shock. Foge went down to Atlanta on Tuesday and visited with the people there, and he called me late that afternoon and said he'd been offered the job and really felt like he needed to accept it. They put together a great financial package for him, and that made it difficult to turn down. He and I agreed it probably was in his best interests to take the job.

Foge is a fine individual and an excellent coach. I hated to lose our defensive coordinator, especially one of his caliber. But I knew it had been a tough adjustment to make, having been a head coach at Pittsburgh, to go back and be an assistant at the college level, with all the recruiting and other responsibilities involved. Plus, his children were getting ready to go to college, and finances certainly get to be a big priority at that stage.

We asked the Falcons to please wait until the signing date to make the announcement, since we were only talking about one day and Foge was still involved with recruiting. They complied, and by Wednesday night Foge officially was a member of the Atlanta staff.

Terry Forbes, our secondary coach, had been looking into the possibility of starting his own recruiting service for the state of Ohio, where he was from and had coached most of his life. His decision to leave wasn't final until recruiting was over, but that left us with three spots to fill, all of them on defense.

On offense we didn't expect any changes. Pete Cordelli, who had been with me for several years, all the way back to his days as a quarterback at North Carolina State, would continue to coach the wide receivers. Jim Strong would continue with the running backs, Tony Yelovich with the offensive line, and George Stewart with the tight ends and kicking game. On defense we had only one staff member returning, Barry Alvarez. He had just finished his first season at Notre Dame with the outside linebackers, but I felt he was an outstanding coach.

It's easy to hire coaches to come to Notre Dame, because virtually everyone wants to coach here. What's important is to find out *why* they want to come to Notre Dame. Are they interested in Notre Dame as just another step on the ladder—a stop before they move on? Do they really and truly understand and believe in what Notre Dame is all about—or do we have to train them about the Notre Dame athlete, the commitment to excellence in academics and all the other areas in which Notre Dame is different?

It's the same way Gene Corrigan talked to me about the head coaching job. Right at the beginning he wanted to explain why it's a little more difficult at Notre Dame. You do have demanding admissions standards, you do have a difficult schedule, you don't get to redshirt—the practice of holding players out for a year so they end up using their eligibility over a five-year period—you don't have an athletic dorm, you don't have all the time in the world for practice and meetings, and there is a tremendous commitment to academics. If you understand and accept all those things and you're still excited about Notre Dame, it will be a great experience. That's the case either as the head coach or as an assistant.

In trying to fill the defensive coordinator's role, I sat down and visited with Barry Alvarez at great length on three different occasions. I was most impressed with him on the field in the one year he had been with us. He had great rapport with the players, and that's so important. The other thing that impressed me was that he did not have a large ego. He just wanted to win, and I felt our philosophies in that regard were very similar.

After visiting with Barry for the third time, I came to the conclusion he was the individual who would give us the best chance to win as our defensive coordinator. He knew our players, he knew me, he knew where we wanted to go. After being with me for a year, I think he knew what I wanted out of a defensive coordinator. He had all the right answers.

Barry had coached the outside linebackers his first year, but now we were going to have him handle the inside linebackers, so he'd be working with Wes Pritchett, Ned Bolcar, and Michael Stonebreaker.

Next, we hired John Palermo from Minnesota as our defensive line coach. John had coached with me the two seasons I was at Minnesota. He is an excellent young coach, a great family man, and a great recruiter. I felt he would blend in very well with the coaches we already had, and he obviously already knew Jim Strong, Pete Cordelli, George Stewart, and Vinny Cerrato from our days together on the Minnesota staff. John has excellent motivational talents and is a good teacher. He was just the person we needed to develop a young, inexperienced defensive line.

John Palermo, defensive line coach

Coach Holtz doesn't just coach players—he coaches coaches, on a daily basis. There are certain things he believes in, and he wants them accomplished, wants them done. He's as demanding of the coaches as he is of the players. But we're just like players. When we see ourselves getting better, we feel good about ourselves.

There are certain things he believes in, in terms of fundamentals. If you adhere to those things and your kids believe in them, your kids will get better. If they feel better about themselves, you're going to play better on Sunday.

Shortly after I hired Barry as the defensive coordinator, he came to me while we were formulating our staff and said he'd like to have George Stewart switch to the other side of the line and coach the outside linebackers—or the defensive ends, as we call them now. George had played on the offensive line for me at Arkansas and had coached for me at Minnesota and Notre Dame. He'd never been on the other side of the ball before. That's always a concern, if a coach is going to be starting from scratch in a particular area. But George seemed extremely excited about the idea, and he may have even approached Barry about the opportunity to coach defense.

Barry wanted George because of his rapport with the players. They have a lot in common in that regard. George is tough and demanding, and he's basically responsible for working with our athletes in terms of setting disciplinary measures. He's exceptionally articulate, and he's always positive with the athletes. I've never heard him criticize a player in front of someone else. He'll get upset, but he'll bite his tongue and won't say anything at that moment but you can bet he'll get the problem rectified before they leave the field. He can be tough with an individual on a one-on-one basis, but he won't be negative with anyone in front of others. I've always admired this in him, and I wish I could be more like him in that respect.

Once we agreed on that move, I felt we would have good chemistry if we could settle on a secondary coach. I'd interviewed an awful lot of different coaches for that spot, before Earle Bruce called me one day. He told me he'd had a great secondary coach at Ohio State, a guy named Chuck Heater, and that I ought to think about hiring him.

I was good friends with Dave McClain, who became head coach at Wisconsin, because he and I had coached together at Ohio State as assistants. About a month before Dave died, we were talking on the phone about staff members and I asked him who he thought were some of the better secondary coaches around the nation. We often compared notes on subjects like this.

Ironically, Dave really was high on Chuck Heater, who had played at Michigan and coached at Toledo and for Dave at Wisconsin. So when Earle mentioned his name, it rang a bell for me. I hadn't realized that Chuck was their secondary coach, because I thought it was a young man named Gary Blackney, who had played for me when I was at Connecticut. As it turned out, Gary had been promoted to defensive coordinator, and that's when Earle hired Chuck.

I was impressed with what Earle said about Chuck and with the job Ohio State had done the year before in the Cotton Bowl against a great Texas A&M passing game and Kevin Murray, a great quarterback. And I was even more impressed after visiting with Chuck personally, so I hired him. That took care of everything on defense.

Chuck Heater, secondary coach

Right away when I started in the spring, I thought we had some talented players, though many were very raw. There was a tremendous opportunity to develop the young players. On the defensive side of the ball we had a lot of people with talent, and yet they were the kind of players who were just going to get better and better and better. During the season, we became a better team as the kids matured and grew. It also struck me that basically we had a whole new defensive staff.

It was really interesting how the chemistry of the staff came together. It's pretty unusual to get a whole new staff and have it work so well. For all of us to bring the experience we had—and we had a good bit of experience from wherever we'd been—and have it just kind of meld together, that was great. I've been part of staffs where that hasn't been the case. So I felt we had a tremendous opportunity to develop as a defensive team.

We still had one vacancy on offense, because George Stewart had switched to defense. One of the things I wanted to do was to even up the

17

coaching assignments on the offensive line. The last two years, George had worked with the tight ends, while Tony Yelovich coached the guards, tackles, and centers. Now we were looking at having to rebuild our whole offensive line, so I wanted to make sure we could give them individual attention as they would need it. It wasn't fair to expect Tony to coach the entire line, even though he had done a fine job the year before, when Chuck Lanza, Byron Spruell, and five other seniors did the majority of playing. So we decided to have Tony coach the guards and centers and hire someone new to handle the tackles and tight ends.

Jackie Sherrill and I had been talking about assistant coaches one day during our week in Dallas for the Cotton Bowl. One of the things Jackie said was that he'd never had a better assistant than Joe Moore, who had been his offensive line coach at Pittsburgh. I hadn't forgotten that conversation. Joe had been at Temple the last two years, since Foge left Pittsburgh, and I felt he was the best coach we could hire.

When Jackie had told me Joe was one of the best assistants he'd seen, I'd asked, "In what area?" He said, "In every area." I asked him why he hadn't brought Joe with him to Texas A&M, and he said Joe didn't want to leave that general area of the country. So I thought we would have a chance to get him.

Joe Moore is an old-fashioned guy. He's tough and hard-nosed. I felt the offensive line was going to be our biggest challenge, and it would help to have two people of Tony and Joe's caliber working with that group. I thought that would give us our best chance to win in the fall. It would be a change, but it could pay great dividends.

I remember talking to Joe during a staff meeting later in the year. I like the way he has of putting things in perspective. I told him we had a problem in one area on the team. He said, "Coach, I know we have a problem when teams do that against us. But if we do this, then they've got a problem."

Joe's an excellent teacher, and that's so important. He's very subtle, and he's one of the funniest guys I've ever met. But he never talks to me. I mean, he doesn't talk to me at all. I heard about a story he told his players. He said, "When I went to school and did something wrong, I got whipped. When I went home and did something wrong, I got whipped. Here I am at Notre Dame, and when you guys do something wrong, I get whipped in staff meetings. This is going to change. Now you guys are going to start getting whipped for what you do." The players thought that was great.

We got our entire staff together for the first time the last week of February, and I felt very good about it.

There were no guarantees for September, but I was satisfied that we'd filled the vacancies we had with the best individuals available. Now we just had to wait to see how things would fall in place. Spring football was less than a month away, so it wouldn't take long to find out.

RECRUITING:
SPEED, QUICKNESS, AND MORE

I don't know if there's anything more important to the long-range success of a football program than recruiting. I'm talking about the necessity for *consistently good recruiting*, because you can't compete on the major-college level without it. One off-year can really put you in a hole. It's no different at Notre Dame than it is anywhere else. You've got to have great athletes to win, I don't care *who* the coach is. You cannot win without good athletes, but you can lose with them. This is where coaching can make a difference.

We get incredible cooperation in recruiting from the people at Notre Dame. During weekends in January, and usually a few in December, we have athletes come to the campus to visit. The coaching staff has a meeting each Sunday afternoon to go over where we stand, then Sunday night we all go out on the road. We're in the young men's homes Sunday through Thursday, and then come back to the office by early Friday. We have athletes in for the weekend, meet Sunday, and go back out again.

On a typical weekend a young man will fly into South Bend on Friday and arrive sometime in the afternoon. We immediately take him over to meet with the admissions people in Kevin Rooney's office. Then he'll have the opportunity to visit with some of our athletes and have dinner.

Early Saturday morning the academic meetings start. He'll meet with Dr. Mike DeCicco, our academic advisor for athletics. He'll meet with various faculty members and professors, and that takes most of the morning. We then have a luncheon for the athletes, their parents, and the faculty. The professors devote a tremendous amount of time to helping us continue to strive for excellence in recruiting. We encourage parents to come here to visit with their sons, and a great number of them do so. It's a great chance to see our commitments in both the academic and athletic areas.

After lunch they visit with our trainer and get a chance to see our facilities and talk about our training procedures. They talk to our strength coach, see our weight room, and see the computer programs each athlete uses for his workouts. We take them on a campus tour, and then it's time for dinner. The athletes generally go to eat with our players, and the parents have dinner with our assistant coaches.

At Notre Dame we don't have an athletic dorm, and approximately eighty-five percent of our students live on campus. I think maybe only the service academies have that kind of percentage of their students on campus.

Sunday morning the young men go to the church of their choice and then we have brunch at my home. I always visit with each athlete individually at that time. I'm honest with these young men when I tell them Notre Dame is not the place they want if they're interested strictly in social life. Nor is it the place for spending all their time lifting weights and working on football and not making an academic commitment. But there is great spirit here, and I think that's far more important. They'll be much more prone to remember that twenty years from now. You don't come to Notre Dame to learn to do something. You come to Notre Dame to learn to be someone.

In recruiting, we try to sell forty years, not just four. We certainly want people at Notre Dame who are going to be great football players. But we also want people here who are going to excel and achieve in all areas. If an individual is fortunate enough to play in the National Football League, he is a rare exception. The average NFL player plays approximately four years. Consequently, if a player graduates from Notre Dame at twenty-one and has an average NFL career, at age twenty-five his football career is over. Yet his life is only one third over. What is he going to do with his life for the next fifty years? That's where Notre Dame really excels. We've graduated 98.9 percent of our athletes over the last twenty years. That's a tribute to Dr. Emil T. Hofman, who has worked with the Freshman Year of Studies, and Mike DeCicco, and the other people here who handle our academic office.

Every recruiting season produces memories, but Derek Brown this year was an unusual story. He was considered the best football player in the country. He was selected for that honor by *USA Today*. He's a six-six,

240-pound tight end, a very fine student and a fine leader, who lives in Merritt Island, Florida. Vinny Cerrato, our recruiting coordinator, did an outstanding job in exposing Derek to the positive aspects of Notre Dame. Miami, Florida, and Florida State were heavily recruiting him. He was a player any coach in the country would have loved to have had.

I believe the reason we convinced Derek to come to Notre Dame was his two younger twin sisters. I visited Derek and his mother and sisters— who were twelve or thirteen and quite intelligent—in Merritt Island. As we sat around the table I started telling Derek and his mother a little more about Notre Dame, with his sisters listening in. Quite often when I would make a comment about Notre Dame, one of Derek's sisters would either correct me or add to it. If I said a building was built in 1892, they would say, with exceptional politeness, "Sir, I think if you check that, you'll find it was 1894." They finally admitted that they had read every bit of information that Vinny had sent Derek about Notre Dame. I felt we had the best recruiters in the world, right there in Derek's home.

I was very impressed with the love and closeness in that home, and I had a good feeling as I walked out. But, as in so many cases when you recruit all over the country, as we do, I didn't know if Derek would seriously consider going that far away from home to attend school. We also had recruited an outstanding tight end the year before in Frank Jacobs, and we hoped to move Andy Heck to offensive tackle to free up a position for Derek Brown on our football team. Yet ironically, it was Frank who did as much as any of our players to help recruit Derek, even though he knew they would be competing for the same position.

I'll never forget calling Derek and hearing him tell me, "Coach, I've made a decision, I'm coming to Notre Dame. But don't tell Vinny Cerrato yet, because I want to see his face when I tell him." He then said, "Coach, you have to promise me that we will win at least one national championship before I graduate." I said, "Derek, I think we will, but you control that more than I do." I was elated, but I had to keep it a secret from everybody, including our staff, for four days. I was relieved when Vinny called me, all excited, to tell me Derek Brown was coming to Notre Dame. I just said, "That's great. We're very, very happy."

Lindsay Knapp's high-school coach in Chicago had been ultra-successful. When we went up there to recruit Lindsay, we had some time to sit around and I said, "Coach, why are you successful?" I ask everybody questions. I've never learned anything by talking. He didn't react, so I said again, "Why do you win every year?" He said, "I don't know." I said, "Sure you do. Why do you win?" He then said the most profound thing I have ever heard, and it really affected me. He said, "We don't get bored running the same play over and over." That's what it means to emphasize fundamentals.

I visited with Gene McGuire and his mother after the two of them had been to our campus, and there was no doubt she really wanted him to come to Notre Dame. They've had a great football program for years at his high school. And it is an impressive organization from the principal down to the students. I think I met every person in the school the day I was there. And their enthusiasm and pride were very obvious. This is true of all good organizations.

Justin Hall's father, Skip, is from my hometown, East Liverpool, Ohio, and he was two years behind me in high school. We had a big, all-class reunion where I was honored a couple of years ago, and Skip introduced me to his son Justin and mentioned that he thought he'd be a pretty decent college football player. I was aware that his high school, Plano, Texas, produced great athletes every year—Bill Ray Smith was from his high school and made all-American for three years for us at Arkansas. They win the state title in Texas about every other year. After the reunion many of our mutual friends wrote me and told me what a good player Justin Hall was, but not many of them had seen his team play.

The typical scenario in a situation like that is the young man usually doesn't turn out to be much of a football player. Well, this case is the exact opposite. I stayed in touch, found out that Skip's son really was a good football player, and we recruited him. When we went to the Cotton Bowl, Justin and his father came over to practice, and he eventually decided to come to Notre Dame. Justin is going to be one fine player before he graduates. He's going to make a contribution to our team this year, and that doesn't normally happen much with freshmen who play on the offensive line. But he's going to be fun to watch in about two years.

I visited Raghib Ismail's high school and met his twin brother Qadry, who ended up going to Syracuse on a scholarship. I didn't get to visit his high school until after Raghib already committed to attend Notre Dame, and while I knew he really hadn't visited many schools, I did not know how good he was. I knew he was fast but not very big. The thing that did impress me was the sincere respect everyone at that school held for him.

I went to Devon McDonald's high school in New Jersey and discovered he had a twin brother who played for a different high school. Devon's team at Kennedy High School won the state title, and the only blemish on their record was a tie against the school where his brother Ricardo played. I thought, well, if you have twins going to different high schools, maybe they'll go to different colleges. It looked like his brother was going to Pitt. Devon came out and visited and we really liked him, and I think he's going to be a heck of a football player.

23

I think there was a lot of pressure on Arnold Ale to go to USC. The one question he asked was how cold it would get, because he did not like cold weather. Michael Smalls, also being from California, felt the same way. We were getting ready to practice one day in October when I looked out my office window. Here came Arnold Ale and Michael Smalls, and they've got on toboggan hats, gloves, scarves, jackets—and it was a little over 50 degrees. I thought, they are in severe trouble when it really gets cold. I didn't tell them how Notre Dame was founded in South Bend. The story goes that in 1842 Father Sorin and a brave group of five French priests set out from Baltimore, Maryland, and headed for San Diego, where they were going to start this great Catholic university. As they came across northern Indiana, it was cold and miserable. Father Sorin said, "I can't go any further tonight, so we will set up camp here and leave when the weather gets better." It never did.

Overall, I think we had a decent recruiting year, though every coach says that every year. It's amazing if we did, because the weather generally was terrible on the weekends we had players in to visit. One area we didn't solve was quarterback. The only quarterback we signed was George Poorman out of the Chicago area, but he'll probably end up in the secondary. That means recruiting two quarterbacks will be of paramount importance next year.

Skill-position players were a major priority for us this year, and I think we met that need. I don't know whether the *Parade* team is any better reference than anything else, but we signed six running backs off that team—Rocket Ismail from Pennsylvania, Rod Smith from Minnesota, Rusty Setzer from Indiana, Walter Boyd from North Carolina, Kenny Spears from Georgia, and Rodney Culver from Michigan. They won't all end up playing as running backs, but they're the kind of athletes we need. Most of those athletes are small, and their skills will dictate moving some of them to different positions, but they know this.

We came up with a class that represented the entire country, with two athletes from California, two from Texas, two from Florida, two from Georgia. I don't know whether we'll continue to recruit nationally like that every year. We've talked about trying to make the Catholic schools here in the Midwest our base, but I think we will seek to continue to recruit players nationally.

Vinny Cerrato is one of the keys to our recruiting. He's young and single and loves his job. If he ever gets married, we're finished. Vinny worked with us at Minnesota, and when I came to Notre Dame, I decided I wanted him as one of our full-time coaches so he could go on the road and recruit. Some head coaches aren't willing to give up one of their coaches on the field to be a recruiter, but that's how important I think recruiting is to our program. It has paid great dividends. Vinny does an outstanding job, is organized, works hard, and takes great pride in his job. We have a lot of pluses here at Notre Dame, but they don't mean much if you don't work at it. When you recruit nationally, you must have a full-time recruiter or you will waste a lot of time and money with poor results.

The assets Notre Dame has in recruiting are unbelievable. You have instant respect when you walk into a high school. People in the guidance office and others seem to go overboard to help you. It's not because of who you are, but what Notre Dame represents.

There are some things about Notre Dame that are different. As someone once told me, Notre Dame does not exist to educate the masses. But if an individual really and truly wants to get a good education, wants to play a national schedule, wants to receive some recognition, wants to be part of a great tradition—I could go on and on—then there is no place like it. If you can't recruit at Notre Dame, you can't recruit anywhere.

People have said a lot about the speed we've recruited, and there's some truth in that. I'm sure some of our freshmen like Rocket Ismail and Rusty Setzer and maybe some others would be welcome on Joe Piane's track team. But there's more to it than just speed.

There is a sign that says "Speed Kills," and I think that is true. If you have speed with intelligence, you've got an unbeatable combination. But speed with a lack of intelligence gets you in trouble.

I would rather have a slow guy going in the right direction than a fast guy going in the wrong direction. At least the slow guy won't be as far out of position as the fast guy. But it helps to have speed and an ability to run. You can be the toughest, most hard-nosed football player on the field, but if you can't get to where the hitting is going on, you're of no value to the team. Your value to the team is inversely proportionate to your distance from the football. If you're on one 10-yard line and the guy with the ball is on the other 10-yard line, you're of no value, even if you're an all-American.

Sometimes a guy has great speed, but if he can run a 4.5 in the 40, but only runs a 4.9 when he's chasing the ball, then he isn't very quick. I'll take the guy who is 4.7 all the time on the field.

Everybody worries about how fast an athlete can run the 40, but I've never been interested in that. Our athletes like to be timed because it's good for morale. It makes them feel better, feel quicker.

We have tried to recruit football players with speed, not track people who we think might be able to play football. One guy who will help us this year is John Foley, because he can run a 4.6 even at six-five and 250 pounds. Chris Zorich is 270 but he is fast. Jeff Alm used to be an outside linebacker, so you know he has good speed for a tackle. George Williams is one of the slower people we have on defense, yet he's still at 4.95 for 275 pounds.

Frank Stams isn't a speed demon, but he was good enough to play fullback at one time, so his speed as a linebacker isn't bad. Michael Stonebreaker has excellent speed. I think we've got a number of people in the secondary with good speed, especially a guy like Stan Smagala, who is really deceiving with his quickness.

Part of the reason we may look at Ricky Watters as a flanker is because of his speed. He can flat-out run and he's a threat on the outside. Frank Jacobs has excellent speed for a tight end, and Tony Rice ranks right up there at quarterback. Anthony Johnson's speed is deceiving at fullback.

We've tried to put speed on defense, and tried to put quick people on the offensive line. You look at our special teams, and I guarantee you there'll be people who can run. We still don't match up with teams like Miami, but we are getting better. And a big part of it is recruiting.

Vinny Cerrato, recruiting coordinator

When you go on the road recruiting with Coach Holtz, you pick him up at the airport, and you better know exactly where you're going. You dry-run the whole situation just so everything goes right. When he comes in, you want everything to go smooth. He's going to ask me, "What do I need to know about this individual? What are the important areas to him? What will sell him on Notre Dame?"

When we go into the home of a player we're recruiting, he's not going to cover those things right away. He starts with academics, then the university in general—then he gets into football, and finally he'll hit on what they really want to know. It's not going to be a long home visit. It's going to be short and to the point, and it's going to be very informative. He's always outstanding. It's impressive to listen to him. When I'm with him, all I do is introduce him and then say goodbye. That's about it. He's going to carry the rest of it, because they are there to meet him.

Sometimes these visits really turn into public appearances. People in the neighborhood know he's coming, and he ends up signing all kinds of autographs. When the head coach at Notre Dame comes in, it's a big deal, it's probably been in the newspaper. If I could take any coach in the country for a home visit, it would be Lou Holtz. It's fun knowing you're going into a high school with someone like him. They stop you and want to meet him, talk to him, take pictures, get autographs. You feel like a big shot.

He's great at salesmanship, and all you're doing in recruiting is selling yourself and selling the university. He usually is the last person to come in—he'll use the last of the three home visits we have. With Derek Brown, for example, I was the first one to visit, just to go over the basic groundwork of Notre Dame. Next, I went with George Stewart, because he was the tight-end coach at the time. Then, Lou was third. A lot of times the head coach has to visit because every other head coach is doing it, especially with a great player.

But we don't feel that Coach Holtz has to go in to see every player. And he doesn't want to have to go in there and convince the player to come to Notre Dame. When the athletes visit our campus, his role is not to sell them on the university. He just wants to see how they fit in and what they think of the place, if they have the right kind of chemistry to fit in at Notre Dame. He really hates to go out thinking he has to talk someone into coming to Notre Dame. He wants them to come to Notre Dame for the right reasons. They are the players who'll do better when they come here.

He does an unbelievable job on a home visit. He can be tired coming off the plane and completely worn out. But when he's in the home for those forty-five minutes, he's upbeat and on top of his game. Then he may get on the plane and fall asleep for two hours. But when he's in that home, he's outstanding.

At Minnesota he had to do a lot more recruiting. The first thing the athletes thought of when you said Minnesota was cold weather. At Notre Dame you can get into anyone's door, and he doesn't even need to see every player we're after. If he sees them when they come on a campus visit, that's enough. I went with him on home visits to see Derek Brown, Kenny Spears, and Bernard Mannelly. He probably went into fifteen homes for the class we signed in February of 1988, and maybe seventy-five the year before, when we signed thirty players.

It's fun to go out recruiting, because it's easy to sell Notre Dame and Lou Holtz and everything that happens here. Even if you're tired from traveling, you get jacked up because you're going to see the best players in the country. You know the type of impact they can have. A lot of games are won in December and January like that. So you can't help but get excited. When you see someone like Derek Brown, you know he's the best player in the country.

Coach Holtz likes to go into the home after the player has committed. He wants the player to already decide to come to Notre Dame. Then he'll come in to meet the family, and it will be more relaxing. When we went to see Kenny Spears, it was very relaxing, and Kenny took him in his room and showed him all his trophies. It was like a conversation with friends. We just talked about when he would report and what he could expect.

Everything kind of fell our way this year, even the national championship. It was almost like it was supposed to happen, with the missed field goal in the Michigan game saying it was our turn. The biggest thing was

27

getting off to a good start with all the young people we had playing. Once they gained the confidence and continued to get better, we were pretty good by the end of the year. So when we go out to recruit now, we're not out to rebuild, we're out to reload at certain positions.

Coach Holtz says, "I want to have the best recruiting class in the country." He says, "It's yours, you handle it, you go do it and just let me know where we are." We don't talk about recruiting much. We don't meet about it all that much. He asked me, "What can I do as far as recruiting during the season?" I said, "Coach, the biggest thing you can do is win football games. You win football games, and recruiting will handle itself." I don't feel he really has to spend a lot of time worrying about recruiting. If we continue to be successful on the field, I think the recruiting will continue to go well.

A few weeks before spring practice began, President Reagan came to Notre Dame for the dedication of the Knute Rockne postage stamp on March 9. It was the first time in history an athletic coach, college or professional, has been featured on a stamp. It was a natural for Reagan to come, since he had played George Gipp in the movie, *Knute Rockne—All-American.* Our basketball arena was filled to capacity, and the entire football squad had a chance to attend.

At one point in the ceremony Moose Krause, our former athletic director, presented the President with a football. President Reagan tossed it into the audience, and Tim Brown, of all people, caught it. As far as I know, it was strictly coincidence. But it did remind me that it wouldn't be long before spring practice would begin, and we'd have to find someone to take Tim Brown's place. Those won't be easy shoes to fill.

SPRING PRACTICE:
THE DEFENSE REIGNS

SPRING practice is like starting all over again. You're 0–0, everyone's upbeat, and it's a time to get a handle on your football team. It's also a time to find out who your leaders are.

Notre Dame's traditional leaders have been the captains. In the middle of our first meeting after the trip to the Japan Bowl, we selected captains by having the players vote. We ask them to try to make it a senior, but that's not a necessity. We talk about the qualities we want in a captain, how important it is for a captain be a positive leader.

I've always been opposed to electing captains before a season. I'd rather elect honorary captains after the season is over and you've determined who has done the best job of leading the team. Many times an individual may be elected a captain and end up not playing very much. This was what I was afraid might happen. However, a preseason election has been a tradition at Notre Dame, and we had to vote on the captains so the athletic board could approve it.

We said we wanted an individual who was unselfish, who cared about Notre Dame. Vote for somebody you completely trust, not just someone who is your buddy off the field or whose personality you like.

Second, vote for someone really committed to excellence, not just in football, but in every phase of his life—somebody who absolutely couldn't live with losing. We don't ask our athletes how many want to win. The questions I always ask are: Can you live with losing? Can you live with mediocrity? Can you live with failure?

Third, we ask them to vote for somebody who genuinely cares about the University of Notre Dame and about them as an individual. There were several seniors who earned votes, but the obvious choices were Ned Bolcar, Mark Green, and Andy Heck.

All three are great young men, and I congratulated the players for their decisions. We met with the captains and talked to them about the role they would play. If we were to become a good football team, our seniors would have to become positive leaders. One of the other reasons I don't like to elect captains is that the minute you elect someone, the other seniors sort of have a tendency to sit back and say, "Well, it's up to them." If you're going to have a good football team, your seniors are going to have to play the best football of their careers. This is not going to happen if they sit back and let the others assume the leadership roles. We told the captains it was imperative they bring out the leadership qualities in the other members of the senior class. They've done this very well thus far.

Looking at last year's defense as we went into spring practice, I thought we did not put good pressure on the passer, we did not play with good pressure overall, and were not as fundamentally sound as we needed to be, but I felt, personnelwise, we were solid. We had four good linebackers in Wes Pritchett, Ned Bolcar, Michael Stonebreaker, who had missed the preceding year, and Donn Grimm. We had four good outside linebackers in Flash Gordon, Frank Stams, Scott Kowalkowski, and Andre Jones. We had a chance to be pretty good in the defensive secondary with Todd Lyght, D'Juan Francisco, and Stan Smagala at corner, plus George Streeter and Corny Southall at safety. However, we had some problems with depth in the secondary.

On the defensive line we were counting on Chris Zorich and John Foley to really come forward and be outstanding football players. Along with them we had Tom Gorman, Jeff Alm, and Bryan Flannery, who were solid individuals, plus George Williams, George Marshall, and Bob Dahl, all of whom had had a chance as freshmen. So with some depth in the secondary, and the development of some of our young defensive linemen, I thought we'd have a very solid defense.

On offense it was just the opposite. We did have Tony Rice back at quarterback, but who was going to play behind him? Kent Graham had done some good things as a freshman, but he had difficulty putting the ball in the end zone. I was anxious to see Steve Belles, because I thought he'd made a great deal of progress the preceding year and maybe was ready to blossom. I commented on several occasions that I thought Belles would challenge Tony for the starting quarterback position.

I felt good at tailback with Mark Green, Ricky Watters, and Tony Brooks. But one thing was obvious to me—we could not have three players of that caliber at one position. It didn't make sense. Consequently, since Green had been a wide receiver as a freshman and we had to move him to tailback out of absolute necessity, I thought it might be in his best interests to move to flanker to replace Tim Brown. Then we would go with two upcoming sophomores, Brooks and Watters, at tailback.

I felt very solid at fullback with Anthony Johnson and Braxston Banks. The wide-receiver position was a question mark. The only individual who had played at all there was Pat Terrell, but we did have two good young freshmen in Pierre Martin and Bobby Carpenter, neither of whom ever played in a game as freshmen. Both were outstanding athletes. We put Pat Eilers at flanker because he's a tough, hard-nosed, dedicated individual. I thought he could help us there, particularly with the running game.

From the offensive line we had lost four of last year's starters. I was concerned about the center position, but we felt Mike Heldt, a rising sophomore, would just have to come along and do it. We moved Tim Ryan from linebacker to center, thinking this would be a natural position for him even though he had lettered as a linebacker the year before. We thought he could develop into a capable backup for Mike.

At one guard position we had Tim Grunhard, who was solid, but otherwise we were really looking. Dean Brown, who had been rather inconsistent at guard even though he hadn't played a lot in two years, moved out to tackle along with a freshman, Joe Allen, and a senior, Marty Lippincott. We took Andy Heck from tight end and put him at what we call quick tackle, along with Peter Rausch and Darryl Wodecki. At the other guard position we were going to try everybody, including Winston Sandri, a sophomore who never played as a freshman.

We thought we'd be all right at quarterback, tailback, and fullback. But the wide-receiver spots, tight end, and the offensive line would be questionable. It was very important that Frank Jacobs come through for us at tight end, because moving Heck to tackle put a lot of pressure on Jacobs. We also felt Rod West would come along at tight end and that we might be all right with the addition of Derek Brown out of our incoming freshman class. It was more important to solidify the offensive line than to worry about tight end.

We started spring practice March 20, and one thing was certain from the first minute the whistle blew: the defense flat-out came to play.

The very first day out there, we lost Chris Zorich with a knee injury. When he first got hurt, they told us he would be out just for four or five days, but he was gone the entire spring. Still, I had the feeling he would become an outstanding middle guard. John Foley missed all of spring practice because of a nerve problem in his right arm, an injury left over from the Cotton Bowl. Our doctors hoped he would be all right by the end of spring practice. So the two individuals we were really looking forward to seeing on the defensive line missed all but one hour.

The chemistry of our defense was outstanding from day one, even with those two players missing. Barry Alvarez and the rest of the defensive staff got through to the players, and they were having fun. Our defense just kept getting better and better.

I knew we were going to have some problems on offense. Our coaches did a nice job of teaching, but we did not have much success. It was difficult to have any consistency. The defense completely dominated practices. However, I wasn't too concerned, because I felt we would get better.

During our first eight days of practice we installed the whole offense and defense and tried to improve everybody. From the ninth day on we scrimmaged every other day. If somebody was injured in a scrimmage— unless it's a freak accident like with Zorich—he at least would be involved for the installation of the offense and defense. Overall, we did not have many players injured during the course of spring practice. That was a tribute to the attitude of the players in terms of improving their fundamentals. It's hard to evaluate your defense against your own offense, but I felt we dominated the offense. We also were fundamentally sound overall and probably a lot quicker than what we had been.

I'd go home at night and say, "I hope we're better on defense, because if we're not, it's going to be one long season, because we may not be able to do much on offense."

The offensive line never did come along during the entire course of spring practice. But that was not unusual.

Frank Stams, senior defensive end

Coach Holtz has a better sense of humor than I do, that's for sure. He's always one step ahead of the players.

There was a time in the spring last year [1988] when I thought I'd pull a gag on some of the freshmen and sophomores and I'd send 'em up to Coach Holtz in practice. For most of them, it was their very first spring.

I'd say, "Listen, Scott Kowalkowski, or whoever, Coach Holtz wants to see you."

So he'd go up to Coach and say, "Coach, did you want to see me?"

Coach would say, "No, son, I don't want to see you."

Then Andre Jones would go up to see him.

"Coach, did you want to see me?"

And Coach is thinking, why are these guys coming to see me?
So he says, "Son, who sent you to see me?"
"Frank Stams did, Coach."
Then the next guy went up to him—I forget who it was, might have been
Kevin McShane—"Coach, did you want to see me?"
"Son, did Frank Stams send you over here?"
"Yes, sir."
"Well, you tell your buddies to take it on in and hit the showers."
Before I knew it I was out there practicing by myself. That's the last
time I fooled around with Coach Holtz and his sense of humor.

At the end of spring we appeared to be a veteran team. I say that because we probably scrimmaged as much as any team I've ever been associated with. But I felt it was a necessity, because at six positions— split end, flanker, right tackle, center, left guard, and left tackle—we had a combined playing time of four minutes and fifteen seconds, in terms of how much our players had been at those spots last year. I had never seen as inexperienced a football team going into a season.

We went three scrimmages in a row where we did not score against either our first or second defenses. I've seen teams have trouble moving the football in the spring against the number-one defense, but never against the number-two unit. This was a little disappointing, because we weren't running a lot of stunts or doing anything to try to confuse the offense, nor were we blitzing. We were just trying to play good, solid, fundamental football and get to the ball. The defense's confidence grew every day, while the offense's deteriorated a great deal.

It was obvious to me midway through spring practice that we weren't coming together as a football team in terms of chemistry, even though I saw a great deal of improvement individually. For example, Dean Brown and Andy Heck have a chance to be outstanding offensive tackles. After our first scrimmage I could see they had a chance to be good, and they were only going to get better as spring practice went along, because the position was new to both of them. But they'd just never played there before.

Tim Grunhard was a solid football player, and I like some of the things I saw Winston Sandri and Mike Heldt and Tim Ryan do. Heldt and Ryan weren't going to be as solid as Chuck Lanza right away, but they had a chance to be good. I thought Sandri, Heldt, and Ryan were going to be fine linemen. It was just a question of when.

We weren't very productive at tight end during the spring, and even though Frank Jacobs showed improvement, he wasn't the dominating player we had to have. We were fumbling quite a bit, even though Ricky Watters and Tony Brooks were playing very well. We just were missing something as far as chemistry and leadership.

Mark Green was going to be a fine flanker, but I felt we needed his consistent leadership a little bit closer to the center of the action. Maybe we needed him back at tailback. So, for several practices, we put Watters in for a few plays at a time at flanker. From the first time he was there, it was obvious he was a natural. He has a good feel for the position, and he would give us some of the same explosiveness that Timmy Brown gave us. Timmy could accelerate with one step faster than anyone I've ever seen. Ricky may not have that same sort of quickness, but he is 204 pounds, a very elusive football player, and an excellent competitor.

However, Ricky didn't want to be a flanker—he wanted to be a tailback, and I could understand that, because he's a good, solid one. I felt, though, that in the best interests of the football team he should be a flanker. I got a call at home on a Sunday night after our fourteenth practice, and it was from Ricky. He said, "Coach, if you really want me to be a flanker, I will do whatever will help the team the most." I told Ricky I hadn't made a decision yet, but that I really appreciated that. The decision wasn't finalized until after our seventeenth practice, with a week to go in spring ball. Even though Ricky hadn't practiced at flanker very much, it was easy to see the feel he already had for it. I thought he'd be very solid. And Mark Green moving back to the tailback position gave us a serenity in the offense that we had not seen previously.

Steve Belles came along very well in spring practice, as I had envisioned, and he gave Tony Rice a good run for his money. But Tony had an outstanding spring. I was disappointed in the play of our split ends, however. They weren't very productive, and after the seventh practice we decided that if we were going to be good on defense, we needed to solve some of our depth problems there. So we moved Patrick Terrell, who is a great talent, to free safety. He had started some for us at split end last year and only caught three passes, but he's a tough, hard-nosed young man with all the ingredients you want. He's a winner, a competitor you can trust; he's committed, and he genuinely cares about other people. Chuck Heater fell in love with him in the secondary, but consequently our problems at split end became a little bit larger. At that point, though, I was more concerned with getting our defense where we wanted it to be.

Chuck Heater, secondary coach

The defense looked good in the spring, but we didn't know if we were good or if our offense wasn't as strong. There was no standard, so you

34

couldn't quite give it the seal of approval. But there sure was potential. And we knew we couldn't get where we wanted to go until our defense was good. Lou said so many times, and I've heard that everywhere I've been—you can't be dominant without a great defense. Even after twenty days of practice in the spring, I'm not sure we knew whether we could be dominant on defense. Barry [Alvarez, defensive coordinator] had great confidence, but it wasn't until we lined up in August and realized the offense was better than what we'd thought in the spring, that we thought maybe we were pretty good on defense.

Pete Cordelli, receiver coach

One thing that really helped us offensively in the spring was to go up against a defense as good as ours in practice. That's only going to make you better. That's why we had our top offense go against the top defense so much. When you don't see the type of speed, quickness, and strength out of your second-line people, it's not the same. You can't go out there on Saturday and say, "Gee, we didn't see anything like this all week." You go one against one, and you know you experienced the best. It's like a boxer—you try to find the best sparring partner you can, to simulate what you're going to see in the ring. In football you make it tough during the week so you're not caught off guard on Saturday.

We ended up with a spring game that was vanilla. The defense only ran one front and one coverage, and we narrowed what we did on offense. Steve Belles finished a fine spring and definitely moved ahead as the number-two quarterback. Tony Rice's stats during spring practice weren't impressive, but he had a tremendous amount of passes dropped, including six in the spring game alone.

We never try to do much with our spring game because we know there are scouts from Michigan in the press box, so it doesn't make sense to show your entire package and give away all your secrets. Instead, we try to make it fun and competitive for the players. We let the coaches or the captains draft teams, and try to keep them as even as possible. Lots of times we only have one practice for the teams to work together, and with the different combinations, it doesn't make for great execution. But that's all right.

The winners in the spring game eat steak, and the losers eat hot dogs. The losers also have to do a hundred hours of community service; that provides a little motivation for everyone. The fan interest in this game is amazing, especially if the weather is nice. This year we had almost 16,000 people, but I hoped they were not judging our football team by what they saw. The weather made it very difficult to throw the ball, with twenty-five-mile gusts, and I think our quarterbacks combined for 12 passes in 41 attempts and had 5 intercepted.

Ricky Watters earned half of the offensive MVP award for scoring two touchdowns, and Belles got the other half for leading his team on two second-half touchdown drives. George Streeter blocked a punt and recovered a fumble and won the defensive MVP award.

We also present awards at halftime to the most improved players during the spring. This year they went to Dean Brown on the offensive line, Bobby Carpenter among the skill positions on offense, Jeff Alm among the defensive linemen, and D'Juan Francisco among the defensive backs. Steve Roddy got one for his second effort, after having a great spring with Chris Zorich out. Walk-on Doug DiOrio got the pit-bull award for his toughness. These awards have been given for years and are named after Frank Hering, Notre Dame's first paid football coach.

We finish up spring practice by the end of April so our athletes have a week to get ready academically for final exams. Our spring season usually ends the same weekend the Bookstore Basketball tournament finishes up. I've always felt it's important to have the players still involved in as many aspects of campus life as possible. Bookstore certainly qualifies, because I'm not sure there's anything else more important on campus. There are 666 five-man teams this year, and they will play to 21 points, one point per basket, single-elimination format, with every game played outdoors, regardless of the weather. If there's a snowstorm going on, you still play.

My first year I didn't play Bookstore Basketball. My second year I played with Mike Bobinski, our ticket manager; Jim Dolan, a former varsity basketball player; George Stewart, one of our assistant coaches; and Chuck Lennon, from the Alumni Association. We did well that year, as we got to the final 16 only to lose to the eventual champions, a team that included Tim Brown and varsity-basketball captain Donald Royal, in overtime.

This year I convinced Tony Rice and Kent Graham to play with me because I felt they were as good as any football players on the basketball court. I always get concerned about injuries, but it's tough to fight something as important as Bookstore Basketball. So I just decided to cooperate, and we even let players out of spring practice early if they have a Bookstore game.

We lost in the semifinals in front of a couple of thousand people on the Stepan Center courts. The game began an hour after the conclusion of the spring game, and it was cold and miserable . . . and I played horrendously. It was right after that game my wife told me she thought I ought to retire because I was embarrassing myself.

As long as I was playing against the average student, I guess I wasn't too bad for a fifty-one-year-old man. But Ricky Watters stole the ball from me one time and went down to the other end and dunked it, and I wanted to run him into the backboard as he went up for the layup. Two things prevented me from doing it. Number one, he was our best football player, maybe our best athlete. Second, I couldn't catch up with him.

With spring practice behind us I'm trying to get a handle on where we are with three months to go before practice begins again in August.

I really like the way our staff complements one another. They get along exceptionally well, they're very conscientious, and have a lot of self-pride. I think the changes we've made have turned out to be positive ones— Chuck Heater handling the secondary, John Palermo the defensive line, and Joe Moore with the tackles and tight ends. Scott Raridon has done an excellent job with our weight program. Scott has gotten the body-fat numbers down, and that has made us quicker. We've gotten great results there, and the overall talent, though exceptionally young, is still the best we've had since I've been here.

As I've said, we thought we would have some problems on offense, but the key to our team would be defense. I am impressed with the progress we made in this area. We seem to be a little quicker than we have been in the past. Our linebackers are very good. Frank Stams and Flash Gordon had fine springs, and they are being pushed by two freshmen—Scott Kowalkowski and Andre Jones. I think Wes Pritchett had his best spring by far, and Michael Stonebreaker is one of the finest linebackers I've had the opportunity to coach. Ned Bolcar had a sore ankle and consequently missed a lot of practice this spring, but we all know what a fine player he is. With Ned out, the development of Donn Grimm was a pleasant surprise.

The secondary has some question marks, but the two pleasant surprises there have been the consistent play of George Streeter and the development of D'Juan Francisco. Todd Lyght is a great athlete, and Stan Smagala is definitely a winner. We have to develop some depth there, but overall it's encouraging. We moved Pat Terrell to the secondary because he has great speed and can cover up some mistakes back there. We definitely need some freshmen there to provide depth.

Ara Parseghian, former Notre Dame head coach
When I saw Notre Dame in the spring, I thought they were going to be a

solid football team. I'd heard a lot of comments about improvements on the defensive side, which I'm always impressed by, because that's one of the prerequisites for any kind of championship season. You can't just continue to try to outscore everybody, because somewhere you're going to get caught.

The offense is a question mark. We have fine tailbacks in Mark Green and Tony Brooks, and two good fullbacks in Braxston Banks and Anthony Johnson. Our freshman split receivers, Bobby Carpenter and Pierre Martin, will be improved over our split-end positions last year.

Our tight-end situation is a little weak because we moved Andy Heck away from there, but I feel Frank Jacobs can be a good one. If we don't have a freshman or two come along in the fall, we may have to move Andy back.

The most disturbing thing about spring practice was the play of our young offensive line. We know that Tim Grunhard and Jeff Pearson can be pretty good football players, but their consistency was not what we needed during the spring. We moved Dean Brown to tackle, where we think he has a chance to be excellent. The other tackle, Andy Heck, will be very good. If we have to move him back to tight end, I don't have any qualms about Peter Rausch stepping in there and playing that position. Our play at center was up and down. We tried so many people there. The best chance to win is with Mike Heldt and Tim Ryan, who moved there from linebacker. Winston Sandri and Ryan Mihalko will be fine guards behind Pearson and Grunhard.

Tony Rice threw the ball better than we ever envisioned he could, but we still are not as consistent at quarterback as we need to be.

Even though we had problems on offense during the spring, I will be disappointed if we aren't a good offensive team because of the new staff. With Jim Strong coaching the backs, I know they will run hard, protect the ball, and block. His backs are always as well-coached as any in the country, and he is a great motivator and hard worker. Pete Cordelli is as knowledgeable as any receiver coach and has great rapport with his players. Tony Yelovich and Joe Moore have a proven track record as great coaches. Joe, with his unique ability to motivate and teach players, is particularly impressive. Tony is a great guy, hard worker, and outstanding technician.

I think our placekickers will be fine. Reggie Ho is a good, consistent short kicker and Bill Hackett is very good on long field goals. Ricky Watters and Mark Green give us two good return men.

Coming out of spring practice, our big concern was the punting. Sean was a fine basketball player who came to one of our coaches in the spring and said he'd like to come out as a punter. I said he couldn't until I spoke to Digger Phelps about it. I thought Sean could play both sports, but Digger felt otherwise. I have great respect for Digger, and he voiced what he felt was fair to the young man and the basketball team.

I sat down with Sean and told him I felt he ought to think about this seriously. Maybe he ought to stay with basketball. He said he didn't wish to play basketball any longer and that he wanted to be the punter on the Notre Dame football team. He understood there was no guarantee he would be our punter.

One of the reasons kickers don't punt the ball particularly well during the spring is that they've been inside all winter and never had a chance to work. Hopefully, Jim Sexton or Connor will become a very good punter.

I do feel we have a chance to be a very competitive football team if we get a lot better, a lot stronger, and grow up and mature much more rapidly than the three months allow before the season starts. The attitude of the team is very good right now, but we'll just have to wait and see what happens. Because of the youth, if we can get off to a good start this year, I think we will pick up momentum and become an excellent football team. However, if we don't start well, our confidence may be shot and it could be a very long year.

Barry Alvarez, defensive coordinator

Lou always talks about defense, about how you can't be a great team until you're great on defense. We knew that would be a key coming into the '88 season—we had to be better defensively.

I really believe our success defensively had an awful lot to do with the attitude that Frank Stams and Wes Pritchett took. I can't overemphasize that, because, as fifth-year guys [five academic years, four football years], everybody was looking at them to see how they took to things.

Don't forget, we had a whole new defensive staff. Every single defensive player had a new position coach. Yet Pritchett and Stams set the example, as far as showing a great enthusiasm for everything we told them. I think that carried over to a tremendous extent. From day one they had fun. They bought everything we told them. They just want to do it. I just can't emphasize that enough. Everybody took their cue from those guys because they'd been here longer than anyone else.

I think Lou's emphasis with the kids on staying healthy and on fundamentals was key. He almost overemphasizes fundamentals, that's how important he thinks they are. He wants to make sure you teach kids how to be in a good football position, because that keeps them from being injured. If they were injured, it was because they had a bad atti-

39

tude. If you got hurt, you were in trouble. So we very seldom missed anyone defensively, even for practice. We had a couple of defensive backs get nicked up, but you look at Stams and the linebackers, and they never missed a day. It was a rarity down in Phoenix [for the Fiesta Bowl] when Stams got sick one day and so did Michael Stonebreaker. They just didn't miss any time, and it was the same with the defensive line. We started the same group there every week.

A lot of that is attitude. Sometimes you can't help injuries, but our kids were afraid to get hurt because they were afraid if they sat down, they might never get back in there again. The Miami game was a great example, when Pritchett wouldn't come out of the game even though he had a broken hand. That type of attitude was instilled in everybody.

The way Lou approaches things is so important. People questioned why he was always so concerned about every team we played, but that's the way we did things. We beat Rice 54–11, but if we played them again the next week, the approach would have been exactly the same. I could look our kids in the eye and say we should win this game, but Rice moved the ball against everybody, and we had the film to prove it. If you take them lightly, they can hurt you.

That's what was unique about this team. They listened. I tried to be honest with them. We'd give them a scouting report on Monday, and we'd go right through the week with them. On Thursday we'd meet with the defense down in the corner of the field and we'd go over the gameplan and say, this is what we want to do. On first down it's imperative they don't rush for more than three yards. We can't be in second and short all day. We try to find their cutoff to throw. When we can get them in third and whatever it would be for them to throw, then we've got them where we want them. Then we can do this or do that. The kids were smart that way—they knew exactly what we wanted, and they knew whenever we lied to them. All they had to do was look at film and see Rice go right down the field against Texas A&M and Arkansas.

The players read us well as coaches, so that's the way we approached it. If we coaches took a team lightly and didn't work and prepare the same way each week, the kids picked up on that.

I think we were able to keep a pretty even keel. That was important. The first week the kids were sky high for the first game against Michigan, and for Miami, but not for any other game. Those were the only two games I thought the kids were really cranked.

A lot of coaches make their mistake by thinking you can set the tone and establish an attitude in the middle of August or the week of a game. We made our approach completely clear in January, after we lost the Cotton Bowl. We weren't going to do anyone any favors. Even during the winter program you better be up for breakfast and you better be going to class. I don't care if you're an all-American—you're going to make that commitment or you're going to run. We weren't going to let anything slide. Lou really stays on top of things like that.

He really knows what kind of approach to take from week to week. The game I'll always remember was our '87 opener at Michigan, my first game here at Notre Dame. We'd been 5–6 the year before and we had a new quarterback and didn't know how good we could be. But Lou kept saying the game didn't have to be close, even though we were playing in Ann Arbor, and it wasn't close.

Lou can anticipate or almost predict exactly what's going to happen. He writes his postgame remarks before the game. He walks in and knows what he's going to say, and in most cases he's right on the mark. He knows if we've had a bad week of practice.

Most coaches are pretty good at going before a team and talking off the top of their head, and Lou could do that better than anybody if he wanted to. But he'll never go in front of the team unless he's totally prepared. Even if it's just a routine practice, he always has his notes with him. I think that's what's unique about him—his preparation. It's so easy to get caught up in everything that's going on, especially at Notre Dame, but he always makes sure he has time to prepare himself for everything that comes along. He keeps up with it all.

Lou always wanted to know what we were going to do defensively. But he challenged us in his own way because he wasn't going to spend a lot of time meeting with the defense unless we made mistakes.

The Pittsburgh game, the first half, was really the only bad half of football we played on defense. So he met with us on Sunday before Miami and he challenged us. He thought we had lost the kids and so on. We didn't have a good scheme. We didn't play well, and we uncharacteristically gave up some big plays. And he wanted to know what was going on. But he never had to meet with us after that.

Our goal coming into the spring was to do so well in practices and do so well in scrimmages each week that he wouldn't come into our defensive meetings. We knew if we kept playing well on defense, he wouldn't worry about us—he'd let us do our thing. But if we screwed up, we knew he'd be right there looking over our shoulder, and that's what happened in the Pitt game. That's what a head coach is for—it's a system of checks and balances.

Defensively, Lou has certain beliefs, and he wants those things adhered to. He couldn't care less how we line up or what formations we use. He wants to know if we're doing the things fundamentally. Are you in good football position? Is your outside shoulder free and clear? I've never seen

41

anybody who's such a stickler on fundamentals. But he saw that every day in the spring, and that's all he worried about. He wanted to be able to look at the film of the defense and see us doing the right things fundamentally. The things we emphasize are the things he believes in, and that's all he ever wanted.

People see Lou calling the plays offensively on the sideline, but they forget that most of his years as an assistant coach were spent on defense. Against Air Force, for example, we played fairly well the first two periods, but he made a quick adjustment in our defensive alignment at halftime. Air Force was the number-one rushing team in the country, averaging 432 yards a game, and we held them to 29 in the last two quarters.

5

THOUGHTS ON LIFE:
THE HOLTZ VIEWPOINT

THE only things that are going to change you from where you are today to where you are going to be five years from now are the people you meet and the books you read. Consequently, I think it is exceptionally important to identify with the proper people and read outstanding books. I have several favorite authors, with Zig Zigler and the Reverend Dr. Robert Schuller being two of them. Consequently, in my philosophy of life you are going to come across a lot of Zig Zigler, Dr. Schuller, Norman Vincent Peale, Og Mandino, and the list goes on and on.

When I was in college I had a professor who asked us to write a philosophy of life. I had never done it before, nor was I looking forward to it. But it was one of the more enjoyable things I have done, and also one of the most profitable. Anytime you write a philosophy of life, it forces you to think about what you really believe in and what you value and cherish. It also can serve as a gameplan for where you want to go and how you are going to get there. I encourage our senior football players to write a philosophy of life before they leave Notre Dame, because I think it is exceptionally important for us to have a blueprint for the future.

Life is really quite exciting. One day you're drinking the wine, and the next day you're picking the grapes. There are certain things in this world we all have in common, such as time. Everybody has sixty seconds to a minute, sixty minutes to an hour, twenty-four hours to a day; the difference is what we do with that time and how we use it. As Reverend Harrington says, "If you're killing time it's not murder, but pure suicide."

Another thing we all have in common is facing competition. So many times people are afraid of competition, when it should bring out the best

43

in us. We all have talents and abilities, so why be intimidated by other people's skills? It is only natural that our own talents often differ from those of our peers.

Everybody gets discouraged at one time or another. I hate to tell you this, but during the next twelve months you're probably going to have at least three crises in your life. This does not mean that a crisis is bad. It's only bad if you react negatively to it. If you take a positive approach to everything that happens, you'll have experiences that improve you for the future.

I don't ask our athletes how many of them want to win. Everybody wants to win when the bands are playing, the crowds are cheering, and the television lights are on. The question I ask is, Can you live with losing, can you live with failure, can you live with mediocrity? A great individual is the one who can get up off the ground after he has been knocked down by adversity.

The one thing that is guaranteed to get you up off the ground the quickest and most consistently is a realistic list of dreams and goals. I am not talking about a wish list. Sometimes people make up a list and say, "Boy, I wish this would happen," but they never do anything to see that these things come to pass. We use the word WIN, which means to me: What's Important Now. You must have goals and dreams if you are ever going to achieve anything in this world.

Can you imagine walking up to a ticket counter at the airport and saying to the airline employee, "Give me a ticket," and they say, "Where do you want to go?" and you reply, "I don't know, but I'm in a hurry, so give me a ticket, quickly, please." "Well, what price do you want to pay, how much are you willing to sacrifice?" "Well, I really haven't given that any thought, but I would like to get a ticket."

I believe that if you are bored with life, that if you don't have a burning desire to get up in the morning with an urgent desire to do things, your problem is you do not have an awful lot of goals. Many times we do not understand the positive effect goal-setting has upon the people who are around us.

I remember when we lived in McGregor Downs in Raleigh, North Carolina, and our youngest son, K.R., was five years old. He'd say, "Hurry up with dinner, Mom, because I want to go to bed." Now, you have to understand K.R. He would never go to bed unless you threatened his life at least four separate times and convinced him you would carry out your threat. Consequently, we suspected he had an ulterior motive. I said, "Why do you want to go to bed so early, Kevin, are you sick?" He said, "No, but I got to get a good night's rest because I'm swimming tomorrow in the contest for five-year-olds at the swimming pool." I said,

"Well, Kevin, that is really amazing. Do you think you can win?" He said, "Oh, Dad, there isn't any doubt in my mind. I've been thinking about it and dreaming about it, and I'm going to win that race."

I admired and respected this, knowing Kevin couldn't swim. But sure enough, he gets up there, dives in the pool, dog paddles, and somehow got to the other side and won a ribbon for second place. Goals just don't happen. You have to believe, you have to be willing to work on them.

Can you imagine walking up to Sir Edmund Hillary after he scaled Mt. Everest and asking, "Hey, how did you get here?" And he said, "I don't know. I went for a walk and here I am."

Most of the time you aren't going to experience success immediately, but you can't give up your goals and get discouraged. When things go awry, you have to step back, evaluate the situation, make whatever adjustments are necessary, and start again. Can you imagine the perseverance that Thomas Edison possessed? We're all aware that he invented the light bulb, but not many people realize that he did so after thousands of unsuccessful experiments. They asked him if he got discouraged after so many failures. He said, "I never failed. After every experiment I realized I was successful in proving that you couldn't make a light bulb in that manner." This is a very unique approach to research, and perhaps it accounts for the reason Thomas Edison is considered the father of invention.

Also, your work may not always be appreciated. When Marconi said, "I have the theory that will enable man to transmit sound through space," they considered committing him to the insane asylum.

And as for failure, take Babe Ruth. Most of us know that the legendary Babe blasted 714 home runs, but how many know that he held the major-league record for striking out . . . over 1300 times!

You have to have goals and dreams, or life isn't very exciting and has no purpose. Can you imagine going out on the golf course, hitting a great drive, and following this up with a tremendous four iron to the green, only to discover that when you approached the putting surface, there was no cup? How long do you think you could shoot baskets if there wasn't a goal? I bet you would lose interest rapidly, and yet this analogy is no different than going through life without goals. It's impossible to get really involved and make a commitment without them. Sometimes your family or athletic teams can set goals for you.

A case in point is the salesman who felt his life was floundering. He rarely enjoyed success in sales. He finally came to the conclusion that he needed direction, so he decided to set some goals. He decided he wanted a gold automobile and firmly vowed that after he made a major sale, he would put a hundred-dollar bill in a shoe box under his bed when he received his commission. He set a time limit of one year to reach his goal, but didn't tell anybody about it.

Suddenly he was exceptionally motivated, and, oh, did he work. Now he didn't get discouraged with a few no's. He became very positive and his whole life changed. He obtained pictures of the gold car he desired and he put them everywhere, on the mirror where he shaved, the bureau where he dressed, the table where he ate, the dashboard of his car. Every month he would go down to the car dealership and sit in that beautiful gold automobile. Everybody at the dealership thought he was crazy, but they didn't say anything to him or pay much attention. Strange as it may seem, in eleven months he had enough money to pay cash for the gold car. He was so proud of himself that he went down to the automobile dealership and counted out the money, $19,000 in cash, on the hood of the gold car.

He drove it home, parked it out front of the house, but didn't say anything to his wife. He ate, went for a ride, returned home, and went directly to bed. His wife thought about the gold car in the picture and the automobile in front of their house, but she didn't say anything. The next morning the gentleman got up, went in to shave, and there on the mirror was a picture of a diamond ring and a fur coat. Once you establish your abilities to achieve something, everybody's expectations of you will rise dramatically.

We all have more talent than we will probably ever use. So many times we put limitations on ourselves. Anybody reading this book could take a three-foot board, suspend it one foot off the ground, and walk across it blindfolded. There would be absolutely no problem, because we wouldn't even think of falling off. But if we took that same board, extended it between two skyscrapers two thousand feet up in the air, how many of us would even try to walk across? Now, I ask you, why not? It's the same board, the same width—the only difference is that the board is suspended at a much greater height.

It seems the higher our challenge, the more we concentrate on failure rather than success. I believe we shouldn't concern ourselves with the difficulty of a challenge. Just take a good mental approach to the task and make your best effort on a continuous basis. I would like to think we all understand the necessity of working hard, as well as the benefits.

Years ago the people of a very successful civilization thought they had all the answers to success. The king called the wisest people in the kingdom together and said, "I want you to put down all the reasons why we are successful. Place them in writing so future generations will be able to read it and duplicate our success." They worked for approximately two years and came back with the answer, and it consisted of nine volumes.

The ruler looked at it and said, "This is great, but it's too large." He then challenged them to simplify their findings. They worked another year and finally narrowed it down to one book. The king said, "This is fine, but it is still too lengthy. Refine it." They worked another year, and finally reported back with their findings, now contained on one page. The king said, "You have done a great job, but it is still too long. Please reduce our formula for success to the lowest common denominator." They worked another year and had it down to one paragraph. The king said, "That's great, but it is still far too complicated. Keep working until everyone understands why we are successful."

Six months later they came back with their findings confined to one sentence. The king looked at it and said it was absolutely great. If all future generations understood this, they would be in a position to conquer anything. The sentence read, "There ain't no free lunch," which says it all.

Everybody is always looking for the quick fix or instant success in today's society. We all want to win the multimillion-dollar lottery or inherit a large sum of money. But you build a successful life a day at a time. No business goes bankrupt if it makes a profit every day. If you take good, hard work, and combine it with real enthusiasm, you have a chance to be ultra-successful. Enthusiasm is contagious. Everybody has enthusiasm. Some people have it for thirty seconds, some have it for thirty minutes, some have it for thirty days, but the individual who can possess enthusiasm for thirty years will be the one people feel has been born on third base.

I'm not a very smart individual, but I try to put signs in various places that will remind me of life's important matters. On my desk, for example, I have four signs. One says, "Nothing is as good as it seems, and nothing is as bad as it seems, but somewhere in between there reality falls." Another one of my favorites is, "This too shall pass." And the third one says, "The time to worry is before you place your bet, not after they spin the wheel." In other words, don't worry about something once you start it. Weigh and evaluate everything before then, and then proceed forward. And the last one is, "May God give me the courage to change the things I can, the serenity to accept the things I can't, and the wisdom to know the difference between the two." These four signs carry a special significance in my life.

I think, basically, there are four things that any organization needs to possess to be number one. First and foremost, you have to make a commitment to excellence. Decide once a year what you are going to do with your life. You don't have to get up every single day and make that decision. When I decided to go to the New York Jets in 1976, I didn't do so with a firm commitment. Nobody could have been any nicer than the owner, Leon Hess. He's a winner in every sense of the word. I was totally unfair to the New York Jets because I did not make a commitment and say I was going to see it through. I got up every day saying, "I'm not sure this is what I want to do, and I'm not sure this is going to work out," and consequently, one day when things weren't going well, I made a bad decision by resigning. What a disservice I did to the New York Jets and the people of New York. But, hopefully, we all have benefited from this experience.

Speaking about successful people, consider Ben Feldman, one of the most successful insurance agents in the entire country. Ben happens to be a resident of my hometown, East Liverpool, Ohio. He is a remarkable man, yet a very shy and unassuming individual. You couldn't pick him out of a crowd as the best salesman in the country. Because he had such resounding success as an insurance salesman, he was called upon to speak at various conventions. I've heard that initially he would only do it if he could speak from behind a curtain. If you listed all the ingredients somebody needed to be a successful salesman, Ben Feldman would not have many of them except for one thing—he had a burning desire to be number one. Don't get me wrong, he is a highly respected individual, but his success can be attributed to a commitment to being the best.

The second thing I think you need to be number one is complete attention to detail. There are so many little things in this world that absolutely have to be attended to, details that can be tedious and boring. In football, most teams will do the big things, but it is the teams that pay strict attention to little things that win. I don't know whether we can be as good this coming season as we were last year, but I do know that if we are to have a chance, we're going to have to pay close attention to details, no matter how trivial. If two seminars were held at the same time, one conducted by successful teams and one by losing teams, the similarities between the two would be amazing. The offensive and defensive theories both employed would be virtually identical. The amount of time they spend practicing wouldn't vary by more than a few minutes, and their practice format would be the same. The main differences would be the attention to detail. In the successful organization, no detail is too small to receive close attention. No job or assignment is minor, and everyone takes great pride in realizing they are important and their responsibilities are critical to the unit's success.

History has taught us time and again that accomplishments are achieved in areas that losers thought were not important and winners did. For Notre Dame to be successful this year, we will have to get rid of all the excuses losers cite. Unsuccessful people always have a million

48

different reasons why they can't be successful. You and I could compile a long list. At the top of it would be the belief that we are not appreciated. There is a saying, "We the willing, led by the unknowing, are doing the impossible for the ungrateful." We have done so much with so little for so long, we now think we can do the impossible with nothing. If you tackle a task just so you will receive recognition, you are going to be disappointed most of your life.

Naturally, when you're successful, you are going to surprise a lot of people. When I coached at Ohio State there was a big billboard at the entrance to the Columbus airport that said, "Behind every successful man stands a very surprised mother-in-law." I think that is certainly true in my case, and I'm sure it's true in many.

The third thing I think you have to do to be number one is be fundamentally sound. All football teams have a tendency to become bored with such basic things as blocking and tackling. Yet if we are ever going to be successful, we'll have to build our empire on a firm foundation. They tell the story about three people who were going to be guillotined—a priest, a lawyer, and a coach. They were allowed to make one statement prior to the execution. As the priest stood up, he said, "Cheer, cheer, for old Notre Dame." The guillotine dropped on the priest, came within two inches of his neck and mysteriously stopped. Everybody thought it was a miracle, so they let the priest go free. They then approached the lawyer, who said, "Justice for all"; once again the guillotine mysteriously stopped inches from its destination. Thinking this was a message that the lawyer was innocent, they let him go free as well. Next, it was the coach's turn. His last statement was "If you tighten the two bolts on the left, the guillotine will work as intended." You see, coaches think they have all the answers. I guess it's sometimes better to keep your mouth shut and let people think you're a fool than to open it and leave absolutely no doubt.

I've been around Billy Ray Smith, Dan Hampton, Tim Brown, Gary Anderson, all great football players—not because they never got knocked down, but because they refused to stay down. When you knocked them down, they got up, took the shortest route to the ball carrier, and arrived there in a bad mood. In addition, they were exceptionally good players fundamentally.

Firm, fundamental principles are what guide my wife and me in bringing up four wonderful children. Those principles are: religious atmosphere, an obligation to each other, and a lot of love and caring for each other.

I think it's also important to be a self-starter. Nobody is going to wind you up in the morning and give you a pep talk and push you out. You have to have a firm faith and belief in yourself, and this, along with good, fundamental principles, will allow you to move your life in the proper direction.

The fourth requirement necessary to be number one is discipline. As I noted earlier, I find it amazing that we can conquer outer space and travel to the depth of the oceans, yet most of the time, we can't win one of life's most important battles—a victory over ourselves. If there is one absolute in our society, I think it's that *abuse leads to restrictions*. Most rules and laws in our society derive from the fact that too many people did not have the self-discipline to refrain from taking advantage of the liberties this country offers. Nobody can enjoy success for an extended period of time if they do not possess discipline.

Ted Williams is another of my favorite heroes, because he's a class gentleman who also happened to be a great athlete. However, the thing he did that impressed me was serving his country on two different occasions during the peak of his career, and doing it without complaining. He also is a hero of mine because he was a self-disciplined person who worked long hours to perfect his absolutely wonderful skills. Going into the last day of the season in 1941, Ted Williams was batting something like .39955, and if you rounded it off, you could honestly say that Ted Williams was a .400 hitter. This is as rare as a lucky rabbit's foot. He could have sat out the doubleheader on the last day of the season, but decided against it.

Most of us probably would have decided not to play, but not Ted Williams. He said that if he were a .400 hitter, he would get enough hits in the doubleheader to be one. He ended up batting .406 for the season. Ted Williams wasn't born this way—you aren't born a winner or loser, but you are what you think you are. Ted Williams had tremendous confidence in himself, in his talents and his abilities.

Nobody wants to be mediocre in life or accept being a second-class citizen. The mediocre are the top of the bottom, the best of the worst, or the bottom of the top, the worst of the best. I know I would like to be a great golfer. Unfortunately, I don't have the time, but I do enjoy the game. I think it was Zig Zigler who said, "I choose not to be a great golfer because I choose to excel in other areas of my life."

When I was coaching at North Carolina State I got a call from Jimmy Durer to come down and play golf with him at Pinehurst. Jimmy Durer was a television golf commentator at that time. I drove down and played with him, and I was doing fairly well until we came to the fifth hole. It was a par 3, and I thought I should hit a six iron, but Jimmy recommended I hit a five iron. I succumbed to his wishes and used a five iron to hit my career shot. It went over the pin, over the green, and finally came to rest underneath a tree. I was quite upset and didn't make an effort to hide my feelings when Jimmy said to me, "If you look north, south, east, or west you will find four places worse off than where you are."

As I examined the situation, he was absolutely right. I was under a tree, but I did have a shot and could still make the par. I could have been in the water to my left, or in the hedges on my right, or in the trap in front of me. Unfortunately, I made a double bogey and it didn't do an awful lot for my attitude.

We got up on the next tee and I hit a bad shot and threw my golf club. Jimmy looked at me and said, "You don't hit the ball well enough to get upset. That's reserved for a good golfer, and you aren't a good golfer." Ever since then I've never once thought about throwing a club after a bad shot. I just say I'm not good enough to get mad, and that's been the extent of it. I think it shows great self-discipline not to lose your temper. I wish I could control mine better, and I have made progress in this area.

You can't flinch if you want to win. Why do some people think very positively and others negatively? Most psychologists will tell you we basically have two thought processes in our mind. One says why we can do something, and the other one tells us why we can't. If you put negative thoughts into your mind, you're going to get negative results. It's just as true that if you put positive thoughts in your mind, you will be a recipient of positive results. There are great opportunities available to us if we will just open our minds to this. It's one reason why we conduct the relaxation period with our athletes the night before the game. I wish we could do it more often, but time prohibits it.

We have a tendency to look at things as they are, without seeing the wonderful opportunities that are available. It is really our choice, nobody else's. Almost everything that happens to us, either good or bad, is a result of the decisions we make. It is popular to point a finger and blame everybody else for the situations we find ourselves in, but everybody has the opportunity to make the choices that govern their lives. We choose whether we are going to be happy or sad, believe or doubt, pray or curse, help or heal, work or loaf, succeed or fail.

There is virtually nothing impossible in this world if you just put your mind to it and maintain a positive attitude. In Zig Zigler's outstanding book, *See You at the Top*, he discussed the ability of the bumblebee to fly. According to Zig, most aeronautical engineers will tell you that there is no possible way the bumblebee can fly. His wingspan isn't broad enough, he is too heavy, and his body build makes it impossible for him to fly. Fortunately, the bumblebee doesn't understand aeronautics, so he just goes along and flies.

It is imperative for all of us to remember that success is not going to happen overnight. Patience is not only a virtue, it is a necessity. I reminded one of the players when I was coaching at Arkansas that Rome wasn't built in a day. He told a teammate that it was strictly because I wasn't the foreman. I'm not very patient, but I am a firm believer that good things can and will happen if you are persistent.

There are some people who will attempt to discourage you. When I first went to Kent State University I was warned by Miss Sloane, our academic advisor, that I would not succeed in college because I did not have the academic background. Based on my high-school transcript, I think this was an accurate evaluation. I also understood that I would have to compete with such outstanding students as Witt Matthews, the valedictorian of our class.

The very first college course I had at Kent State was an English class taught by Dr. Marshall. I walked in the class at the same time as Dr. Marshall, so I quickly took the first open seat I could find and waited for him to say, "Good morning, welcome to Kent State." He didn't. The first words I heard him utter were these: "I want you to look at the person on your left, then look at the person on your right, because two out of three of you are going to flunk this class." I turned to my left, and there sat Witt Matthews. I looked to the young lady on my right and said, "I hope you ain't no good in English." Then I noticed a National Honor Society button on her chest. So I did the only thing I could possibly do to pass English. I got up and went down to the registrar's office and dropped the class and enrolled in one I had a chance to pass.

There were some professors such as Dr. Kaplan, Dr. Sheiver, and Dr. Roberts, three history professors, who encouraged you and believed in you, and for some reason I always performed much better in that atmosphere. I wish I could say I always coach that way, but I don't. However, I do try to be positive, and I have always believed in our players. I'm sure that many members of the news media will say that we are always downplaying our football team and bragging about our opponents. I can honestly say that when we leave a team meeting we always believe that we are going to be successful and that we control our own destiny.

This chapter could easily turn into a book solely on motivation, and maybe someday it will. But for now, suffice it to say that self-image is of paramount importance if you are to be successful and happy. We have inherited five college situations at William & Mary, North Carolina State, Arkansas, Minnesota, and Notre Dame, and never have we inherited a winner. Yet we have taken every school to a bowl game during the second season, at the latest. This was not accomplished by just coaching or by constantly standing on a soap box to sing the athlete's praises, but by a philosophy of making them feel good about themselves. We have been successful because of three simple rules:

1. Do what is right. You know the difference, and if you have any doubt, get out the Bible. It's right to be on time, polite, honest, to remain free from drugs.
2. Do your best. We do not help people at all by accepting mediocrity when they are capable of being better. Don't worry about being popular. Many times we don't encourage others to do their best because we are more concerned with our player's appraisal of our efforts than we are with them.
3. Treat others as you would like to be treated (golden rule). I have never seen a team, a family, or a business that can't become better by emphasizing love and understanding.

There are three universal questions everyone asks of each other's spouse, players, coaches, parents, children, customers, and clients.

1. Can I trust you? Without trust there is no marriage, etc. The only way you can generate trust is *do what is right* all the time.
2. *Are you committed to excellence?* Everyone wants to be identified with someone who aspires to be the best. Not the largest, but certainly the best. The only way you can show you are committed to excellence is to always DO YOUR BEST.
3. *Do you care about me?* Do you care about me because I can run or pass? This question is critical if teamwork is to be achieved. The only way to show people you care about them is to *treat people as you would like to be treated.*

Remember you are special. God does love you, and you are special. Everyone has a God. For me, it is Christianity. For some people it may be Judaism or Hinduism. Unfortunately, for some people their God is money, drugs, alcohol, sex, or power. One thing is for certain: there will be one thing that will dominate your life. I strongly suggest it be something you can be proud of. I have never known anyone who stood up and said the reason I'm successful is drugs or alcohol, but I have seen and read of thousands who said my life is a mess because of drugs and alcohol.

You build a successful life day by day. My good friend Frank "Digger" Dawson from East Liverpool sent me a poem titled "The Builder" that will close this chapter:

THE FIGHTING SPIRIT

I saw a group of men in my hometown.
I saw a group of men tearing a building down.
With a heave and a ho and a mighty yell,
They swung a beam and the sidewalk fell.
And I said to the foreman, "Are these men skilled,
The type you'd hire if you wanted to build?"
And he laughed and said, "Why, no indeed."
He said, "Common labor's all I need.
For I can tear down in a day or two
What it took a builder ten years to do."
And I thought to myself as I walked away,
"Which of these roles am I going to play?
Am I the type that constantly tears down
As I make my way, foolishly, around?
Or am I the type that's trying to build with care,
In hopes that my organization'll be glad I was there?"

6

THE SUMMER:
GRADES AND GOLF

As we pointed toward August and our preseason camp, I felt our good attitude was exemplified by the players' grades in the spring semester. For the most part our defense did a fine job academically.

However, we lost Bobby Carpenter and Pierre Martin because of grades, and this was really discouraging. Pierre, disappointed in his performance academically, wrote a long, impassioned letter to the university. In it he said that he was going to do everything he possibly could to come back to Notre Dame. He'll have to go to school somewhere else for a year, but if he's that committed, then maybe we'll see him back here someday. The loss of those two players was unfortunate, not just for their welfare, but because of our needs at split end. We'd moved Pat Terrell from end to defense, thinking we'd have Carpenter and Martin at split end, and the two of them had some bright spots during the spring, even if they weren't consistent. We didn't want to move Terrell back, but Steve Alaniz is now the only split end with any experience.

Notre Dame has had 508 out of 514 football players graduate in the last twenty years, and to have two athletes dismissed from school for academic reasons was a tremendous shock to the entire university. We always look for something positive in everything that happens. In this case, it meant, first, that Notre Dame would not rubber-stamp its athletes for graduation, that they're going to have to do the work. If they don't have the discipline necessary to graduate, they're going to become a casualty.

Second, it forced us to take a long, hard look at how we could do a better job of motivating our athletes academically.

Ned Bolcar, senior linebacker

Coach Holtz says, "I'd rather be 0–11 than be here as a coach and not have a player graduate."

Mike DeCicco's office, along with Emil T. Hofman's, has had so much success in the past, I naturally assumed that if the players were having problems academically, the responsibility did not rest in their offices, but in ours.

In the past, the football office has had absolutely nothing to do with academics. But after the loss of Carpenter and Martin, we came up with a truth statement. We asked our athletes ten questions each week, and they had to sign the statement and answer it honestly. We asked them questions about their class attendance and things of that nature. If an individual wanted to sit in the union and eat hot dogs and drink Coke and flunk out, we were going to make him the most miserable individual there has ever been.

In addition, many of our freshmen hadn't performed in the classroom as well as they should or could. We also lost Peter Rausch, who was permitted to remain in school but was ineligible to play in the fall. I was disappointed at the number of players we had in summer school—more than fifty. I really didn't care if we ever fielded a football team again.

It is important that when a young man comes to Notre Dame, he learn how to discipline himself and grow and mature and develop, and we obviously had not done the job in the last twelve months. We decided to make some changes. Our players must understand they are students first.

We would never talk to a professor or tell a player what class to take or drop. But by having them fill out the truth statement, we would know everything about them academically each and every week.

I visited with Dr. Hofman and told him what we wanted to do. He is an incredible person, one of the most remarkable men I've ever met. He is in charge of the Freshman Year of Studies program and is responsible for all freshmen. Before we did anything with the truth statement, we needed his consent. His office was aware of the situation, and he approved our statement. We are all here for the same purpose, and that's to see that our students graduate.

In addition to overseeing the academics of all our upperclass athletes, Dr. DeCicco is also Notre Dame's fencing coach and has won several national championships. I tell him I will come to his fencing matches if they use real swords so I can tell who wins.

One of the most impressive displays of leadership is to watch Mike

DeCicco come onto the football field and yank a player out of practice because he missed a class or a tutoring session. I guarantee you our players support Dr. Hofman, Dr. DeCicco, and their style as much as any coach.

With the help of the truth statements, our grades were tremendous. Our overall grade-point average for the entire summer was better than a 3.0, and Mike DeCicco told me it was the best job he had ever seen by a football team during the summer. People like Tony Rice never set foot in the weight room or threw a football all summer. He spent fourteen hours a day with academics. We put curfews on them. We jumped on top of them. We did everything we had to do to make them realize we were serious.

The most impressive thing was that the attitude of our whole team became one of academic seriousness. The players talked about academics with one another. They took pride in what they did. They accepted the challenge. It was one of the most rewarding things that has happened to me in eighteen years as a head coach.

I've always felt that a student's priorities ought to be, in this order: faith, family, academics, football, and finally, social life.

The summer was very hectic in many respects. Wesley Pritchett's father went into a coma and remained comatose as we got ready to begin practice in August. Wes is very close with his father, and it hasn't been easy for him. Peter Graham's father and Ned Bolcar's father both had heart bypass surgery. In addition, we had some problems with my mother's health. I'm always greatly concerned, because she's seventy-two years old, had a stroke eight years ago, is completely paralyzed, and can't speak. She is confined to a wheelchair. I wish I could get back to Ohio a little more often to see her, but it's just not possible. She's a beautiful lady and can understand. She's very proud I'm at the University of Notre Dame, but worries about her only son being under so much pressure.

I had the opportunity to play some golf, and I ended up playing very well by the end of the summer. I even had a hole-in-one—my second in a year—playing with Father Bill Beauchamp, Dick Rosenthal, and Roger Valdiserri.

One of the most memorable experiences I had all summer was when I played at the Bing Crosby Pro-Am for charity. I didn't play particularly well, but there were approximately 45,000 spectators on both Saturday and Sunday. It was a wonderful time, a chance to visit with Daryle Lamonica, a former Notre Dame quarterback who loves this university and has a very fine football mind.

Although I didn't play well, I was able to designate $11,000—our share of the winnings—to go to diabetes. That's always been our special charity.

I didn't have any free time the entire summer, but I went out the last weekend before the freshmen reported for practice in August and stayed with Dick and Marylyn Rosenthal in Vail, Colorado. My wife Beth, my daughter Liz, and I were only there two days, but it was very relaxing and the companionship was excellent. We didn't talk business at all, but we did play golf.

The last round of golf I played for the year was on Arrowhead, a very difficult Jack Nicklaus course. I shot a 78 and missed seven putts inside six feet. Six of them were for birdies. I've never hit the ball that well in my entire life. I was proud of the fact I got most of my money back from Dick that day, after he'd beaten me most of the summer.

A bizarre incident occurred just as summer school ended. Tony Rice, our starting quarterback, needed to do well academically in summer school. The unfortunate thing was that everyone, even in the media, seemed to know that Tony needed to do well. The possibility that he might not be eligible seemed to get an abnormally large amount of publicity.

We made certain that Tony understood that football was his last priority during the summer. We couldn't have cared less if he didn't throw, run, lift, or work out in any way, shape, or form. All we wanted him to do was take care of his academics.

I have to congratulate Tony because he worked his tail off. After his final exams he checked with all three of his professors, so he knew exactly what grades he would be getting before he left for South Carolina for a few days. I know he sat in Mike DeCicco's office when Mike double-checked them, and I know Tony went home feeling absolutely certain that he was eligible to play.

On the Friday afternoon of summer-school commencement, after all classes and exams were finished, our sports information office got a call from Mitch Henck, the sports director at WSBT-TV, the CBS affiliate in town. Mitch said he had heard that Tony was going to be ineligible and wanted to know if that could be confirmed. Our sports-information people were on top of the situation and told Mitch that even though we couldn't say for sure because the grades would not be official and certified by the registrar's office until Monday, Tony was okay as far as everyone knew.

Well, Mitch chose not to believe that. He stuck with his story and ran it on the air at six on Friday night. That immediately created a huge furor, which was particularly difficult because there was no way anyone could deny the story since the grades were not yet official. Even though all of us felt certain that we knew where Tony stood, we were not in a position to release the grades.

Poor Tony had to read in the newspaper back home in South Carolina that the television station had reported he was ineligible. I read it in the paper in Vail, where we were with the Rosenthals. Both of us wondered what in the world was going on.

By Monday the grades became official, and Tony was indeed eligible, just as we expected. But it publicized a situation that never should have become such a big deal, and it unfairly cast Tony in a bad light. He deserved better than that, since he had worked so hard.

As it turned out, the station issued an apology, but Mitch refused to reveal his source for the report. By putting the report on the air, Mitch put Tony in a position of having to defend himself when he never should have had to in the first place.

In any event, I was happy to be able to put all this behind us and start thinking about football.

7

REPORTING FOR DUTY: ADDRESSING THE TROOPS

I don't spend a great deal of time talking to the football team on a regular basis, because after a while talking loses its impact. However, I do think it's important that everyone is on the same page when we're ready to go into a season.

It's particularly important with the freshmen, because you want them to understand where you're coming from and what our goals and philosophies are going to be. We like to visit with them as soon as they get to campus, because what happens those first few days can set the tone for the next four years. Here's what I said to the freshmen one evening in early August just after they had arrived on campus:

"Welcome to Notre Dame. For the next few minutes we're going to go over some things and try to get you off on the right foot. I assume you know the coaching staff. If not, you'll have plenty of chances to work with them and get to know them over the next four years.

"For the next four years this is going to be your home away from home. What's important right now is to reminisce about why you decided to come to Notre Dame. Why did you make that decision? Let's put these up on the board. Gene McGuire says tradition. Derek Brown says academics. Who else came here for a different reason? Someone said honesty—honesty in the people and in the program here. What else? Graduation rate. Graduation and academics go hand in hand. The environment—you like the environment. Opportunity for a national championship. Family-type atmosphere.

"This is the one that counts—academics and graduation. The rest of these things are all built because of this. I want you to read my lips when I say this. You are here to get an education. You are here to get a degree.

"We had two athletes flunk out here last spring, something that's almost unheard of. Those two athletes had better credentials than most of the people sitting in this room. We've had dozens of people graduate from the University of Notre Dame who do not have the credentials you have. In other words, there have been athletes who came here far less prepared for college than you are, and they graduated.

"What is the difference? There are two things you're going to need in order to graduate from the University of Notre Dame. Number one is respect. You are going to respect everyone here at the Notre Dame. Like they used to say in the Army—if it moves, salute it. If it doesn't move, pick it up. If you can't pick it up, paint it white. I don't care if you're talking about a player, a coach, a graduate assistant, someone in the dorm, a trainer or a manager or anyone else, you will show respect to that person. You must be able to respect the tradition. You must be able to respect people to get anywhere here. If you do not respect people, you're going to have a difficult time.

"The second thing you're going to have to do at the University of Notre Dame is work. I'll promise you this. If you show people respect and you do the work, there isn't anything in this world that will keep anyone in this room from graduating from Notre Dame. They do not give you grades here. They do not push you through. But they will work to the nth degree to help you.

"You may not become a pro football player. I hope you aspire to that. Nothing would please me more. One in ten thousand people makes it in professional football. The average length of a pro football player's career in the NFL is 3.9 years. If you graduate from the University of Notre Dame at age twenty-one and you play four years in the NFL, your football career is over at the age of twenty-five. It's done. They expect you to live to age seventy-five. You have fifty years of your life to live after football is over. What are you going to do with it? You can't peel that football and eat it like it's a banana.

"So our number-one objective is to set a standard academically to achieve and strive for. I'm going to tell you how to get an education here. Show people respect and work for it. There's no other way. There was a report that came out a week ago that said Tony Rice flunked out of school. It was an erroneous report. Tony Rice this summer got one A, an A-minus, and a B-minus. You know how much time Tony spent in the weight room? You know how much time Tony spent throwing the ball this summer? Zero hours. He worked fourteen hours a day with a tutor. He will never be an academic problem at Notre Dame again. If you're willing to work, there are people who are willing to work with you. But you are going to have to work—there is no other way around it.

"Let me tell you what we expect from you. It's very simple. We expect you to do three things here at the University of Notre Dame. One, do what's right. If you have any doubt about the difference between what's right and what's wrong, get out the Bible. It's right to be on time. It's right to be loyal. It's right to be honest. It's right not to be on drugs. It's right not to be involved with alcohol. Just ask yourself what's the right thing to do. It's not right to find somebody's wallet before they lose it.

"During the next four days your schedule is going to be cramped. But you're going to receive ten hours of instruction on academics. You'll be given a booklet that lists thirty-three ways not to graduate. Listen to them. Do the things that need to be done in the proper manner.

"On the football field every day all we want you to do is the best you can. Ask yourself every day: Did I do the best I could? We will provide you with the best coaching we possibly can. We'll make every effort and preparation that can possibly be done. But nobody expects you to do the impossible. Nobody expects you to be all-world. But we aren't going to accept less than the best you can possibly do.

"The third rule we have is very simple. Treat others as you'd like to be treated. Being a student here is going to set you apart from other people, whether you like it or not. Everything you do is going to be magnified, whether it be good or bad. If you do something good for somebody, they're going to talk about what a great guy you are. On the other hand, if you do something negative, that's going to be blown out of proportion, too. Treat people as you'd like to be treated. It's not a real complicated rule.

"We have a lot of meetings. Some will be interesting, some will be boring. The reason to have a meeting is to convey information. When we have a meeting, I expect you to sit up in your chair, look alert, and look me in the eye. I'll look you in the eye right from the word go. We aren't going to slouch down in our seats, we aren't going to stretch out and cross our legs.

"I don't have many other things to say, and I'm not lecturing to you or preaching to you. But attitude is where it all starts. You're coming here with a clean slate. What you did in high school really isn't important anymore. But the attitude you take here is the most important thing in this world. If you have the right attitude, you're going to get teamwork. If you have teamwork, you're going to get great performance. If you have great performance, you're going to have success. The attitude you have in the classroom, toward the university, toward yourself, is going to determine your happiness and your success not only here, but everywhere you go the rest of your life. You control your attitude. The door's open in my office and the other coaches' offices. Go in and sit down and ask questions. Above all, make up your mind that you're going to have a positive attitude and nothing is going to get you down.

"One year ago last week Notre Dame never stood any taller or any brighter when six thousand Special Olympians came here for the International Games. I wish you could have been here. Some of these people can't walk. Some are confined to a wheelchair. Some are mentally short— people that really and truly have handicaps. I wish you could have seen the love and the determination and the positive attitude that those people had. When I look around this room and I see the talents and the gifts and the God-given ability that you have and the future and opportunities you have, you can't help but tell yourself that you're lucky and you have a lot to be thankful for.

"Your future here at Notre Dame is in your hands. You can find twenty different things you don't like, but it's losers who look for excuses. The guy with a million excuses is looking for a way to excuse himself for not being successful. You've got so much going for you. Your future can be absolutely outstanding. But nothing is more important than your attitude —toward Notre Dame, toward your teammates and your coaches. If we have the right attitude at Notre Dame this year, we will have one great football team.

"We are expected to win here at Notre Dame. I expect us to win. I don't expect this football team to lose a football game in the four years you're here. Now, you're going to say that's impossible. But it happened right here at Notre Dame. The class that was here in '46, '47, '48, and '49 never lost a football game in four years.

"We control our own destiny, nobody else. How good do we want to be? It's going to depend on our attitude and how well we play together as a team. Some will play, some will not. Who will play will be determined by you. We have a need at several positions here. But nobody is just going to step in and play—you earn the right.

"Last year these two people—Chris Zorich and Winston Sandri—did not play, not a single down. Chris Zorich, I think, is going to be a great football player. Winston Sandri never played at all last year, but he is going to start out as the number-one left guard. One of you may beat them out. But Winston Sandri didn't get downhearted even when he didn't play a down last year.

"We lettered eleven freshmen last year. How many will we letter this year? I don't have any idea. We have a young man here named Steve Roddy who is going to be a senior. Steve Roddy has played very, very little. But the sucker never gave up, never got discouraged, worked his rear end off. Steve Roddy will play at the University of Notre Dame this fall. It's because of his attitude.

"We have a young man named Dean Brown. He will be a junior. He played a little bit as a guard as a freshman. He played a little as a sophomore. Right now, Dean Brown is the starting offensive right tackle. I think he can be an outstanding one. What does all that tell you? It tells you you may play as a freshman, you may not. But if you do not play as a freshman, it does not mean that you aren't an outstanding athlete. It just means your time has not arrived yet.

"There won't be another school in America that will play as many freshmen as the University of Notre Dame will find it necessary to play this year. I don't like to play freshmen. The reason I don't like to play freshmen is that not enough of them care about winning. But you will be treated like everybody else.

"There are three criteria as far as who will play. One, you must stay healthy. If you cannot stay healthy and stay on the football field, you cannot expect to play. If you miss two practices, it's almost impossible to play. We don't expect anyone to play with injuries, but you must play with pain.

"Second, you must learn your assignments. A lot of things will be thrown at you in a short period of time. If you cannot learn your assignments, you do not have a chance to play.

"Third, can you help us win? That's the key word. If you can, you will play.

"There isn't an athlete in this room that isn't outstanding. When you were in high school, the coach had enough problems coaching the other guys who weren't gifted and talented. So consequently, you come here to Notre Dame with a tendency not to have been coached. I don't mean the coach didn't spend time with you or didn't talk to you. But he did not coach you like you will be coached here, where every little thing will be scrutinized.

"You are going to think—my goodness gracious, I can't do anything right. It's going to be a transition for you, and you must be able to take coaching. Because you were gifted and talented in high school, you did not receive this kind of coaching. You're used to running a pattern and catching the ball and that's it. It's different here. You're going to have to come off the ball a certain way, read coverages, make route adjustments. It's going to be entirely different for you—but I don't want anyone to think we're picking on you.

"If a coach stops getting on you, that's when you should worry. We're going to make you as good as we can possibly make you. If you're an all-American, we're going to develop you. We're going to raise everybody's expectation level up one notch. But you're going to have to accept coaching all the way down the line, because it is going to happen.

"Let me give you a couple of pieces of advice. Make friends. That's the same thing I told my sons and my daughter when they came here. I cannot emphasize how important it is for you to make friends. You're going to be homesick. It's normal for people at Notre Dame, because our students come from all over the country. Everybody in this room basically comes from a long way away. Make friends on the football field, in this room, in the dorm, on campus. If you have friends, you've got a base for support. You've got to remember that all that support you used to receive at home is gone now. We are your family now—Notre Dame is your family away from home. If you have friends, you'll have no problems.

"The second thing is budget your time. You have never spent as much time on football as you will here at Notre Dame. I don't care how much time you spent in high school. You will spend a lot more time academically than you ever have in your life.

"Third, identify with good people. Woody Hayes used to say it. Identify with people who think academics are important and you'll be a better student. Identify with people who think football is important and you'll be a better football player. But above all, run with people who do what's right.

"Last, have fun. You will have more fun playing football at Notre Dame than you've ever had in your entire life. Take the right approach. Don't compare your senior year in high school with your freshman year in college. Your senior year in high school you were the star. Now you come here as a freshman and it's different. You'll be treated first class, you'll do things first class, and you'll be on national television every week. You'll play in bowl games. But it isn't going to be fun out on that field unless you have a burning desire to get better.

"We're here to make this the greatest experience you've ever had. We're here to help you graduate. We're here to help you win a national championship. I'm proud that you're here at the University of Notre Dame. I am very proud to be at the University of Notre Dame. I will never do anything to embarrass you. What I do is a reflection on you and on the school. But I don't want you to embarrass me, either. Everything you do for the next four years, you represent me and all your coaches, your family, your teammates.

"My door is always open. We're here to help you. But I'm not here to be your buddy. I'm not here to party with you. I'm not here to impress you or have you like me. I'm here to have the best football program for the best university in the entire world. And to see that you graduate.

"I'm here to see that you graduate and become a multimillionaire so you can call me up and say, 'Coach, I want to take care of you. Don't worry about working anymore. I'm going to put you on my board of directors.'"

On August 12 I spoke to the entire team for the first time as a group. I hit on a variety of subjects, and I think it turned out to be a key evening in terms of making our football players make a realistic assessment of themselves and yet still believe they could win:

"There are a lot of things we need to cover tonight, even though you may not want to hear some of them.

"The first thing is the situation at the University of Minnesota, besides welcoming you back. You probably read and heard a lot of accusations and everything else. I could talk about this situation for about an hour but I don't think that would serve a useful purpose.

"I've been a head football coach for eighteen years and been involved in the game of football as a coach for twenty-eight. In twenty-eight years, I've never done anything illegal to gain an advantage. I have never cheated.

"There's one thing you should always remember, and that's to keep your name and my name clean. There's an old poem that goes like this:

YOUR NAME

"You got it from your father.
It was all he had to give,
So it's yours to use and cherish
For as long as you may live.

If you lose the watch he gave you,
It can always be replaced.
But a black mark on your name, son,
Can never be erased.

It was clean the day you took it,
And a worthy name to bear.
When he got it from his father,
There was no dishonor there.

66

So make sure you guard it wisely.
After all is said and done,
You'll be glad the name is spotless
When you give it to your son.

"We will have a big-brother program again this year. We just assigned everyone, we didn't even ask the freshmen who they wanted. See that they become a part of the group. Let them know the *dos* and *don'ts*. Encourage them to ask questions about anything and come to you when they're down.

"We will not drink during the course of the season, and we will have a curfew during the week. It will be eleven P.M.

"I don't like to have to talk to you about agents, but I feel I must. It's my understanding that some athletes around the country have signed with an agent before their senior year and this is going to be revealed in the future. If you do sign with an agent, men, you lose your eligibilty. You run into problems with the IRS. More than anything else, you embarrass you, you embarrass me, and you embarrass people in this room and the University of Notre Dame.

"We will not vote on a bowl game. How many wish to go to a bowl game when this season is over? Opposed? We're going to a bowl, it's a question of which one. You will have no voice in which bowl we attend. This will be determined by the administration and the coaches.

"This meeting is going to be a little different than some we've had. We look into the season and we take a look at the schedule. We open up with Michigan, which is picked to be the number-one team in the country by *The Sporting News*. They are supposed to have the best offensive line in the country. It's supposed to be a great football team.

"The second game is with Michigan State, which returns seventeen starters from last year's team, which won the Big Ten. The third game will be against a vastly improved football team from Purdue. The fourth one is against Stanford, a team that is awfully good. When we play Stanford, they'll either be 4–0, or 3–1 at worst. Next we play Pittsburgh at Pittsburgh at night on AstroTurf—a team we haven't beaten the last two years.

"Then we come home and in our sixth football game play the University of Miami, a football team that's supposed to be outstanding. Jimmy Johnson has made the comment that this defense is the best he's ever had, that Florida State will not be able to run the ball in their opening game. The closest Notre Dame has come the last five games to Miami has been 24 points.

"Our seventh game is against Air Force. Dee Dowis is an all-America candidate at quarterback, and they have had some success moving the football against us the last several years. After that, we play the Naval Academy. They've got a great quarterback and should be improved. Following that, we play Rice, a very explosive, offensive football team.

"In our tenth football game we play here against Penn State, a team we haven't defeated the last few years. The eleventh game, we go out to USC, a football team that may be the best team on our schedule.

"Our schedule is a demanding one, but last year's was also. Last year we ended up playing nine teams that went to bowl games, and yet we went into our tenth game with a chance to play for the national championship.

"What do the prognosticators say about the University of Notre Dame? Virtually everybody picks us about seventeenth or eighteenth. You know what that means? That means they really don't think we'll have a good football team. They always pick us in the top twenty because Notre Dame has so many supporters that everybody will buy the magazine and read about us. Nobody picked us to win the national championship, nobody thinks we can go against the schedule we have and go undefeated. Most folks believe we cannot get through our first two football games and remain undefeated. We beat both those teams last year, Michigan and Michigan State, and there's no doubt they'll be ready to play.

"Why do people have questions about the University of Notre Dame? Number one, we lost our last three football games last year, including the bowl game. We gave up 80 points in three games. We lost Tim Brown, the Heisman Trophy winner. We lost Terry Andrysiak at quarterback. We lost our split end and our entire offensive line, all five starters. People just don't believe we can be very good on offense. They don't believe we can throw the football. They don't believe we have the receivers to get open or catch it. They don't believe we have an offensive line to protect, nor do they believe we have a quarterback who can throw.

"On defense, the general conception is we aren't very big on the defensive line. We aren't very strong. We can't rush the passer. With our secondary, people question the amount of turnovers we'll be able to generate.

"I'm not painting a dark picture to you, but that's basically what people believe. That's not what I believe. But if you look at it on paper, those are some of the question marks we have.

"Now let's get to what my expectations are honestly here at the University of Notre Dame. My expectations are that nobody will beat us this year. Nobody. There isn't any reason for it. I expect us to be a far better football team this year than last year.

"Let me start with our defense. If our defense does not dominate every single opponent we play, I will be surprised. I think we have the makings of the best defense in the country. We have some people that have to come along. We have to develop and we have to play hard and get better fundamentally. But based on what I see, I expect our defense to be a swarming defense, to have fun and to knock the heck out of people. I don't believe anybody in the country is capable of scoring more than 17 points against us.

"I believe defensively we are capable of shutting out every team we play. I believe we are capable of completely dominating a football game on defense. I think our defensive line is going to be the biggest shock people have seen. I don't think there's any doubt our linebackers are the best group I've been associated with. Our outside linebackers can be big-play people. We've got more speed on the corners than I've ever seen. We can play man, we can play zone. Our attitude last spring was unbelievable on defense.

"We lost our placekicker, but I believe Billy Hackett is a fine placekicker, and I've never seen anyone work any harder than Reggie Ho. I believe Reggie is as accurate as anybody I've seen—from the four-yard line in. We will find a punter. I think our kicking game can be outstanding. Last year we had the best punt-return team in the country, and this year I expect us to have the best punt-return team in the country. But I also expect us to be a dominating force in blocking punts. I think we will have some help from the incoming freshmen. Just in working with them a short period of time, we've got some people who can run and who like the game.

"On offense I might shock you. I've never seen a year on offense that presents more challenges on paper. But I think we're going to be outstanding on offense. I think our offensive line will be excellent. I don't believe there's any doubt Mike Heldt and Tim Ryan can be fine centers. Winston Sandri will be a fine guard, and we've got to find somebody else there. Tim Grunhard at the other guard has got to be one of the leaders and be a dominating football player like I think he is. I think we have two outstanding tackles. I think Andy Heck will be as fine as there is in the country, barring none. What I saw of Dean Brown tells me he can be outstanding, too. Our offensive line will be better this year than last year. We've got to get better fundamentally, and you've got to believe it.

"Our receivers will be fine. I want to tell you right now, there are a couple of freshmen who can flat play. I just don't think there's any doubt that Ricky Watters can be outstanding as a flanker. At quarterback, Steve Belles has worked hard this summer. I think it will pay off. I've always been a Tony Rice booster. I think Tony Rice can be as fine a quarterback as there is in the country. Not an athlete, I don't want to hear that anymore. We've got a heck of a quarterback. We will be a fine offensive team.

"At tailback we've got to find some help for Mark Green. Mark Green has done it for two years and he's going to do it for a third. If he makes as much improvement this year as he did last year, he'll be great. We have good fullbacks. Anthony Johnson and Braxston Banks are outstanding.

"I look at our football team and I expect us to be good and achieve every goal that we have. Our goals are, number one, to win the national championship. Number two, to be a top-ten team. Be a top-twenty team. Go to the bowl of our choice on January 1. Go to a bowl. Have a winning season. Those are our goals. We start at the bottom and cross them off one at a time.

"I do not want you to worry about winning. I do not want you to even think about winning. All I want you to think about is making a commitment to excellence and being the best you can possibly be.

"What are we going to have to do to reach my goals, to reach my expectations? The most important thing we have to do is have the right attitude. Have the proper attitude, a positive attitude toward one another, and the right attitude about making that commitment to excellence. That's where it all starts.

"I'm talking about our attitude toward school as well. I've never been more disappointed with our performance academically than I was last spring. On the other hand, I can't do anything but stand here and applaud the fifty-two players who were in summer school. Almost without exception, they did an unbelievable job. It's unfortunate the news media jumped to a conclusion on Tony Rice that had absolutely no foundation. Tony Rice got an A, an A-minus, and a B-minus. Chris Zorich got two A's. Todd Lyght got a B-minus in finite math and an A in psychology. Dean Brown got an A and a B in two difficult courses. Ricky Watters did a tremendous job, and the people in the School of Architecture called me and said if he's interested in going into that area, they'd love to have him. Our overall grade-point average this summer was well over a 3.0. There's got to be that attitude and that commitment to excellence in everything we do.

"I want to talk a little bit about quitting. Last year we got through two-a-days, and Steve Huffman, our second-string center, came up and said, 'I quit.' I've never seen anyone put a football team in a bind like an individual does by quitting. Once you start something, you let everybody in this room down if you quit. I never said anything to Steve. I never said anything publicly. But I want to tell you, it's totally unfair to the group to quit on them. It almost seemed like he planned to put his teammates in checkmate. So then we moved Matt Dingens over to center. We work with him for five days and then Matt comes in and says 'I quit.' Then we go out there in our last scrimmage and Chuck Lanza gets hurt. Fortunately, Lanza played with pain, and thank goodness we had a guy like Tim Grunhard, who stepped in there at center and worked that whole week. ·

"But all the work and effort that everybody put forth last year could have gone down the drain because two people quit in the middle of the battle. I'll tell you right now, if you want to quit, please do it tonight. If you're in this meeting room tomorrow, I don't care what your role on this team is, your attitude better be, 'I'm gonna see this sucker through this year.' Our attitude cannot be, 'I'm gonna be with you only as long as everything goes well.' Anyone who quits is quitting on himself, and that's a bad habit to start. We aren't going to have that situation anymore.

"We have a great group of guys here. Individually, you're outstanding. Our attitude toward one another has to be the same way. Our attitude better be the same toward competitiveness, toward our desire to go out there and compete against the best. Not to be afraid to lose. The attitude ought to be, 'I want to show the world what kind of team I'm part of, not what I am. I want to show the world the amount of love and feeling that is on this football team. I want to show 'em. I want to set an example for everyone who might be down and out, that Notre Dame is totally committed to excellence in everything they do.'

"I'm not a very good athlete. You've seen me try to run. You've seen me try to catch. I cannot throw. Golf is probably the most difficult game in this world to play. I've never been below a 16 handicap in my life. Any good teaching pro will tell you that if you just do the fundamentals, golf's not a real complicated game. The fundamentals are boring and tedious, but you've got to master them.

"I played my last round of golf this afternoon just to relax. On the back nine, I three-putted 18. I never missed a fairway, never missed a green, never made a putt longer than seven feet. I shot a 34, three under par on the backside alone going into 18. Am I a good golfer? No. But if you have good fundamentals, you can become a great golfer. You can become a great football player if you adhere to the fundamentals. There are fundamentals in punting, in shooting a basketball, in tackling, blocking— and you've got to take the attitude that you're going to be a good fundamental player.

"If you have the right attitude, you have togetherness. If you have

71

togetherness, you have a commitment to excellence. When you have a commitment to excellence, success is inevitable. But it all starts with a basic attitude.

"The freshmen will show great respect for the upperclassmen, regardless of their athletic abilities. You will respect them because they have proven they have the talent and ability to persevere. On the other hand, I expect the upperclassmen to show the freshmen how we do things the Notre Dame way. I truly expect them to help and guide the freshmen and incorporate them into the team.

"Who will play at the University of Notre Dame? I'm going to tell you. If you can help us win, if you can help us be successful, you will play. If you can't, you will not play. It's that simple.

"In closing, I believe you're a member of a very special team. I believe that from the bottom of my heart. Because you've chosen to become a part of this football team, it means you're going to have to sacrifice. You're going to have to pay the price and totally dedicate yourself. Football is the greatest game in the world, just like a war. It's a physical contest, and on every play there's a winner and a loser. It's the guys that are totally dedicated, the guys that absolutely refuse to lose, who are going to be successful.

"Intensity is to do something with a purpose. You practice and play with intensity because you have a purpose. We talk about six seconds from the time the ball is snapped until the play ends. Intensity is to have a purpose for those entire six seconds. From the minute the ball is snapped until it's blown dead I'm going to bust my butt. If you can't have intensity for six seconds, then we don't have the right attitude toward dedication.

"I hope you can dedicate the next three months to have that kind of attitude. I think we've got the ingredients to have something special happen here. But you've all got to lead in your own way. Be the first one in line, I don't care if you are a freshman. Be a leader, and if you can't lead, then follow. If you can't lead and you can't follow, then get the hell out of the way, because I don't want anything slowing us down. I want us to make that commitment to excellence, because if we do, then success is inevitable. You are a special team, and something great will happen to you. We will be lucky and we won't know why, but it will happen, and don't you forget it."

Wes Pritchett, senior linebacker

Coach Holtz said that this was a special team and that he didn't know what it was, but just that this team had some special qualities. He said from the beginning of the season—this was really strange—that this was a team of destiny. He said it was special because we were so close as a team and everybody seemed to be so willing to sacrifice, to work hard, to not accept mediocrity, and things like that. He stressed that from the very beginning of the season. I mean, he said those things in the very first team meeting.

THE PRESEASON, PART I: OPENING FALL CAMP

THE freshmen came in August 8, three days earlier than the veterans, as the NCAA allows for indoctrination. We tested them and we knew right away they had speed. We got on the field and there definitely were some players who could move. Rocket Ismail runs a 4.28 in the 40, and there are seven or eight guys right behind him.

What really impressed me was that this was a great group of young men. For us to be successful at Notre Dame, this is a must. You put them through ten hours worth of academic orientation the first few days, and that's always a good indication of how well they'll fit in here. Fitting in at Notre Dame is based on a lot more than how fast you can run the 40. This group seems to fit in the best of all the groups we've brought in.

Once we got on the field, because we only had twenty-one scholarship athletes and a couple of walk-ons, we couldn't do much teamwork or many drills. You try to put them in the right places. But we tell the upperclassmen that if they stay healthy and practice and progress, they should never lose out to a freshman, even if the freshman is the better athlete. There's just too much to learn when you're new to the program.

So after a few days on the field you have a few freshmen who can play and a few others who could play but they aren't going to know enough in time to do it. It's different now than in our first two years at Notre Dame, when we had to play freshmen anyway, no matter how much they knew. The first year, in 1986, they knew just about as much as the upperclassmen, even though those players had had twenty days of spring practice. But this was a good group and there were no problems, and I felt very good about the freshmen.

74

Next we had to find out how they'd blend in with the upperclassmen. We had one evening session with the freshmen that stands out in my mind. We asked them to put themselves in the position of the seniors and asked them what they would think about the freshmen. What's your reaction to the freshmen when you're a senior and you've been here three years and you've busted your butt and you've got a chance to have a good football team? The first reaction is, hey, I don't want them to take my position. That's the way freshmen will think.

When freshmen come in, they're not that interested in winning, they're interested in playing. As sophomores they're more interested in starting. As juniors they're interested in winning. As seniors they're interested in individual honors and awards. It always falls that way. I said to the freshmen, "If I'm a senior, I would tell you not to screw it up and not to embarrass us. Don't embarrass me by your conduct in the dorm or your performance on the practice field. I've been here and I've paid my dues."

That's the difference between the way a senior thinks and a freshman thinks. When you take a young football team and you've got to put it all together in a short time, it's very difficult to get everyone to blend in. It isn't just a case of sending someone out and saying this is so and so, and you're going to become a player.

We had one scrimmage where we put Gene McGuire, who's going to be a fine player, at center. He'd never been a center before. We taught him to snap just before we started the scrimmage. After a couple of snaps Tony Rice said, "Boy, he really gets the ball up well." I said, "Yeah." So Tony goes over and introduces himself to Gene McGuire in the huddle. He said, "I'm Tony Rice." This is not unnatural, it's not uncommon. That's why we have a big brother program, since our players all live in different dorms all over campus. You want somebody who's a little older, who you can go to with problems or concerns. You need someone who can bring you into the rest of the squad. That way you have a friend in the upperclassmen. So blending the new people in successfully is always a concern.

Pete Cordelli, receiver coach
I don't think anyone ever could have expected freshmen Derek Brown and Rocket Ismail to come in and play the way they did. Their consistency was amazing. That's a tribute to the upperclassmen, because when your upperclassmen are playing well, they raise everyone's level of expectation and performance.

The upperclassmen came in August 12 in great shape, probably the best physical shape I've ever seen a football squad in from top to bottom. You go out in shorts, and the enthusiasm is always good and the retention is good. But we had a problem on offense. We had to build an offense despite the additional losses we had. From the very beginning of spring practice we knew we lost four offensive linemen and two wide-outs. Now,just since spring practice ended, we've lost another offensive lineman and two more wide-outs, so we had to start all over to build that sucker.

It's almost an impossible task—and I'm not saying that from a coach's point of view. We had to find another guard because of the loss of Jeff Pearson, who'd transferred, and we don't have Peter Rausch, who I felt sure would be a contributor but is not eligible this fall. Those two guys were prominent, and so were Bobby Carpenter and Pierre Martin. Four guys we were counting on at the end of spring practice were not here anymore. We were starting completely from scratch.

But there were some pleasant surprises in two-a-days. If he could get the snap down, Tim Ryan could be a fine center. Mike Heldt also had progressed well there. It's asking a lot to have a couple of people who should be in their freshman redshirt year to carry the load at center. They probably ought to have been on the third team, but now one of them has to start, and they'd never played to speak of. Winston Sandri was forced to come along at guard. We still have Andy Heck and Dean Brown at tackle, but Dean hadn't played all that much.

You start putting the team together with no offensive line. We moved two defensive linemen to offensive guard at the start of fall practice. They had no idea what was going on, and yet George Marshall and Brian Shannon were going to be good football players. But it isn't like moving a tackle to guard. So we had a bit of a problem getting the snap from our centers, and we had two people brand new to the guard position in backup roles. We had a freshman in Justin Hall, and he was a backup at tackle already. The last transition was moving Mike Brennan from tight end to quick tackle behind Andy Heck, and I thought that would be our two deep.

Derek Brown, a freshman, would have to make a major contribution at tight end. At split end Steve Alaniz was the only individual, although we did have Ray Dumas back, which we didn't expect. We also didn't expect Ray to get injured early and end up missing most of the year. Rocket Ismail was a young man who not only is very talented, but has great intensity and great awareness. He may help at split end. Rod Smith probably shouldn't be playing flanker right now, but he's there because Aaron Robb has been injured during most of preseason drills. So you're constantly adjusting the pieces. Ricky Watters has nine million things to learn at flanker, Pat Eilers is just getting back to flanker after playing some at tailback.

How do you put all that together and build a football team and still improve when you have inconsistencies at every single place? I don't mind it if it's one or two. The one place we think we can be solid is in the backfield. But you move Ricky Watters to flanker because you've got a problem there with Tim Brown gone. Anthony Johnson hurts an ankle and misses most of two-a-days. Then, after two weeks of Tony Brooks looking good at tailback, you get a call saying he may be out for the year. So the two positions you really thought you could count on aren't the same anymore. One saving grace is that Braxston Banks had a great fall camp and showed some leadership.

I never see anybody get hurt on the practice field, but we do seem to end up with our share of fluke injuries. Tony Brooks had a little soreness in his foot one day, and the next day they decided to X-ray it and found a slight crack in the bone. It's the same kind of injury Keith Byars of Ohio State had a few years ago. If it gets any worse, he may miss the whole year.

As it was, we held him out for a few days and then had to be careful what we did with him. He may go through the whole year like this and still be able to play. But you always feel like the next cut he makes may be his last. That's rather disconcerting, considering he's a player we expect to be a big contributor. However, I have complete faith in our doctors and trainers. They will do what is in the best interests of Tony first and the team second, and that's the way it should be.

Our trainers fixed him up with a special shoe with a steel shank, and got him an orthotic, a hard plastic piece of molding that fits his foot. That's as much as you can do to protect it, and even then, he's one wrong move away from surgery. It might happen tomorrow or it might never happen. We actually had him back out scrimmaging within a week after we discovered the injury, and he didn't look bad. He does look awfully slow in the high-top shoes he's wearing now, but we'll have to wait and see what he can do in game conditions.

The key is deciding about his future by the end of September. He could play in up to three games and still qualify for an extra year of eligibility because of the injury. But if he plays in the Stanford game or any after that, it counts as a full season. If Tony is still having problems and pain and can't be in more than a few plays, it may be difficult for all of us.

We have not put the offense together yet, per se. One day we scrimmaged with only ten players on offense. I told the team there is no difference if we line up without a guard or if we line up with him and he doesn't block. Either way we are playing with ten men. We might as well line up that way and let everybody know we're at a disadvantage. If we've only got eight guys out there who are going to play, let's line up that way.

People will say, "Boy, they're doing a great job out there, because it's eight guys on eleven."

We have not been able to develop the respect and confidence among one another because of the total inconsistencies. Offensively, Heldt and Ryan and Sandri are going to be outstanding, but they're just sophomores. Justin Hall's a true freshman, and he's going to end up playing, maybe even starting. We could start Derek Brown and Justin and Rocket Ismail before it's over. I look at that and I think, How do we bring that all together? At the same time, you're trying to teach and correct things, and improve them. It drives you crazy.

George Kelly, special assistant to the athletic director

I was surprised because right after the first two weeks of practice in August, Lou said to me he thought this team was good enough to win it all. He just felt very confident after we came out of two-a-days. He did have some concerns about the offensive line and the depth there, and he did project that there would have to be continued improvement there, which there was. He foresaw something else that not a lot of people did. He felt the strength of our quarterback was far greater than most other people felt at that point. He was a believer in Tony Rice long before I was.

You always, as a coach, are optimistic in August before the season ever starts. Yet he was far stronger in his beliefs this year compared to the first two. In August he talked about the idea of being able to win every football game, and that was not something he had done either of the first two years. He was much more convincing in his approach this year, even though there weren't a lot of reasons on paper for it. It was a team that was rather young in terms of chronological age, and one that certainly didn't have much experience. But he just said he had a feeling. He had a feel for people that surprised me, and Tony Rice was a great example. Stan Smagala was another individual. He felt that not only could Smagala play for us, but he also could be one of the best in the country. He felt our secondary would be as strong as any we would play all year. The only question defensively was the front line, and yet once we played a game or two, he began to exude great confidence in that part of it.

Corny Southall, senior free safety

The first Sunday we came into camp, we all sat down in the auditorium at Loftus and Coach Holtz told us that day, "This team will be blessed and will be looked over. Things will go our way and we will become champions."

He said it that day and he stood behind it the entire season, every week, week after week.

That stuck out in my mind because I felt the same way. But he put it out there. He put everything on the line and said, "We have the potential. We just have to work for it."

It really wasn't a topic of conversation among the players after that meeting, because Coach Holtz says a lot of things that are important, and you have to keep things in perspective. We were six months away from actually winning it. But we knew that he knew that we could do it. And that meant a lot to the team.

Frank Stams, senior defensive end

It's uncanny. Coach Holtz just told us what we needed to do, and all those goals we accomplished. In order to win the national championship, he said, the seniors are going to have to play their best ball—which they did—and we have to have good senior leadership—and I thought that was provided. He said—and this is all before the season—the defense is going to have to be the catalyst of this team. He said that was what we needed to do, and we did it. It's just amazing how it worked out just like he said it. We talked about it in the very first meeting before the year.

As September approached, it was obvious to me the offensive players had a tendency to say, "Boy, that guy next to me isn't very good. He's always making a mistake. It doesn't matter whether I make my block or not because someone else will miss their man anyway. I wish that player over there would get better or listen to the coach."

So we started running plays in a series of eight. If the team ran a play right with no missed assignments they received 1/8 of a plus. If they made a mistake they received a minus. At the end of the day we would total up the plusses and minuses and inform the team how many failures each position had experienced. The players were now held accountable for their performance, and could not remain anonymous when making a mistake. Even though we just started this system a week ago I really am encouraged by the way the team is starting to accept responsibility for their actions. We have a long way to go but the honor and respect is starting to build.

We don't have many injuries considering we've hit a lot and try to go against one another a lot. The players have to determine the difference between pain and injury. Ted FitzGerald has a sprained knee. Ray Dumas had arthoscopic surgery on his knee in the off-season, and he still can only practice once a day during two-a-days. I keep hearing that everybody will be okay for the Michigan game. What people don't understand is that you don't show up the night of the game and say, "Okay, I'm here and ready to play." If they miss all this work, they might as well miss the Michigan game.

With Tom Gorman out with a chest muscle from our first day in pads, we took a look at Boo Williams, who finished the spring as our number-one middle guard but did not pass the running test this fall when we came back. He came close, but we had a rule that if you can't pass the test, you move down one position. So we moved him down one spot at middle guard, Gorman gets hurt, and we move Boo to the first team at left tackle. He is really starting to come on now.

Jeff Alm has been at right tackle and has stayed healthy. Bryan Flannery will not be a starter at any of the spots because he's got to be able to help us at all three spots, though he's not very big or particularly quick. He's a Notre Dame overachiever, he knows all three positions, and he doesn't make a mental error. He's a good technique player. Utilizing Bryan at all three spots elevated Chris Zorich at middle guard, even after he missed all spring practice. Zorich was one of those guys who hurt a knee the first day of spring practice and ended up missing the entire spring. Maybe Gorman getting hurt has been kind of a blessing in disguise for the younger players, because it has given Williams a lot of time at left tackle and Zorich a lot of time at middle guard.

We had another young man in Mirko Jurkovic who we looked at on offense and then on defense. He was only a freshman, but with all the injuries we had on defense, we thought he might stay on there. I remember his saying, "Coach, what position am I going to play? I worked a little on offense and a little on defense." I said, "Mirko, you probably aren't going to play this year. It's going to be difficult because there's just too much to learn on offense." We had to make a decision to go with the upperclassmen we moved over there, like George Marshall and Brian Shannon, rather than go with a Mirko Jurkovic.

So we said, "Well, we're just going to move you over here on defense and work with you a little. Don't get too alarmed. We'll look at you a little on offense, a little on defense. You aren't going to play this year anyway, but we're going to find out *where* you can play. We won't go into spring practice saying 'Where is Mirko going to play?'" I said, "Just take care of your academics, do the best you can, and don't worry about it. I do believe you're a player. It's not a question of whether or not you're going to play, it's a question of where and when. When, isn't going to be this year."

Well, we put him over there on defense at Gorman's spot, and four days later he's number two on the depth chart. It may end up that George Williams and Mirko are our two left tackles this year. Gorman may end up going back to right tackle with Alm. Mirko and Boo Williams are physical football players, and so is Gorman. Jeff Alm has made great progress in that regard. So with Zorich and Roddy, who is a spot player, and Bob Dahl, if we get him back from an injury, we might not be too bad.

At safety George Streeter is really starting to come along. Greg Davis could have made a contribution, but he's got a thigh problem. Rodney Culver could have, but we had to move him over to tailback with Brooks hurt. So we moved David Jandric in there and he showed signs for the first time of being a pretty physical football player. We knew he was an excellent athlete. Patrick Terrell is going to be fine at free safety. He'll back up Corny Southall, who is not just a great competitor, but also one of the finest young men I know and a true team player in every sense of the word.

That's where we are right now. Defensively, we've just had more continuity and better chemistry. We have more experience and better confidence. It's basically the same team that came out of spring practice, and we know this group is quicker than what we've had before. Are we any good on defense? I really don't know, because our offense hasn't been able to test them. We've had so many missed assignments on offense due to lack of technique and lack of experience.

With the kicking game, we think Reggie Ho is going to be a fine extra-point and short field-goal man, and Billy Hackett will handle long field goals and kickoffs. The punting has driven us up a wall because of total inconsistency. We've had some days where we punt the ball well, and others where we don't, and we're going to have to live with that. We really wanted to recruit a punter badly last year. We looked all over the country, but we couldn't find one that met our needs and could qualify here. Fortunately, there are some next year.

I told the media after one of our Saturday scrimmages that we were going to vote on whether or not to punt this year. Right now, I would vote against it based on what I've seen from our punters. However, the punters are great competitors, and while I don't know who will punt, I have a feeling we will be okay.

The scariest thing right now is thinking what we would do if something happened to Tony Rice. Steve Belles always looks good in spring games and I'm hopeful he'll become a field general. It doesn't help that we don't have a veteran second offense to work with Steve. You've got brand-new linemen, Rodney Culver at tailback, and Ryan Mihalko at fullback, so there's not much continuity with that whole group. There's a freshman at tight end, split end, and flanker. You've got a new center, a freshman at tackle, and two guys at guard who played defense last year. So that created a little havoc. We are still moving people around, looking for the proper chemistry.

But Tony can do so many things for us. If we didn't ask Tony to do so much, he would be outstanding. But because of the multitude of things we have to prepare ourselves for this fall, Tony is going to have to carry a tremendous burden. We've got to be able to throw the ball. We've got to be able to run the ball. We've got to be able to check off. We've got to run the option and play-action passing. We may have to do those things because we may not be able to block anybody. If we don't block anybody, at least you can still run the option. Tony does those things well. If we lose his dimension—especially his leadership and the confidence the players have in him—we're in trouble. He had a good air of confidence last year, but he really has it now. He's running the show.

It was important in our last scrimmage to see Ricky Watters at flanker, work him some at tailback, and see him on punt and kickoff returns. However, he had to go to Chicago on a field trip. His academics come first, no question about that, but this was not an ordinary practice, because we're treating it like a game, trying to iron out everything we can.

I wanted to know two things about Ricky's field trip. One, was there another time he could go? Or, was this the only time possible? I would have really felt bad if there was another trip on Monday that he could have made. But Friday was the only time he could have made the trip. Two, what other obligations does he have this year, because we need to plug that into our program? What if he has another field trip the day we play Penn State?

Ricky Watters has wanted to be an architect since the first day we recruited him. In summer school he took an architectural course, and they told me he has a lot of natural talent and ability. So they accepted him into the architecture program. We're extremely happy about that. Under no circumstances will we allow Ricky Watters to say, "Well, I'll give up architecture, because it conflicts with football." But we will find somebody to replace Ricky on the football team if we find out on the day we play Michigan he has to go to Detroit. I'm not trying to be funny, I'm trying to be honest. Traveling on game days is fine if that's the only time he can go. We can live with that as long as he doesn't have a whole list of obligations that are going to produce conflicts. He may not be a football player, but he is going to be an architect.

With Tony Brooks a question because of his foot, who, then, do we have at tailback other than Mark Green? We could play Ricky there. We could play Pat Eilers there, but then who do you have at flanker other than Rod Smith? It really presents a problem.

Sometimes our number-one offense hasn't been able to make a first down against the number-one defense, let alone score. But I also think this—we are not as far away from being a good offensive football team as it appears to the outsider who just sees our inability to move the football. Some good things are starting to be done on offense. They just aren't done by all eleven people on every play. But there are blocks being made and assignments being kept and commitments being honored. It's not a case where you think this is hopeless. Not at all. But it's all going to have to come from chemistry, and we don't have that on offense. At least we're aware of that deficiency.

Our first season at Notre Dame, in 1986, I didn't know where we were at this time. But at least we had the same team in the fall that we had come out of spring practice with, unlike this year.

For two years we were a team with a lot of seniors. Now we're a junior-sophomore-freshman team, and many of them have been moved to other positions.

Two years from now, if these people continue to progress, we're going to be outstanding. But right now we have so many unknowns. Mike Heldt, Tim Ryan, and Winston Sandri are going to be fine players, but they are not close to being ready. All our linemen are young.

How do I feel? If we were healthier, if we had a punter I knew we could count on, I'd feel better. However, Jim Sexton does show signs of being an excellent punter. But I've got a lot of confidence in the coaching staff and in my ability. I think we can go into a season, no matter what has happened, and get a lot of things accomplished on game day.

THE PRESEASON, PART II:
PUTTING AWAY THE WHISTLE

T HE South Bend/Mishawaka Area Chamber of Commerce held its annual Kickoff Luncheon at the Joyce Center on August 24, the second day of classes, and had a record crowd of more than eight hundred people. It's the first big football-oriented affair of the year, and signals that the season isn't far away.

Chuck Roemer, who emceed the luncheon, pointed out that six of our nine assistant coaches are thirty-six or under. I hadn't realized what a young staff we had become, not including me. I guess it all fits right in with how young our team is going to be this fall.

Our three captains spoke briefly, and if they represent us with the team as well as they do at the microphone, we'll be fine. Mark Green told a great story about taking his responsibilities as a captain seriously. Mark mentioned that both Braxston Banks and Ryan Mihalko had come up to him after practice the day before and talked about how things hadn't gone very well on the practice field. It hit home with Mark, because he said, "I will never again go out there and not give my all. I'm going to make sure that I'm being as good an example as I can every day."

I think Mark was very serious about this, and I can only hope the rest of our seniors are this committed about being leaders. I continue to think Mark will be one of the great captains we've had, because he takes his responsibility seriously, perhaps too seriously—but that's the way things are done here. Nobody at Notre Dame seems to do much of anything without a strong commitment.

Andy Heck had some of the funniest lines of the day, and I think he impressed the audience. Andy takes public speaking very seriously. He might make it in politics someday. He had a great story about people criticizing the offensive line and saying how that would be this team's weak spot.

"Coach [Joe] Moore always tells us that the coaches can't win games for us, but they can teach us how to be winners. He says the winners in life get the best of everything—the best jobs, the best salaries, the best-looking girls. I just want people to know that everyone on the offensive line has a great-looking girlfriend."

Andy also poked fun at us a little bit when he said he didn't know what promises we had made in recruiting, but he found it interesting that the day after we signed Derek Brown, he was moved to tackle. That brought a great response from the audience, and Andy was smiling the whole time. But I think he knows we'll be a better football team this way. He's seen what Derek can do, and I think he knows he's probably better off at tackle in the long run—especially if he wants to have a future in football after Notre Dame. He gives us some game experience and some leadership in the offensive line, even if he's new to playing tackle.

Joe Moore, who coaches the tackles and tight ends, got up and said Derek Brown had as much talent as any freshman he'd seen at any position. That's a strong statement from a guy like Joe, who's been around for a while—and it was probably premature, considering we were two and a half weeks from a game—but Derek has been impressive.

Barry Alvarez, our defensive coordinator, went through the whole defense by position. He had a good line about Chris Zorich. Apparently an official at one of our practices came up to him and said Zorich ought to be worth two holding calls a game because he didn't see how anyone could block him one on one. I hope he's right. Chris certainly has the enthusiasm to help us up there, if not the game experience.

Chris Zorich, sophomore defensive tackle

In one of the first practices of the fall, all the players felt, "Are you sure we're going to win a game?" All the time, we just hit and hit and hit. We knew that we would be a good team. In that practice, we weren't supposed to be that aggressive against our own team. But we were piling up, and there were fifteen or sixteen people on a tackle. That's when we realized we'd be okay. I couldn't believe we were going so hard. Our defense was kicking our own offense's butt. If we could do that, we could have a great season.

I tried to be optimistic yet realistic in talking about our team. I feel inside, even with a ways to go before our first game, that we're going to be a better team than last year and that we're going to become even better as the year goes along.

I want people to say two things about us when they see us play. We're good fundamentally. We're a team of overachievers.

We had our second full-scale scrimmage of the preseason on August 27, two weeks before the Michigan night game. I had made a commitment to fly to New York that day for a press conference at the Kickoff Classic, where Nebraska and Texas A&M were playing. So I could get there in time, we moved the scrimmage to eleven A.M., which worked out well because it started raining hard just as we finished.

We spent about twenty minutes before the scrimmage going over exactly what would happen the weekend of the Michigan game. We went through Friday's agenda, with meetings, dinner, then the pep rally. Then we're going to take fifty-five or sixty players to the Holiday Inn in Plymouth, about a half hour south of the campus, for the night. It'll be the first time we haven't stayed at Moreau Seminary on the other side of the lake.

It's difficult as coaches to figure out how to handle a night game in terms of the players. You can't really let them go all day long, and yet you can't keep them cooped up all day, either. At least going to Plymouth gives us a little more control of the atmosphere. Then we'll come back to campus for a pregame meal at three P.M., go to mass, and then go to the stadium.

We talked in detail about what we do in pregame warm-ups and who goes where on the field. We talked about philosophy on the coin toss, something we'll go over in more detail with the captains later. If we win, I'd rather defer until the second half. If we have to, we'll take the ball, but we really like the idea of kicking off and going on defense first, especially if our defense continues to look strong.

I emphasized the importance of being positive on the field. We don't want any negative words out there. We want everyone to be involved, organized, and enthusiastic.

Last year we established an attitude by winning all our home games. Teams didn't enjoy it when they had to come to our stadium. This is our field, we should dominate here, and I told the players to start getting that in their mind right now. That means even more this year, with seven home games.

On one of the early plays of the scrimmage, Tony Rice got great protection and threw the ball to Steve Alaniz. But Frank Jacobs pushed somebody from behind and got called for clipping. I got all over him and pulled him out of the lineup. Those are the mental things we can't afford two weeks from now. Frank is a fine tight end. He's a great youngster and good worker. But those are things we don't need.

Overall, our progress was encouraging, other than the offensive line. The defense was outstanding again, and I complimented them when we finished.

For a change all three of our punters looked good. Maybe we can punt after all now. Jim Sexton works hard and is getting better and better. Sean Connor has great potential, but is not real consistent.

Ricky Watters had two beautiful punt returns, and Tony Rice threw the ball as well as I can remember. He really has matured as a quarterback. But even that may not be enough if our offensive line doesn't come around. Today we couldn't get to the line of scrimmage to get the tough yards. We tried just about everybody at center. Mike Heldt still isn't quite ready. Tim Ryan can block but he doesn't have the snap down. We even threw Gene McGuire, a freshman, in there for a few plays, and he did quite well.

I'm not sure our backs ran as hard as they need to today, either. Our linemen just aren't as tough and physical as they need to be, and the backs were the same way most of the scrimmage. Steve Belles played some tailback, and he comes as close as anyone to running with the authority we want. But his heart isn't really there, because he's a quarterback. And the way our line blocked at times, everybody in the backfield must have felt like a turkey at Thanksgiving. They had no chance.

Derek Brown had another solid scrimmage for a freshman, leading us in receptions. He may be tough to keep off the field, although Frank Jacobs continues to be impressive, too. Tony Brooks didn't play because of his foot, and I don't like that. I want to be able to leave Ricky Watters at flanker, but maybe we can't afford that luxury if Mark Green is our only healthy, proven tailback.

I told the media I thought Tony Rice showed he can do more than be a great athlete. We want people to think of him as a good quarterback, not just a good athlete who happens to play quarterback. But we know only game production will convince some of our fans who still think he can't throw well enough for us to win. Tony understands that, too.

I tried to encourage Frank Jacobs when he walked off the field after we had finished. I know he was down about my getting on him, but we want him to understand we're all just trying to get better.

I told Frank to try to do something with the rest of the offensive line to encourage us. Maybe they should all shave their heads. I mentioned that to Frank, and then I thought better of it and told him I wasn't really serious. We did that once in college, but then we got beat and it was terrible. We'll find other ways to make the commitment.

After the scrimmage my son Kevin flew with me to New York, so I had a chance to spend some time with him. I sat with Bobby Bowden of Florida State at the Kickoff Classic and we talked a lot about Skip and how he's doing at Florida State. The press conference before the game seemed to go well. They had Bobby and me briefly on live at halftime on television—and I do mean briefly.

At the press conference we talked about polls. I said that, in my opinion, the second dumbest group of people in the world is the writers, who do nothing but vote for the teams with the best records. Who they play means nothing, and that's unfair. The dumbest people in the world are the coaches, because they do the same thing. There's a reason the writers do it, but no reason coaches should. That was the biggest point I wanted to make.

Maybe we'll look back after the season and talk about how much our practice on August 29 had to do with our becoming a football team.

We went through the film of the scrimmage from the previous Saturday with the players, and the performance of the offensive line didn't look any better on the big screen than it had on the field. The players quickly got the idea that I wasn't happy.

It's very simple. Either we're going to attack the problem and work to become better or we're not going to be a very good offensive team.

Steve Belles, senior quarterback
We knew it was going to be a pretty tough scrimmage. Before practice Coach Holtz sort of said this would be the day he would find out what kind of team we could be. The defense had been knocking us around pretty good all during the preseason, so that was really a day when the offense learned what it was made of.

It's a good thing you don't take a poll of players to elect the head coach. I would have been a big loser today. I asked one player if he was mad at me, and he said "Yes" rather emphatically and without hesitation. I didn't push my luck. I didn't ask him any more questions, and I didn't ask any of anybody else, either.

We really went after it with the offense today. It was a question of finding out what it takes to win.

It was one of those situations where you put your whistle in your pocket. Most days when you're hitting, there's a quick whistle to make sure no one gets hurt. Sometimes players have a tendency to ease up a little early that way. They are used to going until the whistle blows, and until they think the guy is down. So we didn't blow it. Well, I did blow it—once an hour.

Frank Stams, senior defensive end

I usually didn't last too long with those long scrimmages. When I see coaches take their whistles off during a scrimmage, that's when the hamstring starts bothering me.

We told them to block someone and keep blocking and not worry about when the whistle blows. We had people piling on each other, and fortunately no one got injured. The backs had to keep running, and if they got to the end zone, they had to come back and the defense had to keep chasing. The offense had to keep blocking, and if a guy got knocked down, he had to get up. You just kept looking for whatever wrong-color jersey you could find and you went after them.

I think the message got across, but I think the players got upset with me. I was even a little different out there. Halfway through, one player said to me, "Coach, I don't think I can make it through this." But when we were finished, many of them said, "That was the shortest practice we ever had." It wasn't necessarily fun while it was going on, but I think the players understood when we were done what the idea was.

Corny Southall, senior free safety

I remember that day. What happened was that the defense was playing really well. At that time of year the defense is always ahead of the offense, and it usually went first team against second, and second against first, and back and forth like that.

But since the first team defense, and the second team, too, were doing so well, Coach Holtz wasn't getting enough plays for us. It was three downs and out. If you stop the offense, then the next group comes in. The offense was getting a lot more plays only because the defense was stopping them. Coach had to extend it, and it kept getting longer and longer for everyone to get enough plays in. It was really tiring, and at the end Coach Holtz came up with one of his lines. He said, "Well, we've been out here for about four hours now, and I think we'll run afterward."

But that was the end of it. He had a few words for us—"We need to improve, but we'll be a good team." That was probably the longest scrimmage in my four years here.

I don't know if there has ever been a practice like that at Notre Dame, though I've had them occasionally at other places. It bordered on being brutal, but I liked the way everyone responded. As a matter of fact, I questioned them afterward, and some of the players thought it was one of the more fun days they had had. I thought then that maybe we would be all right.

Tony Yelovich, offensive line coach

We really noticed the attitude coming into fall camp. The kids were ready. They didn't care whether they had played or not played. The only thing they knew was they had a chance to play now. The experience factor didn't matter to them. But they had the right attitude to make some progress rather quickly. They went after it pretty hard. There was a steady progression in terms of improvement.

I remember the August 29 practice very well. The kids said, "Hey, we've got to get it done. We've got a great opportunity in front of us. We do have a lot of talent here, so let's do it. Let's not talk about it, let's do it." And they did it.

With the type of attitude we saw when people reported in August, I felt like, Something good is going to happen. The freshmen came in and their attitude was great. A number of them were in great shape from having played in all-star games. They weren't looking for starting roles, they just wanted to contribute. They kept up that attitude. The older guys showed up and they knew the kind of leadership it would take.

The thing that impressed me was the attitude. It was like "Coach, whatever you think it takes, we are going to do." No one questioned it, there was no mumbling, no grumbling. They said, "Hey, if that's the way it is, okay." If they're going to take coaching like that without questioning what we're doing, then we've got a chance. That kind of attitude needs to permeate the entire team.

I think we built a little character today.

10

MICHIGAN:
HO, HO, HO, HO

WE traded all of last year's game films with the University of Michigan, and we charted every one of them. We've got files from each game with a sheet for each play. We can go through and see the exact alignment for every play they ran. I'm certain they do the same thing with their film.

You can go crazy with a first game like this because there's so much to work from. But I prefer to look at what the opponent has done against teams I've coached—what Michigan has done against us at Notre Dame, against the teams I had at Minnesota. After you play somebody four or five years, you get a feel for what their philosophy is, what their thinking is. That means more to me than what they did against Iowa or Illinois. I want to know what they did against us.

My first year here, we were interested more in what Michigan had done against our teams at Minnesota than in what Michigan had done against Notre Dame the year before. We ended up taking advantage of the abilities of our quarterback, Steve Beuerlein, in that first game in '86. While we had some good gains and moved the ball, Michigan still beat us.

Michigan is one of the better teams in the country year in and year out, and in 1988 they may be the best. Bo Schembechler is one of the great coaches of all time. His teams are physical, very good fundamentally, and rarely do they ever make themselves lose. They play together as a team and with great confidence. For us to win, we are going to have to be the same type of team. We cannot play stupidly and expect to come out on top.

With a young football team, we decided to spend two weeks getting ready for Michigan rather than one. By doing this, we were running the risk of our players peaking too soon, but that is a gamble we are going to have to take.

The kicking game is always critical when you play against Michigan. They have good athletes and a lot of pride in what they do. Their ability to play error-free football, week in and week out, is impressive. However, they seem to make more mistakes against Notre Dame than their other opponents. As crazy as it sounds, their headgear intimidates some teams, but it won't bother us. We may not beat Michigan, but we are going to play awfully well.

We have to win the kicking game, and that scares me. I know they have a much better punter than we do. Consequently, we've got to be able to block a punt or run one back or something along that line. I think we have a chance to block one or return one against Michigan. We've tried to emphasize to our players that blocking a punt means as much as returning one. Rocket Ismail could be a key here.

It will be critical that we play people who really want to win. We're not putting anybody on that field who doesn't believe in Notre Dame. You can't have anybody in that locker room who has any purpose for being there other than to help Notre Dame, or who's thinking of anything but "How can I help us win?" At the end of practice every day we say "We are," and the players say, "N.D." I think that says it all.

The last and most difficult thing is for us to remain very positive no matter what happens. We have to remember that we aren't playing against an opponent as much as we are playing ourselves.

The type of preparation for each game can vary, but we do have a regular game-week routine, and it begins as we get into Monday of the first week of the season.

I get up about six every day and come into the office for a staff meeting at seven. We meet and watch film all morning. I meet with the news media at noon and try to return phone calls right after that. Then I meet with the athletes or watch some video or prepare for practice. I go to practice and then look at some of the video of it right after we're finished.

Then I go home and prepare for the next day. I'm very involved in coaching, and that may be a little different than at some places. We don't have an offensive coordinator, and that's not because Jim Strong or Pete Cordelli or someone else couldn't handle it. It's just that I want to be involved in it all. I don't know how much longer I can do that with all the demands on my time. It's often twelve-thirty or one o'clock before I get to bed.

Also, the volume of mail around here is tremendous. I depend on Jan

Blazi, my secretary, to make a lot of decisions, because it's impossible to read all the fan mail individually. It's the same way with tickets—I don't have time to get involved with that. I just try to coach football. Thank goodness for Jan, because she is exceptional.

People think this life is so glamorous—I suppose that's because of what they see on Saturday. The fans don't see what we put into it the other days of the week. I very seldom get out for lunch. Sometimes you feel like a hermit, but that's the only way to get things done in the time that's available. If I didn't get a chance to watch CNN or ESPN for a few minutes when I get home at night, it would be easy to spend the entire season in my own little world and never know what's going on in the real world.

I'm worried about fielding punts and kickoffs. Ricky Watters does it well in practice, but I don't know how well he'll do in a game. Ricky is the only guy I've ever seen who can catch punts but not kickoffs. Kickoffs normally are a lot easier to catch. I'd like to have Mark Green back deep on kickoff returns, but he's the only healthy tailback we've got. Yet I hated to put Rocket Ismail back there as a freshman and run the risk of what might happen. Even though I wasn't there, I know what happened to Tim Brown when he was back there for the first kickoff his freshman year, and that goes through my mind. I'm still undecided about who will run the first one back if it's the opening kickoff.

Rodney Culver has had a crash course, but he's not ready to be thrown in there at a critical time when this is his first game. And Tony Brooks looks awfully slow in those big high-topped shoes. But he is a great competitor. A normal person wouldn't even be playing. So we really only have one tailback, and if we lose Mark Green early, what little leadership and stability we have is gone.

We started backing off on the hitting early this week. I worry about our receivers' legs getting a little tired—nobody else's. Tony Rice hasn't thrown the ball well the last couple of days, and that scares me. I don't know if he's getting tight or what. The younger players in particular are very tight right now, though we haven't talked about Michigan much. You try to avoid it as much as you can, but you really can't.

Fundamentally, I think we'll do some good things. I think we turned the corner with Tim Ryan on Tuesday. He kept fumbling the snap, and I made up my mind that he wasn't going to be a center. We told him we would move him anywhere he wanted to move. He's frustrated. He said he couldn't block and he hadn't made a good block all year. I asked him why, and he said because he can't get his right hand up after he snaps the ball. I asked him how he would block me if he had lost his right arm.

So we had him block with his right arm behind his back. We called him Napoleon and Lefty and kept reminding him of that. You need a great athlete at center because you have to play one-handed. Tim has not had a bad snap since.

The attitude of the squad is good in terms of being together and wanting to play. I don't know how confident they are. But the only thing worse than no confidence is false confidence. It doesn't do any good for people to tell you you're really good, then go in the stadium and have somebody beat the daylights out of you.

Ricky Watters isn't ready at flanker, and we can't get him the ball enough, anyway. He just doesn't have a good strong feeling for the different patterns he has to run. But, boy, is he talented. We'll get the ball in his hands even if we have to put him at tailback some. Rod Smith isn't ready yet as a freshman to help us at flanker, but he will be before he leaves. Rocket Ismail can get open, but I don't think he'll catch the ball consistently. He dropped six out of seven long ones in practice this week. The only thing I told him Thursday was that, hey, I don't expect you to catch it yet. I just want to bring the crowd to its feet. If you catch it, it's a bonus. Just run fast and far and get the crowd excited and scare Michigan a little bit. That'll open up the intermediate routes. He'll just have to keep learning. He'll get a feel for it. He is going to be great, eventually.

If something happens to Tony Rice, we'll go with either Steve Belles or Kent Graham, depending upon the situation. Belles is a great competitor. But he has put the ball on the ground a lot and thrown into coverages. It's different in the spring when you play against one defense. Kent has done some good things recently and has really started to come on.

There's a problem at linebacker only in terms of who is going to play. But I expect to play all three at the same time if Michigan comes out with two tight ends, which I think they'll do.

The biggest things we worry about are turnovers, the kicking game, and Michigan's ability to dominate the line of scrimmage—blow us off the ball when they've got it and stuff us on offense. Those are going to be the three big keys to this game.

I talked to the squad about this being a physical game. Some of our younger players don't understand that. You make a great hit and everybody jumps up and down and the crowd cheers and they replay it on television. Everybody gets excited. You get up and your head hurts, your shoulder hurts, every bone in your body hurts. Everybody feels good except you. Ten seconds later the pain leaves. The pain and embarrassment that come from getting beat last a lifetime compared to the ten seconds of pain that come from making a physical play.

I've pushed this team harder than the last two here—harder, and yet with more compassion and patience. I think we've been more patient because our staff has done an unbelievable job of getting these players prepared. Secondly, our players have been a joy to be with. There isn't a guy on the team who's on a different page than the rest of us. We pushed them harder because we had further to go. I knew in the summer because of the personnel changes we'd had that this would be the most challenging year that I've ever put in.

You have two options. One is to say that we can't be real good, so let's lower the standards. That's not the answer. So if you've got further to go and you want to go beyond where you were before, then you *have* to push them. We worked longer and we worked harder, and consequently we may be a little bit tired going into this game. The only thing I dislike more than being tired is not being prepared.

You go home at night and you weigh your options. I think our defense and our kicking game will have to carry this team. But we're not naive enough to think we're going to completely stop our opponents. We're going to have to play well on offense with our schedule. With some teams defense and the kicking game are enough. But not against the people we have on our schedule.

We didn't have many tedious moments this last month we've worked, because the players are so young and there's so much to learn and so much to cover in practice. If players have bad practices, it's because coaches have bad practices. We had one bad practice, and I told the players it was my fault. If the coaches don't go out there with the enthusiasm and excitement necessary to get things done, that's conveyed to the players. So we've said, "Don't count the days, make the days count." Every day I've tried to talk to them about something—whether it be feeling good about themselves or where they are or what they're doing or the direction they're going. We try to be honest and talk about problem areas.

Every day during two-a-day practices, I mentioned to the players that I talked to Bo Schembechler. I did the same thing last year. I'd ask him, "Bo, you going to give your guys today off?" And he'd say, "No, we've got a tough game against Miami the second week. We can't afford to take a day with Miami on the horizon. The only thing these guys have to worry about is Miami. We'll start on Notre Dame maybe the Wednesday of that week." I joked with them along that line every day. They knew I was kidding, but they seemed to enjoy it and we just wanted to stay loose.

I talked to them Thursday about a guy from ESPN asking me in an interview about Michigan being embarrassed because they lost to Notre Dame last year. That just illustrates how strong their football program is, because they didn't think anyone should beat them. I hope our team can progress to that point.

I have tremendous respect for Michigan. This will be the kind of game where, if we don't have turnovers, we play well in the kicking game, and if we don't let them dominate us physically, we will have a chance to win. But I sense this may be one of Bo's better teams at Michigan, and that's saying something.

I told the staff early in the week there were certain things we had to do to beat Michigan. First and foremost was to play with confidence, and that wouldn't be easy with a young squad. It also was important that our tailbacks be productive. Michigan always has a great tailback and fullback.

You have no idea how your players will perform in an opening game. More upsets probably occur in the opening game than in all the other weeks combined. The biggest improvement a team will make is between its first and second game.

We also felt we had to have the gameplan in so our players understood what we were going to do and why we were going to do it. We haven't executed as well as I would like, but we did get it in early and we have had a lot of reps on it.

The players know what to do, but some days they get bored. Sometimes you run the same play a thousand times because 999 isn't enough. They run it over and over and lose their concentration. If they lose their concentration and can still do it, then you've got it ingrained, but the biggest concern I have is whether or not our players will check their low hole card the first time we face adversity.

I get concerned about how the officials will call things like holding in a game like this. I watched some of our opponents' all-Americans on film, and they get their hands outside the defensive player's body and are never called for holding. Yet, in our scrimmage last Saturday, with our own officials, Frank Jacobs gets called for holding with his hands inside his body. The official says, "I thought he might have had hold of his jersey." So if those officials intimidate us during fall practice and then let it go Saturday, I am really going to be upset. I firmly believe we should have a national officials group. One of the reasons is because of the different interpretations of holding by various conferences around the country.

You're not often going to catch Michigan off guard, because they are so sound. But one thing we're going to do is show a lot of motion. We're going to put the formation to the short side of the field. We're going to start the flanker one way and then have him come back the other. We're going to run some ace formations and run some counters out of the single back, which we've never done before. There'll be a few things they probably haven't seen before. The more things we can do without creating a problem for us, the better off we are.

They have three new players in the secondary—I understand they're great athletes. I know they aren't going to let themselves get beat deep. But I think Raghib Ismail has a chance on the play-action pass if we put the formation to the boundary, motion away, and throw back to Rocket on a go pattern. They're going to see that early. They are going to see us go deep early. We are going to send a message—you better stay deep and let us hit some things over the middle. Whether we can do these things or not, I don't know.

We'll just have to see what we do on defense. That dictates so much of how you play on offense. You don't have to be a genius to figure that Bo is going to count on that great offensive line, with its size and experience, and outstanding tailbacks, to control the game. They figure the only thing that beat 'em last year was their own mistakes, and they would be accurate in that assumption. I think Bo will throw deep and he'll throw screen passes, because he likes to do those two things in a big game. I must add that this is a pretty good strategy.

They'll try to control the ball, because they feel they did it the last two years and we've got a defensive line that hasn't played. They figure they've got all the experience and are playing a bunch of young guys who've never played before. They figure they've got an all-American at center going against our nose guard, who hasn't played a single play.

Against Michigan and Michigan State last year we did not run a single option play. Against Purdue we moved the football and we ended up running a lot of option with great success. If we throw it eighteen to twenty-two times, we'll be okay. If we throw it more than that, we'll be in trouble.

I plan to talk to the squad the night before the game about the last three games of last year and how we lost them. I still think back to the Cotton Bowl, when we had A&M right where we wanted them. We've got the ball on their 18-yard line with a 10–3 lead and three-and-a-half minutes left in the half. The worst we're going to do is kick a field goal and be up 13–3. Then it all turns around with the interception and the bomb and the turnover. And the next thing you know we're down 18–10 at halftime.

The third quarter was an even game except we couldn't play catch-up with them. We tried to play catch-up in the final period, but that's not our game and we got blown out. So you take three quarters, and except for that two-and-a-half minutes in there, we had a chance to win the game.

It's important for our players to understand all that and why it happened. We can't make critical errors against our schedule and succeed.

The Friday afternoon before the game I had a good visit with the squad. We talked about what we had to do and why we had to do it. Predominantly, I tried to build their confidence—that I believed our players were better this year, that if we just played our total game, we would be okay.

We went to the pep rally next, and it was outstanding. The crowd was tremendous, and we had it outside of Stepan Center because of the huge number of people—about four thousand.

Then we went back to the Loftus Center. We didn't have time to have a movie, but we did have a meeting. We have fourteen players who've hardly played, and they're going to have to play key roles for us. I knew they were nervous.

So we had about fifteen or sixteen players get up, and we asked them, "What do you remember about the first time you played?" Some guys remembered the first time because they went on field in a mop-up role and it didn't mean much. Others played a more prominent role.

But I think Wesley Pritchett did a particularly great job. He said, "It's a great thrill to come out of the tunnel, and you feel excited and everything else. But don't make it out to be more than what it is. It's just a game. It's no different than practice. You're well-prepared. Your coaches have you well-prepared. Just go out and act like it's practice and you'll be fine. You'll have butterflies, but the first time you get hit, you'll forget all about it. If you make it out to be a big thing, you're making a mistake."

We had a lot of laughs. Tony Rice talked about coming in at halftime against Pittsburgh last year. The first thing he did was line up behind the guard. Anthony Johnson said to him, "Tony, move over, please." He ran a naked play and got thrown for a seven-yard loss, but then he hit his first pass and was fine. The younger players got a good feeling from this—that, hey, it really isn't that much different.

Then we went in and had a relaxation period. I have the players lay down and relax. We do this every Friday night, but I wanted to go longer tonight. Your legs will recover quicker if your whole body is relaxed. The tension goes away and you sleep better. I went through getting ready in the stadium, going through the plays, the signals, and the kicking game. You ask each player to visualize being in the huddle and looking at his teammates. The signals are called, you execute the play, and you're always looking for success. If you're a placekicker, visualize the ball going through the goalposts. Concentrate on what your job is.

We talked about how fortunate our players are. I told them to think about all the great things they have going for them, like going to a terrific school. I then said to them, "You could play for a lot of other head coaches who are different and maybe a lot nicer. But everything we do is done to prepare you, not just for the game, but for life. You have great assistant coaches. I promised you a year ago when we had some staff changes that I would provide you with the best staff possible, and I think we've done that."

I told them there may be better head coaches in the country, but I doubt it. They started laughing, so I knew they were listening to me. But I feel that way, and you've got to feel that way. I don't do everything right. But I believe we know what we're doing and where we're going.

After twenty-five minutes in the relaxation period, they got on the bus and headed for Plymouth. I went home and had some phone calls to make and some relatives to visit, but that didn't last long. Then I went upstairs and worked.

I got up Saturday morning and did some more work relating to the game and then went to the pregame meeting. We went over the kicking game and made sure we had all the proper people. Then the players had kicking-game meetings and individual meetings, and I went back home to get my things together.

I wanted to go to the luncheon to dedicate the Notre Dame Monogram Club's Sports Heritage Hall, but it was impossible to do that on game day. I visited the officials for a few minutes at the stadium, then went to the locker room. There was good tension there. It wasn't hard to sense that.

During the pregame workouts I visited with Bo Schembechler, who now serves as Michigan's athletic director in addition to coaching football. I had seen him quoted about the huge deficit his Michigan athletic program was facing. I figured the first thing he did as athletic director was build himself a home. I kidded him that it must be something special to have that big deficit in the athletic department.

We laughed about that, but Bo said we wouldn't want to compete against them in swimming or several other sports because Michigan had made a financial commitment that should eventually breed success.

He and I have a good relationship. I have great respect for Bo, and I hope Bo respects what we do as well. I love to compete with him because he may be the best. He is the Woody Hayes of college football today. I don't think there is much doubt that he was Woody's favorite disciple, and I can understand why.

Ned Bolcar, senior linebacker

Coach Holtz told us before the Michigan game that he called Bo.

"I called Bo," Coach would say. Then Corny Southall would ask Coach Holtz what he said.

"Bo said we had to give you guys a day off, that his players were tired and bloody and they've got to beat you on Saturday. I told him that I wouldn't give you a day off."

Later, one of the players said he called Bo. Coach asked him what he said. "Well, Bo said the team is having shrimp, lobster, and prime rib."

Our players were finishing the last part of the pregame workout when the Michigan players tried to run through us on their way to the tunnel down in the north end zone. That made for an ugly scene, and that wasn't like Michigan. But the tensions were high on both teams.

In the past when something like that happened, our players just dropped their heads. They didn't this time. I felt then that our players were ready to compete. In the locker room they were really fired up. I calmed them down and the last thing I said to them was how difficult it was to be at Notre Dame. I didn't mean it in reference to Michigan. But I told them it's tough to win at Notre Dame:

"You don't have easy classes here. You don't get a certificate for good attendance. You don't get any leniency because you're a football player. You've got to compete with the best students in the country because you're a full-time student. You don't live in a fancy athletic dorm. You live with all the other students. You don't have a fancy training table, where they cater to you with steak every night. There aren't any fancy cars in our parking lot, unless it's Andy Heck's, which is a '48 Pontiac. There aren't any patsies on our schedule. Everybody we play is tough as all get-out. You aren't afforded the luxury of lifting weights whenever you want. And your social life here is curtailed a little bit. There aren't steroids here to help you get stronger, and there's no redshirting.

"Everybody is saying that because of all these things, we can't be great. They think because you've paid a price academically and are disciplined and make sacrifices, that you can't be tough. That you can't be physical. Because the game has changed so much, with redshirting and all the rest, there are people who say Notre Dame can't win anymore. I don't believe that. I don't believe that we need to have that image any longer."

Opening in our stadium against Michigan made me think back to 1986 and my first game at Notre Dame, which also was at home against Michigan. In the locker room this time before we went down, I was very emotional about taking the field at Notre Dame, much more so than the first year.

The first time I came down that tunnel against Michigan in '86, I didn't understand what it was all about. I was aware of the tradition, but I was more intimidated than anything else. I hadn't added to the tradition, I just happened to be there. I hadn't done anything to prove I was deserving of being at Notre Dame.

Going into my third year now, with a young developing team, and having played on January 1 last year, I felt an awesome responsibility to field a great team. Three years is ample time to do it. We were young, but as Darrell Royal used to say, "If a dog is going to bite you, he'll do it as a pup."

I felt a lot of emotion because this was Notre Dame, and I'm part of Notre Dame. The longer you're here, the deeper the feeling.

THE GAME

SOUTH BEND—Americans do love their heroes.

Notre Dame fans particularly love them when they come in the form of an unsuspecting, 135-pound, walk-on placekicker who came to school bent on pursuing his premedical studies as opposed to achieving gridiron glory.

Enter Reggie Ho, the 5–5 senior with the suddenly golden toe.

The bashful Hawaiian didn't seem to fit the hero's clothes—not with more familar Irish names like Rice and Green and Stonebreaker around. In fact, Fighting Irish coach Lou Holtz didn't especially think Ho did anything he hadn't been expected to do.

Still, there wasn't much question that Notre Dame's neophyte soccer-style kicker stole the show in the prime-time season opener against Michigan. His record-tying four field goals—even if they were from quite-makeable distances—turned out to be ever so helpful in enabling Notre Dame to preserve a spine-tingling 19–17 triumph over the ninth-rated Wolverines.

Holtz unearthed more than his share of answers under the portable lights at Notre Dame Stadium. He learned that Notre Dame's youthful offensive and defensive lines might not be liabilities after all. He learned that a year away from football hadn't diminished the skills of linebacker Michael Stonebreaker, who made 16 tackles.

But Reggie Ho? He hadn't even been part of the question.

In the end, give credit to the special teams, coached by every member of the staff, as they produced every one of Notre Dame's points. A very talented Ricky Watters returned a punt for 81 yards for the lone Irish touchdown. Reggie Ho scored 13 points by adding the PAT on Watters's touchdown and kicking 4 field goals without a miss—from distances of 31, 38, 26, and, again, 26 yards away.

101

Holtz typically masked his pleasure with the season-opening win by suggesting that Ho had done only what was expected of him. In truth, Holtz had been telling the media for months that Ho was exceptionally accurate on PATs and short field goals.

But, in this instance, the timing was everything.

The ending of this game proved strikingly similar to that of Michigan's last visit to Notre Dame Stadium in 1986 in Holtz's first game as Irish head coach. In that game, Notre Dame played well but lost 24–23 when a last-second field goal by John Carney from the Michigan 35-yard line was just wide.

This time, it was Michigan's Mike Gillette who suffered that same fate. A native of nearby St. Joseph, Michigan, Gillette had just successfully kicked a 49-yarder in the fourth quarter with just more than five minutes left for a 17–16 Wolverine lead. However, Reggie Ho made good on his field-goal attempt from 26 yards with 1:13 left in the game to give Notre Dame a 19–17 lead. Michigan, though, responded very well by driving down the field only to have Gillette's 48-yarder at the final gun veer off to the right.

As Ho then proceeded to tell his life story, he explained that being a football star had been the furthest thing from his mind when he came to Notre Dame. He didn't even go out for the team as a freshman, preferring instead to concentrate on his studies. He appeared uncomfortable under the unaccustomed media scrutiny, but there was no avoiding the spotlight of this prime-time encounter.

Both teams played it relatively close to the vest, preferring to jockey for field position and depend on their defenses as opposed to throwing the football all over the lot or attempting other risky offensive maneuvers.

That was hardly a surprise to Notre Dame fans, who had heard Holtz suggest for weeks that the Irish defense would have to shoulder the brunt of the load early. With a retooled offensive line combined with the loss of Heisman Trophy winner Tim Brown, Notre Dame didn't figure to outscore many opponents. And the Irish won't have to if their defense continues its opening-night performance.

Defense, maybe not so ironically, had been one of the sore points when the Irish ended their campaign a year ago in three straight losses that featured 80 combined points by Penn State, Miami, and Texas A&M. No doubt, Holtz vowed his team would be vastly improved in that area. But, the first-game matchup—featuring Michigan's gargantuan offensive line, rated best in the nation by *The Sporting News*, against a Notre Dame defense line with three brand-new starters—seemed a mite unsettling.

Michigan was picked to be one of the top three teams in the country, and this prognostication turned out to be quite accurate. What no one realized on September 12 was that Notre Dame was a little better than people had anticipated.

With the kicking units providing all the Irish scoring, Michigan's special teams were outstanding also. Both Wolverine touchdowns were set up by excellent effort and execution. First, they swarmed Ricky Watters on a punt and forced a fumble which they recovered on Notre Dame's 14-yard line, and this led to a touchdown. Next they returned a kickoff 59 yards to set the stage for a second score. For its part, the Notre Dame defense proved downright stingy.

Zorich had never played a down as a rookie, but he debuted with 10 tackles plus a sack and a half. The Irish hadn't seen such a dominant performer in that spot since Bob Golic. Stonebreaker captured national defensive player of the week honors from *The Sporting News* in his first outing after missing all of '87.

The Irish were not dominating in offense, but nobody is against Michigan. Their secondary presented Rice with all kinds of problems throwing, and he went none for eight in the first half and finished three of 12 for 40 yards. Despite all the new faces on the offensive line, Notre Dame ground out 226 rushing yards, including 69 by Mark Green, 52 by Tony Rice, 49 by Anthony Johnson, and 48 by Tony Brooks.

Holtz—to his credit—had avoided comparing Watters with Brown. But that became difficult when Watters did a rather delightful impersonation of Brown returning two Michigan punts less than five minutes into the game.

Notre Dame actually made it look like they might win convincingly by taking an early 13–0 lead. Michigan failed to score on any of its three first-period possessions. In the first quarter, the Irish used runs of 19 yards by Brooks and 16 by Rice to set up the first of Ho's field goals with only 35 seconds left in the initial quarter. Freshman Arnold Ale recovered a Michigan fumble on the ensuing kickoff, and three plays later Ho made it 13–0. However, Michigan retaliated when Tony Boles made a beautiful return with the kickoff, running it all the way to Notre Dame's 38-yard line. The Wolverines used 12 plays to negotiate the 38 yards, and Leroy Hoard's one-yard touchdown cut the advantage to 13–7 midway through the second period. Notre Dame threatened later in the quarter, but the drive ended when a Rice pass hit the receiver in the numbers, bounced up in the air, and was picked off by Michigan.

The game was very intensely played, and it was quite obvious the two teams were evenly matched. Michigan got a break when Watters fumbled a Michigan punt, and this set up the Wolverines at the Notre Dame 14. Michael Taylor, Michigan's quarterback, ran on fourth-down into the end zone, providing a 14–13 Michigan lead. The drive was kept alive by a

Notre Dame penalty which gave Michigan first and goal on the 6. The Irish came right back, driving 68 yards for another Ho field goal. Tony Rice made a great throw to Steve Alaniz that was the key play in the drive. That made it 16–14 for Notre Dame.

It was Michigan's turn next, and Schembechler's crew converted three times on third down on its way to Gillette's long field goal that made it 17–16 at the 5:39 juncture.

The Irish benefited from three big plays on their march to the winning points. First, Michigan was called for pass interference on the first play from scrimmage. Second, Rice scampered for 21 yards on the next play. Third, Brooks gained another 18 on a quick flip from Rice.

Michigan tried to ice Ho with a time-out, but the little guy pounded through the 26-yarder and earned yet another hug from holder Peter Graham. Taylor hit a pair of passes to give Gillette his final fling, but this time the ball slid off to the right.

"In my judgment, they deserved to win," said Schembechler. However this was debatable as both teams played very well.

And what of Reggie Ho? Well, he managed to praise everyone from Graham to snapper Tim Grunhard to the student trainer who taped his ankle. He allowed that his anatomy studies still outweigh football in importance. And he expressed no interest in inquiring about the possibility of a scholarship.

"I'd never take money from Notre Dame," he said sheepishly.

Just another day in the life of Notre Dame's latest local hero.

Michigan played very well, too. Through the course of the game I knew it would be difficult because Michigan would not make mistakes. In a game like this, there are no winners, only survivors. The two areas I was disappointed in were our pass defense and the way we moved to the ball on offense.

I thought our offensive line and defensive line played well through the course of the game, but I was disappointed with our passing game. Our kickoff coverage left some things to be desired. I had been concerned about our guys not keeping the return inside and in front of them, and that came back to haunt us when Michigan ran one back to set up a touchdown. I was disappointed with our punt returns, other than Ricky Watters's for the touchdown. Our kickoff return, with a lot of young kids in there, did not get executed the way it needed to be.

But it was a great contest, a very physical game.

At halftime I didn't know what would happen. We weren't real fired up. Momentum was going their way. It did not look good. But it's up to us to control that as coaches. We talked about what we did wrong. We had turnovers, we made mistakes on the kickoff return, but we were still ahead. "Let's go out and play this half even," I said. "We're not behind. It's a thirty-minute ballgame."

We really hadn't played that badly in the first half. Ricky Watters's long punt return was a big lift emotionally. Then, we came back down and got a field goal and then another one after they fumbled the kickoff. Michigan did get one touchdown, but that was after we let them return a kickoff of fifty-nine yards. We had another chance to score but we didn't because of an interception. It wasn't anyone's fault. Tony threw it to the right place, and Ricky was wide open. He just slipped, and the ball bounced high off his pads. We held Michigan much better than I ever envisioned, but I should reiterate that no one stops Michigan.

The first touchdown they got in the third period came after they started on their own 38 after a kickoff return. Three times Michigan converted—on third and 9, third and 8, and third and 5—and that disappointed me. On third and 7 or more they converted 5 out of 7, which is a tribute to them. In the spring I thought our pass defense would be our strong point. But as I mentioned, I did not think we were playing the ball well in some of those passing situations, and I think that was evident.

After they scored to make it 14–13, we knew we would find out what kind of team we had. We talk about answering the challenge after the opposition scores. They take the lead on you and you have no choice. You have to answer. And we did that. Once we got it down close to the goal line, we played very conservatively. We felt our defense was playing well, and we didn't want to put them in a bad position. We kicked a field goal, and almost before we could put it on the scoreboard, Michigan came back to kick one of its own.

What makes for a great contest is when the momentum swings back and forth like in a heavyweight fight. You are down and then you are up. This game was a great one because each team refused to lose.

When Reggie Ho got ready to kick the last field goal, I really wasn't worried. We chart field goals every day. Every time we look, Reggie is 24 of 24, or 22 of 22, or 23 of 24, and from both hashes. When we ran the draw to Anthony Johnson on the third down, I said, "Stay in the middle of the field." But he tried to break it, and we ended up on the hash. Michigan called time-out, and we brought our team over to the sideline. We had visualized kicking a last-minute field goal to win the game, and I felt very confident with Reggie. The only thing I felt might cause us to miss it was if we tried to make it. I said to them, "This is just like practice. Reggie's made this 24 of 24 times. All you've got to do is snap it like in practice, hold it like in practice, and Reggie will kick it like in practice." If they would do as we did it in practice, I felt 19 times out of 20, minimum, we would make it. Those are pretty good odds.

I said before the game I was not worried about placekicking. Not once have we questioned our ability to placekick. We knew Reggie Ho was going to be fine on short field goals and Billy Hackett would be excellent on kickoffs.

Initially, I didn't think Reggie would be a good placekicker. I thought he was a bit different and he was. He had a 3.8 grade-point average in premed. He was out there all the time kicking, but he wasn't one of our top three kickers and that made no sense. I talked to Ted Gradel—who kicked for us last year—before he left, and Ted said Reggie was the most dedicated guy out there. He went out and kicked every day, even in the snow. Ted said, "Don't undersell Reggie."

During the spring, Reggie always made 'em. You go back to the spring game two years ago, and he kicked a long field goal. He does work hard and the kids love Reggie, and they have from day one.

We ended up getting the fourth field goal by Reggie to lead 19–17. But here came Michigan once more. Gillette had a chance to kick one on the last play. It was about the same distance as the one he hit to put them ahead 17–16. This time he missed, but it was one of those plays that easily could have gone the other way. At the end of a season you sit down and think about how the complexion of your year changes based on what happens on a play like that. You play for fifty-nine minutes, and it all comes down to that.

When Michigan came back and moved down the field after Reggie put us ahead with a minute to go, it was a great display of passing by Michael Taylor. I thought our pass coverage last spring was great but it's obvious we hadn't been tested. They made some great throws and catches to put themselves in field-goal range. Gillette had already made one from there which surprised me. This was about the same distance and the same angle. The chances of his making two in a row weren't good.

They called time-out, then we used our last time-out. The biggest concern I had was that we would rough the kicker. I said, "Don't rough the kicker. I don't think he's going to make it." Frank Stams said, "I'm going to block it." I said, "That's fine, but don't rough the kicker, because he's not gonna make it." I really didn't think he would make it. But when he kicked the ball, I thought, Oh, that sucker might be good. Of course, bedlam broke out when he missed. There isn't anything else you can do there, but it's a lot tougher than you think with the game on the line. John Carney missed one for Notre Dame that was a lot closer than that in 1986 in his own park in our 24–23 loss to Michigan.

Things got a little wild then, and I had difficulty finding Bo. He was class. He said it was a great football game. Looking at the film, we beat an awfully fine team.

The television people had to love the finish, because CBS had moved the game to prime time, thinking it would be a great start for their season. I'm not sure it was deserved, but the television people loved Reggie and made him into a hero. It was a storybook ending for him.

In any event, it was a great way to start, especially when it's at home and on national television. We didn't set the world on fire offensively, but the confidence we gained as a team is the biggest thing we got out of the game.

I think I was probably calmer during the football game than I've ever been in my life. When Ricky Watters fumbled the punt and showed all kinds of emotion, I put my arm around him and said, "Hey, that's over, we don't show emotion. We get other chances. Forget about that."

When you show frustration, you send a message to everybody that the game's over, instead of having the team come away with a firm resolution that we'll get that sucker back. You can't show that frustration. It is exceptionally difficult not to get frustrated with officials, and I don't handle this very well. Officials are the only factor I know of in a game you can't neutralize. A coach has no control over them. They can take the game right away from the players. This is true in basketball as well as football. In all other sports, you can see the penalty, not in football. So much officiating in football is strictly judgment. We had one opponent called thirteen times for holding in one game and none the next.

I don't understand how we can take a team to Michigan one year and get called for delay of game because we can't hear the snap count. The referee would give us no relief. Then this year we're charged with a time-out because Michigan can't hear the signals. This is Bo's way of trying to take the crowd out of the game. He complains about it everywhere he goes. We aren't playing tennis or golf. The crowd shouldn't have to remain silent.

I don't talk to officials very often. But during the Michigan game I said to one official, "Sir, they credited the back with zero yards and gave you a two-yard gain. That's the only way they could account for that play." I know that's not true, but sometimes I think they ought to pay the officials half their fee because they only watch one team.

After the game the players were excited as could be. It wasn't just the people who played or played well. Everybody on the squad was hugging each other. We passed out game balls and I gave them to the three fifth-year seniors. Wes Pritchett had been out of school one year, Frank

Stams hurt his leg, and Flash Gordon sat out his freshman season. And I gave one to Reggie Ho. Then we gave one to Father Joe Carey for allowing us to use Dillon Hall for our team mass over the last couple years. I had the players in that dorm take it to him.

John Palermo, defensive line coach

That first game against Michigan was a huge factor, particularly for the defensive coaching staff. At the end of that game we felt like we were doing the right things and the players were responding to what we were telling them.

The only injury that concerned me that night was to me. When a Michigan player went out of bounds by our sideline, where there isn't much room, he inadvertently tore a deep gash on my middle finger. I went home after the game and my in-laws were there already and my uncle Lou. We sat and visited briefly about the game. But my mind was on Michigan State. I tried to go to sleep, but I don't think I did until about three-thirty. I woke up about six and my finger was throbbing. I took a shower, and that hurt. I finally took some Excedrin and the pain started to simmer down. I went to early mass, looked at the film of the Michigan game, and did my television show.

We met with the squad Sunday and went over all our goals and objectives, where we faltered and fell, why the game was closer than it should have been. I mentioned at the coaching-staff meeting that it's nice to make corrections after a win. But there were a lot of things we had to correct.

Steve Belles, senior quarterback

The thing that stands out in my mind is that after each win Coach Holtz used to say, "Well, where does that put us now? What are you going to do with this win?"

The whole idea was that it was just one win. He said that after the Michigan game in the film session on Sunday, and it really struck me because it got us into a one-game-at-a-time frame of mind.

I visited with Tony Rice and let him know that we've got to be able to throw the football. I had even thought about going with another quarterback during the Michigan game. Once I looked at the film, I felt a little better. Tony did play well the second half. In fact, he made one great throw over the middle to Steve Alaniz. But the one thing that really upsets me is when an individual does not perform in a game the way he does in practice. Tony did not, but neither did his receivers. We had to be able to throw, and Tony said he would get it done. We told him we could not live without the ability to throw the ball—that we were being unfair to the team. We don't need a running back—we need a quarterback. His leadership qualities and competitiveness cannot be underestimated. I was always positive with him. I knew he could do it and would do it. It was just a matter of time.

I thought Tony Brooks ran well, considering his injury. But I thought all our backs ran exceptionally and blocked very well for each other. They had two mental errors, one missed assignment, no penalties, no turn-overs. They played big-time. Jim Strong has done an incredible job with them. He is a bright individual who will be an outstanding head coach in the near future. His players are always productive.

We still have a lot of games left and they are all big. But there were so many positive things in the Michigan game that we have to feel encouraged. Had we lost that game, you would still have had to say it was a heck of a football game. That was a Notre Dame team that played in that stadium. Many times after an opening game you don't know how good the opposition is, but there is no doubt in my mind we beat one of the ten best teams in the country.

Chuck Heater, secondary coach

In the first game against Michigan, there was pressure on us because they had a pretty good idea where they were going to be. They were a good football team, and they knew it. We weren't quite sure. And Michigan is not an easy team to beat. Some people don't know how to win. Lou Holtz knows how to win ballgames, and so does Bo Schembechler. They know early in the season how to keep from losing games. You don't win by throwing the ball all over the lot and throwing it over the middle.

We dominated in so many ways, and yet they were in the game. It probably shouldn't have come down to the field goals at the end. But that's the respect you have to have for Michigan. They're going to be in the football game. They had the experienced offensive line, and those kids knew that. We were the new kids on the block.

We were playing so many people up front who hadn't been there before. But I thought we took it to them on the line of scrimmage and won it up front. Lou has a way of taking something like that and turning it into a positive.

John Palermo

Going into spring practice, it was a major concern to find out who the defensive linemen were going to be. Bryan Flannery was a dependable

109

player who had played all three positions. Jeff Alm was a big question mark because he had been injured a great deal. As it turned out, he started all twelve football games for us during the year and only missed one practice with the flu.

George Williams was a question mark because he was heavy and out of shape. Even coming out of spring practice, I wasn't sure about his commitment to excellence and whether he was going to be a starter in the fall. He was still a little heavy when he came back in the summer, but he started losing some weight, and he started the season at 280 pounds. At that point he was really moving well and doing a super job for us.

The big surprise was Chris Zorich. Zoro wasn't a surprise to Coach Holtz, but he was to me. He had adapted from the linebacker position to a down spot, but we only saw him one day in the spring because he hurt a knee. Bob Dahl came in and did a good job in a cleanup role, and Steve Roddy gave us some good leadership.

The defensive line was a big gray area going into the Michigan game. But after that game, I had great respect for those guys. I felt like we had a pretty decent defensive line.

I didn't believe it when I heard it, but people told me when the Notre Dame football players take the field, they kick it up a notch. It's not the same team that practices all week. I didn't believe that until I saw it that first game against Michigan.

The biggest high for me in football was that first game in Notre Dame Stadium against Michigan. The gold helmets shine and the band plays. I knew we were going to play hard.

11

NED BOLCAR:
THREE STARS FOR TWO JOBS

I know having captains has been a long tradition at Notre Dame, and I don't intend to debate that. But the risk you run in electing captains before the season is that one of them may end up not playing, for one reason or another—as much as they would like—and that's what was happening this year.

I knew we had the potential for a problem back in the spring when Ned Bolcar hurt his ankle playing basketball and missed our first practices. We told our players that there were no returning starters and we were starting from scratch. Nobody had any money in the bank, and we would come out of spring practice with a starting lineup based solely on what happened in those twenty practices. Wes Pritchett and Michael Stonebreaker performed well and never missed a practice. Ned is an excellent player, and all three had good chemistry with the other players. But Pritchett and Stonebreaker had earned the right to start against Michigan.

When you win you have problems, just like when you lose—only of a different nature. Herb Gould, a fine sportswriter from the *Chicago Sun-Times*, interviewed Ned after the Michigan game and wrote a story that was detrimental to what we were trying to build. The article insinuated that we had promised Ned equal time with Stonebreaker and Pritchett, and he suggested we purposely were keeping him on the bench this year so that he would have to come back in '89 for a fifth year. I would have been really upset, except no one loves or belongs at Notre Dame more than Ned Bolcar. He was selected by the team for the right reasons.

111

We all get frustrated, and don't always react in a constructive manner, and that includes Lou Holtz.

I had talked to the squad the day before the Michigan game about game conduct, what happens when we travel, talking to the news media, which I'd discussed with them before. I wanted them to understand completely how everything that happens at Notre Dame is a national story. I also talked to them about treating the media with respect, being on time for interviews, everything that's in our player policy book—with special emphasis on our rule not to take complaints to the newspapers. So when Herb called me Tuesday afternoon and told me what Ned had said, I was surprised and disappointed that Ned would suggest we were trying to hold him back for a fifth year. I'm just worried about who can help us win, period. As I told Herb, I wasn't worried about Ned being back for a fifth year. I was worried about my being back for a fifth year.

I immediately got Barry Alvarez and we found Ned and sat him down. I explained to him that I wasn't interested in anything but this year. I wasn't interested in doing anything but being fair. We were firm in our discussion, but I wanted to hear Ned's side of it as well. You should always try to look at it from the player's side of it, and I had. I knew it was hard for Ned when he was a second-team all-American the year before.

I said there were three questions I had to ask. One, had I ever given him any reason to mistrust me? I wanted to know when and where I ever told him anything that was not true or did not come to pass. If I tell somebody something, I do everything I can to honor and adhere to that. It's important to me that players trust me.

Second, I asked him if he knew of anyone—whether me or a member of the staff—who worked harder, cared more about the program, was better prepared or more committed to success than we were.

The third question was—did we care about him? I told him, "You obviously have a problem with that because you're saying we don't." There isn't anybody I like more than Ned Bolcar. He's enthusiastic and he's a wonderful young man. But I wanted to know if I had done anything to give him any indication that I didn't care about him. I wouldn't do something for him personally at the expense of the team or a team member, but other than that, was there anything I could have ever done for him legally or honestly that I hadn't done?

If Ned had a complaint and it fell into any of those three areas, I wanted to hear it. Not to defend myself, but to make sure he knew he could trust us, we were committed, and we cared about him.

We talk about these three questions, and having examined them from both the coach's and player's side, we have usually pinpointed the problem, and that was the case in this situation.

I said, "Ned, when you come back here ten years from now, what will they say about your career?" He played in the Cotton Bowl, was voted CBS defensive player of the year, was second team all-American, and was voted captain of the team. I said, "You've had a career already. The only thing missing is a national championship. I know you don't want to hurt Notre Dame or the football team, but it is happening. It's time you sat down and evaluated some things, because we're going to go forward." He said it would never happen again. I said, "I promise you it isn't going to happen again."

He left the office, and I felt the situation would not be a problem again, and it wasn't. The whole conversation took about twenty-five minutes. I said very little to the squad about it. Ned did end up helping us at both inside positions. And he ended up playing extensively in the Fiesta Bowl after Stonebreaker was injured, and he was outstanding.

But it's a typical example of when outside expectations—which are unrealistic—can have a negative effect on something within the team. Would Ned's situation have been different if he hadn't been a captain? It might not have gotten quite so much attention.

As it was, after our final talk following the *Sun-Times* story, it was a tribute to Ned that he did everything he could for the good of the football team. He may not have liked the decisions we made. As a matter of fact, I didn't like them, either. But we felt it was fair.

If Stonebreaker or Pritchett had played poorly, it would have been different. It was a credit to the three of them that they ended up contributing as much as they did—whether they were starting or not.

12

MICHIGAN STATE: A DOSE OF THEIR OWN MEDICINE

As I drove to the stadium for our game against the University of Michigan, I listened to Michigan State's postgame show on the radio after the Spartans' loss to Rutgers. In the locker room interviews, their players talked about putting the Rutgers game behind them and bouncing back against Notre Dame. I was sure they would.

Michigan State had returned seventeen starters from last year's team, which won the Rose Bowl and the Big Ten. We've never been able to run the ball against them. What little degree of success we've had against them has been through the air, and that's a real liability for us now. Our protection has been good, but we didn't throw the ball well and our receivers haven't been productive. So for us to think we could move the ball against Michigan State on a regular basis would be foolish.

Everybody thinks right now that all we're worried about is our passing game, based on what they saw in the Michigan game. But that's not true. We did not run the ball as efficiently as we needed to if we were going to have a good year.

I'm worried about our kicking game, especially the kickoff coverage. We still don't seem to grasp that the key is to keep the ball inside and in front of you. Our coaches really do a good job in the kicking game and they understand the importance of it. Why we don't execute better is a mystery that Ellery Queen couldn't solve. However, we'd better solve it soon or it will cost us a game.

It really cost us against Michigan, when they ran a kickoff back 59 yards and gained the momentum at that time. We'll assign each coach a position in the kicking game and we will just have to do a better job in this area.

I am also concerned about our punt return. We've had Ricky Watters, Rocket Ismail, and Pat Eilers, our three potent return men, catch twenty-five a day. But they still have a problem getting under the punt. The punt return is supposed to be an exciting play, but not because we might fumble it.

The other thing that keeps me awake is the play of our offensive guards and centers. Mike Heldt is going to be a good football player, but this must happen sooner than Mother Nature intended. We've had a problem at left guard since the first day of spring practice. It's been unsettled for a long time. A decision was made in our Sunday staff meeting to move Tim Ryan to left guard and start him against Michigan State.

That may solve the guard position, but where does it leave us at center, with Ryan switching positions? We must be more productive at guard. That's frustrating and upsetting to me, and I've let it show in a lot of areas on the practice field. I can hide my happiness as well as a child can hide a poor report card, but I can't hide frustration.

Our receivers are still not doing the things we need them to do, and that's got me frustrated, too. Now we've been told Tony Brooks may be out for the year. He hurt his knee reaching back for a ball in practice, and I'm afraid that favoring the foot is going to cause problems. His foot isn't creating any more problems than we anticipated, but favoring it may make him vulnerable to other injuries. If he's out, we have to move Ricky Watters back from flanker, which would minimize our big-play potential at that position.

I was satisfied with Brooks's effort against Michigan. It wasn't the typical Tony Brooks, but it was pretty doggone good. I think we could live with that the rest of the year, though we have to keep evaluating the situation. Is it getting worse, is he favoring it, is it getting sore? He hurt the knee opposite the foot injury, and that's not good. We may have to look closer at Rusty Setzer and Rodney Culver sooner than we think. We're going to start Steve Alaniz and Eilers at the receiver spots, and that type of speed won't win a track meet. But hopefully it will allow us to win a football game.

Kent Graham has had a good week of practice. His execution with the running game isn't real good, but he is throwing the ball well. Our first unit isn't cohesive, but it looks like superglue compared to our second unit. All these things make it much more difficult for Kent to look impressive.

The guy who really throws well is Peter Graham. His arm is not very strong, but he's done a nice job on the scout squad. There's nobody I respect more. He's more valuable to us as a scout-team quarterback than he would be as our second- or third-string quarterback. If Tony Rice went down, I would not dismiss the possibility that Peter Graham would be our starting quarterback. That sounds crazy, but he controls the huddle and the team better than anybody else.

You look at our situation and you say, "Well, let's go to the passing game." Number one, what kind of receivers do we have? People say, well, put this guy or that guy in and throw the ball. That's not the answer. I get frustrated in practice, but just dropping back and throwing the ball right now is not the answer. We do know we haven't been able to throw, and this must change.

I'm not concerned about building Tony Rice's confidence right now. Maybe it's the other way around. Wednesday, Tony threw the ball poorly once. I got upset and he got frustrated, which is rare for Tony. The next play he just threw the ball away, and that's the first time he's ever done that. I sent him down to the scout squad and he spent half of practice down there. I didn't know if I was even going to bring him back, and I don't think he did either. It is absurd to send your starting quarterback to the scout squad for most of practice the week you are playing Michigan State. However, the next day Tony performed well. I told him I was always open on the sideline, so when in doubt, throw it to me.

I decided after practice Tuesday that Tony's not going to complete more than one third of his passes, because we're going to go deep one heck of a lot. We have some speed in Rocket and Ricky, so we will get it out.

We'll go deep for several reasons. Number one, Tony throws the deep ball better. Number two, there's less chance of its being intercepted. Number three, if we do hit it, it will be worthwhile.

If he throws a 12-yard out, there are three possibilities—it's caught, it's in the stands, or it's intercepted. If we make people honor us deep, it's going to be different. So his percentage is not going to bother me—his productivity is. In addition, this should make our screens, draws, and delays more effective. I don't think anybody can stop our running game if we execute. However, executing it is another story. We don't run much true option. We pitched the ball one time against Michigan and didn't make any yardage because of a missed assignment.

We are not an option football team, but we run the option. There's a distinct difference. One of the reasons we can run the ball is that people have to play us a certain way because of the threat of the option. They know it's there. We get some good yardage from our fullbacks on the hard dives that are predetermined so we don't have a turnover.

Reggie Ho, senior placekicker
When the ball popped loose in practice, Coach Holtz would scurry after it and say, "See what an old man can do?"

We came out of our staff meeting Monday and went into practice with several things we thought could hurt them. A play that's a regular part of our offense, you better run a hundred times before you run it in a game. But new wrinkles are different. We put in a pass play we ran when I was a graduate assistant at Iowa back in 1960. We haven't run it since '63, but I brought it out and I think it'll be wide open. It's two tight ends form a wishbone formation, and we'll end up with Mark Green wide open down the middle. But will we call it? Will we throw it? Will we catch it? I don't know. We also put in a halfback pass from Steve Belles that we will use sometime this year.

We had the worst Wednesday practice we've had in a long time. We came out of there with more errors than I make on a golf course, and that is a lot.

Offensively, I'm very concerned. Michigan State always gives up less than a hundred yards rushing, and they did a good job against us last year. However, I think we have a great gameplan against them on both offense and defense. If we execute, I think we'll run the ball better against Michigan State than anybody has run it on them in a long, long time. If we don't execute, it'll be a long day and a longer bus ride home.

Joe Moore summed it up best talking to his players. He said, "I understand Michigan State really likes to beat Notre Dame. I understand, as a matter of fact, they downright have a crusade. The thing that concerns me, looking at the film from last year, is that our offensive line didn't give them any reason to believe that we like to beat them. They have outhit us the last couple of years. Let's show them we want to win, too."

We never have a fight on the field, because we're not going to allow it, but Wednesday one defensive player and another player from the scout squad got into a fight, then somebody else jumped in, and first thing you know, we've got a free-for-all. That's never happened before, and I hope it doesn't ever happen again.

I started at the end of the fight and worked my way to the beginning. One defensive player said to one of the scout-squaders that it was his fault. Then they both ended up apologizing. Maybe we were just getting a little edgy, a little tense.

Corny Southall, senior free safety

Practice was pretty intense the week before the Michigan State game. There was a little pushing and shoving going on between the players because we were so worked up.

One time Coach Holtz called Michael Stonebreaker and me over be-

117

cause we had a few choice words for each other—nothing bad, but everyone was just hyper. Coach Holtz asked what happened. Stoney and I had a little difference of opinion, and Coach Holtz played it cool. He turned to us and said, "Corny, are you mad at me?" And I looked at him and I was puzzled because he had nothing to do with the situation. I said, "No, sir." And he turned to Stoney and said, "Stoney, are you upset with me?" And Stoney said, "No, sir." Then he turned back to me and he said, "Corny , are you upset with Stoney?" And I said, "No, sir! Not at all, sir." And Stoney replied the same way, and Coach Holtz said, "Well I guess there's no problem then, is there, men?" We said, "No, sir, not at all."

And we shook hands and shook Coach Holtz's hand and joked around. Things were just really intense, and Coach Holtz had to break the ice somehow. Instead of coming down and chewing us out, he let us know that he understood that things were pretty intense and he just wanted us to relax.

Rusty Setzer gave us a great look in practice, impersonating Blake Ezor, Michigan State's tailback who leads the nation in rushing this week. We're going to have to contain their quarterback, Bobby McAllister. That's an absolute necessity. If we allow him to break containment, we've got huge problems. Ezor is a north-south runner and may actually present more of a problem than their star running back, Lorenzo White, did last year, because Lorenzo had a tendency to stutter and bounce and cut back.

I told the squad this week, we'd have to do a lot of the same things we did against Michigan. I fully expected us to show great improvement over our performance against Michigan.

In practice I talked to the defense separately about how well they played against Michigan, about how many comments I hear, about how many letters I get telling about how good they are and how well they pursue. It's fun to watch them play with togetherness. But I told them it's something that should be synonymous with Notre Dame. Efforts like that shouldn't stand out because they're the exceptions. We should play like that routinely.

I didn't vote Notre Dame in my top fifteen this week for the UPI poll. Anybody can do something one week when you have all fall to work on it. Let's see what happens this week. If we can win this week away from home, then I'll start to feel like maybe we're legitimate. We beat Michigan last year because they made mistakes. We beat Michigan this year despite the fact we made mistakes of our own. The most impressive thing that happened against Michigan was that we had the lead, then fell behind in the fourth quarter and came back to win. We did that not once, but twice. Not too long ago if Notre Dame fell behind, it was all over. But we came back twice in the fourth quarter of the opening ballgame; I thought that was encouraging. However that was at home. On the road it's different.

On Friday we almost decided to go up late to East Lansing. We had so many players with late classes that were important to their academic future, and that's why they're in college.

Two of the freshmen, Troy Ridgley and Mirko Jurkovic, had a history class. I asked them what history class it was, because I was a history major. I figured I could tutor them. Ridgley said, "Well, it's just history. We study about the past." I said, "Mirko, tell me what it is." He said, "Well, we read this book, then we talk about it." I told him, you both better play hard as freshmen, because you may not be here as sophomores.

So, with all the players with classes, we moved our meeting back and had lunch at Notre Dame before we left. We made good time and got to the Radisson in downtown Lansing ahead of schedule.

There were a couple of local television stations that wanted to do an interview, then I spent forty-five minutes with Gary Bender, Dick Vermeil, and Becky Dixon from ABC. They do their homework, and it's always interesting to see what they want to ask. They had many questions about individual players.

Ricky Watters's name always comes up, especially after he returned the punt for the touchdown against Michigan. Gary asked me what his most impressive characteristic was, and I said, "Ricky just thinks he's good." I didn't mean that in a derogatory manner. It's just that Ricky has all the confidence in the world. Everything he does leads you to believe he wants to say, "Coach, just give me the ball." I like that.

We're still going to start Pat Eilers at flanker, because I feel he played a better all-around game against Michigan than Ricky did. Pat is a tough young man who showed up in my office one day after transferring from Yale and said he wanted to play football. I didn't have any idea how good he was. But we played him in the secondary last year, worked him a little at tailback, and now he's a flanker. Gary asked me what Pat's strengths are, and I said, "He doesn't have any." I meant that as a compliment. He is talented, but he doesn't have tremendous physical skills. He sure impresses you with his blocking, his toughness, and his willingness to do whatever it takes to help the football team. I appreciate players like that. Pat came into the locker room after the Michigan game and said, "This is the most fun I've ever had." I thought that was great.

119

They asked about the difference between our fullbacks, Braxston Banks and Anthony Johnson. There aren't many. Banks's runs are a little more exciting, and Johnson's are kind of boring. But when you look at it, Anthony gets a few more yards out of his boring runs than Braxston does out of his exciting ones. But both are productive.

We're going to start Tim Ryan at guard. That's a position that's still unsettled. I hadn't intended to start Tim because we just moved him over from center on Monday. But he worked in rather quickly, so we decided to stay with him. I'm still concerned about center, though, because with Ryan going to guard, we've moved up a freshman, Gene McGuire, and he's just learning what that job is all about.

All the media want to know what's wrong with the Big Ten. Their teams haven't won many games yet, and everybody's jumping to conclusions about what's wrong with the league. I told Gary and Dick that someday I wanted to have a chance to go back to the Rose Bowl so I could offer my explanation on why the Big Ten hasn't won there. I believe it has something to do with the Big Ten going from grass to artificial turf. The Big Ten has become a league of artificial surfaces—everywhere but Purdue, I believe. Yet in the Pac-10, the Arizona schools, Stanford, USC, and UCLA all play on grass. I think there's something to it. It's one reason I'm concerned about Michigan State. We're used to playing on grass, and I think it is much more difficult to go from grass to turf than the other way around.

We had a good relaxation period Friday night with the players. We went longer than usual, but I think that's important when we go on the road. Some people may think it's strange, but I've been a real believer in doing this before games. Sometimes it's not easy in a hotel, but we find a large room where all the players can lay down and relax. We talk about thinking about positive things, about making the plays you're supposed to make the next day and visualizing it in your mind. We've even done it before scrimmages on Saturdays. I believe it helps us get ready. I don't take a poll and see how much the players like it, but I've never had one complain or say he didn't want to go through it. I have had some athletes tell me they do it before exams and that it has helped them.

I try to sleep well on Friday night before a game. That can be tough when you're in a strange hotel. This was the first time we'd stayed at the Radisson, because it's fairly new, but it was surprisingly quiet. Usually when we go on the road there are hundreds of fans milling around in the hotel. I saw Ned Bolcar's parents and Peter Graham's parents and a few others, but things were quieter than we're used to.

I left a wakeup call for seven o'clock to get up for seven-thirty mass, and I never got the call. I got to mass late, and that's never happened to me before. That's a real no-no with me because I'm always very punctual with the squad at all times.

Our police escort to the stadium was unbelievable. Their main job seemed to me to be to make sure that our buses didn't cut in front of anybody. Coming back, we finally excused the police escort. But some people who left after we did beat us back because they didn't have the disadvantage of an escort. This is the second trip to Michigan State for me, and my experiences have always been the same with the escort. We just followed the regular traffic like everybody else, only a little slower.

I think Michigan State has one of the worst visiting dressing rooms I've ever been in, and that includes some rather small schools we played against during my first few years in coaching. It's a depressing atmosphere, but there's nothing you can do about it so you make the best of it. We had seventy-seven players, and it was like we were all dressing on top of each other, but it always works out.

THE GAME

EAST LANSING—Michigan State was coming off a great season having won the Big Ten and the Rose Bowl in 1987. They returned many of their starters and may be the best defense in the country. Last year they led the nation in rushing defense, and George Perles's defense is very sound but unusual, and nobody has been able to solve it. Even though Michigan State had lost Lorenzo White, Blake Ezor is a fine tailback, as he proved in Michigan State's opening game by rushing for 196 yards against Rutgers. On the other hand, Notre Dame has not been able to run against Michigan State, and no one saw any reason for this trend to continue. Most of the Notre Dame coaches felt that if Notre Dame was to have a chance to win, Tony Rice would have to have a good day passing. This did not materialize, as Tony only completed 2 of 9 passes for a measly 53 yards. When Anthony Johnson and Braxston Banks went out of the game with injuries on the first five plays of the game, any reason for optimism on the Notre Dame sideline should have eaporated. Fortunately, Tony Brooks and Ryan Mihalko performed very well at fullback. Notre Dame's defense once again turned in a stellar performance limiting Michigan State to 89-yards rushing, including 66 on 22 carries by Ezor. This was the primary reason Notre Dame escaped with a 20–3 victory.

On the sixth play of the game Michigan State intercepted a Tony Rice pass and converted into a John Langeloh 39-yard field goal to make it 3–0. Only a holding penalty may have prevented Michigan State from scoring a touchdown. Once again Notre Dame could not move the ball against the outstanding Spartan defense and was forced to punt. Michigan State drove down the field once again, before the Irish defense stiffened, and John Langeloh missed a 29-yard field goal. The Irish got a big play from Mark Green as he took a swing pass from Rice and with good blocking from Heldt and Ryan, turned it into a 38-yard gain. Seven plays later, Reggie Ho tied the contest at 3–3 when he was successful on a 31-yard field goal.

The rest of the half was a defensive struggle, and the only score came when Raghib Ismail blocked a Josh Butland punt at the Spartan 7. Stymied at the 5, Ho made it 6–3 with a 22-yarder. Both teams threatened just before the half, but Kent Graham threw an interception deep in Spartan territory. The first half ended with Notre Dame gaining only 100 total yards.

Notre Dame came out after intermission a changed team. Brooks rumbled for 37 yards on the first Irish play from scrimmage, and Rice ended up cutting against the grain for eight yards and the touchdown that gave the visitors a 13–3 cushion. Michigan State got as far as the Irish 49, only to have a Wes Pritchett sack force a punt.

Notre Dame's offense took over and played very methodically by putting together an 84-yard drive that unfortunately produced no points. The Irish started with a crucial 23-yard carry by Green on third and 10 from their own 10. Rice had a 25-yard run on third and 3 and another 10-yard run on third and 3. All these successful third-down plays were nullified when Tim Grunhard's snap zipped through Peter Graham's fingers on an attempted field goal from the Spartan 6.

Notre Dame's next possession started on their own 38, and keeping it exclusively on the ground, they moved the ball down to the Michigan State 9, only to see Rice fumble the football away midway through the final period. With the Spartans now forced to throw, Stonebreaker celebrated his second-straight outstanding game by stepping in front of a would-be receiver and taking a McAllister pass 38 yards to the end zone for the clinching points and a 20–3 advantage. For the game Stonebreaker finished with 17 tackles, 2 interceptions, and 1 touchdown. Notre Dame played exceptionally well the second half despite the fact it did not complete a pass. In fairness to Tony, though, he only had two attempts. They ran the ball 35 times for 195 yards, but the real reason Notre Dame won was its defense played exceptionally well.

"Notre Dame is the best option team we've faced in six years," said Perles. "They ran it well, they pitched it well, and Rice knew when to keep it. They got a lead and played ball control. It's been quite some time since someone has gained that many yards on us. They did a great job of getting the ball outside. They didn't throw much, but we didn't force them to."

The Irish numbers were all the more amazing due to the injuries to Banks and Johnson and the crash course given to Brooks on playing fullback. He responded with 66 rushing yards on 11 carries.

Notre Dame boarded the buses for the three-hour ride home 2–0, but the question still lingers, how much longer can they win without throwing the ball?

Our gameplan was typical Notre Dame—run our fullback up inside, get Mark Green on the outside, and mix in the passing. We like to defer the toss of the coin. We always choose tails, and that's why we normally win on the road. The official will show you the coin. He'll always flip it heads up and it'll usually come down tails. We chose heads and we lost. I did not want the ball to start the game, but for the second straight week we lost the toss and the other team deferred and we had no choice but to take the football.

We got the ball and we were on our 20, and within the first five plays we lost both fullbacks. Braxston Banks went out on the third play when he tried to block somebody. He tore a ligament in his knee and he's out indefinitely, maybe four to eight weeks. These things always happen when we play on artificial turf. Last year we only played two games on AstroTurf during the regular season, but players got hurt each time. At Michigan we lost Braxston and Brandy Wells; at Pitt, Corny Southall and Terry Andrysiak. Now this. A couple of plays later Anthony Johnson resprained the ankle he'd already had problems with twice before this fall.

So now we throw Ryan Mihalko in at fullback, and he's never played in a game before at Notre Dame. He practiced at fullback as a freshman, but last spring we looked at him at guard, at linebacker, at defensive tackle. We ended up leaving him at fullback, and maybe it was a good thing. Tony Brooks isn't healthy and he hadn't played a down at fullback, but we still ended up going with him a lot in the second half. We didn't have many alternatives, because you just don't expect to lose your top two players at a position that quickly. Anthony Johnson came up to me at halftime and asked me if he could try the ankle in the second half. But I did not want to do anything that might jeopardize his ability to help us the rest of the season. This is the third time he's had the bad ankle, and we may have to give him a week off.

So, we lost both fullbacks and then Tony Rice got a little pressure and threw an interception at midfield on our very first series. He threw it into the coverage and he missed Ricky Watters, who was wide open underneath, even though his route wasn't as deep as it should have been.

Our defense came in and we really weren't into the tempo of the game. One of our goals was to contain Bobby McAllister, and we didn't do that early in the game. He ended up running for first downs three different times. We let him scramble around, but he is such a talented athlete, it is hard to keep him contained.

We were a little soft on defense inside. Michigan State was getting four or five yards a crack early. In addition we had poor field position and had to hang on early. With our fullbacks gone, we never could make more than three yards running up inside. That really narrowed what we could do in terms of offense.

Michigan State drove down the field and our defense forced them to kick a second field goal, which missed. This gave us a mental lift, and we came right back on first down with a little slip pass to Mark Green. He got great blocks from Steve Alaniz and Andy Heck and it went for 38 yards. We continued the drive deep into their territory before we faltered and kicked a field goal.

Our field position wasn't very good in the first half, partly because we had a couple of good punt returns brought back by penalties, both against freshmen. The most difficult things a freshman faces are, one, becoming a sophomore, and, two, coming to the bench after he is called for a penalty nullifying a big gain.

We thought a good punt return would help our punt-block possibilities, and that seemed to be the case. We put a punt block on in the second period and got a tremendous effort from Rocket Ismail, who blocked it. Michael Stonebreaker ended up having a great day, and he almost picked this one up and went in with it. But once again we couldn't take advantage of the field position, especially since we normally run the fullback so much when we're that close. We kicked a field goal and led 6–3 at the half. But I didn't feel comfortable, because we really hadn't done anything on offense in the first half. We'd actually been outplayed the first half, and all we wanted to do was get to the locker room without surrendering.

At halftime we talked about the things we had to do. We felt we would have to get the ball on the corner because we weren't controlling the inside. So when the defense held them right away thanks to George Williams, who got a sack, we went to work. We were going to try to run inside on the first play, but Tony Rice checked into a sweep and Tony Brooks made an excellent run for 38 yards from the fullback position. We'd talked to Tony Brooks at halftime about fullback and what he needed to look for in terms of blocking, and he just took it from there. It was impressive for him to make adjustments like that in the course of the game.

I thought Pat Eilers played a great football game for us, but Ricky Watters really came of age. I'm not talking about a game in which he had great stats or anything like that, but there were other things. He had one play where he didn't get any blocking at all and still made 12 yards on a pass. I paid special tribute to him in front of the football team because he played as a team man for the first time, and that is what football and life are all about. He was encouraging guys on the sidelines, and I was impressed with that.

But Pat did a great job blocking on the perimeter, and Tony Rice was excellent running the option. He ran it as well as you could. It's unusual because when you're going with the option, you should be able to get some yards inside, but we never could. Usually if you can't get anything inside, you're not going to get anything outside.

Our tackles played especially well, particularly Andy Heck. We had Michael Stonebreaker for seventeen tackles, plus we have something we figure out called factor points. He was a 2.8, which is the highest we've ever heard of. He played outstanding in the kicking game, and he almost blocked a punt when he came free. He ran an interception back for a touchdown for our final points in the 20–3 win.

We still aren't an excellent team, because we didn't take advantage of the opportunities our defense gave us. We missed a chance at a field goal because the snap went through the holder's hands. Little things like that should never happen in a game if they don't happen in practice. A game is no different except there are 76,000 people watching and screaming.

Against Michigan State our secondary still hadn't come of age, as Andre Rison caught one for thirty-eight yards as he was double-covered. We aren't breaking on the ball as well as we have in practice, but I think that will come.

This game illustrates that we have quite a few deficiencies. They have me concerned right now. But we do have a lot of good things—most importantly, finding a way to win. We controlled the ball, and I thought the third quarter was an awesome display of football.

Even with our fullbacks out and Brooks having to play a new spot, Mark Green had a sensational day with 125 yards. We ran for 245 yards, 195 in the second half. This is impressive against anyone. Against Michigan State, it's sensational.

We gave game balls to the three captains for doing a great job with leadership in our first road game and to Stonebreaker because he played great. And we gave one to Father Tom King in Zahm Hall.

I tried to watch a little of the Michigan–Miami game on a Watchman on the bus home, but we weren't getting good reception. So I popped in a tape of our game and watched most of that. We were home by six o'clock, which was nice because it gave everybody a few hours to themselves.

I couldn't sleep Saturday night. I went to bed about midnight, after watching the end of the Michigan game and seeing most of the Ohio State–Pitt game on ESPN. I woke up at three-thirty and piddled around, finally went to six o'clock mass. I was at the office by seven and watched film for two and a half hours.

We've got some personnel decisions to make at fullback. I think Tim Ryan has established himself at guard, even after one game. Our secondary has got to get better, and they will; Chuck Heater is doing a fine job coaching them. Corny Southall is playing well at free safety, but Pat Terrell is really improving. George Streeter is coming rapidly at strong safety and may be a dominant player.

The next five teams we play averaged forty points a game this weekend, so we'd better know that we are going to be challenged on defense.

I'm disappointed that we aren't making more progress at the receiver spots, although we're awfully inexperienced there. Some things you can correct in a practice, some in a week, some in a year. Our problems may be with us awhile.

I'm concerned because everybody on campus will start telling the players how good they are and they'll start talking about Miami. We're not a team that can afford that.

There'll probably be one change in the starting lineup for the Purdue game. Andre Jones will be replaced at end by Flash Gordon. Flash played very well against Michigan State. Todd Lyght played a great football game. He has the potential to be one of the best I've ever been around. When he is emotionally ready, like he was at Michigan State, he can be incredible. We'd like to see him be consistent.

I don't think Jim Sexton is punting the ball as well as he has in practice. The ball is bouncing a lot and giving him a good average (I think we've had forty-some yards in bounces), but that won't last. He has a strong leg, but he's got his toe pointed up when he kicks the ball and you can't punt like that. If he changes that, he will be productive.

Bill Bilinski, who covers us for the *South Bend Tribune*, always comes by on Thursday night and asks me how I feel. When he asked me about the Michigan State game, I said, "Off the record?" And he said, "Sure, off the record." I said, "We're going to win, but I don't know how." Fortunately, our players did.

I was hoping we might develop our passing game against Michigan

State. But that was being very optimistic, like doing a crossword puzzle with a pen. We're not a unit on offense yet, not at all. I've seen cops and robbers who have better rapport with each other than our offense does. We cannot run the option as much as we were forced to on Saturday. There's no way.

We've always been better running the football than passing it, but this is the first time I've seen the other team laugh out loud when we drop back to pass. We've told our team that defense and the kicking game and not making mistakes on offense can win for us. We can't say, "If we don't come out and complete some passes, we'll be in trouble."

I now worry about how we're going to react to the accolades that will be coming our way. I was pretty tough on our team in the meeting the day after the Michigan State game. Last year after our first two games we were ranked fourth in the country. The difference is, this is a much better fundamental football team—on offense, on defense, in the kicking game.

13

THE ULTIMATE JOB: HEAD FOOTBALL COACH AT NOTRE DAME

George Kelly, special assistant to the athletic director
I think Lou has been amazed at what the Notre Dame football coach means to people. He's still in awe of that because I don't think he really had that in mind when he came here. Year after year it becomes more challenging to cope with that aspect. You create your own monster, and that happens when you have success. The more success you have, the more is demanded of you. The more that's demanded of you, the more you wonder how in the world you're supposed to relax. He does enjoy golf and he thoroughly enjoys speaking, and he has to save some time for himself to do those things. I honestly think speaking is one of his forms of relaxation.

I don't think I can even begin to scratch the surface, in terms of making anyone appreciate what it's like to be head football coach at Notre Dame. I didn't go through an interview during that first year without people asking me what it's like. Even now, after three years at Notre Dame, it comes up. I guess everyone just wants to know what it's like to sit in my chair.

I didn't take anything for granted when I accepted this job. Ara Parseghian always emphasized how much he needed all the experience he'd gotten at Miami and Northwestern when he came to Notre Dame. I talked to him, Gerry Faust, Dan Devine, and I called Terry Brennan. I felt certain that each of them would have at least one thought that would help me do a better job.

Ara Parseghian, former Notre Dame head coach

Lou and I talked on a regular basis during the season, including just about every Friday. I was interested in learning more about the team. Having sat in that chair before and knowing the pressures that went with it, I think I understand the importance of having a sounding board. Even though the head coach at Notre Dame has many, many people around him, he's isolated, in a sense. He can't air his own personal concerns with the public, with the team, not even with his staff. He's kind of contained in a little box because everybody is leaning on him.

With me doing some television commentary, it was very helpful to me to know what was going on. But I think it also gave Lou an opportunity to talk to a former football coach who understood some of the problems. I certainly would have welcomed that opportunity as a coach, to be able on Friday or Saturday morning to talk to somebody that understood what I was doing. I didn't give him any advice—he didn't need any advice. It was just a matter of two coaches talking about his team, about what was going on in college athletics, about evaluating the opponent. It was a matter of expressing some feelings and sentiments that he couldn't express anywhere else, even with his own staff or team. Even when you're at the top, it's a bit lonely at times. I welcomed the opportunity to talk to him. And after a while, when you're on a winning streak, you don't want to change that habit. So that's the way it developed.

George Kelly

Lou really wants to know everything he can about Notre Dame. He reads a great deal, particularly biographical and historical material about people he admires. Maybe that comes a little bit from Woody Hayes's training. He's extremely interested in fighters. In fact, he referred many times this year to the current heavyweight champion, Mike Tyson—not necessarily who he is or what he does, but because of the way he approaches his work in a businesslike fashion.

His interest always has been about the Notre Dame community, the Notre Dame family, and the approach former coaches have had to the big games. When I bring players in to see him who have played here in the past, he's extremely interested in them as Notre Dame people and in knowing why they were successful. What made them win here? Was it something beyond the work ethic? Was it something he could employ in what he did from week to week?

It doesn't take long to find out how many people want a piece of your time. I'd been warned that you had to make sure you left time for football because this position could end up being a full-time public relations position. I remember a couple of things Gene Corrigan, then our athletic director, told me when I started. He said, "You have two things to worry about at Notre Dame. You have to coach the football team and you have to deal with the news media. That's all. Don't underestimate either of those assignments, but that's all you have to do. You don't have to raise money. You don't have to build up interest in the program. You don't have to sell tickets. All that is done for you here."

No matter where you go, in airports or restaurants or anywhere else, you have no privacy. We're on national television eight or nine times a year, and CBS, ESPN, and ABC carry the majority of our games. Plus there are countless interviews done with the coach of Notre Dame. Consequently, many people recognize you as you travel around the country. Thank goodness most of them are awfully nice, even if they aren't always Notre Dame fans.

One thing that is obvious to me is the tremendous respect people have for the University of Notre Dame. As I travel to Universal Notre Dame Nights, the yearly alumni gatherings in cities all over the country, it is comforting to witness the love, the warmth, and the feeling people have for Notre Dame. You develop a great feeling for Notre Dame in a short period.

My first year here, we had 1,804 freshmen, and 1,798 came back as sophomores. Three flunked out and three dropped out. We were the only school in America that lost more football games than students. It's my job to see that never happens again.

Chuck Heater, secondary coach

I've had the good fortune to have played at Michigan and coached at Ohio State—two schools with great tradition. You walk on this campus, though, and you just get entrenched in the tradition here. It may be the size of the campus. It may be the people who have been here. It's hard to articulate, but you know it exists even if it's hard to describe. You feel an obligation here to carry on what has happened before. You feel to properly represent this school, you should know the history. I read five or six books when I came here, just to learn the history and tradition of the school. I'm so impressed with the people I've met here, some of the great players from past years. The people who have been here have great respect for Notre Dame. It's a big thing, no matter what else they've accomplished.

Notre Dame has a beautiful campus, but more importantly, it's comprised of beautiful people. Their affection for each other, the commitment to excellence—that comes through whether you're talking to the security officer or the equipment people or anybody else. The faculty here and their dedication to excellence never ceases to amaze me.

John Palermo, defensive line coach

The biggest thing that hit me was the way the Notre Dame football team plays in its home stadium on Saturdays. That surprised me a little bit. You hear about that, how tough it's supposed to be to come here to play Notre Dame. But you don't believe it until you experience it for yourself. When I walked down that tunnel for the first time and the band was playing, the hair stands up on the back of your neck. The kids are wide-eyed and they're ready to go.

Soon we will have had three children graduate from the University of Notre Dame. It's an expensive school, but I can't think of anything more important than to give your children a good education. I consider it a privilege to be able to pay for my children's education here. A lot of people think my children receive free education at Notre Dame and that's why they went here. Not true. I paid full tuition, room, board, books, and everything else for my children, and consider it a small price for the great education an individual receives here.

My oldest son, Skip, started at Holy Cross Junior College across the street from Notre Dame, then transferred. My younger son, Kevin, started at Minnesota, but he made the tough decision to come to Notre Dame after I came here—and now my youngest, Liz, is a sophomore here.

The demands of the news media here are incredible, but that's just another thing that attests to the greatness of the University of Notre Dame. Sometimes I wish I could have more privacy than I do, but I think an inmate in prison would be glad to trade place with me. I can assure you I wouldn't with him.

Part of the answer is trying to be as organized as possible in dealing with the media. If I did an interview with every newspaper and radio station that wanted one during the football season, I'd never get anything else done.

To help that situation, we have regularly scheduled press conferences that are available to media around the country. During the season, we have an hour-long press conference every Tuesday. There is a nationwide teleconference hookup that enables media from anywhere in the country to call a number and hear everything that's being said, and be able to ask questions. This year, during the week of the USC game, one of our teleconferences had sixty phone lines in use. In addition to the audio hookup, the Tuesday conferences are available via satellite. That way, television stations around the country can receive an hour's worth of video each week of me, a different player each week, plus five minutes of highlights from the previous week's game.

The weekly press conference doesn't take care of all the requests for interviews, so normally I allocate an hour each day from twelve noon until one o'clock for the media. I don't normally go out for lunch, but the demands on my time would make that impossible anyway. I have a sandwich sent in and hope I can find time to eat it.

The Mutual Radio Network has been broadcasting Notre Dame games for years on radio—which I'm fairly certain means we have the largest radio network of any school in the country. I think there were something like 250 stations that carried our games in 1988. In addition, I do an hour-long call-in show with an 800 number each Tuesday night during the season with Larry Michael of Mutual. This is a fun thing to do when you win, but because we have only done it for one year, I don't know about after a loss.

The games that weren't televised by the major networks in 1988 we syndicated through WGN-TV in Chicago, which distributed them to cable systems all over the country. The old Sunday-morning replays put together by the C. D. Chesley company used to be the way that most of the country saw Notre Dame, with Lindsey Nelson doing the games for so many years.

Now every one of our games is televised live to something close to a national audience. For example, in 1988 Notre Dame had three games shown nationally on CBS, two on ABC, two on ESPN, and four on WGN. I also have a weekly television show that's done by Sports-Channel in Chicago. It's distributed to more than six million people via cable.

Even with all this exposure, we get an amazing amount of mail from people asking questions or just making comments. We make sure everyone who writes receives an answer. That alone is a full-time job. If anyone wants to know what this job is like, all they have to do is see the mail and phone calls we get in a week.

A great example is a series of letters I've received from an eleven-year-old girl from Spokane, Washington, named Allyson Treloar. She sent me several letters, as well as a worry rock that I'm supposed to hold and rub to relieve tension. I do keep it on my desk. She and her family came out for the Purdue game this year, and they stopped by the office and I had a chance to meet all of them.

I wish I had more time to visit with people like Allyson, but it simply isn't possible much of the year.

Jan Blazi, secretary to Lou Holtz

It's amazing the volume of mail that the office receives. I think that still amazes Coach Holtz, that so many people write. They ask for auto-graphs. They offer congratulations. They ask for letters to be written to people who are sick. They ask for coaching advice. They ask for secrets to his success in life. I can't tell you how many letters we got this year asking for a copy of his list of the 107 things he wanted to accomplish.

As Gene Corrigan suggested, it is important to find time somewhere in there for coaching.

I think it helps to appreciate the tradition at Notre Dame. I grew up with it in East Liverpool and attended St. Aloysius grade school. Let's not forget that during my formative years, 1946–50, Notre Dame didn't lose a football game.

I wasn't a good enough athlete to attend Notre Dame for football, and I certainly wasn't smart enough to get in academically. But isn't it ironic that I'm smart enough to coach at Notre Dame? I guess the standards for being a coach are lower than those to be a student. Notre Dame stood for something special, as far as the people I grew up with were concerned. All the way back to St. Aloysius, we marched in and out of class to the Notre Dame Victory March on the jukebox. It's hard to forget that.

There was nothing accidental about the clause I had put in my contract at Minnesota. I was perfectly happy there, but I wanted to make sure that if for any reason I had a chance to go to Notre Dame, that I wouldn't have to worry about a contractual problem. For years I thought Notre Dame considered only alumni for its head coaching job. Then, in 1964 when Ara Parseghian was hired, I realized that wasn't true. I didn't have any idea when I went to Minnesota in 1984 if the Notre Dame job would open up or if I would be considered. But if it did become available, I wanted to be able to be a candidate. So, when I signed my contract at Minnesota, it included a clause that said I could leave if we had accepted a bowl bid at Minnesota and the Notre Dame job were offered to me. Minnesota had lost ten straight games and the average score was 47–13, so the logic was that if we had accepted a bowl bid, that meant the program had achieved respectability and they could have someone else to take it to the next level.

Ara Parseghian

I know I was surprised at the magnitude of the job when I came to Notre Dame. That struck me the first year. Of course, we had one of those sensational first years in 1964, where things went well down to the last

133

minute and a half of the last game. You've heard me say it before. Coming from Northwestern and the Big Ten, I came to Notre Dame and felt, well, I've been through this. But, no, I hadn't been through it. The national interest astounded me. I'm sure Lou has experienced that, particularly with winning a national championship this year. All of a sudden you're in tremendous demand. I was awed and overwhelmed by it all. I couldn't believe it.

But, over a period of years, it also could take its toll. Lou will have to guard himself against that. You do pay a price for the traveling and the schedule that the job demands. I knew what was happening to me after eleven years. Lou really goes at a fast pace. I talk to him quite often, and he mentions that he's headed here or there—and I think, that's shades of me in my early years.

I remember running into Francis Wallace, a Notre Dame guy who used to pick the all-American team for Saturday Evening Post *magazine, back after the 1966 season when we'd won the national championship. I'd been at Notre Dame for three years. He said, "How are you getting along?" I said, "Fine, great." He said, "Is it getting to you yet?" I said, "What the heck are you talking about? This is terrific." But about the ninth or tenth year I was here at Notre Dame, I thought back to his statement. It just took longer to understand, I guess.*

Lou's on a roll and things are going good. And yet it only takes a loss or two to reverse the whole process. After you win it, there are even greater expectations. Lou said it well himself back before the Miami game, when he was using a little psychology in saying, "Winning streaks have to come to an end." Now it's true for Notre Dame, too. You find that over time you become a victim of your own success. But Lou is smart enough and analytical enough to handle and cope with whatever problems come up.

As I told our players back in August, whatever happens at Notre Dame is well-covered by the news media, even if it's not anything noteworthy. Here's a great example:

I drove my 1949 Chevrolet to the office one day the week of the Purdue game, and I think it shook up a few people. Before we were finished with our morning meetings, I already had received a memo from athletic director Dick Rosenthal, offering his support if we'd fallen on hard times. There was more to come.

My interest in that car dates back to my high school days in East Liverpool. Back in those days, life was simple. You had simple goals. I thought life was just about perfect if you had five dollars in your pocket, a girl, and a '49 Chevy. After I'd finished high school, I had to choose between college and the '49 Chevy. I decided to go to Kent State, but I regretted never getting the Chevy.

So, a long time ago, I put that '49 Chevy on my list of things I wanted to do in life. Now that I've got it, I'm going to have it refurbished so it'll look brand new—just like back when I was in high school.

Andy Heck has a car something like this, so he and I will have to compare notes.

The second day I drove the car to the office, ABC called and wanted to do a piece on it. I don't know how they found out about it or why they thought it was a big deal, but it's typical of life at Notre Dame. They sent out a cameraman and wanted me to drive into my parking spot, walk around the car, answer a few questions while sitting in the car, and then drive away in it. This isn't brain surgery, but it's interesting to see what the media thinks is newsworthy.

I've been telling people that my regular car dealer took my new car away because we weren't able to pass the ball. If it wasn't for our running game, I'd be riding a bike to work.

I guess it's fitting. If we can't pass on the field, why should I be able to pass anyone off the field?

14

PURDUE AND STANFORD: YES, VIRGINIA, THERE IS AN OFFENSE

I knew Purdue would play us hard—they always do. Their secondary may be the best we have seen. In two games their pass defense has permitted something like 9 completions in 33 attempts with 6 interceptions.

With stats like that, we ought to feel right at home, because we're not doing any better. I've never had a team that was this inept when it came to throwing the ball. I've seen it like this for a single game, but not two games in a row. I don't know how we beat Michigan State, because we weren't throwing it and couldn't run inside. Somehow we still moved the ball.

Last year we beat Purdue on the road but didn't play very well. We fought for our lives, and it's only because Terry Andrysiak hit Anthony Johnson on a couple of big passes and Tim Brown on one that we won the game.

I really don't know what to expect from our team against Purdue. I suspect we might have a letdown after the Michigan and Michigan State games, but I'm not sure.

We worked awfully hard on offense during the week. We had to get something going with our passing game because our defense simply isn't going to play as well every week as it did against Michigan and Michigan State. We said going into the season that we'd have to lean on the defense early, but I don't want to give them curvature of the spine. The other thing you have to guard against is the defense failing to consider the offense as a part of the team.

Pat Eilers, senior flanker

Rick [Watters] and I were going back and forth, playing at flanker.

The previous year I had been competing with George Streeter for a spot at safety, and we came back in the fall both listed number one on the depth chart. I started trying to force it, trying to do more than I was capable of doing, and I'd screw up. So I came back this year with the attitude that whatever happens I'll just learn from it. I'll just come back and do my best and not worry about the results.

I was put at tailback for a week. Coach Holtz had called me in when I was in summer school and said, "Pat, I'd like to switch you to tailback." And I said, "Whatever's best for the team, Coach, and if that's where the team can best utilize my abilities, then that's fine with me."

But I told him that I came here with the idea in mind that I would be a significant contributor to the football team. And I still had that in mind. And Coach kind of smiled and said, "We'll see."

Then a week or so later, after practice had started, he switched me back to receiver. There was one particular instance where I had started the Michigan State game and we were playing Purdue the next week—a team that plays a lot of man-to-man coverage. It was a Tuesday afternoon— and Rick is a better natural athlete than I am—and Coach Holtz said in the huddle, "Rick, I want you in there." And he turned to me and said, "Pat, we're going to have to start Rick this week. They play a lot of man to man, and we've got to have Rick in there."

I said, "Whatever's best for the team, Coach." That's what Notre Dame is all about. After practice he told me he appreciated that I was more concerned for the team than for myself. I'm not trying to give myself credit for that. I'm saying I maybe wouldn't have had that attitude if it weren't for Coach Holtz and how he always says that you've got to put the team before yourself.

It's amazing. We've won two games—and we were fortunate to win the first one—and already everybody wants to talk about the Miami game, which is three weeks away. We've got to keep things in perspective. People told me it would be like this, but I've never seen a place where people get so carried away by a couple of victories. I'm not talking about the people inside the team or the athletic department or the university— but the average fan.

You win a couple and they want to put you in the hall of fame. You lose two and they think you're deemphasizing football. All I can do is make sure our players understand where we are. We've won only two games, and that doesn't mean much because about four dozen other teams have done that, too.

THE GAME

SOUTH BEND—All week Lou Holtz lamented that Knute Rockne and Gus Dorais invented the forward pass while playing for Notre Dame, and now, seventy years later, we were in danger of making that phase of the game more extinct than a dinosaur.

How can the Irish possibly win another football game if they can't throw the football? Isn't that Notre Dame, ranked last among all Division I teams in passing after two weeks, with 21 attempts, 5 completions, and 3 interceptions? Why, it surely is.

And, golly, isn't this Purdue coming to Notre Dame Stadium this week? Isn't this the same Purdue team that is ranked number one in the country in pass defense at 59.0 yards per game? Why, it surely is.

Okay, sports fans, but let's not give up on Tony Rice yet. He may not earn a comparison to Dan Marino or John Elway before he's through, but maybe he's not such a bad passer after all.

What do you think, Lou Holtz?

"Tony threw the ball in the game today more like he does in practice. Don't get me wrong—he's not ready to play on Sunday. But this was the Tony Rice I'd seen in practice."

How about you, Fred Akers?

"We knew Notre Dame could throw. Tony didn't forget how to throw just because he came to South Bend."

If passing was supposed to be one of Notre Dame's Achilles' heels, then maybe the Irish are becoming an awfully good football team. The final score was 52–7, and Tony Rice was not able to throw as many passes as the Notre Dame plan had projected.

It was 35–0 by midway through the second period, and the Irish starters were finished for the day. Purdue played valiantly, and even though Notre Dame accumulated 35 points and 335 yards the first half, it was not as easy as it sounded because on three different possessions they were denied by the Boilermakers. Purdue was decimated by injuries and played many young players that will win a lot of games before they graduate.

What about it, Coach Akers?

"It was a devastating score. We got beat up pretty bad. It was their day. It was an incredible first half. They just dominated us."

For the record, Rice completed four of his six passes for 85 yards. Those aren't particularly gaudy numbers, but for Rice they'll do for a period and a half of work. He more than earned his stripes, running 38 yards for Notre Dame's first touchdown, lofting an eight-yarder to rookie tight end

Derek Brown for another, and connecting on a 54-yard bomb to freshman Raghib Ismail for a third. Not too far into the second period, Rice had directed the Irish to 206 yards of total offense.

With Notre Dame's halftime margin its largest in twenty years, the Irish threw only four times in the second half. All told, Notre Dame got eighty-three players into the football game. Purdue threw an interception on its third play from scrimmage, but it didn't hurt them, as a Mark Green touchdown run was called back by penalty. This necessitated a short field-goal attempt by Reggie Ho that was no good.

There is no denying it. Notre Dame played very well, and this fine performance was not confined to the starting team.

Rice certainly went a long way toward answering the questions about his passing ability, while also rushing for 67 yards.

Tony Brooks, filling in for injured Anthony Johnson and Braxston Banks, earned his only start of the season at fullback and responded by gaining 110 rushing yards on 11 carries (all in the first half), plus a 34-yard touchdown reception from Steve Belles.

The Irish had twelve different ball carriers, five different quarterbacks and seven different people scoring touchdowns. The defense substituted liberally and the leading tackler was Ned Bolcar with seven stops.

"We have to keep this game in perspective," said Holtz.

The game got out of hand very quickly. Shawn McCarthy's first play from scrimmage earned a flag for illegal procedure and his second play was a pass that went right into the hands of Notre Dame's George Streeter. Green's score on the second Irish play from the 22 was brought back by a flag, but the reprieve was brief.

Notre Dame's next possession turned into a pretty, 76-yard march, with Rice going half that distance for the six points. 7–0 Irish.

After a Purdue punt, the Irish went 72 yards, with Rice locating Brown for the points. Brooks sparked the drive with a 31-yard gain. 14–0 Irish.

After another punt, Rice threw a long pass on first down to Rocket Ismail for 54 yards and six points. 21–0 Irish.

After another punt, Kent Graham came in at quarterback but threw an interception after leading a drive deep into Boilermaker territory.

After another punt, Notre Dame drove 80 yards, getting 30 from Brooks on the first play, 21 from Rice, 11 more from Brooks, 13 from Ricky Watters, and seven yards and six points from Mark Green. 28–0 Irish.

On the next Purdue punt, Watters ran it back 66 yards to paydirt. 35–0 Irish.

The Irish turned the ball over on downs at the Purdue 35 the next time, but a Pat Terrell interception gave them the ball at the Boiler 36. This time, Belles took over the signalcalling duties and found Brooks on the 34-yard TD play on the third play of the drive. 42–0 Irish.

It was relentless. What happened in the second half mattered little. For the record, the Irish fumbled once, got a field goal from Bill Hackett from 44 yards, got a 36-yard Rodney Culver scoring run on the initial play of a drive. 52–0 Irish.

Purdue got its only points at the 3:20 mark after a 40-yard punt return had put the Boilers at the Irish 15. Earlier, the Notre Dame defense had stopped the visitors on four straight attempts from the Irish four.

"It was one of those days, when it feels like you run into a brick wall and everything goes wrong," said McCarthy.

The usual 59,075 in Notre Dame Stadium couldn't have agreed more.

Despite all my concerns, we played well against Purdue. We got a turnover right off the bat on an interception by George Streeter on the third play, but we had a touchdown called back on a penalty and ended up missing a field goal, which was discouraging. But from that point on, almost everything went our way. We had three possessions in the first half where we didn't put points on the board, but we were still up 42–0 at halftime.

I wanted us to throw the ball more. I wanted to get Tony Rice more work with the passing game. But this wasn't feasible, because the game got out of hand so quickly. We drive 80 yards to score one touchdown, and then Ricky Watters returns a punt for another one, and—boom—boom—all of a sudden it's 42–0. When the game is won, I believe you ought to play as many people as possible. We ended up winning 52–7 and we used just about everybody.

I thought Tony Rice did a nice job throwing for the time he was in there. He connected on a deep one to Rocket Ismail and it went for 54 yards and a touchdown. Derek Brown caught his first pass and that went for a touchdown also. Rodney Culver ran for the first touchdown of his career in the final quarter. Steve Belles threw his first touchdown pass, and Peter Graham completed his first pass ever, and did some other good things. Billy Hackett kicked his first field goal.

Tony Brooks ran for more than a hundred yards, and Streeter intercepted a couple of passes. Everyone had been talking about Purdue's secondary, but our pass defense intercepted five passes. Our defense played outstandingly again and set us up on offense with good field position.

This was the first chance we had this season to play a second-string quarterback, and we gave all three of them an opportunity. All of them did some nice things, but none moved the team consistently, and that is what we used to evaluate them.

We decided at halftime that we'd find out who was our number-two quarterback. This meant we would give all of them a chance. We gave Steve Belles first-shot because he was a senior. Belles comes out, gets us a first down, runs for about eight yards, fumbles the ball, and gets hurt. He banged up a knee and probably could have gone back in later, but that didn't make much sense with the score the way it was. We then gave Kent Graham the opportunity to play, and I thought he did a nice job of running the team.

The Monday after the Purdue game I had a long visit with Kent. We talked about interceptions, how many he's thrown since he's been here, and the large number of sacks that occur while he is the quarterback. The inconsistency of the offense isn't always his fault, but the fact remains that he has to be more productive.

Kent has a lot of talent, and I feel bad that he isn't more consistent. Sometimes a second-team quarterback feels he has to do something spectacular to be recognized. This may be the case with Kent. If he becomes our first-team quarterback, he may be fine. He can do that if he'll read coverage and exhibit leadership in the huddle. We're not looking for somebody to run the option. We're just looking for somebody to help us win.

Reggie Ho finally missed a field goal against Purdue, but thankfully, it didn't affect the game. Someone had given me a copy of *Sports Illustrated*, which included a story about Reggie. When *Sports Illustrated* told us before the Michigan State game that they were sending a writer and photographer to East Lansing for the game, I was surprised. I know the media always loves the new guy on the block, but Reggie had performed as we all expected. However, any time your offense can't score touchdowns, your field-goal kicker is going to get a lot of opportunities.

I like how positive the whole thing is. Here's an unassuming young man who came here to go to school and has done very well in that area. Now he has had some success in football, and that's not bad, either. I'm not sure you could find a negative angle to this story if you wanted to. He seems to be honestly embarrassed about the attention he has received.

Pete Graham, senior quarterback

I got the sense that Coach Holtz was much more confident about things after the Purdue game. We really hadn't done much offensively the first two games, but against Purdue we put 52 points on the board.

I happened to be in his office after the game. I just wanted to thank him because that game was the first time I'd attempted and completed a pass in my career. He said, "We're going to be a pretty good football team this year, but we're really going to be great next year."

We'd had so many questions on offense coming into the year. But, as he said later, the Purdue game was the first time we realized it wasn't illegal to score on offense. I think once we proved we could do some things offensively, he felt a lot better about our chances.

We went into the Stanford week, and we knew we would be challenged. They had an explosive offense that had good balance between the run and pass. They also appeared to have fine talent on defense. They played well against USC, so we know they are a good team. We wanted to keep their offense off the field, which could only be accomplished if we controlled the football.

We practiced long and hard and physical all week. The players didn't especially enjoy it on the practice field, but I felt we had to keep getting better, as we have a tough road ahead. Tim Ryan and Andy Heck and the offensive line are playing very well right now—and I say that despite having so many new people there and so much improving to do. Frank Stams, Jeff Alm, Boo Williams, and Chris Zorich are improving each day. They're really striving for perfection.

We weren't as sharp as usual. Stanford puts a lot of pressure on your defense, but I have to give our guys credit. Stanford never ran more than three plays on any of their first four possessions, and it was 21–0 before they got a first down on their own. We jumped all over them on offense.

Stanford has a great defensive player in Lester Archambeau, who is only a junior. He got hurt against Oregon the week before we played them. They had to carry him off the field and called it a minor knee sprain. I jokingly told our trainer and one of our doctors that I didn't think anybody ever got any minor injury—I thought it was always eight-weeks recovery. They didn't appreciate that, but my joking with them was my way of saying I think you are doing a great job. Archambeau is a great player, and he played great against us.

THE GAME

SOUTH BEND—Maybe, just maybe, Tony Rice can throw the football a little better than anyone anticipated.

Maybe, just maybe, this Notre Dame football team will turn out to be a little better than anyone anticipated.

And maybe, just maybe, it's going to be rather difficult to spot a legitimate weakness on Lou Holtz's third Fighting Irish unit.

It certainly was an impressive performance no matter where you were when you say Notre Dame beat Stanford 42–14. Stanford had their moments of glory, but the night belonged to Notre Dame.

"They took it to us on offense, defense, and the special teams. Notre Dame just dominated us in all three areas. They have an excellent football team," said Cardinal coach Jack Elway.

All indications were that this would be a very close game because Stanford was most impressive in their first three games.

Notre Dame got off to a fast start and generated two turnovers against Stanford out of their first four possessions. The Irish defense held them in check until Notre Dame had a 21–0 lead. The visitors' run-and-shoot offense had been a major concern coming into the game, but Stanford did not establish their offensive rhythm as quickly as they would have liked.

Notre Dame's exceptional balance resulted in no turnovers for the only time in 1988. The Irish utilized eleven ball carriers, seven different receivers, and had a different player gain 100 yards or more for the third straight week.

What Holtz enjoyed seeing most was Rice's improvement in throwing the football. He knows what to expect from his defense, and the running attack has proven to be far more consistent than the most optimistic Irish fan might have guessed. But with Rice constantly tagged as an option quarterback, even Notre Dame's head coach has questioned the team's ultimate capacity for success with the passing game.

Rice may just have changed his coach's thoughts on that subject. That process began a week ago, when he completed his last 4 passes against Purdue. Those, combined with 6 straight completions to start the Stanford game, enabled Rice to tie the Notre Dame record for consecutive completions. What would have been the record-setting eleventh-straight catch was a 65-yard bomb to Raghib Ismail that was caught barely out of bounds. Few Notre Dame fans would have believed Rice could tie a record also held by greats like Angelo Bertelli and Joe Montana after watching him throw the first two weeks of the season.

What was the difference? Rice said it was darts. Holtz had received a letter suggesting dart-throwing as a way to improve his quarterback's touch. Whether they really made a difference—or if it was strictly psychological—became a moot point. Suffice to say, Rice finished with 11 completions in 14 attempts for 129 yards and one touchdown. Those numbers are more than enough to make Notre Dame's multifaceted offense rather difficult to defend. In any event, Rice plans to continue the practice of throwing darts.

"I'm going to keep throwing them," he said. "Maybe Coach Holtz and I will have a contest at the end of the year."

Notre Dame's defensive method of dealing with the run-and-shoot was to put all the pressure possible on Stanford's quarterback. That message came across clearly on the second play of the game when Brian Johnson was forced to unload the ball early with Michael Stonebreaker breathing down his neck. The Irish did the same on the next Cardinal series, with Frank Stams and George Williams forcing incompletions on first and third down. The third time Stanford had the football, Johnson threw a pass which was intercepted by Flash Gordon on first down.

Rice scored from 30-yards out for six points on Notre Dame's initial offensive try. Reggie Ho missed a field goal after the Irish got to the Stanford 5, but after Gordon's pickoff the home team began on the Cardinal 30. From first and goal at the 6, Stanford put on a great goal-line stand and the Irish came away empty in four attempts—with the last three rushing attempts coming from the one.

But on first down, Johnson tried to produce some running room, was hit by Chris Zorich, and fumbled—and Ned Bolcar recovered at the one. This time Green went over for the touchdown on first down, and Rice ran it in for two points and a 14–0 lead.

"I'm not saying it was the turning point, because I thought we deserved to win this game," Holtz said. "But when they stopped us at the goal line, and then our team forced a fumble on the very next play, that was critical."

Notre Dame stopped Stanford once again. Bob Dahl sacked Johnson on first down, Stonebreaker forced another incompletion on second down, and a punt gave the Irish the ball at the Cardinal 46. It took only five plays before Tony Brooks navigated the final 5 yards for a 21–0 advantage.

Stanford fought back with a beautiful 68-yard, 14-play excursion that cut the margin to 21–7, but Notre Dame came right back with an 80-yard drive of its own, just before the half ended. Rice threw once to Ricky Watters for 21 yards and pitched to Green for 26 more before Anthony Johnson bulled for the final yard. By halftime, Notre Dame had 253 total yards and 13 first downs, compared to 111 and 7 for Stanford.

The second half turned out to be one of the more possession-oriented 30-minute periods of football imaginable. First, Notre Dame held it for 10 plays, going 73 yards for a 35–7 lead, when Rice found Derek Brown on a 3-yard scoring pass. Rice had earlier found Watters open for 16 yards and run for 18 himself.

Next, it was Stanford's turn to claim the ball for 13 plays and a 73-yard scoring drive of its own. Its touchdown came on a fourth-down, 27-yard pass play from Jason Palumbis to Henry Green.

Notre Dame responded with an 80-yard march of its own, this one covering 13 plays and ending with a 6-yard Rice keeper.

Stanford came back with a 15-play possession that began at its own 14, advanced as far as the Notre Dame 14—but failed to score when Palumbis's fourth-and-12 completion to Charlie Young accounted for only 8 yards.

Rice finished with 107 rushing yards and a pair of scores, and, combined with his passing, enjoyed his most productive all-around game since matriculating at Notre Dame.

"Don't take anything away from Stanford," said Rice. "They are a good football team, but sometimes you have games where everything goes your way. Tonight was our night."

For the first time in a long time, the Irish stood 4–0 at this point in the season.

"I may have poor eyesight, but anytime I look down the road, all I see are semis coming at us," Holtz said.

We played rather well. We got Tony Rice darts to throw after I got a letter from a fan suggesting that we do this. I figured it couldn't hurt and it might even help. He just kept getting better in practice. He hadn't been in there long enough or been able to throw it enough against Purdue to see his progress. But against Stanford he went 11 for 14, and all three incompletions came on consecutive plays on our possession in the last minute of the first half. In fact, one of the three was really a great throw to Rocket Ismail that was just out of bounds. We all felt better about our passing game, and our receivers played well with and without the ball.

The first two weeks we heard nothing but criticism about Tony and his throwing. Now, two weeks later, he ties a Notre Dame record with ten consecutive completions.

An important key was getting off to a good start, both for Tony and the team. Our defense forced Stanford to punt after the first three downs, and we drove right down the field. We never needed to convert on third down, and Tony took the ball down the sideline on an option play for the last 30 yards for the touchdown. Our defense held again on three plays, and we got the ball back at the Stanford 45. Tony made a nice throw to Steve Alaniz for 26 yards and we got to the 5. Reggie Ho missed a field goal from there, but Flash Gordon intercepted three plays later. We moved the ball down to the one, but we didn't execute our goal-line offense very well and were stopped on downs. We had three chances from the one and couldn't score, with Mark Green trying once and Tony twice. Fortunately, Chris Zorich forced a fumble on Stanford's first play from the one and Ned Bolcar recovered. Mark Green got it in the end zone this time to make it 14–0.

Again our defense held them, and we took over at the Stanford 46. We were helped by a roughing-the-passer penalty, and Tony Brooks made a couple of nice runs, including the last one from 5 yards to make it 21–0. At that point our defense couldn't have played much better and our offense had taken advantage of its opportunities. However, Stanford wouldn't wilt, and marched 68 yards to score on its next possession. Fortunately, Notre Dame answered the challenge with an 80-yard scoring drive of our own. We had some big plays on that drive—with Tony throwing to Ricky Watters for 21 and Mark Green running 26 yards once and 13 yards later. Anthony Johnson scored from the one and it was 28–7 with 1:13 left in the first half. At that point we had taken control of the game, and Tony Rice had yet to throw an incompletion.

We took the second-half kickoff and drove right down the field, 73 yards for a touchdown, and a 35–7 lead that took most of the mystery out of the game. It was a strange second half. We only had the ball three times, and Stanford only had it twice. But we ended up winning 42–14.

I had really been concerned defensively this week, and I talked to our coaches about it. We won convincingly, but we weren't breaking on the ball consistently. They only had the ball two times the second half, but both times they drove the length of the field on us. You either get better or worse. You don't stay the same. We have to make sure we're getting better.

But after we won the ballgame, it's the same old thing. Our fans have a tendency to take the elevator to the top and wait for Miami. Ara was quoted in the *Chicago Tribune* saying it was one of the most impressive all-around efforts he'd seen from a Notre Dame team in a long time. That's high praise, coming from him, because I have great respect for him, but we can't exchange that for points against Pittsburgh at the end of the week.

Ara Parseghian, former Notre Dame head coach

In the early part of the season I thought the team was very impressive. But it wasn't until Stanford that I could pinpoint a game where I saw a lot of impressive things. I was there at Notre Dame stadium; I saw the game in person because my family was in for a reunion. I saw tremendous balance in the team, and I made the comment, which may have been published, that Notre Dame had an excellent chance of having an outstanding year and should be in the hunt for the national championship. I didn't say Notre Dame would go undefeated. But when I watched that game, there were no apparent weaknesses. The defense was solid; the

146

offense was excellent; all phases of the kicking game—the coverages and the returns—were excellent. I know Lou had expressed some concern about the kicking and punting, but that night everything was clicking.

I saw all that against a Stanford team that wasn't that bad, and Notre Dame pretty much manhandled them. It was a balanced team and a solid team. I just felt it was going to take an awfully good football team to beat Notre Dame. That was the general consensus. That's when I first thought that this team had a heck of a chance to go all the way.

I still question how good we are on defense. We got by in this one because we didn't turn the ball over once. We forced each of our last two opponents to change quarterbacks. But our defense still has some question marks, and it's mainly our ability to make people pay a price for throwing.

Ara Parseghian

You have to have a lot of pieces fall into place to win a national championship. It wasn't until that Stanford game at midseason that I felt they had a crack at it. But that's with the full knowledge that the ball can take crazy bounces for you.

Michigan had a chance to kick the field goal at the end, but it was off instead of going through. The two-point play late in the Miami game— you have to have these things fall in place. Those are the kind of things you don't know—whether they'll fall for you or against you. So there was some uncertainty. But against Stanford I saw no apparent weakness. With most teams you can say, well, the defense isn't very good, the secondary's not good, we can run against them and so on.

But I looked at Notre Dame that night and I thought, if I'm another team playing Notre Dame, I better get my team awfully well prepared because they'll come at you from everywhere. They'll run a kickoff or punt return back on you. Or they'll score on a big play or shut you down completely with their defense. All those things were there. There were a lot of challenges ahead, but I thought at that point they were in the hunt.

15

STRATEGY AND PHILOSOPHY: WHAT'S IMPORTANT NOW

WHENEVER you set a goal, you must make sure it isn't a wish list. A wish list is something you want but don't know how to get. A dream is a goal you are acting upon. How do you know the difference? We have a professor here at Notre Dame who says, the word "win" stands for what's important now. We should ask ourselves that in every situation.

What's important now for me as head coach at the University of Notre Dame?

It's not important for me to worry about putting people in the seats or even to worry about money.

My mandate is to provide Notre Dame with the best football team possible within the rules and parameters set forth by the university and the NCAA. We desire to operate our program according to the spirit and the letter of the law. We certainly want to win, but it has been made abundantly clear that we will not compromise our integrity and values.

Tim Grunhard, junior offensive guard
Coach Holtz is not overbearing. He's big in the emotional and psychological impact, but he is definitely not overbearing physically. But by caring and his motivation, we respect him very much.

We certainly want to win every game we play. But winning the national championship is not the most important thing we seek. My obligation is to make playing football here the most worthwhile experience it possibly can be for the athletes. Part of that is dealing with adversity and understanding what happens when you lose and how to deal with it.

I think everyone should experience defeat at least once during their career. You learn a lot from it. We strive to make the football experience something they can apply to their professional careers and family life. We want the lessons here to be with them long after football is over.

Flash Gordon, senior defensive end

I think one of Coach's great assets is the way he motivates us. There are days when we are down and out, when you have four or five exams and you're just not ready to practice. The weather's cold—and you go out to practice and you're just not there. Your mind is somewhere else—you're thinking about home or a warmer place you could be.

Then Coach Holtz comes out and he's smiling. Every day he comes out with the same expression—he's smiling. And he says, "Oh, what a great day! Isn't this a great day?" No matter what. It could be sleeting, snowing, hailing. He comes out to practice and it's "What a great day!" And we go from there.

He cracks a few jokes and is pretty humorous. It loosens you up and motivates you to get going. He's a very positive person. I don't think he brought any of his personal life or any of his problems with the other side of his organization back to us. When he came to see us, it was always "How you doing? It's good to see you."

He really tried to make the team feel closer together. He wants that unity within the team. That's true with any organization—if you have unity within the team, then you'll be successful. That's what we were lacking before, and he's able to do those kind of things. He's able to come up with those things that promote unity.

I remember my first visit with him. I walked into a meeting room because they were reconstructing his office, and I sat down with him. He said, "Okay, Flash Gordon." The first thing he asked me was what did I believe was wrong with the team.

He was ready to correct the problems that were most obvious. He brought everyone into his office and asked each person what they believed was wrong with the team. He acquainted himself with each individual on the team, which is good. Automatically, everyone felt a little special, like he really cares.

When he asked me what was wrong with the team, I said, "Well, I think it's the unity within the team. We're not united. We don't stick close together." He said he had gotten that information from quite a few other athletes as well. As time went on he kept doing things to help us come that much closer. We had more meetings together, more activities together. We just did a lot of things together. I thought that was a good idea on his part, trying to get the unity squared away.

Pete Cordelli, receiver coach

When you lose an offensive line like we'd had in '87 with Tom Rehder, Byron Spruell, Chuck Lanza, Tom Freeman—you always wonder where your senior leadership is going to come from. But Andy Heck accepted the challenge. Mike Heldt really came on. Tim Grunhard accepted the challenge, and so did Dean Brown. They understood what had to get done as a unit. Being a unit comes in at the Miami game, when Tim Ryan and Tim Grunhard are hurt and you've got to call on Joe Allen and Mike Brennan. Mark Green just got better every year he was here. That's the type of character he's got. Rocket Ismail and Derek Brown come in as true freshmen and end up starting. Ricky Watters is like a freshman because he's playing a new position. The most underrated guy on our football team is Anthony Johnson. When they blow the whistle, all he does is play his guts out. So you had a lot of people coming together.

Wes Pritchett, senior linebacker

I think everybody really felt that the greatest thing Coach Holtz does is sell winning. He makes us believe in ourselves. Obviously he's a great coach and he understands the game of football unbelievably well and has great insights as far as strategies and things like that. But he also can make you believe in yourself and feel that you can go out against anybody and beat them. That rubs off.

Coach Holtz has a great sense of humor and the ability to keep things light and keep guys loose when it's a tight situation, like when you're getting ready for a Miami or USC game. He's serious, he expects a lot from us, and he works us hard and tries to prepare us as well as he can for a game. But at the same time he'll be able to throw in a one-liner and keep everybody loose. It helps keep things in perspective.

We operate the football program by basically the same principles by which Notre Dame operates the university. We stress discipline, hard work, a commitment to excellence, being the right type of person, caring about each other and about the university. It's really a simple philosophy.

Skip Holtz, graduate assistant coach at Florida State

One of the things I have always done, even when I was very young, is sit down with my dad and talk about goals. He would sit down with us and say that to be successful you have to have a goal and a plan to get there. You can't develop a plan if you don't know where you're trying to go. Then, I think it helps to be competitive and have an inner drive.

As a coach I think I'm very demanding. I see a lot of my dad in me because he is such a perfectionist. He always said if you let people get by

150

with doing less than their best, you're doing them a disservice. I don't want any of the guys I coach to say, "If Skip had only known how hard I was willing to work. But he just wouldn't push me." Dad was always a stickler for the little things, because he didn't want to look back and have an athlete say that about him.

It's interesting because we had a group of four great receivers at Florida State this year. I think all four of them could play in the NFL. But we get on them about little things just as much as we get on the walk-ons. I see a lot of my dad's coaching philosophy in me. They are things I've heard from him, things I've heard so many times, they've been tattooed in my head. So I have a lot of the same beliefs and ideas.

Some of the things Dad says just stick with you. One of my favorites is "If what you did yesterday seems important, then you haven't accomplished anything today." The other one is "What are you going to do now?" When I was younger he had me ask that question of myself twenty times a day. It's especially applicable after a season like this, where you win a national championship. Are you going to be content with your success and be content with just winning it once and get soft and lazy and sit back—or are you going to bust your butt to get after it and win it again? It comes back to accountability.

Beth Holtz, wife of the head coach

Ever since I've known him, since we were in high school, Lou has been a lot of fun to be around. A lot of that has to do with his sense of humor. He makes people feel good to be around him.

His sense of humor has rubbed off on everyone in the family. Once at Arkansas we lost a particularly disappointing game to Texas. Kevin came home after everyone else, and Lou said, "Do you want to go shoot a game of pool, Kev?" And Kevin said, "I don't know, Dad, do you think you can handle two major setbacks in one day?"

A big difference between Notre Dame and other universities is my role. At most places the football coach has his own little empire. It's his team, his athletic dorm, his training table. He's like a czar. At Notre Dame none of this belongs to me. I am not the owner of the organization. I don't own the team. I happen to be the department head of a publicly owned company. I just keep an eye on it for thousands of other people. I'm the caretaker.

Jan Blazi, secretary to Lou Holtz

He's very much in control at all times. He's very much a perfectionist. He demands the best of others because he demands the best from himself.

151

He doesn't ask any more of others than he does of himself. He's very organized, very meticulous. He doesn't appreciate excuses from people who work for him. If someone is given an assignment, he expects it to be done. He expects the ultimate from himself, and he doesn't look at anyone else any differently. He has great confidence in the ability of those he hires, and he expects those people to take care of their jobs. His attitude is "I hired you to do a job. There's no reason for you to bother me unless you can't handle it." He has a tremendous amount of trust in his staff to handle their assignments.

A lot of my personal philosophy has built up over time. I picked up a lot from Woody Hayes. I only spent one year at Ohio State with him, but we did win the national championship that year, 1968. I don't think you can coach for someone like that without picking up some of his qualities.

George Kelly, special assistant to the athletic director

Lou has a real strong belief in what he's doing, and he has a way of keeping everyone off balance. He keeps you in partial wonderment as to what he's doing, and he does this to draw the best out of you. He has been subject to environments early in his coaching career—certainly with Woody Hayes at Ohio State—that were extremely demanding. Once things reach a status quo, there's a tendency to relax and take things for granted. He never allows that to happen. If things are going extremely well, he has even more input and makes even more demands on those around him and of himself. He has an unbelievable knack of getting the best out of those who do surround him.

From the very beginning, in 1986, he was extremely demanding and wanted the squad to know just what sort of hard work would be required to succeed. He wanted the players to know that winning wasn't something he was going to do by coming in with the option or the wishbone. All the integral parts were there. But maybe the players didn't realize just how hard they would have to work to make it into that winner's circle.

Flash Gordon

Coming into this season, Coach Holtz was really conscious of fundamentals. He wanted us to be the best fundamental team in America. And considering we were young, he thought, well, we have a chance, but fundamentals are the only way we can get through this season.

He really stressed that through the whole year, and as you can see, it paid off. When the defensive team goes out, there's a crispness to it. And when the offense goes out, they're the same way. Everybody was low.

Everybody came off the ball with intensity. That's what his motto was. He wanted everybody fundamentally sound.

John Palermo, defensive line coach

Coach Holtz is pretty consistent. Whether you're a player or a coach, he's going to drum into your head that fundamentals are going to win football games. I think there came a point when he felt comfortable that we were a pretty decent fundamental football team. Him having confidence in us as coaches gave us more confidence to give to the players. He made the comment once, "I think you guys are going to be pretty good on defense." That made us feel good as coaches, and I think we relayed that to our players. Our players gained that confidence, too.

Ara Parseghian

I think the game has changed since I was coaching, in terms of handling the players. There are more great players today than there have ever been. Everybody has top talent, and that makes it very competitive. I still think the ability of a coaching staff to handle a group of football players in a reasonable way on and off the field is a big factor in your success. Maybe the techniques and strategies have changed some. When I was coaching, we had a constant concern over injuries hitting the team. How it could hurt you if you got hit in an area where you weren't that deep. That certainly worked out well for Notre Dame this year, other than going into the Miami game, when they lost both their guards. I think motivating a team, X's and O's and personnel alignment—those areas haven't changed that much in terms of being part of any success.

I don't believe you win with fancy X's and O's. I believe you win because you execute better than the other team, and that all goes back to fundamentals. If you're playing defense, I want you in the right stance, in football position, with your pads out, your shoulders square, your arms free. We are not great believers in running trick plays or using gimmicks to win football games. I've never liked what that tells your team, especially a young team like we have this year. It tells them they can't win straight up—that they have to do something tricky. That's why you won't see us run many fake punts or fake field goals or flea-flickers, and you especially won't see us do anything like that in the key games. Those are the games you win because you execute better than the other guy.

Playing football is a very unnatural sport. The fundamentals in football do not come naturally. Give a football to an Eskimo and the first thing he'll do is try to peel it and eat it. If he can't eat it, he'll either throw it or kick it away.

I have never had to run a football player off the field in my entire coaching career because he wanted to block and tackle more. I've never had anybody say, "Coach, let me block more," or, "Let me tackle more." But they'll stay out there and throw and catch until the cows come home.

Derek Brown, freshman tight end

Everybody has a day where no matter what they do, they're going to do it wrong. I had a bunch of those during two-a-days. But even that day when he said we hadn't run the play enough times and he was getting on me, he comes back into the locker room and pats you on the back, says good job and starts talking to the players. He does that to lift you up.

We have one of the biggest offensive playbooks at Notre Dame that I can imagine. We're obviously fortunate that our players at Notre Dame generally are intelligent and can handle a complex system.

But I'm not interested in having a team make three or four big complicated plays as much as I am in having a team execute the simple things time after time. If you do that, you will win football games. I couldn't care less if we're exciting. I love boring, seventeen-play drives where you convert time after time on third down. You find out if you're a good football team when it's third and 2. Everyone in the stadium knows you've got to run the ball for two yards for the first down. The other team knows that's what you're going to do. The good team is the one that can do that even when everyone knows it's coming. Maybe that's a little bit of the old Woody Hayes's three yards and a cloud of dust. Personally, I believe in seven yards and a cloud of dust. I like to win the hard way. We earn it.

Derek Brown

What I tell my friends, and they always ask, is that Coach Holtz is the biggest perfectionist I know. We work on little, little things. If you're three inches too long on your first step, he's going to get on your case about it.

I remember one time after I'd been here maybe two weeks. We were running pass routes and I thought I was doing it right. He goes, "Derek Brown! No, I'm sorry. It's my fault. We haven't run the play enough times. It's my fault. I'm sorry. We haven't run it enough times. We've only run it forty-two times!" That was funny. Everyone on the team cracked up.

He is definitely a perfectionist. He knows everyone's position like the back of his hand. I'm just amazed at all the stuff he knows. He's a genius on the football field, definitely.

I like the way he coaches, because he's not one of those coaches who stands up in the tower. He's down there with you.

I remember one time he got on Tony Rice's case about throwing the ball to the hole and not to the receiver. He made me go out there, and he goes, "Tony, where's the hole? Even I can do it." So he did it himself and threw it right to me.

Another time he made Rocket [Ismail] go deep on this one pass play, and Tony didn't quite throw it right or the line didn't block right or something. And he says, "Get back there, Rocket!" He must have run about five miles in one little section of turf, because every time he came back, it was "Run it again. Come back. Run it again. Come back."

I think our teams always have been able to run the ball well. You do have to be flexible. The year before I came to Notre Dame, the star of the team was Allen Pinkett, who had been Notre Dame's all-time leading ground gainer. My first year here we didn't have much in the way of a running attack, but we had Steve Beuerlein and Tim Brown and we ended up averaging more passing yards than any team in Notre Dame history. The next year, Beuerlein graduated. We had four fifth-year senior starters back on the offensive line and we basically tried to run the ball right at people.

The offense hasn't changed. It's just that you emphasize different things with different personnel. Obviously you have a different emphasis for a Beuerlein than you do for a Tony Rice. But it all comes out of the same book.

Offensively you've got to be able to do many different things. We've been characterized as an option team. I'm not interested in running the option full-time. But I do feel it's important to be able to run some option, to have the threat of the option there, especially with a quarterback like Rice. That really changes how a defense plays against you.

You've got to have a power running attack. You've got to run draws and delays. You've got to have a pocket passing attack. You've got to throw screens. You've got to be able to run some option and some misdirection. We try to do all those things out of the same basic formations, so a defense has to defend all of those at once. We see what a defense is going to do against us and then we make some decisions. For example, when we would split Tim Brown out wide with Tony Rice at quarterback, it forced a defense to make a decision. It would be very difficult to double-cover Brown and still be able to defend Rice on the option.

We want to force a defense to defend the entire field, because we think we'll find some openings somewhere in there. You set up a defense the same way, by keying on fundamentals. The personnel may change but the philosophy doesn't.

George Kelly

This turned out to be an interesting year. Lou had told me right after the '87 season that he wanted to get away from having such an active coaching role on the field. And yet that's so difficult when he works so closely with the quarterbacks and the offense. During the course of the first two years he had a tendency to gameplan more himself so he knew exactly what the quarterback could do. Now that the quarterback and the offense is in place, he relies more on input from others. He's still calling the plays, but he's interested in hearing series ideas and areas we ought to be attacking, as opposed to specific plays.

The amazing thing about Lou is his ability to go from area to area on the team and actively coach, based on his knowledge of the game. If he has one area where he wants it, he's more than capable of taking on another area and doing whatever needs to be done. He is not the kind of coach who is going to observe from afar in a tower. He's a hands-on coach, no matter where it is on the field he's working.

I've been fortunate to work with three outstanding coaches who are tremendous in their ability to call a game from the sideline and know exactly what needs to be done from play to play during the course of the game. I'm speaking of Bob Devaney at Nebraska, Ara Parseghian, and Lou. They have total command of both offense and defense, not just an expertise on one side of the ball.

When I first met Lou I got the sense that, like a lot of head coaches, he might have been a little more oriented toward the offense. I hadn't even realized that he had been the secondary coach of a national championship team at Ohio State. He does have great expertise in that area, and I think his abilities defensively are nearly what they are with the offense. In Ara's case, most people thought he was terribly ingenious in his ability to call and direct plays from the sideline offensively. But I always felt his greatest forte in coaching was defense. His initial approach on Sunday was to set up the defense before he would go to the offense. And I think we saw a little of that this year in terms of the way Lou and Barry Alvarez got our defense where he wanted it.

People think I've gotten the reputation of being a disciplinarian. I don't agree with that. Discipline is what you do for someone, not to someone. Then they have the option of getting better or bitter.

I'm extremely intense about how I approach things. That's the way I am. I don't believe in compromising anything. If it's worth doing, it's worth doing with a commitment to excellence and a hard-work ethic. I don't see any reason to just go through the motions.

George Kelly

Everybody has the opinion that Lou Holtz does Rocknelike scenes in the locker room before a game. He's like every great coach—he works. That worked for Rockne, but there's no way anyone is really going to emulate that. Lou's approach is all work. He gets his coaches together and he approaches the squad on a total thought more than a specific breakdown. He's not a screamer. He's very calm in his approach. At halftime and pregame the volume may increase a little bit just before he sends the team out. But it's not a perpetual tirade of emotion and hype. It's work. It's appealing to the players to do the things they worked so hard on all week long.

Ara Parseghian

One of Lou's greatest attributes is that he understands there's one constant in all of life, and certainly football—and that's change. He's certainly very knowledgeable about the game. If somebody else has a better idea, Lou has never hesitated to ask about it. I've seen him in an environment with other coaches, and if somebody makes a comment, his ears perk up. He probes into it right now to see if it might be of help to him in his preparation or the team's preparation. Some coaches with big egos wouldn't consider lowering themselves to borrow an idea from somewhere else or ask a question about how somebody else does something. I think that's one of the reasons Lou's so successful. Nothing escapes him. I've admired that quality in him.

When we talk, we don't talk X's and O's. In fact, out of our talks, there may not have been anything that was of any help to him. I'll say this, if something came up, he wasn't afraid to ask. That's a quality that most successful people embrace. I've seen him do it many, many times. He wants to know, and he doesn't hesitate. He tucks those things in the back of his head, and that's what has made him a great coach. Over a period of years, he has built a good backlog of coaching experiences.

Frank "Digger" Dawson, longtime friend of Lou Holtz from East Liverpool, Ohio

Lou Holtz is the same person I've known since back in the 1940s. When he slips into town, he's very low-key. He comes to see his mom and he likes to go over to the old pizza parlor.

I'm two years older than he is, but we met because my father was the parish funeral director and he was an altar boy. We became good friends because of football. Wade Watts became our football coach in 1949. I was the manager and Lou was the 98-pound guy who got killed on every play.

One time we had football practice down at Patterson Field, which went underwater when the river got too high. There was a huge pileup and we heard this voice say, "Help, help, I'm drowning." We unpiled about eight guys, and Lou was on the bottom. His face was totally plastered with mud. But he had such a desire to play. In the old team pictures, he's always sitting next to Wade Watts.

Lou was a great guy to go downtown with, which we all did in those days, and stand on the street corner and swap stories. We stood on the Dairyland corner, which is where the old Lincoln Highway came through East Liverpool. We would swap tales and stories and talk sports and play trivia before anybody knew what trivia was.

Lou wasn't a great student. But if the football coach said to run through a brick wall, you did it. There were never any questions or challenges to authority like that.

Our town clock was taken down a number of years ago, but the city fathers wanted to see it back up. So we organized, and he and I headed up a fund-raising drive for East Liverpool High School alumni. We've raised over $200,000, given out three $1000 scholarships, and we had four thousand alumni come back for a reunion. He was our featured speaker and one of our six outstanding graduates. He's been great about coming back, making speeches, and calling on people. He raised $3000 one afternoon just on the phone.

Some people have a magic about themselves. Ronald Reagan's got it, Bill Cosby's got it, and Lou's got it. If you could bottle it and sell it, you'd be the king.

My relationship with him is one of my treasured assets. My life would have been different had I not known him. What makes him different are his humility and his ability to listen and ask questions. He's always asking you questions. He's always trying to learn. He's got a tremendous open mind. He knows what he wants in life and knows what he has to do to achieve it. He's willing to work with all his heart and soul to reach his goals. My biggest concern is that he works too hard. He pushes himself awfully hard.

I've learned things from everybody along the way in my coaching career.

My high school coach, Wade Watts, ran a very tough program. He said we would be committed and we would be disciplined and we would become part of the team. He made it very difficult for people who were not totally committed. He wasn't going to let you find out how warm the water was.

Either you were going to dive in or not. But there was going to be a total commitment.

Paul Dietzel made a decision at South Carolina to bring in his own staff when he was hired. It was tough for me because I had been hired by Marvin Bass, but now Paul came in as the new head coach. My salary was going to be reduced from $11,000 to $7000 and my responsibilities were reduced from being defensive backfield coach to taking care of academics and running the scout squad, which is nothing more than what a graduate assistant does today. It also was tough because my wife was eight months pregnant with our third child. But you have to make those decisions as a head coach and do what's in the best interests of your program.

The thing I learned from Paul was great organization and the effect organization has on your players. All the t's were crossed, the i's were dotted, and every practice was planned all the way down the line. Everything that happened was so well-organized that the players knew a lot of thought went into it. Nothing happened by accident. He also was an excellent salesman. He could project optimism. He could take a catastrophe and make it look like a great thing and that we should be thankful it happened. I have never learned that talent. It's a quality that Jimmy Johnson, Miami's coach, possesses—no matter what happens, things are really good and no one has made a mistake. It's a great quality, and it's all about thinking positive.

Ara Parseghian

I got to know Lou best when I was at ABC and did several games when he was at Arkansas. I also did several games for CBS when he was at Minnesota. I had the opportunity to watch the guy operate. You go in a couple of days before the game. You get a chance to watch practice, to sit in his office and talk to him, to watch the gameplan being formulated—and you form opinions about coaches. I was very impressed with his organizational ability, his attention to detail, his recognition that it wasn't just X's and O's—that emotion and inspiration had a big part to play in a game. I remember one game vividly when Arkansas was a 13-point underdog and yet they just blew Texas away and it wasn't close. It was a tremendous job of preparation. He can take apart a defense, and once they get on the scoreboard and get that momentum going, they're very tough to stop.

Chuck Heater, secondary coach

In coaching, there's always another battle. I think we've all been around long enough to know we've got to go out there ready to play. The great thing about Lou is that he has a plan. If you follow the plan—the fundamentals and the other things he believes in—and you are good enough, you will win. So there's really no fear of losing. He's a very positive individual. He communicates that positiveness to the team. So it was a little different perspective on things than other places I've been. He has the relaxation session on Friday nights before the games, and all that plays into the idea of staying relaxed and just going out and doing what you're supposed to do. You've prepared Monday through Friday, and Saturday should just be a conditioned response.

Chris Zorich, sophomore defensive tackle

Coach Holtz is the kind of individual that, if you have a problem, you can go talk to him. My friends at other schools just get sent to their position coaches.

Woody Hayes really didn't care what other people thought. He cared about his players and he expected to win. He felt you were hired to win. You weren't hired to shake hands and be a nice guy. He was a fanatic about winning. But he also was a fanatic about seeing that the players derived the same benefit as the contribution they were making. There was a love-hate relationship with Woody and his players. But when they left, they loved him dearly. Anybody who coached for him felt the same way, including myself.

I learned at both William & Mary and North Carolina State that you don't worry about the other team. You don't worry about the schedule. You worry about your team. When I was at William & Mary, we played in the Southern Conference. But we also played West Virginia, Virginia Tech, North Carolina, Wake Forest, Miami of Florida, and Tulane. That was rather demanding. At North Carolina State, in addition to the Atlantic Coast Conference schools, we played East Carolina, South Carolina, and then we played a lot of games on the road against people like Georgia, Penn State, Nebraska, Florida, Syracuse, Arizona State, Indiana, Michigan State.

My first six years as a full-time coach we went to five postseason bowl games. Looking back on that, you can't worry about who you play. We set up our offense and defense to compete with the very best teams on our schedule. We didn't say, well, we can probably beat these teams, but we can't compete with these others. If you gear up to play the best and you recruit that way, you don't complain about your schedule or write it off and think you're in an unbelievable situation. Obviously, we couldn't be as good as some of those teams overall, but we weren't going to worry about that.

At Arkansas I learned what pressure is all about. That's one place where people expect to win—not just some of the time, but all of the time. At William & Mary and North Carolina State, we were always the underdog. At Arkansas that wasn't the case. We were usually the predominant favorite, and you learn to live with that. You also learn that you can't please everybody.

At Minnesota we didn't really do anything any differently than at William & Mary or North Carolina State or Arkansas. Nothing is as good or as bad as it seems. There were certain areas at Minnesota that looked absolutely horrendous. We had lost seventeen straight conference games. The average score from the preceding year was 47–13. That's not an exaggeration. We had only forty-two total athletes on scholarship when I got there. The facilities were poor. The attendance was down. But eighteen months later we were in a bowl game and had sold the stadium out on a season-ticket basis. We built a $5 million football facility.

There are positives to build upon anywhere if everybody pulls together. Sometimes it takes a catastrophe to get everybody together. That's the one thing about Minnesota—the people in that state, the administration, the coaches, they all pulled together. That was a unique experience, because so many times not everybody pulls for you and supports you and wants to see you be successful. That's why we have had some success here at Notre Dame—because Notre Dame is the epitome of everybody pulling together all the way along the line—all sports, all the people at the university, and all the students.

One area that has received a great deal of attention recently in college athletics is the use of steroids. At one time there was a general feeling among athletes and the general public that steroids did nothing but help you and that the negative effects were minimal. That has been proven to be a complete inaccuracy.

Here at Notre Dame we test for steroids and we will not tolerate them. I assume most schools feel the same way. If you're observant, you often can recognize an individual using steroids. You may see a sudden weight gain. When you see someone come out of nowhere to bench-press 550 pounds, you have to wonder. Steroids may make you a better athlete in some ways, but I think we've got to do everything we can to get rid of them. Some people are tempted to go to steroids to remain competitive. We've got to get rid of them to remove that lure.

When I came here, Notre Dame explained to me exactly what my mandate was. It was not to win a national championship, nor to change Notre Dame's priorities, either directly or indirectly, nor to have any input into admissions or academics. The administration, faculty, stu-

161

dents, and other people at Notre Dame are always saying to us, "Boy, we want to be good," or, "It was a great year." But in the same breath they say, "But the thing we're most pleased about is that it's an honest program. It's aboveboard. We do have student/athletes—and this school is not ever going to be a football factory."

When an athlete makes a bad decision, which is going to happen, it's amazing the letters you get from people saying that this is not the way Notre Dame should be. You get more letters when something like that happens than you do when you do not win, or letters of congratulations when you do win. The message that keeps coming back to you over and over here is that we want to win and that's great, but character and integrity are more important. This is not something that they just say. It's reinforced over and over and over again. If all the administration talks about is winning and losing, the coach reads the message that winning is the most important thing. Notre Dame will never get to that point.

As far as NCAA Proposition 48 is concerned, it comes back to the idea that abuse leads to restriction. That's true anywhere in life. Proposition 48 came into existence because everybody talked about accepting only academically qualified student/athletes. People who had a legitimate chance to graduate. People who had adequately prepared themselves to go to college. But the schools would not discipline themselves to do that.

I think it's a mistake to enroll an individual who doesn't have a chance to graduate. I've heard the argument that he'll be better off even if he doesn't graduate, just because he's been exposed to it. I don't believe that. He has seen a different lifestyle which he isn't going to be able to embrace. That's one of the biggest problems you have in professional athletics. You have the individuals who are no longer playing sports and now they have to go back into the mainstream of society, but they are not adequately prepared mentally to do that.

Because schools would not discipline themselves to take the proper student/athletes, Prop 48 was passed. Prop 48 says if an individual doesn't have a core curriculum of classes, a 2.0 average in those core courses, and a certain college-board score, then he is not going to be eligible to play as a freshman. (By the way, I am against college-board scores. I don't believe they are accurate criteria to determine who does well in college. I don't think there's any doubt that the college boards are somewhat biased in favor of certain social and economic groups.)

The intention of Prop 48 was to keep schools from recruiting these individuals. Some schools said, even if the athlete was going to miss a year, they would recruit him and play him for three. Some schools were recruiting 50, 60, and even 70 percent of their athletes who were Prop 48.

That was the abuse of Prop 48. Next, they passed Proposal 42, which said you cannot give these individuals a scholarship at all. Why did we need Proposal 42? Because people refused to acknowledge the fact that we should take qualified student/athletes. Schools recruited Prop 48 players and figured not many freshman football players were ready to play and most were redshirted anyway. The only difference was that they could play only three years instead of four.

I am not passing judgment on Proposal 48 or Proposal 42, but merely explaining why I feel they came about. We should see how many Proposal 48 athletes are graduating before we pass judgment.

Keeping everything in perspective anywhere, but especially at Notre Dame—where there are so many demands on you—is ultra-important.

Golf is the one thing, maybe the only thing, that gets me away from it all. I cannot go to the beach or a resort and sit around and relax. I can't get away from it that way because in ten minutes my mind is right back in the office. But in golf the intensity and concentration are such that your mind can't be anywhere else.

But during the football season you don't have golf. In fact, during about ten months out of the year, golf is not an option for me. Part of that is the weather.

I always eat dinner during the season once I get home at night. I'll get home at ten o'clock on Monday and Tuesday, maybe nine on Wednesday and Thursday. I'll always have plenty of things to do after I eat, but I'll go home and work instead of staying at the office. My wife will fix me something to eat when I get home and we'll sit and talk. It may only be twenty minutes, but we do get a chance to visit and talk. That's why I wait to go home and eat.

I try not to worry about winning the game. I always have a strong faith in God, and I try to find time to read every day. We had some big ballgames this year, and if you think about the magnitude of them, you're in trouble. If you think about all the things that could go wrong, you become a basket case. Then you become paralyzed and you don't get anything done.

If you keep asking yourself, "What's important now?" you force yourself to take action. What's important now? We have to win this game. Now the question is how we win it. You don't have time to sit around. I could not find five or ten minutes a day to sit and think about the magnitude of the game. Your whole attention is devoted to what you have to do with the squad. I don't spend thirty seconds thinking about what I'm going to say to the media during the season.

People ask me, "How much time do you sleep?" I don't know. I don't worry about the clock. Lots of nights I'll go to bed about two in the morning and I can't sleep, so I'll get up at four or five and go to the office. I have no trouble sleeping. If people have trouble sleeping, I ask them, "Why do you go to bed?" I go to bed when I'm tired. I don't say, "Well, it's eleven o'clock, time to go to bed." If I'm not tired, I don't go to bed. I don't need an awful lot of sleep.

George Kelly

I'm not sure how he really relaxes during the season. He enjoys late movies on television. I know he reads a lot. But, seemingly, when he comes in here at seven o'clock in the morning during the season, he has the whole doggone day planned for everyone. When we go into a meeting, he already has laid out the practice plan. He's already looked at the film and made nine million comments about it on what has to be corrected or done. I think maybe fifty percent of his work is done at night after he goes home. I don't think he sleeps a great deal during the season, and that becomes more evident in his physical appearance during the year. But I don't think he could live any other way. His motor is always in overdrive. He always goes beyond the speed limit.

16

PITTSBURGH:
SETTLING A SCORE

HERE it is, the first week of October. We're 4–0 and ranked fifth in both wire-service polls. I should feel good, yet I am tremendously concerned about Pittsburgh. The reasons are many and varied, but it's primarily because Pitt always plays super against us and we are in mid-semester depression.

I'm not as interested in how well a team plays as how well it's capable of playing. I know Pitt is capable of beating anyone in the country—just as they did last year against us. Everyone wants to talk about the Miami game already, but we have too much respect for Pitt to do that. Pittsburgh has as many great athletes as anyone, and I'm certain they will be one of the better teams we play this year. I know we'll have to make some big plays if we are to win.

Everywhere I go this week people look at me like I'm trying to pull off some big con job about Pitt. They have lost their last two games, to West Virginia and Boston College, but people don't realize we will be facing a different Pitt team. I'm scared to death. I'm not sure how good we are, but I know Pitt can be outstanding, as witnessed by the 42–10 thrashing they gave Ohio State. Meanwhile, back at the ranch, all our fans are gearing up for Miami. It would be nice if Pitt rolled over and died against us, just because they read their obituary in the newspaper, but they won't. They will probably have the biggest bonfire and pep rally they've ever had, but that is a tribute to Notre Dame's teams of the past.

When I think of this situation, I remember a long time ago when I was in Germany and we went to visit the Eagle's Nest, where Adolf Hitler hid during World War II. We started by taking a bus ride up to about 12,000 feet—it's one of the hairiest rides you've ever seen. There are six buses that make the trip together, so in case one bus's brakes fail, the other buses can stop it. It is incredible, because those 12,000 feet are straight up a mountain.

After you get that far, you get into the elevator that was made for Hitler and you go another 4000 feet straight up to his hideaway. It was nice, because we rode the bus and the elevator and I couldn't help but think of those poor guys who built the road out there, how difficult it must have been.

That's the way it is with this football team. All our supporters want to take the elevator. They're already at the top waiting for Notre Dame to show up. They don't understand that we're still down here building the road, climbing the ladder, scaling the mountain. It's a difficult climb, particularly when you have those people up on top this week saying, "Hey, y'all come up here. We're waiting for you."

Well, it isn't quite that easy for us. We've made some improvements, but I have a tendency to look at the negative things that keep us from becoming a good football team. I'm also well aware that every week is a different game in terms of emotions and gameplans and everything else that goes into it.

I don't mean to diminish the great effort put forth by our players in everything they've done, but we are not a great football team by any stretch of the imagination. We are a team that has to go out and work hard every single Saturday.

It's impossible to play great football every single week. I look at the top twenty teams to see who they played last week. There were seven teams in the top twenty last week that could win without having to play their best. We don't ever have that luxury with our schedule. Let's not whistle in the dark and pretend to be brave.

I do think we'll have the players' attention this week, for a couple of reasons. One, we can put on film and see how good Pitt is this year. Two, I think the chemistry with this group is a little bit different than on a lot of football teams we've been around. I think we'll have a good week of practice.

Someone asked at our press conference if I had seen any T-shirts about the Miami game. I have not seen one. None of our secretaries wear them. None of our coaches wear them. None of our players wear them, and my wife does not wear one. Those are the only people I see all day.

The only thing on our mind is Pittsburgh. With our schedule, we can't afford to focus on anything else. We put our attention on Pitt last year and they still whipped us in the rain like a yard dog.

I never get depressed during a game, but at halftime last year against

Pitt, I was as close as I have come. Still, even though we were down 27–0, we had a plan to come back. We didn't have a quarterback, since Terry Andrysiak had broken his collarbone. Somebody would have to pick up the slack. We told the offense it would have to score two touchdowns. The kicking game would have to set up a third, the defense would have to set up a score, and we would have to shut them out. If we did that, we could win. Our kicking game did set up one touchdown, our offense did score two, and should have scored three, but we got down to the 8 and didn't score any points. Our defense held them down to one field goal, which wasn't bad. But we had dug too deep a hole to get out of. Tony Rice was playing his first game, and I thought he played well considering the circumstances. But when I remember him last year and look at him this year, there is no comparison. He'll have a real test this week because Pitt has awfully impressive athletes in its secondary. I've never seen a team that plays the run as well as Pitt does yet still gets tremendous pressure on the passer. They blitz an awful lot, and yet they've only given up something like 2.3 yards per rush.

Troy Washington ties things up nicely at free safety. We know Louis Riddick is an excellent athlete, because he played fullback against us last year and ripped off several big runs. Their coaches feel Alonzo Hampton is the best defensive back they have. They play a lot of man coverage. They blitz you. They put tremendous pressure on you and force you to throw the ball before you have time.

They did give up 31 points to West Virginia. But they come on the type of plays we can't count on. West Virginia's first touchdown came when their quarterback scrambled, threw the ball in desperation as far as he could, and the receiver made a great play. That happened when it was about third and 30 in the third period, with the score 10–7. West Virginia later ran a draw play that went for 80 yards. The other two West Virginia scores occurred when their offensive got the ball in great field position and only had to drive 25 yards or so to score. West Virginia really didn't do a lot offensively against Pitt. However, they were definitely the better team on that day.

Pitt is one of the top ten teams in the country offensively. Their offensive line is huge, most of them have started for several years already, and they dominated us last year. Had it been a fight, the referee would have stopped it. Darnell Dickerson is a pure, raw talent at quarterback. He puts points on the board.

Derek Brown, who's only a freshman, will be in the starting lineup for the first time this week because of Frank Jacobs's arch injury from the Stanford game. He's the best player we have there. He's not quite ready, but we'll be all right as long as we know it and he doesn't. He will be the difference in a lot of games before he leaves here, hopefully in our favor. He is one of those individuals who came here with a great reputation, and yet I think we underestimated him.

Despite Derek's talents, we need to have a healthy Frank Jacobs to be good. We don't have a lot of injuries, but we joke with our players about calling each other Wally Pipp. Wally Pipp was the first baseman for the New York Yankees until he was injured and they put a guy named Lou Gehrig in his place. They never got Gehrig out of the lineup again. I think a lot of our players are starting to understand that it's not a wise move to get hurt.

We're always concerned about our offensive line, but even more so this week because of Pitt's talent and because we are so young. Andy Heck has done a fine job at tackle, but he's only playing his fifth college game there, and he's probably going to line up against Burt Grossman. Tim Ryan wasn't a guard until three weeks ago, and now he's up against Marc Spindler. Mike Heldt is just a sophomore, and Dean Brown hasn't been a tackle until this year. If your offensive line isn't effective, you are merely biding time until they pronounce you dead.

I do think we have improved offensively in the last few weeks, considering we had to completely rebuild the offense starting this fall. I didn't know we would progress as fast as we have. We've had some pleasant surprises on offense but no consistency.

Our defense is pretty good and our linebackers have been excellent. Frank Stams is becoming as good an end as I have seen. Our defensive line has exceeded my wildest expectations, and our secondary is coming. We have good chemistry, and we have made very few personnel changes.

We thought the one strength our football team would possess would be the running backs, but we haven't been able to keep this group healthy. Braxston Banks is out of action as a fullback for an indefinite period since his knee injury in the Michigan State game. Our starting fullback, Anthony Johnson, has missed a couple of games with his ankle. Those two would have been a great pair if they'd stayed healthy. Tony Brooks's performance, despite his foot problems, has generated great respect from our staff and team—even on one foot he has been great—but he is at less than full speed. Mark Green, our captain, has stayed healthy and productive. Despite all the injuries, Jim Strong has had our backs ready.

Overall we've played well enough to win four football games. I don't know if we are playing well enough to win five.

John Palermo, defensive line coach

Michigan had a reputation of being a great running team. Stanford had a reputation of being a great passing team. Being able to handle both of them defensively gave us a good gauge for our team. The second half of the season, I thought our secondary really picked up the pace. We were able to play some man coverage with them, and they were gaining confidence all the time. I thought that made a big difference in our defense.

Tony Rice didn't throw the ball real well this week in practice. I gave him something to read that Norman Vincent Peale wrote about a pitcher in baseball who overstrode because he got anxious. Dr. Peale could have been talking about Tony. It was a fine article, and Tony reacted very positively to it.

We did everything we could to focus our attention on Pitt during the week. During my weekly radio call-in show Tuesday night it seemed all the calls were about Miami. I never said a word about the Miami game to the team all week because, in all honesty, I never thought about it. If we weren't focused on Pittsburgh, the Miami game wasn't going to mean much. We all knew Pitt was going to be difficult for us, despite what happened to them the first part of the season. We were concerned that we could play very well and it still might not be good enough.

Pitt has a history of playing well as a team against Notre Dame. I think remembering last year will help our players. We haven't beaten Pittsburgh since 1982. We weren't able to do it the last two years, when Foge Fazio, who used to be head coach at Pitt, was here and it obviously was an emotional thing for him. Enough said.

Tom Gorman, defensive tackle/offensive guard
We had a pregame meeting and then a defensive-line meeting before the Pitt game. Coach Palermo and Coach Holtz told us they were convinced that if we got by that game, we wouldn't lose at all. They told us that would be the toughest game of the year and it wouldn't be smooth sailing, but that we would get by.

THE GAME

PITTSBURGH—The sigh of relief heaved by Notre Dame football coach Lou Holtz Saturday in the Pitt Stadium could be heard as far away as the Grotto on the campus of the Fighting Irish.

It came about precisely at the same time Mark Green crossed the goal line with 4:32 left in the game, to crown a clinching 14-play drive that consumed nearly seven minutes and provided the final margin in the 30–20 Irish triumph over Pittsburgh.

In reality, there's no relief in sight for Holtz and his Irish. The next item on their menu is top-ranked and unbeaten Miami.

But, at least Green's up-the-middle dash guaranteed the Irish a perfect

5–0 record of their own heading into the Hurricane matchup. It came on an afternoon in which Notre Dame's ground attack proved to the biggest skeptic that it is for real. And it capped off an afternoon in which the Irish won a football game under some rather bizarre circumstances:

Who would have imagined that one of the Irish heroes would be junior fullback Braxston Banks, who wasn't added to the travel list until the last minute and whose appearance in the home game came as a surprise to Mike Gottfried and Pitt?

Banks had been inactive since a knee ligament injury three weeks ago at Michigan State. In fact, he wasn't even listed on the flipcard roster distributed in the press box. But, with Anthony Johnson still hobbled slightly by an ankle injury from that same game, Banks played a critical role in a noteworthy third-period drive that put Notre Dame ahead for good at 23–17.

On second and 11 from the Pitt 43, quarterback Tony Rice looped a swing pass over the linebackers and Banks took it 30 yards down the Notre Dame sideline. Banks ended up touching the football each of the last four plays on the drive—catching another pass for six yards and carrying three times, the last for one yard and the score. Not bad for a guy most had expected to see in the training room, not the interview room.

"It's nice to be back," said Banks, with a knowing grin.

Who would have imagined that Notre Dame's rushing attack would continue to improve in spite of a makeshift offensive line? The Irish lost both guards during the game—Tim Ryan leaving with a shoulder sprain and Tim Grunhard with an ankle injury.

Notre Dame stayed in the game with its running game all day long, totaling 310 yards and all four Irish touchdowns. Sophomore tailback Tony Brooks fought and clawed for 105 yards, including 52 alone on one first-period rumble. Senior tailback Mark Green added 83 difficult yards to go with 69 yards from Rice. Green, Rice, Johnson, and Banks all scored touchdowns. Seventeen of Notre Dame's 27 first downs came via running plays, but the entire Notre Dame team will attest to the fact that very few came easy.

"These backs are a pleasure to block for," said tackle Dean Brown. "You give them a little room and they do the rest."

Who would have imagined that Notre Dame could beat a good team on the road despite playing probably its worst defensive half of the season? However, let's give Pitt credit for an excellent gameplan.

Pitt quarterback Darnell Dickerson threw often and well early in the game as he completed a pair of first-half scoring bombs. Amazing as it sounds, those 42- and 33-yard big plays ended up as the Panthers' only touchdowns. The Irish shored their pass defense up after intermission to limit Dickerson to only 3 completions for 29 yards.

"We found out how we could react to adversity," said linebacker Wes Pritchett.

Pitt jumped out to a 7–0 lead only to see the Irish come back and take command at 14–7. Pitt rebounded to knot the score at 14–14 and, after Notre Dame assumed a 17–14 advantage, tied it once again 17–17. But Pitt lost because of three of the most frustrating plays Mike Gottfried could recall.

First, the Panthers lost a golden opportunity on their initial possession. Pitt started on its own 39 and Dickerson quickly completed passes for 13, 22, and 12 yards. Faced with second down from the Notre Dame 13, they elected to give the ball to Curvin Richards, who broke into the secondary, but a fierce hit by Todd Lyght forced a fumble which Chris Zorich recovered. That was one lost chance.

Second, the Panthers appeared on the verge of taking the lead again just prior to halftime. With Notre Dame on top 17–14, Pitt had marched all the way to the Irish 9 with just over a minute left in the half. This time Dickerson scrambled up the middle, only to have the football come dribbling off his fingertips just as he reached the goal line unmolested. In fact, Dickerson had two more legitimate chances to recover the ball in the end zone, only to see it squirt loose into the hands of Stan Smagala.

"When I fell on it the first time, I thought I had it," said Dickerson. "When it slipped through I couldn't believe it."

Third, the Panthers ultimately stabbed themselves in the back with a costly 12-men-on-the-field penalty midway through Notre Dame's last scoring drive. With the Irish clinging to a 23–20 lead, Pitt apparently had forced Jim Sexton to punt from his own 32 halfway through the fourth period. The momentum definitely seemed to be swinging in Pitt's favor.

However, when the officials discovered the home team had one-too-many men on the field during the punt, Notre Dame retained the football and made the most of the error. Running the ball on 11 consecutive plays, the Irish marched from their own 47 for the clinching touchdown, which was scored by Mark Green. The Irish also ran the clock down to the four-minute mark, which made it virtually impossible for Pitt to mount a legitimate comeback.

Indeed, the luck of the Irish seemed to follow Notre Dame to Pittsburgh. "We could have won the game," said Gottfried, "but we made just enough mistakes to lose. Notre Dame hadn't beaten Pittsburgh since 1982, and the '87 defeat marked Notre Dame's sole blemish the first nine weeks of the season. It came on a rainy night in Pittsburgh when Terry Andrysiak broke his collarbone and Rice made his quarterback debut.

The win also came in a challenging emotional setting in which most Irish fans preferred to look ahead to the long-awaited Miami confrontation as opposed to worrying about a Pitt team coming off consecutive losses to West Virginia and Boston College.

Pitt started the game as impressively as any Notre Dame has seen. Dickerson's aerial thrusts kept the Irish secondary off balance on the first drive, but it ended abruptly when Lyght made a great play on Richards and caused a fumble. On Notre Dame's possession, Rice underthrew a pass intended for Steve Alaniz which was intercepted—and just four plays later, Dickerson hit a 42-yard bomb to Reggie Williams for six points.

Notre Dame wasted little time answering the challenge. It took the Irish only four plays to knot the score at seven, with Brooks's 52-yard run setting up a 2-yard scoring run by Rice.

The Irish, who held the ball offensively for 39:49 compared to 20:11 for Pitt, promptly provided a clear indication of their plans to attempt to play ball-control football. Their following possession lasted almost five minutes, covered 86 yards, and featured 11 running plays. Johnson accounted for the 14–7 advantage by scoring on fourth down and one.

This game would find the momentum swinging back and forth many times before Notre Dame would ultimately claim the victory. With Notre Dame leading 14–7 in the second quarter, Dickerson again found a seam in the secondary—this time locating Henry Tuten from 33 yards out to make it 14–14.

Notre Dame carefully moved into range for a 37-yard Reggie Ho field goal, which was good for a 17–14 lead. This field goal was set up when, on first down, Rice threw to Johnson for 13 yards. Only Dickerson's bizarre and unbelievable fumble on his way to a certain touchdown kept the Irish on top 17–14 at the half.

Notre Dame missed an opportunity to extend their lead when a 48-yard drive to start the second half ended on the Pitt 26 with a Ricky Watters fumble. Pitt took advantage of this opportunity by driving for a field goal to tie the game at 17–17. It was then that Banks came off the Notre Dame bench to ignite a critical 80-yard touchdown drive. Pitt rallied once again with a drive of their own before Dickerson was stopped at the Irish 16. Scott Kaplan then trotted onto the field and calmly kicked a field goal that made the scoreboard read 23–20.

After the ensuing kickoff, Pitt committed its twelfth-man blunder at the most inopportune time possible, and Notre Dame went in for the points it needed to clinch its fifth victory. Rookie Arnold Ale staved off any thought of a Pitt rally with an interception of a Dickerson pass with three minutes left in the game, and for the first time in the game, the

Notre Dame band could play the Notre Dame Victory March with confidence.

"That's a mistake. That just shouldn't happen," said Gottfried of the penalty.

The sigh of relief turned into smiles of belief in the Irish locker room as the Notre Dame victory party was tempered by the thoughts of Miami's visit to Notre Dame Stadium a week away.

To date, the Irish had met every challenge—and that was all Lou Holtz could ask.

We won a wild game by a score of 30–20. Like all victories, you have a sense of relief that you won but you also get a distinct impression this may be your last one.

I only slept a couple of hours after the Pittsburgh game because I got home early in the morning after visiting my mother. I stayed up until four watching the video of the game and then got up at six to go to mass and the office. Sleep doesn't seem important now, when we're playing the number-one team next. After watching the film I don't think our defense played particularly well, although we did play better the second half. We all know the importance of not giving up the big play—and yet that really hurt us against Pitt. You sure don't want to go into a big game like Miami when you're not playing your best on defense. Unlike Winston Churchill, I could not say the Pitt game was our finest hour, but we did win.

The most impressive thing we did in the Pitt game was compete. If our team were to have a physical I think ninety percent of our body would be heart. The players answered every challenge. We'd beaten Purdue and Stanford fairly convincingly. But you never know what's going to happen when you're fighting for your life on the road. This was the treadmill test our team had to pass, our offense in particular. They won our admiration. I have to give our offensive line a lot of credit because we really played well up front against a fine defense.

Tony Rice kept his poise, really threw a nice soft ball, gave us great leadership, and refused to lose.

Tony did a nice job of dropping the ball over the defender on one key pass to Braxston Banks late in the game. It was the kind of play he wouldn't have made a few weeks ago. I don't know if the darts have made a difference, but Tony definitely has improved.

I know Pittsburgh had some injuries on its defensive line, but I still didn't think we could be very effective against them offensively. If I had known before the game that we would need 21 points to win, I would have been a basket case.

Tim Grunhard and Tim Ryan got injured during the game. We flew back from Pitt knowing that both of them would have to be X-rayed when we got to South Bend, that it might have been bad news all the way around, and we were somewhat relieved at the results. Still, those injuries are going to be a problem this week because we have to go into the Miami game without the two of them. That means we'll probably have to make some changes on the offensive line. We probably will move Joe Allen from tackle to guard in place of Grunhard, who's got an ankle-ligament injury. Ryan sprained a shoulder and probably won't play against Miami, either.

I didn't fly home with our team—which I had never done before—but my mother lives about thirty-five miles south of Pittsburgh and I felt it was important to stop and see her. So I flew to East Liverpool and spent a couple of hours with her. My mother, seventy-two now, had a stroke at age sixty-two, and she can't speak and is paralyzed on the right side. The Pitt game had been on ESPN, and they did a live interview with me after the game from the locker room, which she had seen. When I got to the nursing home, she gave me a big hug and wouldn't let go, and she cried. Life gets so crazy during the season, but I was sure glad I stopped, because I don't know when I'll get back again. I told the players next day to remember how important their families should be to them, because it's something all of us take for granted so often, and we shouldn't.

Ten years ago we'd arranged to pick up a new car for my mom at four o'clock one particular day. At one o'clock she had the stroke. I still remember when we played Oklahoma in the Orange Bowl in '77 and beat them 31–6. She came to Miami but wouldn't go to the game and wouldn't even watch it on television. We came back to the hotel and the first thing she wanted to know was "Who won?"

Our football team is tired. They've been involved in midterms for a week and they've got another week of them before we play Miami. I don't know how much concentration we'll have on the practice field next week, but it's been a good group so far, and they've done everything we've asked of them. Our defense hasn't gotten better the last two weeks, but we will get that rectified. Our problems on defense are my fault, and not those of the assistant coaches or the players. I need to look closely at our practice schedule and maybe change our routine a little.

The last two weeks our offense has been productive. That's the way it has been the last two years, and I hope it can continue. However, you can't expect your offense to carry you against good teams. Our offense is gaining confidence each week, and more importantly, they have gained the respect of our defense. But regardless of how much improvement our offense has made, we all realize we aren't going to outscore great teams. Our defense must play well, and they have a better chance to do this if our kicking game is outstanding and our offense controls the football without turnovers.

I am impressed with the offensive line so far. Our assistant coaches, Joe Moore and Tony Yelovich, have done a great job with them, especially considering the injuries we have right now. Andy Heck has become a great tackle, but that doesn't surprise me at all. He's as dedicated as anyone we've ever had, and if you had to pick someone who could change positions as a senior and still be a great player, it's him. Dean Brown has been the most pleasant surprise on the team. Take good athletes who want to get better, and it's usually a matter of time until excellence becomes synonymous with their performance, assuming the assistant coaches provide the leadership.

Somebody suggested that maturity was the reason we won at Pitt this time and not last year. However, we are much younger and less experienced than we were a year ago, so it can't be that. Naturally, Tony Rice is more mature, and that makes a big difference, but on the other hand Arnold Ale clinches the game for us with an interception, and he's a freshman.

No, I don't think it's maturity. I think it's attitude and confidence. It's confidence that comes from practice. We talk about never flinching and about answering the challenge. Pitt scores early and we come back to tie it at 7. It's now a fifty-three-minute game. They get the field goal to tie it at 17 with three minutes left in the third quarter, and it instantly became an eighteen-minute game.

After the Pitt field goal the sold-out stadium is really loud. When you are on the road, this is an intimidating situation. As we lined up to receive the kickoff, Tony Rice comes up to me and says, "This is a great game, isn't it, Coach?" I said, "It's not one of my favorite ways to relax." He was just having a great time because he loves to compete. He doesn't care if the score's close, he just wants to go out there and play.

Our defense was a little discombobulated in the first half. Only a great hit by Todd Lyght kept them from scoring when they drove right down the field on their first possession. Todd's hit forced a fumble on our own 2 that Chris Zorich recovered. We reciprocated their kindness by throwing an interception. The first play after our turnover, Dickerson makes a great throw for a 42-yard touchdown.

We did come right back on offense with two straight scores. The first was set up by a great run of 50 yards by Tony Brooks. The second touchdown came on an impressive 86-yard drive. We couldn't stand prosperity, and threw another interception, and a series later Dickerson threw another long touchdown pass against us. We actually ended up ahead by 3 at the half, but this was only because Dickerson fumbled the ball into our end zone just prior to the half and Stan Smagala recovered it for us. This was the most bizarre play I have ever seen, as Dickerson had three opportunities to recover the fumble before Stan fell on it. Talk about Notre Dame spirit.

The second half the momentum kept changing until late in the third quarter, when Pitt tied it with a field goal. We then took charge of the game with an 80-yard drive that took six and a half minutes off the clock. This was the series where Braxston Banks made several key plays for us. I give Braxston and Jim Russ, our trainer, credit for doing the impossible, because I didn't think Banks could play against Pitt. Oh, but he played well.

Pitt came back with another field goal, but then we held the ball for nearly seven minutes and culminated a fourteen-play drive with a touchdown by Mark Green. The key play of the game was a penalty against Pitt for too many men on the field, which gave us a first down when it looked like our drive had been stopped.

It was a tough, physical game, everything I thought it would be. We did run the ball for over three hundred yards, which I really didn't expect us to do against their defense. Sometimes we're a better running team than I give us credit for.

If there was anything that stood out after watching the Pitt film, it's that we competed and found a way to win. We were very proud of our offensive line's performance, but for that matter, I was very proud of our whole team. Our team made some great plays. Rocket Ismail made one block on Tony Brooks's long run that was as fine as I have seen by a receiver. Tony Rice doesn't throw a lot—only when we need to—but he is effective. I felt that Frank Stams and Chris Zorich played so hard that it will be a total disservice to them if we don't put nine other people out there who'll play every down like they do. However, after looking at the film, we have that type of effort from everyone.

We had three turnovers, and all three were by receivers. If there's one positive, it's that in five games we haven't had a fumble by a tailback or a fullback.

We had twenty mental errors on defense, and that's a mortal sin. We were fortunate that we scored on every opportunity we had inside Pitt's 20-yard line, while Pitt had two fumbles inside our 20. Our kicking game wasn't bad, but that's like recommending your child for college by saying he's not in jail. We have to get better or Webster's dictionary has to rewrite its definition of perfection.

I'm excited about being 5–0, and our players are also. I never thought we'd be undefeated at this point, but then again, I hadn't expected our offense to be as productive as it has been. Our defense is and has been the strength of our team, but we must realize that they have to complement one another. The scoreboard doesn't say offense, nor does it say defense. It merely says Notre Dame, which comprises all facets of our team.

The attitude has to be, "If they score 30 points, we will have to score 31." The defensive attitude has to be, "If we score 3 points on offense, then our defense will have to hold them to 2 or less."

There were some great hits by Todd Lyght, Pat Terrell, and George Streeter. We will need more of these against Miami. Skip, my son, is a graduate assistant at Florida State, which lost to Miami in their opening game by a score of 31–0. It turned out to be Florida State's only loss all year. Skip called me and said Miami was an awesome team, and I believe him because we have taught our children not to lie.

We have two choices—improve fundamentally or try to sign a nonaggression pact with Miami before Saturday.

17

FORMER IRISH COACHES: THE LEGACY CONTINUES

I T is very helpful to know about the history and tradition of Notre Dame if you plan on coaching here long enough to make more than one year's worth of house payments. I have found it beneficial to talk to my contemporaries who have held this position prior to me.

It certainly behooves any coach to study his predecessors and gain an understanding of what they did and why they did it. You can eliminate a lot of mistakes this way. These coaches understand the difficult decisions you are confronted with on an hourly basis. At other schools there may be egos to polish, but here at Notre Dame everyone has the same purpose—to help Notre Dame. I'm certain I will feel the same way when I leave.

Knute Rockne is loved and cherished here as much as he was in 1929 or 1930, when he had his unbeaten teams. His name is still magic. The dedication of the Rockne postage stamp here last year was one of the most amazing things I've ever seen. People came from all over the place to buy stamps and other souvenirs. The fact that President Reagan was here to speak certainly helped.

There aren't a lot of people still alive who were around when Rockne was, but Moose Krause is one of them. He was a freshman in Rockne's last season, and Moose tells some great stories about the guy. Moose is a Notre Dame legend and a great friend. When we were 1–4 in 1986, he told me daily not to worry, that we would succeed.

One reason Rockne was so successful was his intelligence. He probably would have been a great success in any other line of work he might have chosen. As it was, he was a very successful chemistry teacher at Notre

Dame. As a coach, he knew how to motivate his players, and that's a key to long-range success in sports. I don't think it's any accident that he won three national championships and still has the best winning percentage of any coach in college football history. Thank goodness the football coach doesn't have to teach chemistry here anymore. It's always amazed me that I wasn't smart enough to be admitted to Notre Dame as a student but they think I'm smart enough to coach here.

People keep writing more books and articles about Rockne, and the folks in our sports information office tell me it's amazing how many requests they get for pictures of him.

Frank Leahy intrigues me as well, especially because of the reverence that his former players show when talking about him. He coached three national championship teams, too, and he was the coach when I first followed Notre Dame. I hear people like George Connor, Johnny Lujack, Johnny Lattner, and Creighton Miller talk about him, I almost feel I know him.

Leahy was another one who did some interesting things with motivation. He had a way of dealing with his players that made him special. Yet he was so intense about everything that it damaged his health, which has happened to other Notre Dame football coaches.

I had been searching for an out-of-print biography of Leahy written by Wells Twombly, who used to write for one of the San Francisco newspapers. My original copy was given to me by a friend, Frank Fuhrer. So I mentioned on my radio call-in show that I had lost the book Frank had given me and needed another one. Within a week I had received twenty-seven copies of the book in the mail. One person even checked one out from the library and sent me a note letting me know when it was due back.

One individual I've stayed in close touch with is Ara Parseghian. We have a lot in common. We've known each other a long time. We're both from the Mid-American Conference—I played at Kent State while he was coaching at Miami of Ohio. We're both from Ohio. We both worked for Woody Hayes.

I respect Ara greatly. I actually got to know him better after he got out of coaching. When he was doing color commentary on television, he was assigned to several of our games and we had the opportunity to have some long and serious conversations. He was the teacher and I was the student, and I asked him a thousand questions about coaching and motivation.

Ara is one of the most unassuming people you'd ever want to be around. He's a class guy; you just feel good being in his presence. He is one of the best coaches who has ever lived. He still lives right here in South Bend, so I see him a great deal. Ara didn't go to school here, but after coaching at

Notre Dame for eleven years and winning national titles in '66 and '73, I think he has as good a feel for the place as anyone.

We get a chance to play golf a little bit in the off-season and we talk every week during the season. I am constantly asking why and how he did things, and he never fails to give me an honest answer. He is positive, and never offers advice or second-guesses me unless I seek it. Though he has been out of coaching now for fifteen years, I have as much respect for his opinion as anyone I know. We even borrowed our current cadence count from him. But most of the things we talk about aren't technical—they involve his philosophy of doing things at Notre Dame and whether some of those strategies still work. I always feel better after talking to Ara. He's always in control and knows what's going on.

One of the first things I did when it was determined we would go to the Fiesta Bowl was to write a letter to Dan Devine. He lives in Phoenix now and works at Arizona State. I told him he was invited to come out to any of our practices or team functions during our stay for the bowl game. I don't think Dan receives the credit and recognition he should as a former Notre Dame head coach who has won a national championship.

Dan did come to practice one day, spoke to the team, and did an excellent job. He came into the locker room after we won to congratulate us. I didn't follow Notre Dame closely when Dan Devine was here, because I was trying to solve our own problems at Arkansas. However, I have a special appreciation for what it takes to win a national championship, whether at Notre Dame or somewhere else. It doesn't just happen.

That makes all of those guys special.

I have great respect for Terry Brennan, too. I called him not long after I got the job here just to get his impressions of what it was like coaching at Notre Dame. He's a class act in all respects. What's particularly gratifying to me is the loyalty of the former players from the Terry Brennan era: Connor, Lujack, Angelo Bertelli, Miller, Lattner, Leon Hart. The group of guys from that period stays very close to Notre Dame. Terry is an individual I would like to have talk to our squad sometime.

I also hear from Gerry Faust quite often. He has a son still attending Notre Dame, and he still has a particular interest in this team, because he recruited the seniors and because he loves Notre Dame. Gerry is such an optimistic person, you sometimes wonder if he is sincere. But without any equivocation whatsoever, I can say that Gerry Faust is for real. In some ways I wish I could be like him.

I could go on forever about what binds the Notre Dame football coaches together. There is a spirit, and you feel it. You always sense that there are former coaches who not only pull for you, but are willing to help.

18

MIAMI:
THE BUILDUP

THERE will be many keys to the Miami game this week, but I don't know if any of them are bigger than confidence. That is why we started on it in the locker room after the Pitt game.

Miami is an extremely disciplined football team on the field. You can talk about the extracurricular things and the way their players have talked in the past, but from when the ball is snapped until the whistle blows, they are as disciplined and fundamentally sound as any team I have seen. They play with great emotion and confidence, a tribute to the staff. We must generate an atmosphere that we can beat them, even though they beat us decisively last year and they're better this year. Fortunately, we are much better than we were a year ago, though we might not look impressive to our opponents. We do the things to win that don't show up on the statistic sheet.

I told the team I played my last football game in 1957, so there's no way I can help them on the field. We can win this game. It doesn't have to be a fluke for us to win, but it sure won't be easy.

We asked the players in our Sunday meeting to do three things for us.

One, just relax. We don't play for six more days. I told them I called the NCAA but they can't send a team here for us to play until Saturday, so there's no reason to get all pumped up now and have all the adrenaline gone by the time we kick off. If you make a fist and hold it for two hours, you can't pick up a lamp. So there's no reason for anyone to be tense.

Second, we want them to go through our relaxation routine before they go to bed. We want them to lie there for a few minutes and visualize themselves making great plays.

Third, have faith that we will be successful—never doubt it. I don't have proof that we can win. If we had proof, there would be no need for faith. Just have faith that if they listen to what the coaches say, we can win.

Miami comes in here with a 36-game regular-season unbeaten streak, and that is impressive, but all streaks come to an end. Columbia's long losing streak did last Saturday, and maybe Miami's winning streak will this week.

I don't think there's any question Miami has an advantage from having a week off, while we had a tough game against Pittsburgh on the road. Had we had an open date last weekend, in all probability we would not have lost our two starting guards. We would, as a result, be healthier than we are at the present time.

There is no doubt the extra week also gives Miami a better chance to prepare for us. I believe our offense, with its flexibility, is very difficult to prepare for in one week. It also allows them to get healthy, be relaxed, improve fundamentally, perfect some segments of the kicking game, and most importantly, eliminate mental fatigue that occurs about the middle of the season. We have no control over these things, so there's no reason to dwell on them.

Everyone wants to make this into a grudge match, especially the media. They ask a lot of questions, about getting even with Miami. You don't get ahead of someone by getting even. It makes for a lot of hype, and it's unfortunate we can't stick to football.

I like Jimmy Johnson. I have tremendous respect for the Miami program and what it has accomplished. I've known Jimmy since 1977, and Joe Moore, one of our assistants, coached with him at Pittsburgh. We competed against him when he was at Oklahoma State, and we were quite successful. There is no animosity on my part, although I did say to him after last year's loss in Miami to please do me a favor and stay there one more year.

Unfortunately, some students or fans on both sides have written some letters and made some phone calls to both Jimmy and myself. I think that's indicative of the interest in this game. There's a tremendous amount of emotion connected with this rivalry as far as the fans are concerned. I guess it dates back to before I started at Notre Dame, when Miami defeated Notre Dame 58–7 in 1985. Notre Dame fans thought Miami ran up the score, but Jimmy felt they were just running their offense and playing their game. I hope our fans act with a lot of class on Saturday. I think they will, because there's no reason to have anything but respect for Miami and what they've done on the field. Jimmy says

183

Notre Dame fans have sent him hate mail. He is lucky. I received hate mail from both Miami fans and Notre Dame fans.

The amazing thing about Miami is the way they throw the ball without ever paying the price. It's like having a sheriff's badge. They do whatever they want throwing the ball. They seldom get sacked, seldom get called for holding, and rarely throw an interception. It's impossible to defense them if those things hold true against us.

I get advice from a lot of people about how to beat Miami, but few answers. Half the people tell me we need to blitz them. But you can't do that all the time. Florida State tried to blitz them an awful lot, never got a sack, and were beat 31–0. The other half of the people tell me we need to drop back and cover the receivers. But Michigan did this and gave up 31 points, too.

Steve Walsh is the best college quarterback Miami has had. He is better than Bernie Kosar, Jim Kelly, or Vinnie Testaverde. I don't know if he'll be the pro those three are, but I wouldn't bet against it. He is a great quarterback and his team wins. I can't imagine anyone being better than Steve Walsh is right now. He knows when to throw the ball away, and you'd think he would be called for intentional grounding occasionally, but he isn't.

The question I asked was, how did Michigan score 30 points against a great Miami defense? After studying the films it was obvious the answer wasn't because Miami had a weakness. Michigan just made some great throws and catches. Michael Taylor threw two touchdown passes that were as well-covered defensively as you'll ever want to see. Michigan just executed well on some key plays. Michigan didn't establish a ground game, although they ran it better than we could. But let's remember that the Wolverine offensive line is rated the best in the country. Michigan could have won had they gotten a critical first down in the fourth quarter. But again, give credit to Miami.

I'm amazed that some people have suggested this is a game for the national championship. That's idle conversation. You can't even discuss a national championship until the eighth or ninth game, because there are so many things that have to happen. A national championship isn't something you win. You wake up one day when the season is over, and you are national champions. But this is a game that could be very important in determining who has a legitimate chance for a national championship.

This is the type of game where you don't have to get the players ready emotionally. Instead, it's important not to get ready too early. I will pray a lot this week, as I do every week. I don't pray for a victory, but I pray for guidance and direction. It is amazing, but my prayers are usually answered.

In a game of this magnitude, we just want to play up to our potential. The only thing that would disappoint me is if we did not play as well as I think we're capable of playing.

It is imperative that we don't make this game out to be bigger than life. What's the most important is that we just be ourselves. We can't panic, get overly excited, emotional, critical, and tense. If that happens, it will be a normal reaction, but one that will jeopardize our chance for success.

Miami players have talked in the past about how there is no spirit at Notre Dame, but I believe they are trying to convince themselves. We haven't played with the Notre Dame spirit, so how could they believe it existed? I feel we are just starting to resurrect the spirit, particularly at home. Sometimes teams come here and make mistakes they can't believe. That could happen on Saturday. Then again, Miami has played so well on the road in the past, you can't tell if they are at home or on the road. Great teams do that.

I love this situation for our fans, our students, our players and coaches. There is some pressure involved, and you do feel it. But games like this are why you want to be in coaching. It's like working all your life to buy a car and then being afraid to drive it because you might get a scratch on it.

This is where we wanted to be, and I hope we can get through this without going through some bad experiences. Miami has been in three big bowl games in recent years. They lost to Tennessee and Penn State in two consecutive years, which cost them the national championship before they won in their third try. Miami knows how to win. They feel confident because being in a big game is nothing new to them. They relish it, whereas this is a new experience for us. We haven't been there before. I hope we will be in the future.

This is the first time our team has been in a game of this magnitude, with this amount of coverage, with this amount of national interest. Our expectations are high, but deep down inside, I don't know if we really believe we can win. The confidence of our players must go much deeper than standing on a soapbox saying we will win.

I laughed when someone told me Jimmy Johnson said we had more speed than his team. He said he's worried about Notre Dame controlling the football against them. He can't be too desperate if that's all he can find to worry about. He only has to go back to last year. We didn't have the football long enough to know if it was blown up or stuffed. We worked all week on throwing the football, but you couldn't tell it by our performance that Saturday. Knute Rockne and Gus Dorais would have been embarrassed by the way we threw it last year at Miami.

According to Miami's standards, ball control probably means Notre

Dame running four or five plays in a row. We couldn't even do that last year. They run an offense that never get penalities, seldom loses yardage, seldom turns the ball over, seldom puts their defense in a bind, and very seldom has to punt. They have a good kicking game when they use it, so their opponents start 80 yards from the goal line on a regular basis.

Miami knows, and Steve Walsh knows, that if they don't have a pass that's wide open, they just throw the ball away, punt it away, and they know they'll get it back in a minute or two. It's not like they kick it away and worry about not getting it back. That's how good their defense is.

As I mentioned before, the preparations for the Miami game really started in the locker room after the Pitt game. After addressing certain things about the Pitt game, I talked to the players about their conduct, talking to the press, the good things they did that day and a little about our upcoming opponent.

I said Miami was a great football team, but I felt we could beat them if certain things happened. They'd have to believe in one another. They'd have to believe in the coaches and do exactly what they were told, and they'd have to believe in the spirit of Notre Dame. There have been so many games in the past where Notre Dame has played number-one teams and won, and our players had to believe that it could and would happen again. If they didn't have faith, it wouldn't happen.

Sunday morning when I went to church, you could already tell this was going to be a different week. All year people had been talking about the Miami game, but this time it was for real. I figured they didn't think we could win, so they would get the maximum enjoyment out of the pregame excitement.

We were concerned about our team because it appeared that Tim Ryan and Tim Grunhard would miss the game. Miami's defense is such that they play two defensive tackles on your guards and usually get a mismatch in this area. With the loss of our two guards, we felt we needed to move two tackles, Joe Allen and Mike Brennan, to guard, even though they hadn't played there previously.

During the course of the week I called Bo Schembechler, which I do quite often, because I have great respect for him. I asked him about Miami's team, which had come back to beat Michigan by one point the week after we had played Michigan. He said they were an outstanding football team. Did Bo think we had a chance to beat them, since he had seen both of us play? He said yes, he thought we had a chance, but we would have to play very well. This encouraged me greatly, because over the last five years, Miami had beaten us rather decisively. I think the average score had been something like 34–6 during that period.

186

Our practices were more physical during the week than I would have liked, but that was out of necessity because of the personnel changes we had made. We needed to get the other people ready and acquire some continuity so our offense could go into the game with some degree of confidence. To win a game like this, you have to play well on defense and with your kicking game. But I knew we would have to put some points on the board and be productive on offense, too.

Reggie Ho, senior placekicker

Coach always says before practice, "This sucker doesn't even have to be close."

I had hoped we could go into the Miami game undefeated, but more important now was to come out of the game undefeated. This could best be done by creating a positive upbeat environment during practices. This did not transpire as I had hoped.

We had to change too many things in the offensive line, which affected our continuity. Consequently, our coaches could not be as positive as I would have liked. There were a lot of mistakes during the course of practice, and I lost my temper more than a couple of times.

On Monday Digger Phelps came in and talked to me about the game. He'd been the coach here when Notre Dame broke UCLA's 88-game winning streak, and had been in a number of other victories over number-one-ranked teams. He talked a lot about the Notre Dame spirit and how somewhere along the line good things would happen. He also said it was important to make sure people didn't think I was uptight about the game. He said we should take the coaches out on Thursday night for dinner so that everyone would be relaxed.

Digger is a fine basketball coach and a rare individual. He came to my office four or five times during the week. He kept saying, "You'll beat them. I can feel it. It's just like it was when we beat UCLA." What was great was that here you had the basketball coach concerned about how we were going to get ready for Miami. Few people understand the spirit or history of this place more than Digger.

I turned on the television Monday night and watched *The Sportswriters* on SportsVision. This is a show where sports writers from Chicago talk about a lot of different subjects each week. The individuals on it have great insight, and I watch it when possible. One of the items they discussed was our upcoming game with Miami. I was immediately impressed with their intelligence, since none of them gave us a chance to win.

I disagreed, though, with their contention that we didn't have a chance because we run the option and Miami stops option football. One thing I'd like to point out is that Miami doesn't just stop an option offense, Miami stops *all* offenses. Florida State runs a pro-style passing attack, and I don't think Florida State got inside Miami's 30-yard line once in sixty minutes. Because Miami beat Oklahoma decisively three years in a row, we have a tendency to think their ability to stop the option is their only asset. They are a great defensive team overall, which is often forgotten.

I wanted to be positive but realistic with the news media. We took the position that games like this were what Notre Dame was all about—that Notre Dame normally rose to the occasion. Miami is a great football team, but we were getting better rapidly, and if we could ever put the same twenty-two players on the field two weeks in a row, we could be an outstanding team, too.

We talked about how good Miami was. But I also continued to emphasize that somewhere, somehow, Miami's long winning streak was going to come to an end. We knew it. Their players knew it. Their coaches knew it. We just didn't know when. It may very well be this weekend, because Notre Dame has a history of stopping winning streaks.

I received a lot of personal phone calls at the office and at home from friends. Unfortunately, I didn't get a chance to return very many. It's ironic that when you need the most time to prepare, it seems your normal day has been reduced from twenty-four hours to twenty-four minutes and twenty-four seconds.

The phone rings an awful lot more at all hours of the night on weeks like this, which makes it exceptionally hard to get things done. I get upset with my wife every time the phone rings at three o'clock in the morning because it wouldn't happen if we had an unlisted phone number. Our number always has been in the phone book, and she wants to finish our career that way. I'm not sure we can, because of the interest Notre Dame creates. One thing for sure, I can always tell what time the bars close at night based on when the phone stops ringing. We have always had a listed number in the event a parent of one of our athletes had a problem and needed to talk to me.

On Wednesday night I met Father Ned Joyce for a sandwich. I try to do this about every other week during the season, and we talk about our team. I have tremendous respect for him, and even though he's officially retired from his post as executive vice president of the university, I know he's still extremely interested in what happens. He also is the individual who hired me, along with Gene Corrigan.

This was the first really big game most of our players had been involved in, where a lot was expected of them. It's one thing to play in a big game where you're the underdog, such as we were my first year in '86 when we played Penn State. It's something else to play the number-one team when you're ranked number four yourself. We talked to the squad on a daily basis about being positive and getting things done. But conversation won't win this game. What was equally important was that we learn the gameplan inside and out.

I liked our gameplan on both offense and defense, but I wasn't sure how well we would execute. We had elevated Patrick Terrell to the starting free safety starting last week at Pitt, and this week we added Arnold Ale at end. In addition, Frank Jacobs still hadn't recovered from a foot injury during the Stanford game, and Derek Brown would be called upon to start again. Consequently, we were starting three true freshmen in Derek Brown, Ale, and Rocket Ismail—along with Terrell, who a year ago had been a split end for us.

At the Quarterback Club luncheon on Friday I think 1800 people showed up, and the atmosphere was electrifying. Every time you walked out of the office to go to a meeting, it seemed like someone wanted a picture or an autograph. Consequently, when I had to say no because of a team meeting or practice requirement, I felt badly. I'm sure some people got the impression I was too important for them, and they resent it. This wasn't the case at all.

So many people come to a game for pleasure and relaxation. It's different for me. I hope people understand that this is really and truly my profession. I find it's very difficult for even friends and relatives to understand this, but they have to realize that my first obligation is to our players and that we need to give them every opportunity to be successful.

There were a lot of individual interviews this week as well. The Tuesday-night nationwide call-in show on Mutual was exciting because of the interest all the callers had in the Miami game. During the entire week everyone has had positive vibrations. Every time I looked at the film, I could see Miami was outstanding, but I didn't find anyone—player, coach, student, or fan—who didn't feel that we couldn't play with them.

I've been involved in big games before, but I'd never seen anything like this. We'd been in bowl games that meant a lot, and Arkansas–Texas games were generally big deals, but the week before Miami was incredible. I was excited, too, but it was important to put it in perspective. It was tough enough when people were talking about this game before the season even started. I told our players that every time you win a game, the next one becomes bigger than the last one. If they think this is big, then let's keep winning and I'll show them a big game our eleventh and twelfth games of the year.

We had press conferences every day this week; I've never been involved in anything like it for a midseason game. Every time you turned around, there was a television camera. It was fun, in a way, but it's a little strange because next week is fall break and there'll be no classes and all the students will be gone. Everyone has midterms right now, but that's good because it will keep the players from thinking about the game too soon. I've never seen so many people on campus so excited about a football game, and that could have a negative effect. Hopefully, the exams will keep everything in perspective.

There must be a lot of money being made on campus this week, because all you hear about are the T-shirts being sold by the students. I don't get out on campus at all during the season unless it's a special occasion, but you can't help hearing about the T-shirts.

Normally there are a few people around on a Thursday of game week and quite a few on Friday, especially with the Quarterback Club luncheon held at noon. However, I heard a couple of the student trainers say that there were so many people walking around the South quad on Thursday at noon that you would have thought it was game day.

We visited with Brent Musburger and Pat Haden and the CBS people for about an hour Friday afternoon. We talked about the intangibles of the game and tried to give them our sentiments so they could do the best job possible for what appears likely to be a very large television audience.

I've talked to Skip every day this week. Florida State plays East Carolina this week, and he says they're scared of East Carolina. I kidded him that if that was the case, maybe he ought to get out of coaching before he really got into it.

I don't know what to think about our offensive line. Mike Brennan started out as a tight end, then we moved him to tackle, now we will start him at guard. Having a guy who came as a walk-on start his first game at a new position against the number-one team in the country doesn't sound like a very good way to obtain longevity in the coaching profession. But that's what we are going to do.

We even moved Tom Gorman, who had been a defensive tackle but tore the chest muscle in August, to offensive tackle this week to work behind Andy Heck. He is a fine player, but he missed so much practice time because of his injury that some of the younger players have had the opportunity to claim that position. It is obvious that they aren't going to give it up, but we think Tom can help us on offense.

Our feeling is that Miami will not beat us throwing and catching. I don't care how many passes Steve Walsh throws or how great he is or how sophisticated their passing game is. I agree with people who say those things, but what I'm concerned about most is their ability to run with the ball. We absolutely can't let them run the football. I know they will throw for a couple hundred yards, but if they can run it as well as throw it, we will need to use a basketball scoreboard, as Miami may set a new record.

Being in Minneapolis, while Steve Walsh was in high school, I certainly knew about him. We didn't have a chance at him at Minnesota because he made it plain he didn't want to go somewhere where they were building a program. I honestly thought he'd go to Notre Dame. He was a passer, and we couldn't accentuate that at Minnesota. He's a Pat Haden with height. I think his dad bought 180 tickets for this game, and I hear John Sullivan, one of their offensive linemen from Chicago, purchased 130.

It'll be interesting to see how Arnold Ale reacts in the game. We told him the day after the Pittsburgh game that he would be the starter this week. He's from California, and he comes over to practice wearing a scarf and earmuffs when it's 52 degrees. He said that's the coldest he's ever been. I told him it's as warm in South Bend as it is in Los Angeles. The only time he'll notice the difference is when he goes outside.

One key offensively is that we've changed the way we now call our passes. With so many young receivers starting out, and with Tony trying to perfect a lot of things he does, we decided to make the change prior to the Pitt game. This is a drastic change in the middle of the season. But we thought it was important to do so now. That's why our receivers wore wristbands against Pitt—to remind them of their assignments.

The pep rally Friday night was unbelievable. It was outside the Stepan Center, and I've never seen so many people congregated there before. I'm not good at estimating crowds, but there must have been twenty thousand people, or at least it seemed that way. The sound system went out and came back just in time for me to say a few words.

The pep rallies at Notre Dame are something special. This is the first year we've held one outdoors. We used to have them inside Stepan Center, and the atmosphere there was amazing. But we had to move outside because too many people ended up crowding in there and the fire marshals didn't feel it was safe. When we had them at Stepan Center, the band would march across the entire campus, playing the Victory March with the students following. The players would walk onstage with the Victory March playing. Normally there would be two players, an alumnus, and me on the program.

This time when I got up, I asked the fans to do three things. One, I wanted them to conduct themselves with a great deal of class. Two, I wanted them to yell louder than they've ever yelled in their life to support us. Three, I wanted them to go tell Jimmy Johnson that we are going to beat Miami.

191

The crowd went absolutely berserk, and that was all anyone had to say. We walked off the stage and took the team back to our meeting room in the auditorium of the Loftus Center.

I couldn't believe I had predicted we would win. This was totally out of character for me. We went back to the Loftus Center for a meeting and I asked the players why they thought I had said that. They said, "Because you believe it"—and I said, "Yes." I did believe it deep down inside, but I really couldn't explain why. Miami already felt they would win, so they couldn't be any more determined to win no matter what we said or did. It's the mark of a great team to have that kind of confidence. However, what was important to me was that our players knew that I believed we could win.

We started listing all the reasons we thought we could win. We were playing at home. We had a good defense. We had been successful so far this season. We walked out of that room, and I honestly felt we would beat Miami. I didn't know if our players felt in their hearts they could win, but if they didn't, there wasn't anything else we could do to convince them.

I went with the team down to the Holiday Inn in Plymouth and spent the night with them. You could tell the mood was a little different than for the average game, but I liked the fact that the players seemed loose and relaxed.

We got up Saturday morning and it was a dismal day. I hated to see it rain. It turned out to be a beautiful day, but it didn't look very good at eight o'clock. We had our pregame meal, got on the bus, and went back to campus to go to mass. We had an outstanding mass and service, delivered by Father Riehle. You can always tell how ready a football team is at the pregame mass by noticing how the players shake one another's hands and hug each other. It didn't take long to observe this was going to be a special game.

After the mass the players walked over to the stadium, and again the atmosphere was unmistakable. The whole thing was everything you'd ever expect when you talk about playing a big game.

MIAMI:
THE GAME

WE went out for pregame warm-ups and there was a confrontation between the two teams in the end zone before the game even started. Emotions were really high, and it is unfortunate when this happens. This was to be college football at its finest, and to have this happen was depressing to both teams.

I don't know why the emotions in this game are so hostile, because we have lost to other fine teams, such as Michigan and USC, in the past and have had no problems. I do believe Miami was either looking for a confrontation or was attempting to intimidate Notre Dame. Nevertheless, this situation should never occur, and it is up to both schools in the future to see that this contest is a shining example for other schools to emulate, or else we should end the series immediately. Once the game started, both teams competed very hard and played with class.

When I arrived in the locker room for the pregame talk, our players were as emotional and upset as any group I've ever seen. I knew one thing for sure—this was going to be a very physical game. I tried to calm them down.

Chris Zorich, sophomore defensive tackle
Before the game started, after the scuffle in the tunnel, I was in tears. Guys were hitting lockers and I was ready to hit anything. I was really pumped. As a coach, it would have been natural to say, "Let's go!" But Coach Holtz was just the opposite. We had another half hour in the locker room, and he told us to relax. It was awfully hard to do.

During the summer a good friend and successful businessman by the name of Carl Pohlad called me, which was natural because we talk quite often. He said something constructive to me that really got my attention. He said, "You cannot be successful if you flinch." In other words, when things go wrong, you must always act like you are in control of the situation and things are fine. This advice was invaluable to Notre Dame in 1988.

We had to play with a great deal of confidence and never let losing enter our minds. Miami never flinches, and always feels it will win when it's late in the game and it's close. They become even more confident, if that's possible. We had to feel the same way. I told our players if something good didn't happen to us, we'd just have to believe and to hang in there until it did.

Anytime you have a big game, you have certain players who have to play very well. We felt that our entire team had to play well, but Derek Brown, Rocket Ismail, Ricky Watters, Tony Rice, and some of our backs would have to make some big plays for us to be successful. On defense we would have to get a great performance out of our secondary and out of our line, particularly Frank Stams, who was our best pass-rusher. Wes Pritchett and Michael Stonebreaker would have to set the tempo for the game, and they did.

THE GAME

SOUTH BEND—As always, there were 59,075 football fans seated Saturday in Notre Dame Stadium, where unbeatens Miami and Notre Dame fought with teeth bared on a glorious, sun-kissed afternoon for college football.

But, as the years go by, count on that number in attendance growing by leaps and bounds. Like Bobby Thompson's home run for the New York Giants or Don Larsen's perfect game for the New York Yankees or Franco Harris's immaculate reception for the Pittsburgh Steelers, Notre Dame's dramatic 31–30 victory over top-ranked Miami figures to go down as a game for the ages. On a legendary grass field that has seen more than its share of great moments in collegiate football lore, this one might have been the best.

Unlike Larsen's World Series effort in 1956, this one didn't qualify as a perfect game. In fact, the seven turnovers by the Hurricanes had plenty to do with Miami's undoing. But for pure drama, you aren't going to see many more entertaining football games than this one.

Amazingly, the game actually may have been better than the hype. With Miami making its first call at Notre Dame Stadium since the Canes did their 58–7 drubbing of the Irish in Miami in Gerry Faust's last game in 1985, the Notre Dame faithful had been waiting for this moment. Emotions have run strong between the two teams and their fans in recent seasons. In fact, the two squads combined for a minor fracas in the tunnel before the game ever started.

Notre Dame had done its part in prepping for the game, facing another unbeaten opponent while having gone 5–0 or better itself for the first time since 1943. The Irish had been shut out only twice in the last 119 games—both times by the Canes, in '83 and '87. Notre Dame had lost its last four games to Miami by a combined score of 133–20. Motivation did not go lacking.

Miami did its part, too, arriving with the number-one ranking, an overall 16-game winning streak, and a regular-season unbeaten streak of 36 games. Miami had not lost a road game since 1984 and had not lost a network-televised road game since 1979. In fact, the Canes had added to that figure in rather unbelievable fashion just a month earlier in a scintillating 31–30 comeback win at Michigan.

Still, Irish coach Lou Holtz didn't hesitate to play on the thought that the streak had to end somewhere and it might as well be this week.

In the end, Notre Dame didn't beat Miami as much as the Irish somehow outlasted the Hurricanes. Quarterback Steve Walsh put on an awesome show, writing his name in the Notre Dame record books by completing 31 of 50 passes for 424 yards, the most ever surrendered by a Notre Dame team. But Walsh did permit three interceptions, and two of the four fumbles lost by Miami came tumbling from its quarterback's hands.

Maybe the statistics didn't show it, but give Notre Dame's defense a whole lot of credit for simply hanging in there. Despite Walsh's artistry, the never-say-die Irish defenders made sure their adversaries knew they had been in a football game.

Veteran defensive end Frank Stams enjoyed a game for the scrapbooks—while spending most of the afternoon personally harassing Walsh. Stams forced Walsh to fumble twice, recovered a third, and tipped the pass that free safety Pat Terrell ran back 60 yards for a touchdown.

Terrell put the Irish on top 21–7 with the runback of that tipped throw. Then he made what turned out to be the game-saving play when he knocked down Walsh's two-point conversion attempt for Leonard Conley with the game in the balance and 45 seconds on the clock.

Quarterback Tony Rice didn't finish with Walsh-like numbers, but the 195 passing yards he produced still ranked as a career best. He also ran the ball 21 times and scored the first touchdown of the game.

The list went on forever. Wes Pritchett made 15 tackles while playing with a broken hand. Rookie tight end Derek Brown, who had been greatly coveted by Cane coach Jimmy Johnson, made a pair of spectacular catches. Flanker Pat Eilers scored a touchdown on only his fifth career rushing attempt. Raghib Ismail set up the second Notre Dame touchdown with a 57-yard reception, and Ricky Watters's lone grab of the day for 44 yards preceded Eilers's run.

But Holtz had no intention of pointing out heroes.

"This was a win by the Notre Dame spirit," he said. "It was a win by a group of guys who just refused to fold and believed. You can't pick out a hero today. Notre Dame was the hero."

The Irish never trailed in the contest, but that didn't stop Johnson from wondering what might have been had his Canes not been prone to give up the football so many times.

"It should not have come down to a two-point conversion. There is no way we could have made as many mistakes as we did and won the game. If we had played better, it would not have come down to one or two plays."

Once this battle of perfect records got under way, the football game couldn't have been more fun to watch.

Notre Dame's defense wasted little time setting the tempo. On the game's initial series, Stams applied the pressure, Walsh fumbled, and Chris Zorich recovered. The Canes' second possession reached midfield before Stams again nailed Walsh on a judgment call that was ruled an incompletion but easily could have been called another fumble.

After Miami's punt, the Irish constructed their first scoring drive. The 12-play, 75-yard march featured three conversions on third down—a 22-yard pass to Ismail, a 13-yard run by Braxston Banks, and a six-yard keeper by Rice. On third and four from the seven, Rice faked to Banks and waltzed unmolested into the right corner of the end zone.

George Streeter intercepted Walsh and set the Irish up at the Miami 35, only to see Rice fumble the center's snap on first down and the Canes recover. The Irish kept Miami from running the ball on a consistent basis most of the day, so Walsh kept up his relentless aerial assault. Mixing 20-yard strikes to Cleveland Gary and Andre Brown, he finished off the 8-play, 68-yard excursion with an 8-yard throw to Brown—who shoved the ball over the goal line from a prone position to make it 7–7.

Both teams came back with a pair of lightning-quick scores.

Notre Dame began with a 57-yard bomb to Ismail on third and 12 to keynote an 80-yard, 11-play drive. On third and five from the 9, Rice found Banks all alone over the middle on a delay and he scored untouched. Four plays later, the Irish made it 21–7. With Stonebreaker blitzing, Stams got his fingertips on a Walsh throw and Terrell grabbed it in midstride and outlegged Walsh to the flag. But the Notre Dame advantage didn't last long, even with just 5:53 left in the first half.

Walsh continued to pepper away, finally ending a 61-yard, eight-play drive with a 23-yard scoring toss to Leonard Conley on a fourth-and-4 call. After an Irish punt, Miami got it back again at the 1:13 juncture. After a controversial call on an incompletion that could have been ruled a fumble, Walsh fired to Brown for 22, then found a wide-open Gary for 15 yards and the tying points at the 21-second mark.

In the first half alone, Walsh had gone 17 for 29 for 248 yards as the Canes finished with 295 total yards—and a 21–21 tie. Longtime *Miami Herald* columnist Edwin Pope called it the greatest first half of football he'd ever seen.

The two teams exchanged quick jabs early in the third period. Bubba McDowell intercepted a Rice pass on the first possession, but Jeff Alm pried the ball out of Conley's grasp on the very next play and Stams recovered. After four plays moved Notre Dame to the Miami 25, Billy Hackett's 43-yard field-goal attempt was blocked.

On its next drive, Miami made what proved to be a critical mistake. The Canes faced a fourth-and-three call from their own 47 with more than eight minutes left in the third quarter. Johnson opted for the fake, snapping the ball to the upman, Matt Britton—but Notre Dame was alert and quarterback Steve Belles stopped the play for a loss of one.

The Irish wasted no time. Rice connected with Watters in midstride for a 44-yard gain to the two. On the next play, Eilers cut back on a pitch right and stumbled into the end zone for a 28–21 lead.

Seven plays into Miami's next attempt, Alm picked a Walsh pass out of the air and sent his teammates on a 65-yard, nine-play possession. Tony Brooks ran for 22 and Rice hit Derek Brown for 26 before the drive stalled at the Miami 11. Reggie Ho's 27-yard field goal made it 31–21 with 37 seconds remaining in the third period. Miami got those three points back in a hurry. Throwing on seven plays out of nine, Walsh moved his team to the Irish 6—then Carlos Huerta knocked through a 23-yard field goal.

After a Notre Dame punt came a Miami drive and turnover that also turned out to be critical. Starting from their own 46, the Canes got as far as the Irish 11 before facing fourth and 7. This time, Walsh double-pumped and angled one over the middle for Gary, who was hit by Michael Stonebreaker just before reaching the goal line. Miami argued for a touchdown, but the Irish got the ball at the one.

Notre Dame went nowhere on its ensuing drive, but Miami did likewise—with Stams blindsiding Walsh and Zorich recovering the fumble at the Notre Dame 28 at the 3:37 mark. Needing just a couple of first downs to run the clock, Rice was hit while attempting to pass on third down and lost the football at the 2:10 mark. Walsh required just four plays to score, doing it on fourth down on a lob to the right corner of the end zone to Brown at the 45-second stoppage.

After a time-out, Walsh tried to find Conley in about the same spot for the go-ahead points. But George Williams's pressure forced a quicker-than-desired throw that floated short and was routinely knocked down by Terrell.

"I saw him come into the flat and head into the corner of the end zone," said Terrell. "I just jumped in front of him. I don't think Walsh saw me coming and I followed his eyes the whole way and knew where he was going to throw the ball."

The Irish needed only to have Anthony Johnson fall on Huerta's onside kick attempt to ensure its victory—and kick off a party that lasted the rest of the afternoon both inside and outside of Notre Dame Stadium.

"This was a great football game," said Holtz. "I said that I felt Miami was the best football team in the country and I believe that right now. But I've never been prouder of a football team than ours. This was two great teams that competed as hard as anything I've seen."

For the Notre Dame players, it was a moment that had been long-awaited:

"It was like we could feel all those Irish legends out there," said Zorich. "I kept hearing those lines from our fight song about shaking down the thunder and waking up the echoes."

In the end, a banner lost amidst the sea of humanity that engulfed the field after the game ended said it all: "Nobody Leaves Notre Dame No. 1."

Miami came out throwing the ball, and after the first five plays, it was obvious that their passing game was even better than I had envisioned. Steve Walsh displayed excellent talent and vision.

Our football team had a crispness also, and even though we were concerned about our offensive guards, I was positive we would move the football. I just hoped it would be forward. Little things usually determine the outcome of a game when two teams are as evenly matched as Notre Dame and Miami. There were five controversial calls during the course of the game, and four of them went against Notre Dame and in Miami's favor.

The most damaging one was when we had a 21–14 lead just before the half. They completed a pass over the middle to the tight end, Rob Chudzinski, and Stonebreaker put a great hit on him that created a fumble. We recovered it, but they ruled it was an incomplete pass. When I looked at the film later, it confirmed what my initial reaction was during the contest—that it was definitely a completed pass and a fumble. However, officials make mistakes the same as coaches, and you can't worry about it. Barry Alvarez said it best: "Fans go to the game and want to coach. Coaches go to the game and want to officiate. Officials go to the game and want to be a fan."

Late in the first half we had managed to fight and scratch our way into a 14-point lead, 21–7, thanks to a complete team performance. Our defense had covered a couple of turnovers, and our offense had taken advantage of them. In addition, Pat Terrell intercepted a pass and ran it in for a touchdown. However, in the last two minutes of the first half Miami scored 14 points to tie it up, 21–21.

Rather than being down because we didn't have the 14-point lead, I wanted the players to understand that we proved for thirty minutes that we could play with Miami. Now, instead of it being a sixty-minute ballgame, it was a thirty-minute ballgame. Forget about the first half, forget about losing the lead. Happiness is best described as having a poor memory. Let's look forward to the second half. That is why God put eyes in front of our head rather than behind—so we can see where we are going rather than where we have been.

During that first half Miami scored on fourth and 4. Even though we had played great defense for the first three downs, the touchdown still counted six points. We play three great downs on defense and had nothing to show for it.

Pete Cordelli, receiver coach

I thought one of the big things this year was the pride we took in playing at home. We haven't been beaten at home in two years now, and we emphasized that. You don't let somebody come to your home, your stadium, and take something away from you. At halftime of the Miami game you've got the offense on one side and the defense on the other. All of a sudden somebody's hand comes through the defensive blackboard and the whole thing just shatters. It just exploded. Guys are screaming and yelling and everybody's out the door.

We came out for the second half just as excited as when we began the game. The game went back and forth, but we ended up taking the lead on a quick drive after Miami didn't convert on a fake punt. In a great game the momentum swings back and forth because both teams refuse to lose. It was critical that neither team flinched. Finally, Miami did.

We were in a punt return, but we always look for a fake—because in nationally televised games Jimmy Johnson had a history of doing the unusual in the kicking game. Jimmy had done this against Florida State in its season opener and been successful. So we were aware they might try a fake. When they did it and it wasn't successful, it sent a message to our players that Miami had to gamble to be in the game. This was the single most important play in the game. After the game, people talked about the controversial officiating, but I thought it was a smoke screen so nobody would ask about the fake-punt call. I am certainly not second-guessing Jimmy Johnson. He is a great football coach. He's proven it on the college scene and he will do the same in the pros.

On the play immediately after we stopped the fake punt, Tony Rice hit Ricky Watters on a great throw and catch down to the Miami 2-yard line. On the next play Pat Eilers took it in for the lead, one Notre Dame would never surrender. We did fumble deep in our territory, however, and it set up the last Miami touchdown.

Miami, being the great team it was, came back and played valiantly, but the two-point conversion missed when George Williams pressured Walsh and Patrick Terrell had his man well covered in the corner of the end zone.

The Notre Dame spirit is alive and well in South Bend.

Chris Zorich

The best time of the season was when there were only forty-five seconds left in the Miami game. It had come down to the final seconds, and I wasn't scared. I was confident. Coach had all of us confident. I came to Notre Dame for games like that—for pressure like that.

There was never any doubt in our minds that once we got the lead in the second half, we would win. A lot of people said we were lucky to win, but I disagree with that completely. I was disappointed the outcome of the game came down to the closing seconds, because we were in a position to say checkmate much earlier but we were aware that Miami was as dangerous behind as they were ahead.

Once the game ended, my initial reaction was "Boy, will that be a great game next year, when we go down to Miami to play." It was bedlam as everyone rushed onto the field. Thank goodness, I have a gentleman named Paul Harvey who is my chaperon. I've never had one before and never needed one here or anywhere else, until the Miami game. With my size and strength, I'm not sure I wouldn't have been injured. We did a television interview on the field for CBS, and the students were all trying to get on camera and disrupt the interview so much that I got upset. This was the wrong thing to do, but I did get silence, and that was my goal. I wanted to tell the world that our players were great, but that this victory could only be attributed to the Notre Dame spirit and the Lady on the Dome.

In the locker room our football players were very excited. As Frank Stams said, we'd reached our goal of having a winning season. That was true, because we were now 6–0. I liked the fact that he said that, and I hoped that people would remember to keep things in perspective and understand that beating Miami only counts as one win—not two or three. Equally important, we were now through with midterm exams, and I felt we would gain confidence and momentum in the weeks to follow.

Chris Zorich

One of the great moments was all of us holding up our helmets after the Miami game and telling each other we loved each other.

After the press conference I walked out and immediately saw my sister Vicki. She said, "I know this is going to be the year we win the national championship." I got absolutely furious. After a football game I'm tired and worn out, and the last thing I need to hear is someone talking national championship when all I'm worried about is the next ballgame.

I went home and spent a quiet evening with the family. Despite what my sister had said, I was already thinking about Air Force. Her remark kept coming back to me, and I can't tell you how many times that next week I was reminding people that I didn't think it was possible to win a national championship with only six victories.

In reflecting on the game, though, I did feel that for the first time we had proved we were capable of winning it all. For the first time I felt we might really pull this thing off. That wasn't the same as doing it, as I kept emphasizing to the players. But at least we had a chance, and that's all we could ask. We knew we had a long way to go, and we could only play one game a week, but if we were good enough to beat Michigan and Miami and the other teams we'd won against, then we were halfway home. We really and truly had a chance to accomplish something we would all remember long after the cheers faded.

Wes Pritchett, senior linebacker

I don't think anybody knew how good we were going to be, because we had lost a lot of players and didn't have a lot of experience. Everybody was eager to see how the unproven guys would perform. I think as the season progressed, we gained more and more confidence. And I think the turning point of the year definitely was when we beat Miami. That's when we really felt like we were going to win the national championship.

After looking at the film, I didn't feel we played consistently well on offense. There were still many things we needed to correct in practice. But the big question is: Where am I going to find the time? Little did I realize the demands on my time would become so much greater because of one victory over Miami.

The news media made a big deal about the one Miami turnover, but as I said before, I felt there were four others just as controversial that went the other way. It really bothered me when the story came out of Miami suggesting that someone had talked to one of the officials, who said he blew the call on the play at the goal line.

To be kind, I believe someone was misquoted. I won't allow myself to believe it was an out-and-out lie. Never once did I see the name of the official who supposedly said that, so I put no credence in it. Art Hyland, who handles our eastern independent officials, issued a statement after talking to all four officials who worked the game out of his office for the CIFOA (Collegiate Independents Football Officiating Association), including the official who was solely responsible for the call.

The statement said, in part, "In accordance with our longstanding policy, none of the four officials ever made such a comment, or have even talked to a reporter, coach, or any other person about that call or the game. Furthermore, the official who made the call has reviewed tape of the play and is still confident he made the correct call. Any other official who saw the ball dead prior to the fumble had an obligation to overrule the official who ruled the fumble. No official did so, nor was there even discussion at the time. It's unfortunate, and quite frankly, irresponsible, that the alleged quote of the CIFOA official was made public without confirmation. Prior to the release, I indicated to Miami reporters that no CIFOA official had made such a comment, nor could he, under our policies."

The bowl officials are here en masse now. I don't want to get involved in serious discussions with them, but I did sit down after the Miami game with Dick Rosenthal and Father Bill Beauchamp, the executive vice president of the university, and I said we would like to play the best opponent possible in the best situation possible, but that I really don't care to visit with the bowl people. I have great faith in Father Beauchamp and Dick.

My only concern is the University of Notre Dame's football team. They keep me apprised of the bowl situation on a regular basis, but I'm really not much interested. I've always said if you win enough games, the polls and the bowls take care of themselves.

When we had our Sunday squad meeting in Loftus, the first thing I did was to congratulate our team. I've never seen a team compete any better, be more positive, or play any harder. We have played better and we would have to in the future. But there were some areas in which I thought we excelled. Our defensive line and linebackers were outstanding. Jeff Alm has become an outstanding player, and Boo Williams is vastly underrated.

We knew they could throw the ball, and we were willing to concede a lot of yardage, but not four hundred yards. We said before the game that we must make Miami pay a price for throwing the ball as much as they do, and I think we did. We forced seven turnovers, and there wasn't one that was a gift. Every single one of them was accomplished by a fine play.

When I looked back at the film, there were two fumbles we could have had that were ruled incomplete passes—one by a receiver and another by Steve Walsh. However, we won the game, and that was our mandate.

We did commit two serious errors on defense, on fourth down and long plays, which they converted into touchdowns. Had we been able to avoid those two plays, I would have said it was an excellent performance by our defense. We were able to slow down the run, which we felt was of paramount importance.

Offensively, our line did not play as well as we would have liked. Yet I thought the effort was exceptional, considering the personnel changes and Miami's outstanding defense. We had three turnovers, and most of the time that many is disastrous, but we did overcome them. We did have a quarterback-center exchange problem, which we think should never happen in a football game. I think that's the first one we've had since I've been at Notre Dame, and it came at a most inopportune time.

Tony Yelovich, offensive line coach

When the season started, we found out that both Tim Ryan and Tim Grunhard were going to come on pretty well for us at guard. Mike Heldt played very consistently. We lost our guards in the Pitt game when Ryan and Grunhard got hurt, but we moved Mike Brennan in and moved Joe Allen inside. They had to pick up the slack. We were short on depth with our interior people.

The unique thing is that we were very young. Ryan was only a sophomore. Heldt turned nineteen the day of the Fiesta Bowl, so he played a national championship season at the age of eighteen. Their growth and maturity were so impressive.

As the season went along, we gained some continuity. Playing together is so important, learning how to play with the guy next to you. It's not like playing on an island. The center has to get a feel for the two guards next to him. I remember after the Miami game, Mike said, "Coach, it was a lot different with two new people in there." You get used to playing with people, and you know how they're going to react. Mike was hurt going into that game, but he knew the guys on either side of him had gone down. He said, "Let's pull together and let's do it." People like Andy Heck and Dean Brown did everything you could ask to help Brennan and Allen. That attitude just permeated everywhere through there.

You had a national championship potentially staring you in the face, but they didn't care who was in the way. They were going to do it. We had two starters out against Miami, but you didn't have time to think about it. We just looked at Brennan and Allen and said, "You guys have to do it." There was nothing to discuss, there was just work to do. I didn't have time as a coach to sit there and say, "Gee, I've got two guys in here at guard who haven't played before." They just had to do it. That's all there was to it. It was demanding as heck—it was a hard week.

We did the things we had to do in order to win. I don't feel we were fortunate to win, by any stretch of the imagination. After looking at the film, I know our football team deserved to win. I am sure Miami felt the same way, but that's football. It's trite, but beauty lies in the eyes of the beholder.

Chuck Heater, secondary coach

The odd thing about the Miami game was that for other than five minutes, we had control of it. We get ahead 21–7, and then for five minutes they dominated us, and now it's tied at halftime. We go out and knock them in the head pretty good in the third quarter. And the only touchdown they score in the second half comes after we fumble deep in our territory with three minutes left in the game.

Steve Walsh threw the ball fifty times for four-hundred-some yards, but we had a couple of busts. We broke coverage one time and gave them one touchdown. But we tried to tell our players that psychologically, as they ran off that field at halftime, the advantage was to Notre Dame because we had momentum, that Miami was as lucky as the day is long to be in that situation. We were the ones up 21–7, and they were fortunate to get back in it. There was no reason to feel bad about where we were. We were going to come out for the second half and do for the most part what we did in the first half, and we were going to beat these guys. We had to get our kids thinking the right way mentally at halftime. We didn't want our people thinking they were in trouble, that they could lose, that Miami had all the momentum.

Our kids came out the third quarter and just played super. But with a quarterback like Walsh and the great system they have, you have to understand they are going to get some yards and complete some passes. You aren't going to shut them out. They're going to move the chains some. We gave up 30 points, which isn't exactly what you want to do. But we were close to giving up just two touchdowns and maybe a couple of field goals.

Now, if you keep them to 18 or 20 points, you feel pretty good about the game. Later in the season, I don't think we would have given them any more than two touchdowns—maybe three at the most. Because we were a much better football team defensively at the end of the year. They were lucky to catch us when they did, in terms of our defense.

In order to beat Miami we had to play as a complete team. It is unfair to point out individuals, because I could just list our entire roster and I wouldn't be far wrong. Our defensive line really played well, our linebackers were outstanding, our secondary competed well, and the emotion overall on the defense was exceptional.

On offense it wasn't one of our better days. Tony Brooks ran as hard as he has all year. Ricky Watters made only one catch, but it was a key one, and Derek Brown made two critical catches when we were deep in our own territory.

Looking at the kicking game, I thought our punt team was adequate. Our kickoff coverage was excellent. Our PATs were okay. Our kickoff return was good, and the fake punt by Miami was stopped because of a great effort by one of our most valuable players all year, Corny Southall.

Nothing is as good or as bad as it seems, but somewhere in between, reality lies. This win couldn't be as good as it seemed. Regardless of what we are ranked or what people are saying about bowl games, we can't be concerned. We have no control over those things. All it can do is distract us.

When the ratings for the week came out we were second behind UCLA. The news media wanted my reaction to the fact that we beat Miami and we're number two. For some reason they labored under the misconception I thought we should have jumped to number one. I said, "Well, this is the final ranking, right?" And they said, "Oh, no, they vote again next week." I said, "Okay, as long as they're going to continue to vote, then I'm not real concerned about this week. Let me know when the final poll comes out, and that's the time I'm interested in hearing about it."

It's like having all your money bet on a horse and having it in second place at the halfway pole. You sure don't want to tear up your ticket to win, but going to the cashier to get your winnings isn't going to be very profitable, either. To even think about national rankings right now is ludicrous.

We've only won six football games. People ask me if this could be a national championship football team. I think this—if we win twelve games, we've got a chance. Six isn't enough. As a matter of fact I know of no football team that's ever won the championship by winning six games.

When Beano Cook predicted on ESPN before the Miami game that Notre Dame would win, Tim Brando said there was no way. Tim said if Notre Dame won, he'd sing the Notre Dame Victory March in front of our entire team. So Tim flew to South Bend on Thursday following the Miami game and came to practice and they shot a cute little segment for the Gameday show on Saturday.

The manager at the airport had given him a key chain that played the Victory March, so at least Tim could practice. I told Tim in front of the players that if I'd known this would happen, I wouldn't have been so excited about winning the game.

There was no reason to expect much—because if Tim wasn't smart enough to pick us to win, he certainly wasn't smart enough to learn the words. He held up a helmet while he sang, just like our players do after we win. He said to me, "Is this the way they hold up their helmets?" I said, "We do it with bigger arms."

I did say, somewhat seriously, I hoped it would be a heck of a long time before they picked against us again. The players got a kick out of the whole thing, and it was a nice ten-minute break at the start of practice.

Where are we at midseason? I don't know. Starting out the year, I felt we would be a better football team in '88 than '87, even though we had a lot of question marks and we were awfully young. I did know one thing—our defense impressed me in the spring and made a believer out of all of us.

We had a lot of concern going into the Michigan game, because we thought our defense and kicking game would have to carry us. Nonetheless, we did beat Michigan, and I think they've proven to be an exceptional football team. We went up to Michigan State to play on the road, and we found a way to win. Our defense carried us in both of those games.

We expected a difficult game against Purdue because they had given Washington everything it could handle. We were fortunate to play well against Purdue and win decisively. We got by Stanford, a team that lost to USC by four points in the last few minutes and lost by four points to Oregon.

We lost our two guards during the Pitt game, but we rose to the occasion and won that one, too. Coming back to play Miami, we thought we had a chance to win, but I don't think anybody else in the country gave us much of a chance, particularly certain members of the news media.

Now we're 6–0 and looking forward to Air Force. It's one challenge after another.

It has been a fun year to coach so far, even with the trials and tribulations. The season is only half over, but the players have done everything we've asked of them. It's not fair to evaluate the season now, other than to say, "We are where we want to be at the present time, but, boy, do we have a long way to go." I can't help but think of a saying I used all the time when I first came to Notre Dame.

> *We aren't where we should be*
> *We aren't where we are going to be*
> *We aren't where we ought to be*
> *But thank God we aren't where we used to be.*

20

AIR FORCE:
GETTING BACK ON THE GROUND

I wish we could dream about the Miami game for a while, but if we do, we will have a nightmare at Air Force.

I'm sure everyone enjoyed reading the papers Sunday morning after we beat Miami, but I hate to think what the headlines will be a week from now if we take Air Force for granted, because they are capable of beating us. We will play well and hard, but I don't know if it will be good enough. We're not well-disciplined enough right now to be a great team, and we still make too many mistakes to eliminate practice. Our goal is perfection, and while we are closer than we have ever been, we're not as sound fundamentally as we need to be. There's no way in the world we should be satisfied. We've got to put Miami behind us and become a better-disciplined football team.

This was the theme of my talk the week of Air Force, because I know the players want to be great. We have a chance to be. The thing that has really impressed me is that we're a team that wants to get better.

The atmosphere on campus this week will be completely different than it was the week before. Most of the students had already gone home or were in the process of leaving, since we were entering fall break and had no classes all week. I was really concerned about a letdown because the campus was desolate, except for a small number of people, and even they didn't want to put the Miami game behind us.

Air Force beat us four years in a row before I got here, so I don't believe the players will take them lightly. But if we don't have a good week of preparation, and if we aren't ready to play the game this week, then

Irish head coach Lou Holtz makes a point to his players on the field during one of Notre Dame's seven homefield wins in 1988.

Michael and Susan Bennett

Lou Holtz and the Fighting Irish sideline prepare to celebrate another Notre Dame score.

Michael and Susan Bennett

Michael and Susan Bennett

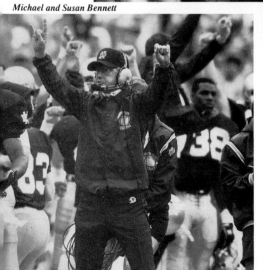

Irish coach Lou Holtz signals for a two-point conversion following Notre Dame's second touchdown in the 34–21 Irish victory over third-ranked West Virginia in the Fiesta Bowl.

Irish quarterback Tony Rice listens carefully to some words of wisdom from Lou Holtz.

University of Notre Dame 1988 National Champions

Action Sports of America

Freshman tight end Derek Brown's catch for a touchdown in Purdue game.

William Panzica

Braxston Banks heads for the end zone on a nine-yard scoring pass from Tony Rice that gave the Irish a 14–7 second-period lead in its win over defending national champion Miami.

Notre Dame players clasp hands as they receive final instructions before the opening kickoff against the USC Trojans.

The action on the Los Angeles Coliseum field captivates Lou Holtz's attention, as he and assistants Tony Yelovich and Mike Dossory keep their eyes riveted on Notre Dame's victory over USC.

Junior cornerback Stan Smagala sprints for the goal line on a second-period 64-yard interception return of a Rodney Peete pass that gave Notre Dame a 20–7 advantage in its win over USC.

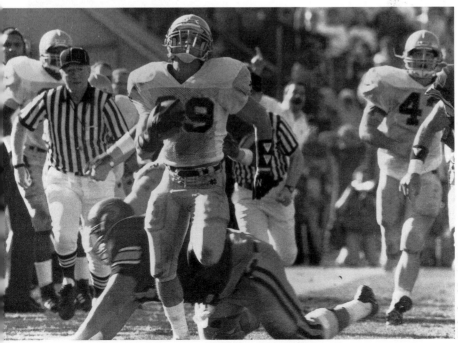

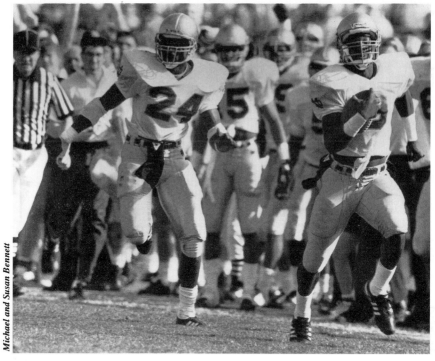

With tailback Mark Green keeping a lookout, quarterback Tony Rice races down the sideline on his way to a 65-yard touchdown run in the first period of Notre Dame's win at USC.

Senior linebacker Wes Pritchett (right) joins his teammates in raising their helmets in tribute to Irish fans in the Los Angeles Coliseum following top-ranked Notre Dame's 27–10 triumph over second-ranked USC in the regular-season finale.

Notre Dame coach Lou Holtz leads his Irish team in singing the Victory March in the locker room following its Fiesta Bowl triumph against West Virginia.

Irish captain and linebacker Ned Bolcar celebrates Notre Dame's '88 national crown as he's carried off the Sun Devil Stadium turf by his teammates.

President Ronald Reagan congratulates the Notre Dame football team on its '88 national championship on its visit to the White House on January 18, 1989. To Reagan's left are '88 Irish captain Ned Bolcar, University President Rev. Edward A. Malloy, C.S.C. and coach Lou Holtz. To Reagan's right are Vice-President-elect Dan Quayle and linebacker Wes Pritchett, who holds the box containing George Gipp's letter sweater that was presented to the outgoing president.

we don't deserve to wear the Notre Dame helmet. I feel that strongly about it.

I didn't need Sherlock Holmes to tell me Air Force is outstanding. Even before I put on the film of this year's team, I knew they would be well-coached and would execute very well, especially in running the option. People try to tag us as an option team, but we're novices compared to Air Force, which does it for a living. They have such incredible statistics this year, but then again, they do every year. The last time they were outgained was in 1945, by George Patton and his Third Army.

However, in keeping up with their scores during the course of the season, I noticed they had given up an awful lot of points. In fact, they won Saturday over Utah, 56–49, despite giving up an incredible number of passing yards. They'd given up at least 23 points in every game, so I felt it would be especially important to play well offensively.

Because there were no classes, we had a lot of meeting time with the players, and that's always good when you are playing against the option, because you have to outexecute them. We're going from facing a Miami team that throws the ball as well as anyone in the country to facing Air Force, which runs it as well as anyone in the country. If there is a plus about having the students gone, it's that we'll have the players' complete attention. We won't have to worry about everyone in the dorms telling them how great they are after beating Miami. Our assistant coaches will make sure everybody gets their feet back on the ground rather quickly.

All three of the military academies run the wishbone because it doesn't place an emphasis on personnel as much as on execution. You win in football and life because you execute, and the service academies all have such tremendous built-in discipline that it's the perfect attack for them. The wishbone can really create some problems for you, even though you may be bigger and stronger, because the team employing it can control the football and consequently the game. The wishbone is the most difficult offense to defense.

Air Force runs the option without paying the price. They don't turn the ball over very often and seldom make an error or a mistake. When you play the wishbone, the most disciplined team is going to be the most successful. Your best chance to win is to get ahead, as it is not a good offense to play catch-up.

Ned Bolcar, senior linebacker
Coach Holtz would tell us that we would have a half-day practice today. We were all excited until he said it would be a half day, eight in the morning until eight at night.

To win, we have to outexecute Air Force. It has nothing to do with talent. If you're going to look at personnel, there is no question we have better talent. But don't labor under the misconception Air Force doesn't have talent. I think this will be the biggest challenge we've had from them since I've been at Notre Dame. Overall, it's the best Air Force team I've seen.

Dee Dowis had a lot of success against us out there last year, and he had two runs of over fifty yards. He has great quickness and he runs the option as well as anybody. Defensively, they've given up some points, as I've said, but most of them came through the air. We're not a team that throws forty passes a game, and I don't believe we intend to do that this week. That would play right into their hands. We never seem to have success when we go into games trying to establish the pass. I know we'll have to throw the ball some—we're just not a team that lives with the pass.

To our credit, we probably have a much better understanding of the wishbone than the average coaching staff, since we run the wishbone occasionally ourselves. We don't know everything there is to know about it, but we know enough to be scared. Sometimes I wish we didn't know how dangerous that sucker can be. Sometimes ignorance is happiness.

Against the wishbone, you have to say you're going to concede certain amounts of yardage to the fullback, or the halfback, or the quarterback, or the pass, and then you have to minimize the damage. You aren't in the wishbone very long if you don't have a great quarterback who can execute it. Either that or you aren't in coaching very long.

Life is a trade-off between positives and negatives. Our students aren't around to tell our athletes how good they are, and we did have more time to practice and meet with the players. But their absence meant there was a general lack of enthusiasm on campus. In addition, I felt many of our freshmen might start to get homesick, since many of their friends had gone home and they would have more free time.

Our injury situation at guard is better this week, although it may never be completely resolved this year. Tim Grunhard probably will fight the ankle problem the rest of the year, unless we can find a way to give him two or three weeks off, which isn't very feasible. We have the same situation at fullback with Anthony Johnson and Braxston Banks, but we've been fortunate that a freshman, Rodney Culver, has been able to help us there.

Considering the intensity and hard hitting in the Miami game, we came out of it very well in terms of injuries. Wes Pritchett did break a bone in his hand, but he put some tape on it and played most of the game. This really impressed some of our younger players. We would never have allowed him to play had we known it was broken or if it jeopardized his future.

I had been kidding the players about an all-American at Minnesota named Pug Lund. He had a little finger that was bothering him when he carried the ball back in 1934, so he asked the doctor to cut it off. I've been telling the players Wes is related to Pug Lund. I guess we'll call Wes Pug Pritchett.

The basic schedule we set up for the week started with breakfast at eight o'clock. The next three hours would be devoted to academics. They were either tutored or attended study hall. That give us a chance to meet as a staff in the mornings and get the gameplan finalized. We met at one o'clock on the kicking game and then we had individual meetings before we went on the field. We were able to finish up a little earlier than usual, with the extra time available, and this enabled us to meet once again after dinner, which we never do when school is in session.

Naturally there were all kinds of interviews and phone calls this week. But it seemed like most of the attention was focused on the Miami game or looking ahead to Penn State or USC. There weren't as many questions about Air Force as I had anticipated. I was pleased with our practices and thought we improved in many areas. One thing was obvious: we were much more confident than before we played Miami. We had our normal Quarterback Club luncheon Friday, but it was very subdued compared to the excitement that we'd seen the previous week. On Saturday the stadium was as full as it always is, but our students weren't out in force the way they normally are. Considering we only have 9,000 students at the games, it's amazing the atmosphere they create. On the other hand, if the students aren't exceptionally excited about the game—as they certainly had been for Miami—then it feels as if there are more spectators in the stands than fans.

Since it's so difficult to get tickets to our games, the contributing alumni have to apply for seats for individual games, and if the demand is greater than the supply, which it always is, the tickets are distributed by lottery. That means many of the 20,000 contributing alumni in the stands may be there for just that one game. They come to watch as spectators, and that's different from our students, who are there every week and qualify as fans. The word "fan" comes from fanatical, and this certainly describes our students. They never sit down during the game, and they create an atmosphere that is second to none.

If we win the toss of the coin to start the game, we prefer to defer our option until the second half. The team that kicks off to start the game will score first seventy percent of the time. We prefer to have the defense start out and establish a tempo for the game, but that doesn't always happen.

THE GAME

SOUTH BEND—Most every Monday morning quarterback in the country had Notre Dame pegged for a letdown against Air Force coming off its triumph over top-rated Miami.

But, if this counts as a letdown, then the rest of Notre Dame's '88 opponents better beware when the Irish get their game back in high gear again.

Their 41–13 win over the Falcons may not have been as emotional or artistic as the events of a week ago on this same field. Nonetheless, Lou Holtz's second-ranked Irish were absolutely outstanding in the second half. They strung together three touchdown passes after intermission and controlled the leading rushing attack in the nation in disposing of the Falcons.

Was Holtz disappointed?

"We won the football game and that's what we wanted. I thought we played very well the second half. We fought for our lives in the first half. At halftime, this was a real football game. But I was impressed with our team the second half."

Air Force had cut the Irish lead to 20–13 at halftime—prompting a few words in the locker room from several Irish players. Whatever their tone, they worked. The Falcons managed only 29 rushing yards in 18 carries the second half—but in fairness to the cadets they were forced to play catch-up. Nevertheless Notre Dame was pleased with its performance against the number-one rushing attack in America with its 432-yard average. Possession time after halftime read 18:10 for Notre Dame to 11:50 for Air Force.

Overall, the Falcons managed 170 rushing yards—44 from the ever dangerous quarterback Dee Dowis. The Notre Dame defense had to make an abrupt change in its strategy after defensing Miami's pass-oriented offense the previous Saturday.

"We had to go back out there in the second half and make something happen," said Air Force coach Fisher DeBerry. "If we could have stopped them and gotten the football, it would have given our team the confidence and momentum it needed."

But that simply didn't happen. Taking the second-half kickoff, Notre Dame ran off eight straight running plays—only one of them netting a gain of more than five yards. Then Tony Rice flipped a flare to the left to

Tony Brooks, who weaved his way 42 yards down the sideline for a 27–13 lead.

After an exchange of punts, the Falcons gambled and lost in an attempt to get back within striking range. On fourth and two at the Notre Dame 34, Michael Stonebraker and Chris Zorich stopped Andy Smith after only a yard. On the fourth play for the Irish, Rice pitched to Steve Belles, who fired 50 yards downfield to Ricky Watters for a 34–13 edge.

Air Force's next two possessions produced a net of minus-eight yards—with a 29-yard punt putting the Irish in position at the Falcon 43. Notre Dame again ran off eight straight running plays, then Rice threw 28 yards to Watters for the final points of the day.

Watters fumbled a punt on his own 37, which Air Force recovered, but the Falcons couldn't take advantage of it. After first and goal at the nine, Air Force was stopped on three runs, and a fourth-down pass from the 15 was broken up by George Streeter.

"Once their defense got into the flow of our offense, they got their rhythm back," said DeBerry. "The defense might be the unsung hero of this team."

Neither team had managed to establish any particular superiority in the first half. Air Force moved the football well on its first drive, only to reach the Irish 18 and have Albert Booker fumble the football to Notre Dame. A great hit by Stan Smagala created a Pat Terrell recovery. The Irish punted the ball and Air Force came right back with a 42-yard, eight-play drive for a Steve Yarbrough field goal. Most of the damage came on Dee Dowis's 22-yard run on first down. Notre Dame promptly answered the challenge with a 71-yard possession of its own. The Irish kept it exclusively on the ground for 11 plays, with Mark Green taking a pitch to the right for seven yards and a 7–3 lead.

After another Yarbrough field goal made it 7–6 to cap a 41-yard march, Notre Dame put together its own 71-yard scoring drive. Rice threw once to Watters, who made a spectacular 22-yard grab, and then staved off trouble with a third-down toss to Derek Brown for 10. Rice—who broke Joe Theismann's single-season rushing record during the contest—got the touchdown himself from four yards out for a 14–6 advantage with 5:55 remaining in the second period.

Buoyed by a 36-yard Watters punt return, the Irish needed but four plays to make it 20–6—with Tony Brooks motoring 27 yards on first down (on his way to a game-high 85-yard day) and Anthony Johnson going 10 yards for the score. But a 60-yard kickoff return by Anthony Roberson set up a 26-yard Air Force drive. Smith's three-yard run at the 44-second mark cut the margin to seven points.

That prompted some interesting thoughts at halftime.

"I did some screaming," said Wes Pritchett, a fifth-year senior. "I told them we had come too far and worked too hard all winter, all summer, to let it slip away today."

Thanks to a second half more befitting a 7–0 team, it didn't.

We kicked off and Air Force returned it to about the 40, which was one of the better returns against us all year. Air Force then proceeded to move it very methodically down the field to our 18 yardline. Our defense stiffened and we got a great hit by Stan Smagala that created a turnover and set the pace for the game.

Offensively, we played very conservatively. We were bigger and stronger than they were up front, and we wanted to make it a physical game. We knew we would have to play sixty minutes against them, but in all honesty, Air Force's team was better on defense than I had anticipated. We played a respectable first half, but the game was far from over.

We didn't play badly in the first half, but Air Force had managed to move the ball with some degree of success. We made a little adjustment at halftime on defense that paid dividends the second half, but the main thing we did was reshape our attitude. Some things were said in the locker room at the half by the players, mainly about not letting anything slip away at this point. Our coaches were very calm, but I think the players sensed that we hadn't approached perfection, which was really our goal.

In the second half we played awfully well. We held Air Force to about thirty rushing yards in the last two quarters, and we controlled their passing game. We scored on three big plays in the second half, all of them passes. Tony Rice threw once to Ricky Watters, once to Tony Brooks on a flare pass, and Steve Belles threw another long one to Watters off a pitch. It was exceptionally disappointing that we couldn't run the ball consistently against Air Force, but give them credit.

We did a nice job defensively the last thirty minutes. Air Force got down to our 34 once, but Michael Stonebreaker and Chris Zorich stopped them on fourth down. Even when we fumbled a punt late and they had first and goal, we kept them off the board. It was a most impressive second half by our defense.

We went on to control the football game and win it rather decisively, 41–13. But the score was not indicative of how well Air Force had played us.

The Air Force contest was the game that all my high-school friends chose to come visit us. There were eight of us who ran around in high school and were and are close. Six of them came back for the weekend and the game.

I don't get a chance to visit with people much before a game, and I'm not really one to do a lot of socializing after a game. But I did get a chance to sit down and visit with my buddies, and we had a great time. Even though it had been thirty-five years since we went to school together, you could tell there was still a good feeling among us. We would do anything for each other, and that is what life is all about. Out of the seven who showed up, there were two who had their Ph.D.s, one in chemistry and one in math. One is a teacher in high school. One is a pharmacist. One holds a very prominent position with Chrysler. One is head of a radio station—plus me.

One of the highlights of the game was the halfback pass Steve Belles threw to Ricky Watters for a touchdown. We had put in this play for Michigan State six weeks ago but had never used it. It became a natural when we moved Steve to tailback in order to help with depth at that position. Steve has a natural knack for finding the hole and he's a good north-south runner. The play really wasn't that open, but Ricky made a great catch. My daughter Liz plays for her dorm football team and she had told me to put the play in that week, as their team ran it and it was always open. Naturally when we ran it she took the credit, and I was happy to give it to her.

When the polls came out on Monday we stayed number two, with UCLA number one. If we kept winning, it was inevitable that we would have a chance to move up to number one. I didn't care to have that happen, but the only other option was for us to lose and move down, and that is bad luck. So the only choice we have is to keep winning on Saturdays, and go back and reload.

21

NAVY:
GOING THROUGH THE MOTIONS

I felt good about going to play Navy. We had beaten them decisively last year, and while I knew they would be much improved, I thought we were in a rhythm. They had a nice quarterback named Alton Grizzard, and I knew they would be tough and well-disciplined, the way all the academy teams are. But it was a neat little challenge for us to go back on the road and play the Naval Academy after two weeks in a row at home.

Navy had given up more than 50 points to Pittsburgh the week before, which I hadn't expected, and I am sure Navy hadn't expected, either. I thought Pitt would win, but not by that wide a margin. It's tough playing a team coming off a bad loss, because they feel like they've got something to prove. They could make their season and ruin ours by beating Notre Dame.

I talked to the squad about the Naval Academy and told them we should win the football game because we're a better team. We had studied the history of the series and knew we had had a lot of trouble with Navy over the years, even though we hadn't lost to them since 1963. I remember one year at the Meadowlands in the early eighties. John Carney had to kick a field goal right at the end to win the game by one point, when Tim Brown was a freshman. You didn't need to understand nuclear physics to realize that we had come too far to falter now.

Navy will be similar to Air Force in a number of respects, although maybe not as quick. No doubt Navy was bigger and stronger physically than Air Force. I guess a ship can hold bigger men than the cockpit of an airplane. Grizzard ran the option well against us last year as a freshman, and Navy has a transfer at quarterback named Gary McIntosh, who has a very strong arm, throws well, and is an excellent athlete.

Statistically, over the whole season, Navy has done some impressive things. Pitt beat them decisively by making a lot of big plays, and we can't count on this. We have more of a plow-horse offense, though we've been productive. Two years ago against Navy in Baltimore we were outplayed in the second half. People think I'm in need of psychiatric help when they hear me say we could lose if we don't play well. They assume we will win by five touchdowns. But you never know what to expect on the road, and I'm not sure how our team will respond.

Our football team is different each and every day. Each week you have to look at your injuries, your attitude, your challenges. You evaluate the current situation and go from there. You cannot say how you are going to handle something two weeks from now. You can't even say necessarily how you are going to handle a football squad tomorrow. You just play it day by day. You go by your gut feelings and speak from the heart. You stick to your beliefs and principles, and you have to understand what you want from your team and your coaches. But you can't predict whether you need to work the team exceptionally hard or whether you need to back off on a particular day. You can't say whether they need a pat on the back or a kick in the tail on a given day. If anybody saw us practice Monday, I think they would have come to the conclusion that we respect Navy and weren't taking anything for granted.

When you win, you have as many problems as when you lose. They are just different problems. You have a player who isn't playing enough. This player isn't getting his picture in the newspaper enough. This player is depressed. This player is getting pressure from home about his performance. That is why it is important that everyone understand their role and accept it. The Notre Dame team comes first. You try to bring it all together, and you can sense the emotional complexity when you deal with the squad. Despite all these decisions, I think you've got to have a respect for your opponent every week, or your players won't respect them and disaster will strike.

Flash Gordon, senior defensive end

My first visit with Coach Holtz about not playing in the Miami and Air Force games came when I went to his office to speak to him. I didn't play a down in either of those two games. He said he wasn't aware of that because he was down with the offense.

He went about it the right way. He sat me down in his office. He listened to my problem and tried to solve it. He brought my position coach in. He brought the defensive coordinator in and we sat down and talked about the entire situation. He was fair with everyone. He didn't take sides with the coaches, and he didn't take sides with me, either. He was just fair about the whole situation. I think that was important, just to show that he cares as much about us as he does the staff.

I was impressed by that—bringing those coaches in and asking them, "Why isn't Flash playing?" He brought out the grading sheets and observed those to make sure everything was going well when I did play. Then, after he observed those notes, he said, "Flash, we're going to get you back in there." I really didn't know why I wasn't playing in the first place. I thought I was playing pretty well. But Coach went about it in the right way.

After I left the office, he spoke with the other coaches, and I really don't know what they talked about. But he was concerned about my welfare, and he was going to be fair about it. That really impressed me.

Everyone thinks your job is easy when you win, and that's not true. I'll take winning over losing, but that doesn't mean we don't have to deal with complex problems.

Football teams start out the year going in a direction. By the middle of the year they change—not always for the better. I don't think attitude or morale are necessarily good just because you're winning. I think attitude and morale are good when players feel they are getting better. The minute you stop getting better on the practice field, your morale and attitude are going to go down.

The worst attitude I think I ever had on a football team was one year when we were 6–0. As coaches all we were trying to do was to keep people from getting injured, because we didn't have a lot of depth. Consequently, we didn't practice with great intensity. Eventually we lost because we weren't all on the same page.

After the loss, we went out there on Monday with an attitude of "A guy who won't do it isn't a bit better than one who can't." We forgot about who was supposed to have talent, and looked for people who were willing to work and improve fundamentally. It was a brutal week working on fundamentals but by the end of it the attitude was the best I had seen for a while, and we did nothing but get better the rest of the year.

Going into the Navy game we felt it was important to sit down with our football team in the middle of the year and go over our notes from that first squad meeting in the middle of August. We reviewed some of our expectations as well as our performances. We had to make sure we got back to basics, and to make sure everyone was on the same page.

We have to keep getting better. How do we do that? One thing we have done virtually every week—though we did not do it last week and we may not this week, because of injuries—is to go first team against first team in practice. We feel it's absolutely essential to spend twenty-five minutes or a half-hour working your top offense against the top defense. You don't scrimmage and you don't tackle, but everything else is live. We get a great look every week from our scout team, or the Kodak team, as I call them. We call them the Kodak team because they should give you a good picture every time.

A member of the news media asked me if there's anything we can do to try to become number one, or do we have to hope UCLA loses a game along the way? Being number one is completely out of my hands. That's like asking how much my wife is going to spend when she goes shopping. I have no control. She has her Ph.D. in shopping, so it's something I can't worry about. There was a saying a long time ago, "May God give me the courage to change the things I can, the serenity to accept the things I cannot change, and the wisdom to know the difference between the two." All we can try to do right now is be 8-0 when the weekend is over.

We don't talk about being number two or number one or number eight. What we talk about is getting better. That's what we can control. We can't control where they vote us in the polls. All we want to do is become 8-0. If we're 8-0, then let's reload and let's try to go 9-0.

When I put on the film of Navy, I was amazed to find out Pitt had punted the ball seven times last week. That told me that though Navy gave up some big plays, they were also capable of playing very well defensively. Anytime you force seven punts, your defense has done some good things. The wishbone once again gave us some concern, though we did have an advantage from having played against it the week before. So we would have a lot of carryover and wouldn't have to change our defensive gameplan much.

On the negative side, the Midshipmen would know exactly how we would try to defend them after watching us play Air Force. Some coaches, when they're preparing for a game they should win, will approach it differently. But we'll use the same approach we used with Miami or anyone else. This was one of the longest weeks we put in.

I got an indication that Tuesday wasn't going to be a very good day when I found out that five of our starters wouldn't be at practice because of academic counseling. I didn't receive the information on three of them until just before the start of practice, and that didn't put me in a particularly good mood. I have nothing but admiration for the University of Notre Dame, and academics is far more important than a single football game. But when we had devoted each morning to academics the whole

219

week before, I did not see how we could run into these kind of problems just forty-eight hours after school had resumed.

It seemed like every time the phone rang there was more bad news. So much for feeling great when you're 7–0 and ranked second in the country. Tony Rice has to do some community service and consequently is going to miss practice. Tony Brooks has a make-up exam, and Ricky Watters is studying for an architecture exam. Our players have to learn that academics here are something to be taken care of time after time and day after day. If they can't handle both academics and football, we will eliminate one of their priorities—and that means no more football for them.

Sometimes I wonder how we're handling success. That's as important as anything right now. I told the team Tuesday something I don't tell many people. I am exceptionally proud of my mother and father. My father died in 1977, and he was a hard-working man who had many great qualities that influenced me.

When I first went to college at Kent State, I only had one shirt, one pair of pants, and a windbreaker. I didn't know if I would make it through the winter. As a matter of fact, I almost died my freshman year with strep throat and pneumonia.

My father had been driving the bus for the Catholic schools in town, and he did a good job. The bus company in East Liverpool had gone out of business because C. A. Smith, a multimillionaire, died and his heirs did not want to run the company and there were no buyers. They asked my father if he would be interested in picking up some of the routes. Well, he was smart enough to pick up the ones that would do well and to decline the ones that wouldn't. Business went well, and by the time I was a junior, I was driving a '56 Buick Riviera and I had more money in my pocket than I ever had before. Unfortunately, my father changed in some ways; like so many others, he had a hard time handling success. Successful people think they become invincible and invulnerable. I'm not sure what happened, but a year later my father was bankrupt. The money was all gone and our family was all alone.

So, as I told the squad, I've seen what happens when you don't handle success the right way. Right now I don't like the way we're handling it.

If we think that because we win a few football games, we can let our academics slide, forget our priorities in life, or that we are more important than someone else, we have serious problems.

Next, I read an article where one of our players said he really didn't start believing in what we were doing until after we beat Alabama last year. I don't ever want to hear that. I told our players, "Either you believe what we're doing completely or you find another school or another sport.

If you aren't a believer, we don't want you around, and we'll close ranks and march on."

Wednesday wasn't a very good practice, either, and we had a couple of other players miss because of make-up exams. It was the same on Thursday.

Maybe our week's preparation wasn't exactly what we wanted, but I first must look at myself and the attitude I had toward the football game. When you play a team you think you should beat, you have a tendency to be a little tougher on the players than normal. I was a little tired and irritated, and I didn't like the continuity of our practices at all during the week.

We played in Baltimore two years, and one of the things I remember about that game against Navy was that it came after an open date and we played a tremendous first half and led 28–0. We took the second-half kickoff, drove to Navy's 2-yard line, and ended up settling for a field goal. I think the game ended 33–14. In other words, we did not play very well in the second half. Consequently I had some trepidation this year, although overall I thought our defense would be very, very solid and that our players would rise to the occasion.

We had scheduled what I thought would be a typical Friday. We met at twelve noon, had lunch at twelve-fifteen, and at one got ready to fly to Baltimore. When we travel on Friday, I like to arrive at the game site at approximately four-thirty to five P.M. That way we can get checked in, have dinner, and go through our normal routine that evening.

This time we were informed that there was no reason to go to the airport for our scheduled one o'clock departure because the plane that was supposed to be ready hadn't been able to leave Minneapolis. So instead, we had another brief meeting, turned the players loose for a bit, and didn't go to the airport until about three-thirty. The plane did not arrive for us, this time because of a problem back in Minneapolis with the brakes. We went back to campus, had dinner at the North Dining Hall, and ended up leaving at seven P.M.

With the hour's time difference, it was well after eleven P.M. before we arrived at the hotel in Baltimore. We'd spent over ten hours trying to get there, and no one was very happy about this, especially me. There was good reason to be irritable. Many of the players who lived on the east coast were looking forward to seeing their parents, who had been waiting for six hours. But this wasn't possible.

We normally have dinner at six the night before a game. Then at seven we have a movie on the road. We tell the players they can bring their pillows and just relax, and we get popcorn and soft drinks. We have a short meeting at nine, then we show the players Captain Video, which is highlights from the game the previous week and the highlights and best hits from the game against that same opponent a year ago. At nine-thirty I visit with them and we have our relaxation period. At about ten we have a snack, then go to bed. In the morning we have our pregame meal and our mass, which is the last thing we do before leaving for the stadium.

Well, this time there was no movie. There was no meeting. There was no relaxation period. There was no dinner, and even the snack was cold, since we got there late. We have a rule that says we wear coats and ties onto the bus and off the bus, into the hotel and out of the hotel, into the stadium and out of the stadium, into the plane and out of the plane. But by the time we finally got to Baltimore that night, we looked like anything but a Notre Dame football team. Little did I realize at that time that we wouldn't look like a Notre Dame football team the next day, either.

We went to the stadium and immediately found out we couldn't warm up when we normally do because the Midshipmen were going to march into the stadium, as was their custom. That was fine, because that's all part of the tradition and we were Navy's guests. However, the Midshipmen arrived late, as their buses took a long time to get to the stadium. It was a perfect example of Murphy's Law. It was nobody's fault in particular, it was just one of those trips where nothing goes right.

THE GAME

BALTIMORE—There were a half-dozen dropped passes, a couple of lost fumbles, 90 yards in penalties, a pair of missed extra points and a 10-yard punt that set up a Navy touchdown.

No, it was anything but a performance to remember for Notre Dame in its 22–7 victory over an outmanned but not outfought Midshipman brigade in Memorial Stadium.

Yet for their trouble, the Irish are almost sure to become the new number-one team, following a UCLA loss to Washington State. That turned out to be the ultimate irony for Irish coach Lou Holtz, who wasn't impressed with his football team for the first time in 1988.

"People will say, 'Hey, it's a win.' But let me tell you something. We've got a lot of serious problems. We're not a very good football team right now," said Holtz.

Notre Dame's head coach might have used an available excuse. His team seemed as out of sync on the field as travel plans had been the day before when flight problems kept the team from arriving in Baltimore until eleven o'clock Friday night.

Even so, the early moments of the contest didn't suggest any of this. Middie quarterback Gary McIntosh fumbled on the second play from scrimmage, and Jeff Alm recovered for the Irish. It took six plays for Notre Dame to get onto the board, with a 10-yard Tony Rice–to–Derek Brown pass doing the job for a 7–0 lead.

From this point on, the Navy defense, which was vastly underestimated, controlled the line of scrimmage. The Irish had used nine plays to drive methodically from their own 22 to the Navy 45 on their second possession, only to lose the ball when a Rice pitch to Tony Brooks went astray. From there, Notre Dame went with its second unit and decided to throw the football, doing that on seven of its next eight plays. However, after getting a couple of first downs the drive ended without a score when Kent Graham threw an interception.

The next time Notre Dame got the ball, the first unit with Tony Rice at quarterback returned to the field and the ground game got rolling again. Five of the next six plays—all rushes—produced seven or more yards. Finally, Rodney Culver broke three different tackles in plowing the last 22 for a 13–0 edge. Reggie Ho's PAT went right.

The Irish got the ball back one more time before the end of the half. With Rice connecting with Anthony Johnson for consecutive gainers of 19 and 13 yards, Notre Dame got as far as the 12 before Ho booted a 29-yard field goal. That made it 16–0, predominantly because Notre Dame's defense was outstanding the first half. They held Navy without a first down until the second period and gave up only two the first half. The Middies' grand total of 46 yards in total offense in the half was a tribute to the fine play of the defensive unit.

Notre Dame took command on the first drive of the third period, using seven straight running plays for a 67-yard touchdown drive. Rice, Johnson, Brooks, and Mark Green all had gains of 10 or more, and Ryan Mihalko bulled over the final yard. That made it 22–0 when Brooks couldn't get it in on the two-point attempt.

From there, the Navy defense dominated the game. Notre Dame didn't get a first down on any of its next three possessions, which is highly unusual, and when they did finally get on track and moved the ball, they fumbled it away on the Navy 31.

In between, Navy had managed a touchdown on a 22-yard Alton Grizzard run to finish off a 33-yard, five-play drive. This touchdown drive came after Notre Dame punted the ball 10 yards.

The Middies came close to making it a bit more exciting until turning the ball over on downs at the Irish 30 with seven minutes to go. Deric Sims came ever so close to gaining the necessary two yards on fourth down, but the officials gave it to Notre Dame and effectively ended any hopes for Navy.

Tony Rice finished with 88 rushing yards, the largest chunk of Notre Dame's 267. The Irish limited Navy to only one pass completion and a grand total of 192 yards. Still, it didn't go down as one of Notre Dame's smoother all-around performances.

"We were not mentally alert, and that's no one's responsibility but mine," Holtz said.

"Fortunately, our defense was ready to compete and really played well, because every time we tried to get something going on offense we had a penalty or some other self-inflicted wound. We didn't have any kind of continuity. But let's give the Midshipmen a great deal of credit for our problems."

Continuity or no continuity, The Irish are going to be number one.

On the first play from scrimmage our defense made a great play and forced a fumble and Jeff Alm recovered at their 27. We struggled to get a couple of first downs, and then Tony Rice made a terrific play to hit Derek Brown for a touchdown. All of a sudden we're up 7–0.

Our next possession ended when we fumbled away a pitch, and I could sense we weren't very sharp. On our next series we threw three straight incompletions and had to punt. We put Kent Graham in the next series and he threw six passes. But once again we were forced to punt. Tony Rice went back in the next series, and we kept it on the ground and went 68 yards for a touchdown. Rodney Culver covered the last 25 yards on an excellent run. However, we missed an extra point for the fifth time this year.

Then, on the last drive of the half, we made it down to Navy's 12 and Reggie Ho kicked a 29-yard field goal as time ran out. We had outgained Navy 231 to 46 in the first half, but we weren't sharp or playing as a team. Thank goodness our defense was excellent. Navy didn't get a first down in the first period, and they got only two in the entire first half. Our defense had carried us.

We didn't play particularly well, but at halftime it was 16–0. We could tell there was something missing, and we certainly didn't find it in the second half.

Anthony Johnson, Mark Green, Tony Brooks, and Tony Rice all made nice runs on our first possession in the third period. Ryan Mihalko scored from a yard out to make it 22–0 early in the third quarter. We made only four first downs the rest of the way. We won the game 22–7, but I certainly wasn't pleased. In the locker room I don't think the players were happy, either. But, then again, I didn't take a poll.

I don't think I've ever been as frustrated after a win as I was then, and I'm afraid I showed it. We won, but we didn't come close to our standard, which was excellence. I certainly didn't want to take anything away from Navy, because they played their hearts out, which had something to do with our performance. But we had a commitment to be as good as we possibly could be, and we weren't, and everyone knew it. I did not use profanity or downgrade anyone personally. But as a total football team, we had fallen below our expectations, and we'd worked too hard to have this happen. Anytime you don't do the best you're capable of, you're cheating yourself. We had plenty of excuses for not playing well, with our travel problems. But the fact remains that we did not play well, and we could not live with that.

I wish I could say it was the football players' fault. But I think it was mine, because in many respects I didn't provide the right leadership. I wasn't mentally prepared for the game, and I didn't do a good job during the course of the game. Fortunately, no one evaluated my performance during the week, because I wouldn't have graded out well.

Our performance was very disappointing to all of us. We showered, dressed, got back on the buses and flew home. I couldn't help but think of a quote I heard, "Aggressive teams don't show up, they just lick themselves like a lion does." By this standard we stayed in the shower until we were waterlogged.

Ironically, we found out, after getting off the plane back in South Bend, that UCLA had been beaten at home by Washington State. That meant we probably would be elevated to number one in the polls after playing our worst football game of the season.

It was humbling. I would hate to guess what my spirits would be like after a loss.

The sun did come up the morning after the Navy game. I hadn't been sure it would after the way things went Saturday. I was in a much better mood Sunday after staying up most of the night looking at the Navy film and spending a great deal of time talking to the coaches the next morning. Our coaches are such positive people, and when the bank asks me to list my assets prior to issuing me a loan, I always start by listing our assistant coaches.

I'm still upset with our attitude on Saturday. However, it would be unfair to complain about our effort, especially on defense. The secondary—George Streeter, Corny Southall, Patrick Terrell, Todd Lyght, Stan Smagala—played very well. George Williams played exceptionally well, and Wes Pritchett improved and stayed on his feet. Jeff Alm and Chris Zorich continue to amaze me. On offense, Andy Heck and Mark Green were outstanding, as you would expect, and Derek Brown made some excellent plays. Kent Graham played well, but Tony Rice was awesome. I've never been around a competitor like him. He is a winner.

But the bad things far outweighed the positive things, and we did some things that were disastrous. We had two turnovers on first down after we'd driven to their 35, seven penalties for 90 yards, and I didn't help our team during the game. It's as poor a coaching job as I've done in eight years. We were impatient and very inconsistent, and these two items must be corrected.

We now control our own destiny, because UCLA lost and in all probability we will be elevated to number one in the polls. This means that if we win the rest of our games, there shouldn't be any question about who finishes on top. That was not true before today.

While we will probably be number one, I will not vote us in the top ten based on Saturday's performance. USC, Arkansas, and West Virginia are still unbeaten, too, and we know Michigan and Miami are fine teams.

But if we get our act together now, we've got a chance. Before UCLA lost, we could have won the rest of the way and still been second.

When I talked to the squad on Sunday afternoon, I was blunt:

"I'm worried about this football team and its attitude. There's something that isn't right with this team. If there are some people interested in transferring, some people who aren't happy about how much they're playing, let's get it resolved. We should never feel bad after a win, and maybe we ought to enjoy it, because it may be our last. If we don't make some changes inside of ourselves, we will live to regret it.

"We're going back to basics. There are going to be some personnel changes, and there are some things you better understand.

"One, the team is more important than the individual. You have to subjugate your welfare for the sake of the team.

"Two, consistency is more important than greatness. I don't care how great a player can be. I want to know what to expect from you day to day.

"Three, it's a privilege to represent Notre Dame.

"Four, it's ability that determines your capability, but your attitude that dictates your performance.

"Five, we're going to select intelligent players who know what they're doing.

"Six, an individual who won't do it is no better than one who can't.

"Seven, we're lacking in certain areas, and even though we've come a long way, we have a long way to go. We definitely have some reasons to change some personnel.

"I feel we're fixing to have the same thing happen to us that happened last year when we lost our last three games, and I'll be darned if we're going to let that happen again without doing something about it.

"There are certain players on this team who have earned the right to speak up, and I'm going to give them the opportunity to do so."

Here's what some of them said:

George Streeter: "I had a chance to win some things when I was in high school, but we never did. We always fell apart and somebody got selfish. I'll tell you one thing, no matter what anybody else thinks, I am going to go out of here a winner."

Frank Stams: "When I was a freshman here, we had a lot of guys on this team who play on Sundays, people like Steve Beuerlein and Allen Pinkett. We had some talent, but something was always missing. There's a fine line to cross to be great. And we've got to get better if we're going to reach that point. We're losing focus on the little things. The season's not over, but we're only as good as our last game, and right now that's not real good."

Pete Graham: "I can't tell you how much things have changed around here in the four years I've been here. When I was a freshman, the upperclassmen wouldn't talk to you. Now we have freshmen come in and contribute and they're no different than anyone else. I haven't played much here, but understand that this is the best thing in the world. I'm leaving after this year, and I know I'm leaving something great."

Andy Heck: "There's a perception about Notre Dame that we're not very tough, that we don't play until the whistle blows. We've got to change that perception."

Mark Green: "We were 5–6 my freshman year, so I know how it felt to be home on New Year's Day. We've come so far, and it has nothing to do with physical ability. No one can tell me we had the same attitude yesterday against Navy that we did against Michigan or Miami. I know we didn't. We have to play that way every down. In the Michigan game I saw guys with tears in their eyes, but not yesterday. We have an opportunity here—let's not let it slip out of our hands."

Wes Pritchett: "Just two years ago we were 5–6. Now we're number one with three more games to go. Anybody who doesn't understand where we are and what we have to do the rest of the way isn't the kind of guy who belongs here at Notre Dame."

There were some other seniors who echoed those thoughts. But it wasn't exactly what they said as much as how they said it. We've got a chance to accomplish something great. Let's not lose sight of where we are and where we're going.

The idea to have our players speak up before their team members came from Barry Alvarez. After the team meeting each individual coach conveyed his feelings to his players and the results on team morale were dramatic.

You may get the impression that the head coach comes up with all the good ideas, but that's not accurate. Our coaches all have the opportunity to voice their opinion on every facet of the program, and their input definitely affects the decision I make. This was never more obvious than the actions we took following the Navy game.

22

BEING NO. 1:
IT'S NO BIG DEAL

UPON my arrival home Sunday night, the day after we'd beaten Navy, I received a phone call from Herschel Nissenson of the Associated Press informing me we were going to be rated number one. I was asked not to say anything about rankings because it wasn't going to be released until Monday and it would be unfair to the wire service if this was printed prematurely.

As I put my head on the pillow that night, I thought to myself, This is ridiculous. We play very poorly against Navy and they elevate us to number one, and we're going to be playing Rice, the team with the longest losing streak in the nation. My last thought as I went to sleep was that we ought to be the underdog in this game. Obviously I'm not very positive early in the week.

I knew the polls would be released at six o'clock that night, so on Monday I talked to the squad before practice about being ranked number one. I felt it was permissable to talk to them at that point, because I was confident the news would be released by the time we left the practice field. I told the squad I was really excited initially about being number one and I hoped that they were also.

However, it was important for them to realize that they weren't being coached by Barry Switzer or Joe Paterno, that this was a new experience for me because I'd never coached a team that had been ranked number one. I told them that when I received the news, I was so excited that I called the NCAA to see what being number one meant. The NCAA said our touchdowns still only count six points and we still have to make ten

229

yards for a first down, not nine. If you're number one and you fumble, and the other team recovers the ball, they get to keep it.

In other words, there's absolutely no benefit to being number one. However, it's very difficult to remain number one because the top-ranked team thinks it has to play spectacularly. They feel if they're number one they have to score two touchdowns on every play and hold the other team without a first down on every possession. I told them the only thing we had to do was remember that we were the same football team we were before they ranked us number one. We weren't any different at all, as players or coaches. It wasn't our goal to do anything other than be the best football team in our stadium on Saturday. We weren't any better-looking, any richer, any stronger, any faster, just more vulnerable to pressure.

Our football players interpreted my message in the proper way, and consequently we had a good week of practice. It was imperative that our players didn't place any added pressure on themselves because of our national ranking. If the pollsters were right, they wouldn't have to vote every week. The only thing I knew for sure was that we had not been the number-one team in the country the preceding week, and we would not stay there long unless we got better.

It's not comforting to be ranked number one this year because it hasn't been very good luck for Florida State, Miami, or UCLA.

It isn't important to be ranked number one at this time of the season, but it sure is important where you're ranked on January 2. While I don't like to be number one in early November, it is better than being number one on September 1. The only advantage to being number one is it means that you control your own destiny. You don't need help from anybody else. If we win the rest of our games, I'll be surprised, but I'll also be part of a national champion. A member of the news media asked me if we were now in the driver's seat, and I said I am just happy to be in the car.

The other thing that surprised me was that when the polls came out, everyone got excited. I don't know why. I don't notice anybody jumping up and down at Hertz Rent-A-Car when I rent a vehicle.

If we get excited now, everybody'll be flat by Saturday and we'll get beat. My thoughts are not carved in granite, because I have never been number one except at Ohio State under Woody Hayes.

I understand that everybody is going to play harder against us. But golly, how much harder can they play against Notre Dame than they have in the past? I believe that same team may not play as confidently against us as they have in the past, so maybe this will be to our advantage. Just like the rat said, "I don't want any cheese, I just want out of the trap." All we want to do is win Saturday, and nothing more.

We can't control the atmosphere on campus. We talked a little bit about that in the staff meeting on Tuesday. There just isn't much we can do. To keep this thing in perspective, you know the players are going to live in the dorms and they are going to go to class and consequently will be vulnerable to the flattery that will come their way. It sure would be nice if we could incubate them from this thinking, but then it wouldn't be Notre Dame.

It's hard to believe that we are exactly the same when we woke up today as when we woke up yesterday. We're not going to change our uniforms or the way we sign our name. People act like we won a million-dollar lottery. On the field, however, it can be a different matter.

I couldn't believe it, but somebody was telling me that this is the first time Notre Dame has played at home and been number one this late in the season since 1970. It is true we won the national championship in 1973 and 1977, when we were elevated to number one after beating Alabama in the Sugar Bowl in '73 and Texas in the Cotton Bowl in '77. It is rare when a team is ranked number one in early November and goes on to win the championship.

There is a theory that I should now be relieved we are ranked number one. The misconception that initiates this thinking is that there is some kind of extraordinary pressure at Notre Dame to reach that goal. That's absolutely not true. I feel absolutely no pressure to win the national championship from the Notre Dame family—which includes administration, student body, the faculty and alumni. However, the subway alumni—those who didn't attend Notre Dame but root extremely hard for us—expect us to win. As a matter of fact, I suspect that they virtually demand that we win. They are the greatest fans in the world and their enthusiasm is unbelievable. However, they are the most demanding group I have ever seen or heard. No matter what you do, it's not good enough, and you've got to live with this, since you can't change it.

Deep down inside I don't feel any pressure to win. When Father Joyce hired me, he told me all the things about Notre Dame that he felt made it difficult to have a good football team. He talked about academics, redshirting, the schedule, and on and on. I asked him one question. "How good does Notre Dame want to be?" He said, "We want to be the best we can be within the rules of the university." I would like to think that we have done that.

We have won without compromising our values, integrity, honesty, or commitment to academic excellence. We have tried to keep football at this university in the proper perspective, and never once have we placed it ahead of academics, which is the way it should be. We have never worried about being in the top twenty or being number one. We have only concerned ourselves with being the best we can be.

I am aware that when I came here, our opponents were telling prospective athletes we were deemphasizing football. Likewise, I read all the comments about how Notre Dame could never be one of the better teams in the country, and the reasons why. According to certain prognosticators Notre Dame could never again be at the top. This didn't faze our players, our coaches, or me.

By the same token we're not at the end of the journey just because we're ranked number one. If we lose next week and I die, my wife would have to hire pall bearers for my funeral, since I would not have six friends. That's life. You're up and you're down, and I hope our players understand this. It is important to understand that this is human nature, and you can't worry about it or let it affect you.

When you have success at Notre Dame, you can become intoxicated with it. They tell the story (and that is just what it is) that when Ara Parseghian came here and made Notre Dame an instant winner, the fans felt he could do anything. One game it was snowing and the students started chanting, "Ara, stop the snow. Ara, stop the snow." Ara supposedly called over Tom Pagna, an assistant coach, and said, "Could I do it?" A few years later, after Ara had established himself as one of the greatest coaches of all time, the same situation occurred, and once again the students responded with the same chant, "Ara, stop the snow. Ara, stop the snow." Once again Ara called Tom Pagna over and said, "Should I do it?"

My last thought on being ranked number one was that it meant we had refused to accept mediocrity. I had this saying on my office wall and had shared it with our squad:

ARE YOU AVERAGE?

"Average" is what the failures claim to be when their family and friends ask them why they are not successful.

"Average" is the top of the bottom, the best of the worst, the bottom of the top, the worst of the best. Which of these are you?

"Average" means being run-of-the-mill, mediocre, insignificant, and also-ran, a nonentity.

Being "average" is the lazy person's cop-out; it's lacking the guts to stand in life; it's living by default.

Being "average" is to take up space for no purpose; to take the trip through life, but to never pay the fare; to return no interest for God's investment in you.

Being "average" is to pass one's life away with time, rather than to pass one's time away with life. It's to kill time, rather than to work it to death.

To be "average" is to be forgotten once you pass from this life. The successful are remembered for their contributions, the failures are remembered because they tried, but the "average," the silent majority, is just forgotten.

To be "average" is to commit the greatest crime one can against one's self, humanity, and one's God. The saddest epitaph is this: "Here lies Mr. or Mrs. Average—here lies the remains of what might have been, except for their belief that they were only 'average.'"

23

RICE:
ROCKETING TO WIN NO. 9

PEOPLE cannot comprehend why I'm concerned about Rice because we're playing at home against a team that hasn't won a game yet, and, in addition, they think we are invincible.

It is true Indiana beat Rice decisively in the season opener, then they lost their second game to Southwest Louisiana. I thought then that Rice must be down this year. The fact they returned most of their football team from 1987 had given everyone ample reason to be positive. When they were 0–2 they changed their quarterback, and this changed their team. They put Quentis Roper at quarterback, and they put their former quarterback at free safety. Their offensive and defensive execution then changed completely.

They went down to Texas A&M and lost a very tough game. Then they traveled up to Arkansas to play the Hogs at Little Rock, and I can assure you this is a difficult place to play. Nevertheless, Rice had a chance to win the game, as it was tied in the fourth quarter. Arkansas came back to score late in the game and won 21–14. It is difficult to believe this team has the longest losing streak in the nation.

In only one of their seven games have they given up more than 24 points. Defensively they are very solid, very quick, and very good fundamentally. Offensively, they can be dangerous. Roper has great speed and quickness, and he has completed fifty-five percent of his passes. This is impressive for any team, but particularly one that has been losing.

Offensively, their style of attack is very similar to Stanford's. They employ what is called the run-and-shoot offense, but they will also run the wishbone. They have the style of passing game that gave us a lot of trouble against Stanford, and they have implemented certain segments of the option that we have trouble defending. Their kicking game is well disciplined and probably superior to ours.

We did not go out in pads on Monday, although I sure thought about it after the way we performed at Navy. We need to fall back into the rhythm we had maintained the first seven weeks of the season. Win on Saturday, relax on Sunday, prepare on Monday, work on Tuesday, polish on Wednesday, perfect on Thursday, get ready emotionally on Friday, and win on Saturday. Now, as we near the end of the season, we can't be as intense in practice as we would like. It's just not feasible. You have to know when to back off the players, and I sense this is the time. We didn't play well at Navy, so it must be because we are tired mentally and physically.

It is a good sign that our players respect how well Rice played against Arkansas and Texas A&M. The Hogs are undefeated and in the top ten. The A&M team that struggled with Rice is similar to the unit that beat us in the Cotton Bowl on January 1, 1987. You have to be impressed with Rice's effort and execution. We should win the game, but I'm always afraid of us playing very poorly and coming out second best. By Tuesday I am mad, because Rice already has caused me two sleepless nights.

It's hard to realize we're sitting here 8–0 in the first week of November. I'm sure it's a surprise to some people, and probably to some coaches and players. So many of the experts thought the team was too young, that we were a year away from being a really good team.

Maybe we are a year away. I don't know. I never said publicly that 1989 was going to be a great year or that 1987 would be a poor one. The experts just said we were a year away, and I never disagreed with them. I think we *might* be a year away. But who knows?

I realize people are already starting to say that with the exception of five or six players, the whole football team is back for 1989. In addition, they will argue that some of our better athletes are in the freshman class. There are some quality freshmen, sophomore, and junior players who haven't had a chance to play for a variety of reasons. However, that doesn't guarantee we are going to be better next year. I don't even look that far. The only thing I know about next year is this—we are going to start out in the spring further ahead than where we were this spring. We will have a lot of players with the same names, but they will be different people. We will start out as a much better football team at the first meeting we have in 1989 than we were at the first meeting in 1988. That's it.

As we work into November, it's hard to avoid the distractions of the bowl situation. The only communication I have had with the bowl representatives is to say hello. I have not sat down and talked to them. I wave at them, or they step into the locker room and congratulate us on our win. I think Dick Rosenthal and Father Beauchamp have probably visited with them extensively, but I haven't. I have no idea what the bowl picture is. My son Skip told me where everybody is going and what's happening. He has it all figured out. I guess if you are a graduate assistant, you can do that.

I addressed the players the day after the Navy game about the possibility of going to a bowl game. I informed them that nobody has come to us and said, "We want you in our bowl game." I read this and I read that in the papers, but nobody has said, "We want you in our bowl." I told Dick Rosenthal, "All we want to do is win." I have really not given a thought to the bowl game.

Someone suggested that if we were going to have a letdown, maybe now would be a good time. It seems most people feel that a letdown is inevitable. I say nonsense. We are not supposed to have one, we already had one last week, and we have practiced too hard to allow this to happen. We realize we can't win all the time, but I can assure you we don't want to lose this one. Having a letdown tells you something about your team, but to have two letdowns in a row tells the country something about your team, and it isn't a good story.

On Sunday and Monday I'm a basket case because whatever film I see of our next opponent looks outstanding. On the other hand, all the film I see of our team is not very impressive because I just notice the mistakes.

That's why, early in the week, I'm not usually very optimistic about our chances to win the upcoming game. It sometimes seems like there's no way we can win. I try to be realistic, and I don't start to feel comfortable about our team's chances of winning until our preparation is complete on Thursday.

When we look at an opponent, we want to know the level of performance they are capable of achieving. If it's very high but still not as good as our worst performance, I'd feel pretty good. But it seems that doesn't ever happen. We see our mistakes and the positive things the opponent does, and I'm a leading candidate to go over Niagara Falls in a barrel.

As we prepared to play Rice, we had a real thrill on November 1 when Vice-President George Bush came to the campus for a campaign speech at Stepan Center. My wife Beth and I had a chance to meet him before the speech, but I didn't stay to see his address because I had to attend practice. Digger Phelps is a close friend of Vice-President Bush, and he mentioned there was a chance the Republican presidential candidate might stop by our practice after his speech. We let him know he was welcome, but we really didn't expect him to make it.

I told the coaches he might stop by and I mentioned it to the players as they were loosening up for practice. I then took a poll, and a large percentage of the players said they were going to vote. The majority said they were voting for Bush, but it was far from unanimous. I jokingly told the ones who said they were voting for Vice-President Bush that they could sit up front if he did come to practice.

Halfway through practice I saw a helicopter go over our heads and I assumed he was leaving the area. Shortly thereafter a Secret Service man came up and said the Vice-President was coming by after all.

His entourage of cars pulled up, and our field looked like a limousine parking lot. The Vice-President was most impressive. He talked about how proud he was of the team and how he followed us. Some of the players remembered when he'd been here for the Penn State game the year the Nittany Lions won the national championship. He and Joe Paterno are great friends. He talked about some of his experiences, and I think the players really enjoyed it, especially since it was impromptu. He did say we had a lot in common. We both were working hard to be number one. I told him his chances were much better than ours. We gave him a football and he wished us well. I honestly was surprised at how young he looked. Our players gave him the old Notre Dame cheer, "He's a man, who's a man, he's a Notre Dame man . . . President Bush."

When I spoke to the squad Friday afternoon, I told them this would be the chance of a lifetime for Rice. The only thing better than beating number one is being number one. It bothers me when somebody plays the role of a spoiler. We can't let that happen to us. In November there are only two types of teams—those going somewhere and those trying to prevent others from going somewhere.

On August 12 we had no worries, no pressure, there was nothing to lose. We were going to go out and play for Notre Dame. We said we would not allow a team to come into our stadium and walk out with the game ball. If we don't have that burning desire to play against Rice, we'll be in severe trouble.

At the relaxation period Friday night we did have a problem getting the players as quiet as I wanted. It wasn't a perfect situation, but staying at the Holiday Inn in Plymouth this year has been a big improvement. For years we had stayed at Moreau Seminary, as it wasn't realistic to let them stay in the dorms the night before a home football game. For a variety of reasons we decided to stay off-campus, and the people at the Holiday Inn have really been great to us and gone out of their way to accommodate our needs.

Frank Stams, senior defensive end

When we were staying at the seminary, all the guys were complaining. They'd say, "I can't sleep. It's too quiet."

Well, it was just our luck that Coach Holtz decided to go over there and spend the night and see what it was really like. With my luck, he stays in the room right next to me.

I always wake up early to come back to my room in the dorm and shower in my room. So I get up early and I'm walking out and this guy bumps into me—this guy with his boxer shorts on. It's dark, and I look and then I look again, and it's Coach Holtz.

All the showers were on—they were all on. One of the managers had gotten up at five-thirty and turned them on for all the players because it takes so long for them to warm up.

Well, Coach was headed for the bathroom when I was getting out of there. So I said, "Hey, Coach. Man, we gotta get out of this place. This place is haunted."

He goes, "Haunted?! What are you talking about? This place isn't haunted."

I go, "This place is haunted. Look in there. All the showers are on but there's no one in there."

That was the last night we stayed in the seminary. After that we always stayed in Plymouth.

THE GAME

SOUTH BEND—After his Fighting Irish rose to the top spot in both wire-service polls, Notre Dame coach Lou Holtz spent most of this week convincing his players that being number one doesn't guarantee anything. Rice had just lost to Arkansas in Little Rock by a score of 21–14 when the Hogs pulled it out in the fourth quarter. In addition, the Owls had taken the Aggies to the wire in College Station before losing to Texas A&M in a close game. It was with good justification that Holtz was concerned about the game with the Rice Owls.

Touchdowns still count six points. Fumbles still mean the other team gets the ball. It still takes 10 yards to get a first down.

Holtz's messages must have been effective. His team played as if nothing fazed it by scoring on five of its first six possessions and waltzing to a 54–11 win in Notre Dame Stadium.

Raghib Ismail tied an NCAA record by running back a pair of kickoffs for touchdowns, and fullback Anthony Johnson added two scores of his own, as the Irish played as if the number-one tag didn't bother them a bit.

"I am in shock," said Holtz. "If you had told me this would be the score, I wouldn't have believed it. We were just a little bit too strong for them overall, but it's just one of those things."

Notre Dame's typically strong running game was as dominant as ever, running up 294 net yards and five rushing scores. The two teams ended up running the same number of plays (70), but Rice managed only 71 net yards in the second half. In the process, the Owls saw their losing streak, the longest in the country, extended to 15.

"Notre Dame is a great football team," said Rice coach Jerry Berndt. "We had to play pretty close to a perfect football game and we didn't do that."

Still, the visitors had a few fans wondering about the accuracy of those rankings in the first few minutes. Rice took the opening kickoff and marched 70 yards downfield in 10 plays for a Clint Parsons field goal and a 3–0 lead. Quarterback Quentis Roper came out throwing, hitting Mike Boudousquie for 23 yards on the very first play.

Then it was time for Notre Dame's "Rocket" to blast off. Taking the kickoff 87 yards up the right sideline, freshman Raghib Ismail officially needed 13 seconds to amend that deficit and make it 7–3 for the Irish. The Owls couldn't get out of their own territory on any of their next four opportunities, and Notre Dame quickly took control.

Mark Green's 40-yard run keyed a 63-yard, five-play drive that made it 14–3. Then Tony Rice threw 41 yards over the middle to tight end Derek Brown on first down and six plays later Johnson scored the first of his touchdowns from the three to make it 20–3.

Ricky Watters fumbled the ball at the Rice 20 and they recovered it on the next Irish possession. However, Jeff Alm's interception two plays later put Notre Dame back on the attack at the Rice 18. Braxston Banks gained three yards, Tony Brooks took a pitch for 14 and then broke a tackle to go the final yard over the stripe. Johnson's two-point conversion run upped the count to 28–3.

Parsons capped a 44-yard drive with another field goal—this time from 41 yards. But Billy Hackett did the same for the Irish, hitting from 42 yards with 19 seconds left after a two-minute drill run by Kent Graham. At the break, the Irish led 31–6 and had 248 total yards.

After an exchange of fumbles, Notre Dame used the big play to string together a 70-yard scoring drive. Brooks went for 20 on first down, Rice followed with a 16-yard gain and Rodney Culver scored on a 19-yard burst. That made it 38–6.

Rice never quit and kicked a third field goal, this one by Parsons good from 45 yards on the first play of the final quarter. This meant Rice would give Ismail one more chance to return a kickoff, and he promptly ran it back 89 yards down the left sideline for a score.

The Irish used up nearly half the period on a 16-play march that ended in a 28-yard Hackett field goal. Then, after Rice fumbled the ball away on its second play, the home team drove another 40 yards, with Joe Jarosz finishing the Irish scoring on a six-yard run.

Rice did have the distinction of becoming the first team in Division I to notch two points on a return of a missed extra point when Bill Stone ran 85 yards with the ball after Hackett's PAT was blocked.

Roper finished with 21 completions in 36 attempts for a respectable 197 yards. But the passing game was about all Rice could muster since Notre Dame limited the Owls to 32 net rushing yards.

No Irish player caught more than two passes. Rice threw only eight, and Notre Dame's leading rusher, Green with 66 yards, did that on only five carries.

"All we wanted to do was be the best team in the stadium today," said Holtz.

There was no question about that.

We played just about everybody in the game because we won it by a rather comfortable margin. However, it didn't start out that way, as Rice drove down the field and kicked a field goal on its first possession. On the ensuing kickoff, Rocket Ismail ran it back for a touchdown. The blocking on our kickoff return was excellent and Rocket made the most of it. We scored on every possession but one in the first half. We fumbled once, but Jeff Alm intercepted a pass two plays later and we ended up leading 31–6 at the half.

Rocket ran another kickoff back for a touchdown in the second half, and that assured him and Notre Dame of leading the country in kickoff returns. Our reserves put together a couple of nice scoring drives in the last quarter. Overall, it was a very impressive performance by Notre Dame, and our players knew it. We wanted to be the best team in the stadium, and we were.

Rice played hard, but we had too many athletes for them, and we won 54–11. One of the thrills was to see the third-teamers play. I knew the game was over at halftime, so we wanted as many to play as possible. Maybe the reason I feel this way is because I was a third-teamer most of my life.

No matter how many games I coach at Notre Dame, I am always thrilled at the conclusion of the game when our team goes over and salutes the student body by raising their helmets. The helmet represents the golden dome and the Lady on the Dome. When we raise it, in essence, we are saying that we praise Our Lady and our school.

There were several people who played well for Notre Dame, and I don't like to point them out because I will invariably overlook some. Nevertheless I need to mention some people on offense because they haven't received much praise.

Mike Heldt, Tim Ryan, and Tim Grunhard are playing exceptionally well inside. We haven't been able to start the same offensive line two weeks in a row, but we know our first-team offensive line has Heldt at center, Ryan at one guard, Grunhard at the other, Andy Heck and Dean Brown at tackle. Derek Brown has really progressed as a freshman. His best football is ahead of him, obviously, and it will help that Frank Jacobs and he will push each other to be better. Tony Rice continues to play well, and fortunately doesn't make too many mistakes. But he makes a lot of great plays. Our backs continue to run well. Anthony Johnson, Tony Brooks, and Mark Green are excellent, and they have so much pride, it shows in every facet of the game. Our receivers aren't very productive, but everyone is trying hard. Tony Rice completed three out of eight, but had three dropped. Our passing game is not as impressive as I would like, but it has been very effective.

On defense we continued to play well. We controlled the line of scrimmage on both offense and defense, and when you do that, you have a pretty good chance to win. George Williams and Jeff Alm continue to play well, and Mirko Jurkovic played very well. Quentis Roper presented some problems with his scrambling, but our secondary responded well. Pat Terrell, George Streeter, Todd Lyght, Stan Smagala, D'Juan Francisco, and Corny Southall are really playing inspired football. It is a great tribute to Chuck Heater, our secondary coach. Chris Zorich lined up against an outstanding center. I don't know if people around the country realize what a good football player Courtney Hall is, but Chris just continues to amaze us all.

Chris's high-school coach was here to see him play in college for the first time. I don't know what his plans are for November 19, but I sure hope they include watching Chris play again. Chris has so much respect for Coach John Potocki, and it showed in his performance.

What concerns us most right now is our inability to throw the ball consistently.

One pleasant plus has been our kicking game. Far too often people evaluate a kicking game predicated entirely upon the performance of the kickers, and this doesn't give you an accurate assessment. There is no doubt in my mind that we have one of the best kicking games in the country. So far we are number one in kickoff returns and tied for number three in punt returns. We haven't had many penalties in this area and have continually gained favorable field position from this phase of the game.

Immediately after the press conference I met with Father Beauchamp and Dick Rosenthal concerning bowl bids. I didn't care if we went to the Cereal Bowl, just so the administration was happy and we were playing for the national championship. The bids go out November 18, the day we play Penn State, which is our next game, but realistically almost everything will be decided next weekend, when we're not scheduled to play due to an open date. Sitting there with a 9–0 record, all indications were that we would probably have our option of going to any bowl we chose. I explained that we wanted to play the best opponent available, and I didn't care where that occurred. It made no difference to our coaches or players whether that opponent was Miami, West Virginia, Auburn, or Florida State. The only thing on our minds was making sure we got better during the open date.

24

THE OPEN DATE:
TAKING A BREAK

TALKED to the squad immediately after the Rice game about the importance of using the open date as a positive experience. It could be a great asset to us if we handle it properly. First, the players would have Sunday off, which normally is a meeting day for us. I told them to spend that time on their academics. Don't waste the day by goofing off, they were told, and I don't think they did.

It is unusual to have an open date so late in the season, with only two games remaining. But we could still make it a plus. It has been a long, taxing season mentally, and while we need to maintain our continuity, we really need to ease the pressure on them. We wanted to keep the momentum we had coming out of the Rice game, so we kept it as similar to a normal game week as we could with the exception of no pressure. The only two exceptions we made were eliminating the Sunday meeting and not scrimmaging on Saturday.

I would have preferred we not have an open date, because we were healthy and had a rhythm going for us. With just two weeks left in the season, we could see the finish line, and we were anxious to sprint there. But as one of my sayings on my desk reads, "This too shall pass."

One thing for certain, we aren't going to pound or beat on the players like we did our first year here, when we had an open date. The situation was different then. After that game we had what amounted to another spring practice, and there is no doubt we accomplished a lot that week.

At that time I told the players we would be a much better football team after the open date, and we were. I felt during the last half of the 1986 season we were one of the twenty best teams in the country.

243

We lost to Penn State, the national championship team, by five points. We had a kickoff return for a touchdown called back for a clip. We had a 58-yard punt return for a touchdown called back for a penalty. We had pass interference called against us on third and 8, which gave Penn State a first and goal situation on our 2. Despite this adversity, our team had a chance to win the game at the end, but we dropped a pass in the end zone with 14 seconds left. We made a lot of great plays, and even though the calls went against us, we played the national champions very even. As a matter of fact, we outgained them by over a hundred yards. But statistics are for losers. The fact remains that Penn State won because they knew how to win and we didn't.

After that disappointment we went down to LSU and lost to them by two points, even though we had a chance to win. They were ranked fifth in the country, and I could believe it. Boy, were they quick. Since those were the only two games we lost after the open date, I felt good about our football team at that stage.

This year's open date will have to be completely different. We would like to work some of the younger players, but we don't want to risk injuries that could jeopardize a young man's performance in the spring. In addition, I feel they just need to escape the pressure that Notre Dame football places upon players. Maybe it's me who needs to escape the pressure, I don't know.

There are different ways coaches deal with an open date. Some will go and watch their next opponent play. Others don't even like to look at an opponent on television, let alone in person. I will not go to the Pitt–Penn State game personally, but I will probably watch it on ESPN. We will have a coach who will scout Penn State, as is customary. We do exchange films, and we know Penn State, having played them for several years. Their philosophy hasn't changed much during that time. I think Joe Paterno is a great coach, and I know Penn State will be as hard to beat as anyone we play.

The morning after the Rice game our coaches spent a normal Sunday. The players were excused, but the coaches weren't. We looked at the Penn State film from last year, as well as some from their recent games. Even though this wasn't as good a Penn State team as we normally see, it's still an excellent team capable of playing very well. Defensively, they're a very good team, as evidenced by giving up just nine points against Alabama despite turning the ball over a lot.

Offensively, they do some very good things. If they had a healthy Blair Thomas, they might be in the top ten. The second half against West Virginia they did some things to get back into the game, even though they lost. They played very well against Maryland and won. We knew there was a chance, if Penn State lost to Pitt, that Penn State would come into our game needing a win over us to avoid their first losing season in fifty years. Our seniors have never beaten Penn State.

We had a typical Monday practice, as was Tuesday and Wednesday. We spent more time on fundamentals than we did on the gameplan for Penn State. On Thursday we practiced again, then gave the players off Friday, Saturday, and Sunday. It was important to give them some time to spend on academics—and we wanted them to get away from football. We don't normally practice on Fridays before games, so the only difference this week was that we did not play on Saturday. I thought about scrimmaging them on Saturday, but it didn't make sense this late in the year. We liked their attitude, and at this stage of the season, that was the most important thing.

I talked to the squad before our last practice on Thursday. You never know what will happen when you give a team three days off, but I tried to get a few messages across. I didn't want anyone to do anything to embarrass himself, his family, or his teammates. Approximately half the players are going home or to visit someone else's home. I didn't want anyone playing basketball. I didn't want anyone even thinking about football all weekend. I wanted them to run for conditioning, and the quarterbacks to throw darts.

The only other thing I wanted them to do is go through the relaxation period every night before they went to sleep and think positively. The one time we played poorly this year was against Navy, and it's ironic that this was the one time all year we didn't have our Friday-night relaxation period.

I told the players it had been a fun year so far. I've never enjoyed working with a group of players and coaches more. The senior leadership has been outstanding. We had all kinds of question marks coming into the season, and yet they've risen to number one and have earned the respect of people around the country. This has transpired because of the way they've practiced and played.

The attitude of the freshmen has been unparalleled in my coaching career—a tribute to the upperclassmen. They never asked, "Is this important?" They only ask, "How can we get better and win?"

Right now it's a two-game season. We need to come back and play against Penn State with the same kind of enthusiasm we did against Michigan or Miami. All we've done is put ourselves in good position. We haven't done anything yet.

I called a friend of mine named Billy Warren and asked if there was any way we could fly down to Augusta, Georgia, one day to play golf. I hadn't held a golf club since July, and I was mentally and physically tired and just wanted to get away from football for twenty-four hours. Billy arranged it, so Dick Rosenthal, Jim Basney, and I flew down there late Thursday night after practice.

We played Augusta National Golf Course on Friday. There is something special about Augusta. It's like you are in fantasy land. It was one of the most enjoyable days I have spent. I did not play especially well. But how can you complain when you are in such a beautiful environment? We played eighteen holes in the morning, and Dick called his wife Marylyn and said, "We voted last night, and no matter what happens, we will be home by Christmas." We had lunch and played eighteen holes in the afternoon. We were walking down the eleventh fairway and I said to Dick, "Maybe you better call Marylyn back and tell her we acted a little hastily, and maybe we won't be home by Christmas after all."

I did play well on the second eighteen, but the course record is still intact. We had a great time. The members, guests, and club personnel all make you feel very special. I have been to Augusta on a couple of other occasions, with Jack Stephens from Stephens, Inc., in Little Rock, and Wheelock Whitney from Minnesota. Even the worst time I ever had at Augusta was still great. I was standing on the ninth green and met a friend, Joe Antonini, chairman of the board of K-Mart and Co. and a big West Virginia fan, walking down the first fairway. We laughed because it looked like we would be playing West Virginia in the Fiesta Bowl.

Now it's on to Penn State, a multiple-defense football team and one that really concerns us. They have run at least forty different defenses this year, and there is no way you can guess exactly what they are going to do.

Their defensive scheme is probably as complex as anybody's we play, and that is one of the reasons they are an outstanding football team. You eliminate their game with West Virginia, and Penn State's defensive statistics are as good as anybody's in the country. They are big, strong, physical, and they run well. In other words, they are a typical Penn State defensive team, which means you had better button your chin strap when you play them.

Penn State has held six opponents to fourteen points or less this year, and that's an impressive statistic if you are playing our Sisters of the Poor, let alone their schedule. Four of the five games that Penn State has lost were against teams whose combined record is 31–5.

It's a typical Penn State team, which up until recently was the fifth-rated defensive team against the rush in the country. That's the one statistic that always catches my attention. Figures don't lie, but liars figure. Statistics can prove anything you desire, but one thing that is absolute is that great defenses are always effective against the run.

As I have said before, I don't look at how a team performs. I'm interested at what level they are capable of performing. That is what concerns us about Penn State. Defensively, they stopped Alabama and a lot of other fine defensive teams. They don't give up many first downs—and that's because they disrupt your rhythm. Last year we were forced to punt seven times. At the conclusion of the game our punter was exhausted, which explains why we lost 21–20 when we missed a two-point conversion with 31 seconds remaining.

Penn State has two excellent linebackers in Andre Collins and Keith Karpinski, who must have gone to grade school on a G.I. bill, because it seems like he has been playing forever. We don't know if Brian Chismar will be healthy enough to play against us, since he's been injured, but he is an awfully good football player. For us to beat Penn State we must play an outstanding defensive game, because they gave up points like a pit bull gives up a bone. Over the years, we have moved the ball against Penn State as well as anybody, but that's still well below our average.

Penn State has done two things in two games that are highly unusual for a Joe Paterno team.

One, they have five turnovers against Pittsburgh. But they very seldom turn the football over against Notre Dame. They play with great concentration and intensity and protect the football very well. I think Penn State has had one turnover against us in the last two times we've played them.

Two, they rarely if ever give up a big gain, but they did against West Virginia. This is a tribute to the Mountaineers' offense, but you can bet it hasn't happened to Penn State since then. I am confident that Penn State will not have a turnover, give up a big play, or suffer a critical penalty.

The other thing that concerns us about Penn State is that they can run the football. Last year they ran against us for 299 yards. That's a lot of yards. It would take me a drive, three-wood, and wedge to equal it. Penn State did have the best back in the country last year in Blair Thomas, and he will be back next year after missing this season with a knee injury.

They have a tailback by the name of Gary Brown, and he has a lot of the same moves and elusiveness that Blair has. Their fullback is very strong, and they have more speed at the wide receiver position than in previous years. I don't know who their quarterback will be, either Lance Lonergan or Tony Sacca, but both of them do some awfully good things. I think Sacca scrambles very well, has an exceptionally strong arm, and has a great future. Lonergan obviously is a winner.

Joe Paterno does as good a job of keeping his team in the game as any coach I have competed against. He is an excellent sideline coach. His team makes few mistakes and very seldom suffers a turnover or a foolish penalty. Penn State's opponents, on the other hand, always seem to suffer critical turnovers and penalties at the most inopportune times. This applies to all of their opponents, not just Notre Dame.

Last year we had the ball on Penn State's 4-yard line with 23 seconds left in the first half, and we had two time-outs. I used one of them and called our team to the sideline. I said, "We have three points on the board, and please do not remove them by throwing an interception." I said, "However, I think we can score a touchdown. We are going to run 325 SQY pass." Now, I know this means nothing to you. What I did not realize at the time was that it meant nothing to our quarterback, either. We threw an interception, took the three points off the board, and consequently, when we scored with 31 seconds to go in the game and were down by 21–20, we were forced to go for a two-point conversion, which was unsuccessful.

I'm always scared to death of every opponent but particularly Penn State, because they have played so well against us. They don't make many mistakes. They play good defense. They run the football, and they always hurt us with big plays.

25

THE SENIORS:
LEADERSHIP PERSONIFIED

THE Penn State game next week will be the last home game for the seniors, and it's a chance for that group to go through a second straight year without losing at home.

Senior leadership is so important with any team, and this one is no different. I still reflect back on the first conversation I had with our captains, Andy Heck, Mark Green, and Ned Bolcar, a meeting held shortly after they were elected captains.

I was very honest with them and said I didn't think the senior group was a great class in terms of talent. As far as leadership was concerned, I wasn't sure. They assured me that this senior class would provide the best senior leadership Notre Dame had experienced in years. They informed me they had already had a meeting with some of the leaders on the team, and they were all on the same page.

As the season winds down, there is no doubt the seniors have been a great group. One of the things they have done exceptionally well is set the tempo. The way they have accepted their role is amazing. It is very difficult to win unless your seniors really play the best football of their careers, and they have this year.

When a freshman comes to college, all he wants to do is play. "Man, if I can just play, come out of the locker room after the game and say I played . . ." He is not embarrassed to go home at Christmas and say, "I know we're 0–11, but I'll tell you, we're building for the future." Then, as a sophomore, they just want to be starters. Winning isn't that important to them. When they become juniors all they want to do is win. They feel that winning is the most important thing in their careers. However, when they become seniors, they want to know, "What legacy am I going to leave? What records? Am I an all-American?"

The biggest thing this senior class has done is accept their leadership role and teach the underclassmen the way a Notre Dame player should conduct himself in the classroom, on the field, and in all social circumstances. I can honestly say I have nothing but respect for the dedication, commitment, love, and unselfishness of the seniors. This would be a good time to acknowledge that they are also fine players.

They have done a tremendous job. Very seldom have I had to ask, "How can I expect the younger players to know what to do, when the older players aren't showing them by example?" When we have our first squad meeting of 1989, I will say to the junior class, "I want you to be exactly like last year's seniors, only better."

An individual's attitude and his willingness to accept his role is of paramount importance. Flash Gordon, for a variety of reasons, didn't play a couple of football games. He never complained, publicly or in the locker room. He is a competitor and wanted to play, but he didn't want to do anything to jeopardize Notre Dame's chances of winning. These are the reasons we win, not because of brilliant strategy. Flash earned his starting position back and played brilliantly down the stretch.

Not everybody can be first team, but you can always put the team first. That is difficult for some people to accept, but that is why some teams lose. There is no doubt our players have made unselfishness a strong priority.

Frank Stams and Wes Pritchett are always laughing and joking and keeping everyone loose. I was being interviewed on the field by CNN prior to practice. Players were throwing and catching in the background, so it appeared practice was under way. Stams and Pritchett are off camera, and they kept hollering, "That's the way to go, Stams. Boy, you look great. That's tremendous, outstanding, Pritchett. You are really going to be a great one." They were attempting to give the viewers the impression that assistant coaches were making these complimentary comments during practice. They find humor in all situations.

I've never seen people having as much fun playing football as Pritchett and Stams. They have a great attitude, and there are no two players on this team who have more intensity. Last spring some seniors came to practice to give Stams and Pritchett a hard time about coming back for their extra year. I guess they're glad they did. I know we are.

You look down the list of seniors, and they've all got a story to tell.

Steve Alaniz isn't the most talented receiver ever to play at Notre Dame, but he made a great contribution.

I have tremendous respect for Steve Belles, because he'll do anything to help this team. He knows Tony Rice is our quarterback, but Steve is tough, a good competitor and leader. How many quarterbacks have you seen making tackles on kicking teams, as he does? You can win with Steve as a starting quarterback.

It's been a tough year in some respects for Ned Bolcar, but we wouldn't be where we are if it weren't for him. His leadership has been excellent, and he is the fourth-leading tackler on our team. When we were having trouble with our kick coverage a few weeks ago, I put Ned in charge. The attitude in the huddle, the tempo and our execution changed dramatically from that point forward.

Let's not forget that Michael Stonebreaker is a great football player. He made first team all-American this year, and Ned made second last year. That's not bad.

Mike Brennan is a real unsung hero of this team. He could have played lacrosse anywhere in the country. He chose to come to Notre Dame, and he was a walk-on football player. I don't know where our offensive line would be this year without him, because he has played three different positions and performed very well at all of them.

Once we moved Ricky Watters to flanker, who would have thought Pat Eilers would get much playing time? Obviously Pat did, because he blocked and carried out his assignments with great intensity. He is a better athlete than we give him credit for being. But no one has ever questioned his courage, competitiveness, and unselfishness. Pat showed up on our doorstep after he transferred from Yale and said, "What can I do to help this team?"

D'Juan Francisco came here as a star running back and was moved to the secondary. He has worked very hard and has reached the point where I believe he will eventually play on Sundays. His position switch was made to benefit the team, but eventually it will be very beneficial to D'Juan personally.

Tom Gorman got hurt early, which prevented him from being a dominant defensive lineman. But even when we moved him to offense, all he wanted to do was help us win.

Peter Graham is another unsung hero. He handles the prep teams at quarterback, and does it as well as anyone I have seen. He is as popular as anyone on our team, and he possesses talent.

One of the greatest young men I've ever been around is Mark Green. He has excellent talent and is willing to exploit those abilities at any position we feel is best for the team. His attitude is terrific, and there's no one who doesn't love and respect Mark. He has as much love and compassion for his teammates as anyone I have known.

I don't know how many people could make a transition like Andy Heck did, from tight end to tackle, and still do all the things he did to help this team—both on and off the field. His coach, Joe Moore, did a super job with him, but the credit has to go to Andy and his parents. I wish I could buy ten percent of his future.

Andy is exceptionally coachable and very conscientious. Last spring we were watching film of a scrimmage. On each play, every player grades out at zero or with a plus. Andy said to Coach Moore, "You gave me a zero on that play, and I thought I did a pretty good job." Coach Moore said, "You did for an average player, but not for the great player I think you are. Do you want me to put a plus for an average player or a zero for a great player?" Andy said, "The zero is fine." I knew then he would be a great one.

Chuck Killian, Marty Lippincott, Steve Roddy, Aaron Robb, and Kurt Zackrison's championship rings will be the same size as Tony Rice's and others, because their contribution has been critical to our success, although people on the outside didn't realize it.

There's no one on this team I respect more than Corny Southall. He has started for two years and will get a chance to play professional football. But if that doesn't work out, he will still be a success in life.

George Streeter is a prime example of a player who has developed into a great strong safety. His leadership role has expanded his senior year, and he may be the most underrated player on our team.

Whatever success these seniors experience this year they will have earned. They have been through hard times, but they are better people for it. Our job at Notre Dame is to prepare young people for life, and the university has done this. Their future, I feel, is secure.

26

PENN STATE:
NO FANFARE, JUST FIESTA

THE physical condition of our team is not as good now as it was before the open date. Anthony Johnson hurt his ankle last week and is unlikely to play. Rodney Culver has a sore shoulder from the Navy game and is practicing on a limited basis, and Braxston Banks still has a bruised knee. Tim Grunhard's ankle doesn't respond as well as we'd like, and he isn't full speed yet. We don't know how productive he'll be the rest of the year. If it weren't for these injuries, this book would be half as long. Patrick Terrell has a fallen arch. He was able to come back Monday but he is not quite full speed, either.

This week we found out from one of our team physicians, Dr. Jim Moriarity, that Derek Brown has the same illness that George Gipp died from. Derek was in St. Joseph's Hospital for a few days, then moved to the infirmary. Derek's illness, as explained to me, is an infection in the soft palate area—near the tonsils. The preceding weekend, when we did not play, he had gone home with another player. On the way back to the campus, because he felt so bad, he had to stop at a hospital for emergency care. If this is the same thing George Gipp died from, it shows you how far medicine has come in seventy years.

The one thing I'm not worried about is our players' enthusiasm to play this football game. I think they understand the difficult time we've had beating Penn Sate the last couple of years, and there is no such thing as a bad Penn State team. Some are better than others, but they are all good.

Our football players came back from their free weekend with a fresher outlook on the season and on life. I think they found out that there is life after football, but it isn't nearly as good as life with football.

253

There are still certain areas where I would like to see a tremendous amount of improvement. One of them is obviously the passing game. We've had a problem recently improving in this area because it gets dark so early, which limits the amount of time we can spend on it. We do have a lighted practice field, but our offense and defense share it once the sun goes down. We know Penn State is very good on pass defense, as Pittsburgh only completed 9 of 22 attempts for 108 yards. We've progressed in the passing game, but we're still not where I would like to see us. However, we're anxious to see if our improvement is as obvious in a game as it has been in the last ten practices.

In all probability, we are not going to run the football against a team like Penn State. They have dominated the run against virtually everybody they have played, including Pittsburgh, which has a great offensive line. Pitt has an explosive offense and is very talented at all offensive positions. They were averaging about 35 points a game, yet only scored 14 against Penn State. We are probably going to have to throw the football, but we still make every effort to establish the run.

This game probably means as much to the Penn State contingent as any game they have played the last five years, and that includes the national championship encounters. The reason is simple. If we beat Penn State, it'll be their first losing season in fifty years. I would like to remind them that this game is just one of eleven Penn State plays, so don't play like it's worth six losses. I get nervous when I think how prepared Joe Paterno will have his team, but my confidence returns when I'm around our coaches and players. They are winners, and they know it, act like it, and prepare like it.

At our press conference this week I was asked if I thought we were ripe for an upset, since we were 9–0 and Penn State was fighting for its life at 5–5. I told the reporter that he sounded like a comedian out of work. Penn State has beaten us the last couple of years, so there is no way in this world our football team is going to have a letdown. Our main concern was not taking Penn State lightly, but making certain we didn't peak too early. As far as we are concerned, we don't even play after this game. This is the end of our season. If you could have been at our practice session Monday, you would know why I'm concerned about us being too emotional too early.

Contrary to public opinion, we aren't in a three-game playoff for the national championship. We are strictly preparing and solely thinking about our game with Penn State. The national championship is the furthest thing from our mind, and it should be. Anyone who follows football knows that Penn State has beaten us for three consecutive years. The only thing worse is to lose to them four consecutive times. While it's possible, I have the feeling our coaches and players aren't going to allow this to happen, especially not in our season's last home football game in the stadium that Rockne built.

One of the touchy subjects that came up this week at the press conference was the Notre Dame–Penn State series and the fact that it might be discontinued. I am not responsible for who we play, when we play, or where we play. I am only held accountable for how we play. I know Penn State is reevaluating its scheduling philosophy and has decided not to play Syracuse in the future. Syracuse is not particularly happy about that, but I'm certain Penn State's reasons are valid and justified. Over the years Penn State has played as tough a schedule as anyone in the country. They are not trying to make it easier, and the same can be said for Notre Dame. Our schedule in the past has been suicidal, but this is normal for Notre Dame.

There are some concerns that Notre Dame might play only eastern independents and Big Ten teams. We have three Big Ten teams on our schedule now, and as I understand it, we play Indiana, Ohio State, and Northwestern in the future. We're beginning a series with Boston College. Then you add Pitt, Penn State, and Navy, and all of a sudden you're locked into eight or nine games a year. Having USC on our schedule is a necessity, because it's a traditional game. This does not give us the opportunity to play other teams around the nation.

We would really be unfair to our fans nationwide if we played only Big Ten teams and eastern independents. If you look at the Notre Dame scheduling history, you will find that we have played a national schedule all the way back to Rockne. In the past, Notre Dame played teams for five, six, seven years, and then scheduled somebody else. There was a time when we used to play Iowa every year, Georgia Tech quite often, and Army annually, as well as Nebraska and Oklahoma. Notre Dame doesn't want to be locked into traditional games every year, but wants the flexibility to continue to play a variety of opponents over a certain number of years. The Penn State game is great for fans of both schools, but when it was scheduled originally, it was with the understanding that it wasn't for infinity.

I know what Notre Dame's scheduling policy has been for the past fifty to seventy-five years, and I can assure you any changes won't ease up the schedule. If we don't play Penn State, we'll play somebody at least as formidable.

The necessity of beating Notre Dame to avoid its first losing season in fifty years is a tremendous motivating factor for Penn State. I know it's going to be a close game. We played Penn State four times when I was at North Carolina State, and the games were always well played and close. When you play Joe Paterno and Penn State, you'd better make sure you wear all your pads, as it will be a physical game. I used to tell the squad they were playing a computer and it wouldn't make a mistake.

Practices this week were pretty good, because we had the advantage of getting the gameplan in early. We knew Penn State would change its defenses to a certain extent, as they always do. You always see a different defense from Penn State than what you anticipate, and that causes some blocking problems for us. Consequently, it's difficult to finalize our offensive gameplan against them because we're going to have to make adjustments during the course of the game.

Last year our last home game was against Alabama and we played impressively and beat them decisively. We kept the gameplan simple so our players could be exceptionally aggressive. We want to be flexible during the course of the football game, but most important of all, we want to be 10–0.

One of the duties I must perform on Friday when we are playing on television (which is every week) is to meet with the commentators. CBS was televising our game with Penn State nationally, so I visited with Tim Brant, John Dockery, and Leslie Visser. This meeting took place immediately after the Quarterback Club luncheon on Friday. We spent a little longer visiting than usual, since Tim and Lesley hadn't seen us play.

We talked about our expectations for this team coming into the year. I said that naturally we've been pleased with the results, but that no team ever exceeds my expectations in terms of execution. As a matter of fact, I honestly felt we would execute better than we have.

We played word association with the players' names. John would give me a name and I would give him the first sentence that came into my mind. Mark Green is a blue-collar worker. When you come to the stadium, he's ready. Ricky Watters is probably a tailback in the future. Wes Pritchett is like money in the bank. You can count on him.

Tony Brooks had his foot X-rayed again after practice Wednesday. I don't know how he has played all season, let alone as well as he has. I said I was thinking about breaking some other people's feet intentionally if it worked out this well.

I told them I'm happy Derek Brown is better and can play tomorrow, but it cost me a great halftime speech. We could have said, "Win one for

Derek." I guess it doesn't have the same ring as "Win one for the Gipper." I'm sure Grantland Rice could have done better with this.

We met with our team at four on Friday, as we normally do. I know they are tired of listening to me.

The main thing that we emphasized was this:

"We control our own destiny. All we're concerned about is winning this game. Nothing in the past, nothing in the future matters. Let's live it one day at a time.

"I know the weather will be bad. We're supposed to have an inch of rain tonight. We've had 2.8 inches so far in November, and by tomorrow it'll be over five inches.

"You may remember the old cartoon where there's a football game going on and it's sunny on one side of the line of scrimmage and raining on the other side. The coach on the rainy side says, 'That is just one of the things I don't like about playing Notre Dame.'

"I don't care if it rains, snows, hails, or if the sun shines, nothing is going to bother us. As long as we don't get concerned about the weather, we'll be fine.

"We want to treat this game like any other. On paper, we should be the best football team, but we don't play on paper. We just need to forget who we're playing, forget the opposition, and just go out and play our own game. We know how to win, and we will win."

I was very positive during the whole meeting, and the players sensed it, but I was just being honest.

It was very important that the seniors treat this game like any other one, and I told them that. It just happens to be their last one in this stadium. "You can think about that when it's over. I told you on August 12 that this was a special group, and now you know it. In a few weeks the entire country will know it.

"In life, you read about people who have achieved greatness when things went against them. Look at Jim Abbott, the pitcher from Michigan with one arm who played in the Olympics and is now with the California Angels.

"We've had a winning season. We're going to a bowl game, and we're going to play on New Year's Day. We have one goal left, and you know what it is, but don't even think about it.

"It's going to be a fun day—and yet, we've just scratched the surface of where we want to be."

For some reason, the weather is normally horrendous when we play

Penn State. The year before it was terrible all week, and when we got to Penn State it was as poor a day as I've ever seen, with the wind-chill factor about 20 below and a thirty-five-mile-per-hour wind. I guess coaches should take a lesson from the weather—it doesn't let criticism affect it.

This time it wasn't too bad for a game on national television. At least we didn't have a lot of snow, although it was rather gray, with the temperature about 40. It never rained to any extent during the game, but it sure looked like it was going to pour.

I talked to Joe Paterno before the game, as I normally do with most opposing coaches. We never talk about the game or anything related to it, but we do touch on a variety of different things. The subject of West Virginia came up, and Joe said they were a great football team. He was tremendously impressed with them, and said offensively they were the best team he had ever seen. I thought, Boy, that's what I need to hear, because I felt we would be playing West Virginia in the Fiesta Bowl. I keep asking Joe and Bo Schembechler when are they going to retire, and they say in four years. They started giving me that answer ten years ago. They both are great for the game, and I hope they stay in it for many years.

During the course of the game, we didn't do anything spectacular. Penn State made absolutely no mistakes, and we made a couple that hurt us and kept us off the board early. We won 21–3, but it wasn't very exciting. It was like watching paint dry. We didn't get many big plays, because Penn State didn't go to school to eat lunch. They play very intelligently and refuse to give you anything cheap. They make you earn everything you get. We did get Rocket Ismail open deep late in the game for a play that put it away.

We controlled the game and ended up with 503 yards in total offense, which is about as good as we have played on offense. We played very well on defense also. We held Penn State to less than 150 yards and three points. We won the game the old fashioned way—we earned it. I should pause here and praise Penn State for a great effort. Joe Paterno was most gracious after the game. Our players felt great about winning, and fortunately we managed to get all the seniors in the game for the last time in our stadium. The preceding year, Penn State introduced all its seniors before the game, and they made us stand out there in the cold, watching it. They wouldn't start introducing the seniors until we came onto the field. That really upset me. At the time I thought that we should do the same thing to Penn State this year, but that's not Notre Dame. We introduced our seniors early, and Penn State came out three minutes before kickoff, which is normal. They didn't need to be out there any earlier.

In the locker room prior to the game and after the seniors had left to be introduced, I told our juniors and underclassmen about the leadership we would have to have next year. The players looked around, and what they saw was next year's team. It didn't look as strong as this year's team. We talked about the things these seniors have sacrificed for the team, their leadership, the type of people they had been, and their desire to leave Notre Dame on top. The players certainly wanted them to go out winners, because it was their way of showing them how much respect they had for the seniors and how much they cherished their leadership. When we took the field, I don't think I have ever seen a group of underclassmen as committed to winning a game for the seniors as these men were.

THE GAME

SOUTH BEND–The last time Penn State paid a visit to Notre Dame Stadium, it was the Nittany Lions who were unbeaten and on their way to a national championship. Notre Dame, in Lou Holtz's first season, was struggling at the .500 mark.

The Irish put up a dogged fight that day but lost 24–19. They haven't lost a home game in 12 outings since.

Two years later, it's Notre Dame that has national championship designs after its 21–3 triumph over Penn State in Notre Dame Stadium. And it's the Nittany Lions who finished the year 5–6 for their first losing season in 50 years.

Holtz's Irish still have two formidable hurdles looming ahead. Top-ranked Notre Dame must travel to Los Angeles to face second-rated USC Saturday—then go to Tempe where a Fiesta Bowl berth awaits against unbeaten West Virginia.

The Irish will have to capitalize better on their scoring opportunities than they did against Penn State to win either of those next two. But Holtz wanted a brief moment to savor the season's tenth victory over an opponent his seniors had never beaten. It marked only the second Irish win over Penn State since the series began in 1981.

"It's a win," said Holtz. "We did what we had to do. We're in double figures now. Our players could not possibly feel good about their playing career unless they had beaten everybody on the schedule once. We had done that with the exception of Penn State. I'm just happy for the seniors."

Penn State and Joe Paterno put up a valiant effort against a good Irish team. Notre Dame's defense kept the visitors from controlling the football as they had done the year before en route to a 21–20 Penn State victory. The Irish rolled up 502 total yards, but suffered some untimely penalties and turnovers deep in enemy territory.

"We just didn't have enough offensively," said Paterno.

The Irish defense held Penn State to 179 total yards, permitting only five pass completions in 24 attempts to go with 105 net rushing yards. Only once in the entire second half did the Nittany Lions cross middlefield —and that ended at the Irish 38 after the visitors misfired on a pass out of punt formation on fourth and 12.

Penn State did get on the scoreboard when a 15-yard facemask penalty against the Irish moved Eric Etze into position for a 52-yard field goal to end the first half.

The Irish, meanwhile, notched 301 rushing yards and held onto the football for nearly 39 of the 60 minutes.

Notre Dame made the scoreboard light up on its very first possession. After a Penn State punt pushed them back to their own 13, Braxston Banks rambled 16 yards on second down to get the Irish out of a hole. Quarterback Tony Rice threw for 31 yards to Ricky Watters, and Tony Brooks converted on fourth and one from the Penn State eight. Rice took it in himself from two yards out for the 7–0 lead at the 5:12 mark. The drive covered 87 yards in 12 plays.

Jeff Alm picked off a Lance Lonergan pass deflected by Arnold Ale late in the first period, but the Irish couldn't take advantage. They had driven 73 yards to the Penn State 10 until a holding penalty and then an interception by Sherrod Rainge put the Nittany Lions back on offense.

Another Rice-to-Watters salvo—this one good for 27 yards—headlined Notre Dame's next drive. Mark Green tip-toed down the right sideline on his way to a 22-yard scoring run to conclude the 60-yard parade. Notre Dame was up 14–0.

The next time Notre Dame got the ball, Reggie Ho missed a short field goal after the Irish had reached the Penn State 18. The offense was on the bench a very short time because Gary Brown fumbled when Jeff Alm hit him, and Wes Pritchett recovered at the Penn State 24. Two plays later Rice threw an interception at the 22-second mark. As the half was getting ready to end, the Irish were penalized for a facemask, and this enabled Etze to kick the field goal that made it 14–3 at the half.

The Irish had totaled 286 yards and 16 first downs in the first half, but the scrappy visitors had kept them from scoring more often.

Notre Dame ruined another chance to score when Green fumbled at the Penn State 14 on its first attempt in the third period. But, after the visitors punted, Rice promptly found Rocket Ismail wide open behind the secondary for a 67-yard scoring pass.

Neither team made a serious threat the remainder of the game as Notre Dame played very conservatively. This showed the amount of respect Notre Dame has for a Joe Paterno team.

Rice led all rushers with 84 yards while also throwing for 191 more. Green added 64 rushing yards to go with 63 from Banks and 54 from Brooks. Notre Dame's Pennsylvania connection at the receiver spots featured two catches for 78 yards and one score by Ismail and four for 71 for Watters.

It was a workmanlike effort for the Irish—just another rung on the ladder.

"This isn't the end of the journey," Holtz said. "This isn't where we want it to end."

The Trojans and Mountaineers await.

In the locker room I thanked the players for their wonderful friendship and their work ethic. Then we talked about what we had to do against USC. I felt confident that USC would beat UCLA. Before the season even began, I felt USC would be as good as any team in the country. That's our next challenge. I hope we can meet it successfully.

As I've told the players so many times, every time you win a game, it makes the next one that much bigger. If USC beats UCLA, that couldn't be more true than this coming week. Then USC would probably be ranked second, and it doesn't get any bigger than number one against number two in the last regular-season game.

Things were rather confusing and hectic in the locker room after the game. The Fiesta Bowl representatives were there to invite us to play West Virginia, but in all honesty, my thoughts were already on USC. I talked to the squad as I normally do and then varied from my normal routine by returning to the field to do an interview for CBS. This was a mistake, because I think they were reenacting World War II on the field with a full cast. I got crushed. I wanted to get out of there and go home because the UCLA–USC game was on television, which would be followed by the West Virginia–Syracuse game on ESPN later that night. I'd have the chance to watch both of our next two opponents. I was rude to some people, and I felt bad about it because that's not treating people the way you want to be treated. I could give you a million reasons why I was short-tempered but not a single excuse.

On the way home it registered on me that we won the football game. We're 10–0 with one more on the horizon. Thanksgiving is coming up and, boy, do we have a lot to be thankful for. It's been a miracle season so far for us, and I can't put into words how thankful I am to be at Notre Dame right now.

It was a special feeling to leave the stadium for the last time this year, knowing we were 10–0. But I also realized this—if we don't beat USC, the whole season somehow will be wasted and a failure in my eyes. Anytime you get this far and don't go all the way, it is a total and complete disappointment. That's why when people would congratulate me, I said, "For what?" We haven't done anything yet. All we've done is put ourselves in a position to do something.

27

BOWLS AND PLAYOFFS: THE RACE FOR NO. 1

A T this time of year the amount of discussion about the postseason bowl games is absolutely amazing. Everyone is trying to get an edge by figuring out exactly where everyone else is going to go.

My philosophy is to stay out of it completely, but to keep informed as to what Father Beauchamp and Dick Rosenthal think. I enjoy the bowl representatives, they are great people and some of my closest friends can be counted among them. I love my wife, but I don't take out my wallet and look at her picture when it's third and 13. By the same token I don't visit with bowl reps during the season because I would have to either show partiality to one of them or to my own football team and game preparation. These are the only two options available when twelve bowl reps attend your game.

I would be doing a grave injustice to our team if I didn't put all my efforts into seeing that we do everything we can to win as many games as possible. If we don't win, we won't get a bowl bid. It's like a bank—you can't withdraw money unless you make a deposit.

The only time we talked with this team about going to a bowl game was on August 12, when I asked them to vote on whether they wished to go to one or not. When we go to a bowl we only have two objectives—win the game and have the best time possible. The players voted to go to a bowl game. They understood they had no say in what bowl we went to, where it was, when it was, when we leave, who goes, how many times we practice, and any other decision related to it. In other words, they voted to go to a bowl game under a complete dictatorship. That's the last time the players had to worry about bowls.

263

On my call-in-radio show on Mutual, someone asked me about the possibility of playing a bowl game against a school I had previously coached. That wouldn't bother me at all. In 1987 Brent Musburger and the people at CBS asked me the same thing when there was a possibility Arkansas might end up in the Cotton Bowl as our opponent. That would have been fine. I would not want to jeopardize a goal our team could accomplish simply because of my personal feelings. When you're a coach, you are a professional. You handle those things in a professional manner.

Arkansas went to the Cotton Bowl following the 1988 season, and I didn't have a great desire to play them—not because I coached there, but because they are awfully good, I didn't want to play Oklahoma or Nebraska or Miami or West Virginia, because they are also awfully good football teams. I went to school at Kent State, but I would be happy to play them in a bowl game. Why? Because I think there's a chance we might beat them. I have a lot of friends in Arkansas, I hope. Ken Hatfield is a great coach, and Frank Broyles is a friend and a very talented individual.

Ara Parseghian, former Notre Dame head coach

I said a while back that I thought Lou would take Notre Dame to a major bowl game in three years after he took over. I didn't want to put pressure on him, but after watching him and knowing what he was capable of doing, I felt he would accomplish that. Well, he made a liar out of me because he did it in two years.

I have been to virtually every post-season bowl game at some point in my career. We went to the Cotton Bowl last year for the first time. It was an outstanding bowl and we had a great time. I realize Notre Dame has had a great relationship with the Cotton Bowl down through the years. This dates back to when they played Texas the first two years that Notre Dame started going to bowl games again.

When I was at Arkansas we played UCLA in the Fiesta Bowl and it was very nice there. The only thing I didn't like about Phoenix was there were no freeways. There are nine million stoplights and they are all red. It's the only place in the world with two million people and no green lights.

I loved the Orange Bowl, which has been very patient with me. While at Arkansas in 1977 we accepted an invitation to the Orange Bowl and then encountered some adversity on our team. I'm sure the Orange Bowl wished they had selected a different team after we made the decision to suspend three of our better players. They still treated us great, it was a super bowl, and the Big Eight champion is always going to be a terrific opponent.

The Sugar Bowl is a super bowl game, and New Orleans is a fun town. The only unfortunate thing about playing in the Superdome was that we had to play Alabama when Bear Bryant was chasing his second national championship. They beat us in a good game. Afterward I went over to congratulate Coach Bryant and the Alabama team on a great performance. Coach Bryant looked at me and said, "Lou, I want you to know that's the best game we played in five years." I said, "Boy, am I glad I had a chance to see it." He just laughed.

Despite all the great experiences I've had with bowl games, I'm still in favor of a playoff. My feelings about the value of a playoff came in 1977, when I felt a great injustice was done to the Arkansas football team. They awarded the national championship to Notre Dame that year, and they deserved it. But I did not feel that was fair to our team. There were three teams that year with an 11–1 records. Three teams finished the season with impressive bowl wins, and three finished very close in the balloting, with over 1000 points.

Arkansas did not win the national championship, and yet I felt we were as good as any team in the country. We could say that at the time because we didn't have to play anyone else. You always become more optimistic when there's no one else left to play.

NCAA Division I football is the only championship that isn't decided on the field.

I do not want to do anything to disrupt the current bowl system, because I think it plays an integral part in college athletics. Bowl games are educational for the athletes. They are fun for the entire program, and they may help many college athletic programs survive financially.

We probably won't see a playoff system in my lifetime because the bowl games divide postseason money on an almost national basis. Almost every conference has a bowl tie-in, and since all league schools share bowl payments, most schools in the country get a share. I don't know what would happen with a playoff system.

Still, I would like to see a two-team playoff on the first Saturday in January. Let a computer pick the top two teams after the bowl games— don't do it by voting. Give each team so many points for every game it wins, so many points for every game its opponents win and its opponents' opponents win, and so on. In other words, I think a team should be rewarded for the type of schedule it plays. You would get no points for beating a Division II school. Total up all the points after the bowl games have been played and take the top two teams pointwise. That way you're selecting the teams that played the best week in and week out. To do it by popular vote, just by win-loss record, is totally unfair.

Right now I think we have some schools changing their schedules to match the capabilities of their team so that they will be successful every year. If you had weekly computer rankings, I think you would find this trend would reverse itself. The process should be similar to some of the state high school systems, where you can go 11–0 and not even make the playoffs.

Our current system has people voting who don't get to see the other teams play every week. It's a misconception to think the number-one team is the best team week in and week out—they're number one just because people voted them the best. We played horrendously against Navy and yet we jumped up to number one. Why? Because of our record. That's why you need a computer.

Maybe the computer would have matched us against Miami again after the bowl games. I think a great rematch would have been Miami and Florida State in 1987. However, we should seriously think about the ramifications a playoff system would have on the student/athlete academic record. After all, that is why they are in college. As important as football is, let's remember that it is still an extracurricular activity.

28

USC:
IT'S *THE* GAME

WELL, USC beat first-ranked UCLA, so it would be Notre Dame, ranked number one, against USC, now ranked at number two.

The USC game is the one I looked forward to all year. Not because I thought USC would be one of the five best teams in the country, but because I thought we'd be able to get all the tickets we needed. I told people, "Boy, I'll be glad when we get to USC because tickets won't be a problem." So you can imagine my predicament when I discovered the game was sold out a month earlier. Obviously, people realized early that this game would have great significance. This is the greatest demand for tickets to this game we witnessed in forty years.

From the time you first put on a pair of football shoes, these are the games you want to play in. These are the games you prepare for all your life. These are the games when the best comes out in Notre Dame. These are the games when Notre Dame memories are made.

When I first came to Notre Dame I knew the USC game was the game, but I didn't know why. After looking into the history of it, I could understand why.

I think the rivalry between Notre Dame and USC is the greatest I have witnessed. The history of this series is rather incredible. It all started sixty years ago, when USC sent an assistant athletic director, who had just gotten married and was with his bride, to Nebraska, where the Irish were playing the Cornhuskers, to talk to Knute Rockne about starting a series. The young man, Gwynn Wilson, and his wife Marion continued on to South Bend because Rockne refused to approve the series. Knute's logic was that the Irish were tired of traveling and were going to stay

267

closer to home. USC wanted to play Notre Dame because they felt this game would give them the national exposure they were seeking. Mrs. Wilson talked to Mrs. Rockne about how nice Southern California was, how they put fruit baskets in the hotel, what a pleasant trip it would be for all concerned. Mrs. Rockne told Knute she thought they ought to agree to the game. Wilson sent a telegram back to California saying, "The game is on."

The first game they played was in California. It was decided by one point, and Notre Dame won a controversial decision. The next year they played in Soldier Field in Chicago, the same year and same place Dempsey fought Tunney in front of 110,000. Notre Dame played USC in front of 120,000. Once again there was a disputed call in that game, and again Notre Dame won by one point. They have played every year since. One team dominates the series for a while, then the other, but it has always been a special game. You can sense it and feel it. Some of the greatest college games ever played have been between USC and Notre Dame.

The year the series began, a paper hanger in Germany wrote a book called *Mein Kampf*. The same year the owner of the New York Yankees fined Babe Ruth $5000 for missing curfew, and at the same time, Wellington Mara bought the New York Giants for $2500. You could buy a Ford for about $300, and Al Capone was making millions selling booze and broads in Chicago.

It's a great game, a great series.

I first really became aware of it when USC played Notre Dame in 1968. I was at Ohio State at the time, USC was number one and undefeated, and Ohio State was ranked number two. Notre Dame had a fine football team and was ranked ninth. The tradition of this series is to expect the unexpected, and it happened when Notre Dame and USC played to a tie. Consequently, USC dropped to number two, Ohio State moved to number one, and when we played and defeated them in the Rose Bowl, we won the national championship.

There've been so many great games, but maybe none more memorable than in 1974, when Notre Dame was ahead 24–0 and Anthony Davis ran the second-half kickoff back to ignite an incredible comeback and a 55–24 victory.

The week of the USC game my first year, I could sense the importance of it by the attitude of the players in practice. The year was 1986, and although we were 4–6 at the time, going out to play USC carried a special significance for all of us. This was going to end our season, but USC was committed to play on January 1 in the Citrus Bowl against Auburn.

USC had a great team, and we were very average, but the game still produced an air of excitement that is rarely duplicated. It was an emotional game played in a loud stadium. Much to my surprise, Notre Dame had a strong, vocal crowd, even though the game was played in the Coliseum. USC runs that horse around so much when they score, for a while I thought I was at the racetrack. I kept looking for a window to bet on that Trojan horse.

After my son Skip roughed their punter with eleven minutes to go in the game, we found ourselves behind 37–20. It was at this precise time that our team's attitude changed. I can't tell you why or how, but they finally came to realize that they no longer wanted to be average. No longer could they live with losing, and they refused to accept defeat. It was an incredible comeback, with Notre Dame winning 38–37. Our national championship in 1988 may have been born that day.

Larry Smith, USC's coach, has three objectives—beat UCLA, beat Notre Dame, and go to the Rose Bowl. USC has achieved the other two objectives this year, and it is up to Notre Dame to make sure he doesn't achieve the third one.

USC has some very impressive defensive rankings, and their offense in big, strong, tough, and aggressive. Erik Affholter is an all–American receiver, and I felt Rodney Peete was a great quarterback last year, even though he didn't have a great day against us. Their backs run as hard as any I've seen. They make too many great plays to call it poor tackling.

The most effective defense I've seen against Peete is to try to block the extra point. I haven't seen anybody really stop him. You run a risk when you blitz him because he has great mobility which allows him to avoid the rush. Any coach will tell you that when a quarterback scrambles, the defense is very vulnerable to a lot of big plays. In addition, they have a very strong running game, so you cannot focus on the passing game exclusively. This presents some serious problems to us.

The passing game sets up their running game because Peete is perhaps as prolific a passer as we have seen. He has a very quick release, a very strong arm, is very intelligent, and possesses excellent peripheral vision. His receivers find the hole in the coverage, and Peete can find the receivers. When that doesn't transpire, Rodney has the ability to run the football and hand it to the receiver.

I don't believe you can actually stop Rodney Peete. If you could, somebody would have done it already. They have tried the measles, laryngitis, blitzing him, and covering him. They have tried virtually everything, and yet Rodney Peete has continually enjoyed success.

I'm very impressed with the togetherness of the USC squad. I saw an inteview with Peete and Affholter where they talked about goals and chemistry. They really seem to have a lot going for them this year. It's their hundredth year of football, just like it was for us last year, so this season is somethng special. They're awfully well-disciplined and one of the best fundamental teams we faced. They never flinch, and they obviously have a great desire to beat Notre Dame. They are an excellent team that possesses all the tangible and intangible ingredients necessary to win the national championship, or else they wouldn't be 10–0 against a very tough schedule.

I told the team on Sunday, "This is *the* game. It's the first time since 1948 this game has been sold out in the Colliseum, and to my knowledge tickets are being scalped for $400. This is like a basketball tournament where two of the better teams in the country end up meeting in the finals. Of course, the USC–Notre Dame game is big even when they aren't the number-one and-two teams. This is what you work for, so I hope everyone enjoys this week. But it's not a matter of life and death, and let's remember it's not for the national championship. The loser may be eliminated, but the winner will not be crowned as national champion.

"Preparation and concentration are going to be exceptionally important this week. Be positive and believe in the Notre Dame spirit. But remember, this is just a football game. Relax, enjoy it and we will win the game. Don't get caught up in the hype, as it will be detrimental to performance.

"How do you prepare off the field? Get your rest and eat right the next few days. How do you prepare on the field? Strive for perfection.

"Tuesday will be our only day in pads. We'll be in shorts on Monday and Thursday.

"Remember our motto: Count on me. This game is going to be won by the Notre Dame team, not by superhuman plays. You can worry about the economy, about physics and chemistry, but don't worry about winning. Just believe in the Notre Dame spirit."

I want the players to understand how much this game means, so I had Dave Duerson talk to the squad Tuesday, since he was down from Chicago to do a television piece. On Thursday I invited Father Ned Joyce to say a few words, because there's nobody who's been around Notre Dame athletics longer or has a better sense of this rivalry than he does.

Greatness is in the mind and in the heart. I'm happy that we're four-point underdogs. I just don't like the reasons we are underdogs. Obviously we still have many people who question our capabilities and will continue to do so regardless of what we accomplish. I'm glad we're playing on the road in front of 93,000 people, because this is a chance for us to prove we are an exceptional team.

I told the players to close their eyes, put their heads down, and then raise their hands if they qualified as a great player. I told them there should be more than that, and a few more raised their hands. I want all of them thinking they have a chance to be great at this point.

All indications are that the weather may be a factor. I welcome the opportunity to play in warm weather, and I think our players do also. There is no way possible we can prepare our players in South Bend for warm weather. The last time we had temperatures of 70 degrees in South Bend, the Cubs were still in the pennant race.

This game's important to people around the country because we're both undefeated. Neither team has flinched. Both teams have absolutely deplored losing and done what they had to do to win. To achieve a perfect record means that the players on both teams have made tremendous sacrifices.

It's imperative that we keep our emotions under control during the week. It's important we don't get too high too early. No doubt both teams will be ready to play at game time. Regardless of how excited our players are, we can't play the game until Saturday afternoon.

I called Jimmy Johnson this week to talk about preparing a team to play on the road. It is not unusual for me to call other coaches; I do it all the time. It is not abnormal, either, to have a variety of head coaches call me and discuss things. I didn't give it a second thought when I picked up the phone and called him. We discussed a variety of things and exchanged thoughts and ideas. I do this quite often with Barry Switzer, Bobby Bowden, and others. On this occasion I was interested in Jimmy's philosophy about going on the road, because Miami has had such an outstanding record on the road. Ed Pope from the *Miami Herald* happened to be in Jimmy's office at the time I called and, ironically, he was talking to Jimmy about the same thing. I appreciated Jimmy's input—though I guess he may have thought it was a little strange to be helping Notre Dame. Nevertheless, the news media thought it was a newsworthy story, but I didn't.

I didn't realize until Monday, when I was interviewed, that this would be the first time the number-one and number-two teams have played each other in a USC–Notre Dame game. I think it is the first time both teams have been undefeated and untied. I had no idea that was the case.

I was doing some work at home while watching the tail end of *Monday Night Football*, and I heard them talking about the Notre Dame–USC game in great detail. There seems to be tremendous interest. Obviously there are a lot of people pulling against us in this game. Anybody who hopes to win the national championship is rooting for USC to win, with the exception of West Virginia. I would hope my native state of West Virginia is pulling very hard for us to win.

If this is a high-scoring football game, we are probably going to lose. A game of this magnitude is usually low scoring, unless one side makes mistakes. If both sides make mistakes, turnovers, fumbles, then the score could mount. In order for us to have a chance, we must keep the scoring low. This is very difficult to do against USC.

The game is different than the Miami game in that it's a road game for us. If the game were played here, and the students were here, finishing up exams, and there was excitement, it could be different. Right now, everybody is packing up their forks and knives and leaving town. We're going to be here all by ourselves, which isn't all bad. For Miami the excitement, the news media, and the television crews were here. The atmosphere on campus this week will be completely different from the Miami game and we will have to approach it differently. This time, by six o'clock Tuesday night, we are going to have to go around and shut out lights on campus.

Last year after we played USC, I said I thought they had a very good chance to play in the Rose Bowl, which they did. You could see their team continue to improve during the course of the season. I saw where they were at the beginning of 1987, where they were when we played them, and projected where I thought they would be at the end of the year. When I talked to our squad on August 12, I'd said USC would probably be the best team we would play this year. Unfortunately, I was correct in my evaluation. They entered the 1988 season as one of the top three teams in the country.

Most folks thought they would be outstanding; however, they are even better this year than I anticipated. I haven't seen Barry Sanders from Oklahoma State enough to evaluate him, but I'm sure that he is a great football player. Still, I don't know if he's played the competition week in and week out that USC and Rodney Peete have. I can't say who will win the Heisman, but if Rodney Peete does, I will not lead a protest.

Rodney Peete, I think, is the best quarterback in the country. He does so many things well. Steve Walsh is a great passer, and Miami is a great passing team. Michigan runs the ball very well. But I don't think we've played any football team that does a combination of run and throw as well as USC. I am convinced this is true because of the multiple talents Rodney Peete possesses.

Their tailbacks, Aaron Emanuel and Scott Lockwood, and fullbacks Leroy Holt and Ricky Ervins, are great runners because they are physical.

272

Their offensive line is big and strong and protects the passer well. Affholter is an outstanding pass receiver, and their flanker, John Jackson, is an excellent receiver as well.

Their tight ends have given them a lot of big plays. Last year Paul Green started at tight end. I thought he was absolutely outstanding. This year Scott Galbraith is even more impressive than Green. This tells us that they have two great tight ends, two fine wide-outs, good running backs, Rodney Peete, and a strong offensive line. Offensively, they are averaging almost 35 points a game, which is incredible, given the schedule USC has played through ten football games.

Defensively, I really am impressed with them. They are leading or were leading the country in defense against the rush, total defense, defense against the score, and perhaps the most important statistic, defense in turnover ratio—giveaways and takeaways. Their defense is dominating up front, but the real strength may be their secondary.

Mark Carrier is a great football player, and you have to be impressed with their cornerback, Ernest Spears. USC plays the ball very well in the air, and they play man coverage. They are very well-coached and well-disciplined, and they are on a mission. We haven't played as well on the road as we have at home, but we accept the challenge of going out there and playing possibly the best team in the country.

Wes Pritchett, senior linebacker
We were the number-one team going into the game, but all they said in the papers was how USC was a better football team. I think Coach Holtz did a great job of using that as a motivating factor on us—"Nobody's giving us any respect. We're the number-one team in the country and everyone thinks we're going to get slaughtered by USC." It really gave the guys another incentive to go out there and play harder and show the rest of the country how good a football team we had.

It has been a week since Rodney Peete first came down with the measles, and it should not pose a problem for us in Los Angeles. But, just to be safe, we had all our players get shots for measles before we left.

I did not get a measles shot, but I did get a flu shot. I have had every type of measles possible. I had seven-day measles. I had German measles. I had three-day measles. I am well over forty, and they told me there is no danger of my getting the measles at my age, so I decided to adhere to my philosophy of never getting a needle shot unless it was a case of life or death.

But I did take my flu shot in front of some players, and never flinched. Passed out, yes, but did not flinch. My arm hurt the next day. They did not give me the flu shot in the muscle. They could not find one. When you get it in the bone, it hurts.

I have been giving our players from California a hard time about the measles situation. I told them that we never have to get shots when we go to the states of Michigan or Pennsylvania to play.

So it comes down to the last football game of the year, number one vs. number two. USC was very impressive against UCLA, but they may have difficulty reaching that level of emotion two weeks in a row. However, it may be possible for them to accomplish this because of the high buildup this game has received and the magnitude of it.

Ara Parseghian always calls me every Friday during the season, but he said he wasn't going to do it this Friday because he never had much luck at the Coliseum and he didn't want to jinx us.

We weren't going to Los Angeles until the Friday before the game, hoping to treat this just like any other road game. In the past, with the students leaving campus for Thanksgiving on Tuesday, we had left for Los Angeles on Wednesday, as we did last year at Miami. But I decided before the season ever began that I didn't want to go until Friday. This would enable us to have better concentration at our practices.

However, after going home Saturday night following the Penn State win and thinking about it, I called Dick Rosenthal and asked him if we could go out Thursday night. We had to be there for a luncheon on Friday, but I wanted us to have all our preparation done here, and therefore not practice out there. I wanted to stay on campus and have our Thanksgiving here, even though there was no one else on campus, because we would have the players' attention and would be able to generate more meeting time with our team.

Our coaches did an exceptional job preparing our players this week. After looking at the film, Chuck Heater, our secondary coach, said he felt our defensive backs had a chance to play the USC receivers man-for-man as long as we didn't do it too often. We would have to select the proper time to play man-for-man, and I have never been around a coach who can do this better than Barry Alvarez. So the decision was made to blitz more often than we have in the past. This goes against our basic philosophy, but it was going to be difficult to win if we didn't do something unusual. Rodney possesses too much talent to play them any other way.

I didn't know how much pressure we could apply even if we blitzed them. Getting a man free was one thing, but to tackle Rodney was another. In addition, their running game concerns us if they catch us in a blitz. Despite our concerns, the fact is, if we couldn't pressure him, it might be a long afternoon.

We practiced indoors all week because we had about five inches of snow and it was exceptionally cold. I worried about the weather in Los Angeles, because we wouldn't be acclimated to it, but we had no control over it.

Classes ended Tuesday at noon. Wednesday was our last hard practice, and I talked to the squad at length about Thanksgiving. Our schedule for Thursday included an optional mass in the morning at ten o'clock. Then we would have our Thanksgiving Day meal at eleven o'clock. We would have nothing else scheduled that morning. I asked our squad to be there promptly at eleven, because I wanted to say a prayer of Thanksgiving and it was imperative the entire squad be present. It was an excellent meal, and we invited the coaches' families and let the players bring girlfriends, family, or other friends with them.

Our schedule was that after eating, we would have a brief meeting, go out and practice, then board the plane for Los Angeles, arriving there at nine P.M. By doing this, we would be there Thursday night with basically all our preparation complete.

We planned to work out briefly on Friday, but it was basically to review kicking-game assignments. I never miss a practice, but the luncheon was a command performance. We wanted to have a relaxing Friday, with plenty of free time for the players, then go play the game on Saturday.

Our squad during the course of the year was not as prompt as they needed to be. Occasionally, people were coming fifteen and twenty seconds or even a minute late to the practice field. We talked to the players and ran them when they were late, but we weren't getting the desired effect. It was normally the same players who were continually late.

I talked to the players at the meeting Wednesday night about promptness. Afterward I went home, got a good night's sleep, and got up Thursday morning for mass. I wanted Thanksgiving dinner to be extra special and make the players aware that they have so much to be thankful for, not just because the season has been a success, but because they are at Notre Dame and have had good things happen to them. We should all feel quite fortunate.

As it turned out, Ricky Watters showed up fifteen minutes late, and Tony Brooks came in twenty minutes late for the eleven o'clock meal. I visited each of them individually about why they were late. This prevented me from sitting down and eating with my family. Ricky said he was late because he was turning in a paper for architecture. I thought this must be true, because no one would make up an excuse that wild. In addition, Ricky is an honest person. Nevertheless, it was an unacceptable excuse because he could have turned in the paper at another time. I told him he had been late previously, we talked about it, and I told him specifically how important it was to be on time. If you aren't on time, you're showing people that you don't respect them and that your time is more important than theirs.

I made it abundantly clear that coming in late was totally unacceptable, and I had a notion not to take him to USC. However, having had this problem previously at Arkansas, I wished to avoid controversy at all costs. I was going to make an exception at this time, but if he were late for anything at USC for any reason—his fault, my fault, heart attack, I didn't care—he would not play in that football game. I wanted him to understand that completely and clearly. I didn't plan on having this conversation again. I prayed this situation wouldn't reach the stage where I had to suspend him, because the athlete invariably will receive adverse publicity, and always more than he deserves. He's a great young man, and he's made a great contribution to our team's success, but rules must apply to everyone.

I talked to Tony Brooks exactly the same way.

We had our typical Thursday practice, got on the airplane and had a routine trip. As soon as classes were over Tuesday, we'd all set our watches on California time so we could get acclimated to the three-hour difference. We went to bed on California time and got up at eleven, which was eight California time. So it wasn't that much of an adjustment for anyone.

It was a good forty-five-minute ride from where we stayed in Newport Beach to the Bonaventure Hotel in downtown Los Angeles, where the "Big Game Luncheon" was held. I had a lot on my mind, so I took the opportunity to finalize some last-minute items that needed to be done. No matter how long you work, you just never seem to get everything done.

There were around 2500 people at the luncheon and it was packed. Craig Fertig, the former USC quarterback, and Tommy Hawkins, who was a great basketball player at Notre Dame and now works in Los Angeles, were the masters of ceremonies.

Fertig told a great story about going back to South Bend in 1967 to play Notre Dame when the Trojans hadn't won in Notre Dame Stadium in thirty-two years. They told him the weather was nice. It was 19 degrees. John McKay informed the officials that he absolutely would not bring his team onto the field until Notre Dame was already there, because he was not going to have his team stand around in the cold while Notre Dame made them wait to play.

It ended up being kind of a Mexican standoff, because neither McKay nor Ara would budge. Finally, an official came to get USC's team and said if they didn't take the field now, they would have to forfeit the game. McKay said, "What would the score be?" The official told him it would be 2–0, and McKay said, "That's the best damn deal we've gotten here yet."

I don't know what will happen during the game tomorrow, but I think we will play well. I think our preparation has been good, and our players are confident yet nervous. Our seniors know the importance of the game, and I'm really pleased with their leadership. They aren't about to let the underclassmen step out of line. For example, at dinner the conversation was louder than usual. The players know I prefer a very quiet environment, and they usually accommodate my wishes, but not this time. I felt the noise could be attributed to nervous energy rather than lack of concentration. However, before I could say anything, Andy Heck stood up and said it was time to start getting serious about what we were here for. Our seniors can get more done with our team than any I've seen. The rest of the meal was quieter than a silent movie.

When I first arrived on campus, I interviewed every one of our players individually for approximately thirty minutes in an effort to understand them and Notre Dame. They were all such fine men and very clean-cut. After five days of interviewing players for ten hours a day, I said to Jan Blazi, my secretary, that I wished occasionally one would drive up on a motorcycle with a week's beard, just so I would know we had some defensive players. I was joking, of course.

It's interesting that this late in the season there are only three undefeated teams left. Ironically, all three are coached by men who came from the same conference. I think that says something positive about the Mid-American Conference. I went to Kent State, and both Larry Smith of USC and Don Nehlen of West Virginia went to Bowling Green. One thing that's similar with all three of us is that we were trained by hard-nosed coaches who liked to win the hard way.

There was a story in the *Los Angeles Times* today with quotes from Steve Beuerlein and Ron Calcagni about how tough I had been with quarterbacks when they were playing. I'm sure Tony Rice would say the same things. There is no way you can win if the quarterback is not mentally tough, yet you can't allow him to take physical pounding in practice. The players must respect the quarterback, and this is best accomplished by putting a lot of mental pressure on him. If I can rattle him, so will the opponents. Many times I will get on a quarterback and the other players get mad at me. When this happens, you know you've found a leader.

We only spend about twenty minutes in the relaxation session. The first time I did it with a squad, I was at Arkansas and we were playing Florida in the Bluebonnet Bowl in '82. Florida had a great team with Wayne Peace, Neal Anderson and Wilbur Marshall. Florida probably was a more talented team than we were. We did the relaxation period for our offense only. I wanted to see the effect it would have on them. Defense had been the strength of our team all year. In the game, we were unbelievably poised on offense and played with great confidence. Just the opposite was true of our defense. We couldn't slow the Florida offense down, but fortunately we controlled the ball for almost forty minutes and won 28–24. There was such a discrepancy that day, we have continued doing the relaxation session for the last eight years. Does it work? I don't know, but I do believe it gives us an edge in the game.

It's amazing how many fans there are in our hotel who think we're here on vacation. I don't wish to be impolite, but it would be awfully difficult to get anything done if I stood in the lobby and signed autographs for people all afternoon. People sometimes don't understand that I'm working. I'm not here just to observe the game. You don't go up to Mike Tyson between rounds and ask for his autograph.

Friday afternoon the players and assistant coaches went to a local high school to loosen up for an hour or so. This was the only thing we had scheduled for the players from the time they arrived Thursday night until Friday at six P.M. dinner. They had all afternoon to themselves, with few restrictions, as I trusted them completely.

When I arrived back at the hotel from the luncheon, I immediately checked with the coaches to see if everything was okay with the team. They assured me it was fine, but there was a little problem at practice, which they perceived to be minor. I felt good, but to show you how optimistic I was, we brought two punters on the trip. That's the first time I have ever done this as a head coach.

I normally will walk into a meeting at precisely the proper time. The first thing we do on a continuous basis is set our watches. We go by LLH time. This stands for Louis Leo Holtz time. At six sharp we close the doors and say our prayer. The managers always tell me who is missing just as I walk into the meeting.

This particular time the managers told me Tony Brooks and Ricky Watters were missing, as well as two other freshmen—who were late for the very first time. Approximately forty minutes later they showed up and said they had lost track of time at a shopping mall.

My mind was made up at that exact moment that they weren't going to play against USC. However, in fairness to them and the team, I wanted other opinions to see if I was making an emotional decision. I listened to assistant coaches for a while and then summoned the leaders of this football team, as I perceived them. I told them the situation and let them speak. I don't think there is any way I would have changed my mind, but by listening to the players I would know what their reaction would be to our decision. If they felt like I did, great; if not, we would still make the same decision but we would have a morale problem which would need to be addressed and solved in the next twelve hours. I wanted the players to express their opinions, and to hear what they felt was proper and fair. They could have possibly persuaded me to change my mind. The important thing, I felt, was let them express themselves.

Andy Heck, senior offensive tackle

We had just had the pregame meal and we were all going to watch a movie, which we usually do the night before a game. That night we were watching The Untouchables.

We were all gathering in the room and one of the managers came up to me and said, "Did you know that Tony Brooks and Ricky Watters weren't at dinner?" I said, "No, I didn't know that. Does Coach Holtz know?" And he said, "Yes, we just told him." Then the guys started whispering it around.

We started watching the movie, knowing that something was going to happen. About halfway through the movie Mike Green—our head manager—came in and grabbed me, Wes Pritchett, Frank Stams, Tim Grunhard, Mark Green, Ned Bolcar, Tony Rice, George Streeter, Corny Southall, Flash Gordon, Pat Terrell, Stan Smagala, and a couple of others. We went into the other room, where we had had our pregame meal.

Coach Holtz was sitting there around a big table with all the coaches. Coach Holtz was smoking a pipe, and it was obvious they'd been discussing something important. Obviously, it was the situation with Ricky and Tony. Coach Holtz had us come over and sit down. He explained the situation—they had been late and had tried to call but weren't successful. He said it was our team—meaning the seniors and the few juniors. It was our team, and he wanted to hear what our feelings were on what we felt should be done in this situation.

I remember I spoke up first and said, "I feel real strongly about it." And Coach Holtz said, "Well, which way do you feel strongly about it?" And I said, "I think we should send them home." I even said that we should kick them off the team.

Wes Pritchett chimed in and said he agreed totally. That was pretty much the consensus. Frank Stams and Mark Green said they agreed also. Everyone in the room had the opportunity to express himself, and it was unanimous to send them home. Coach Holtz took a puff on his pipe, got a smile on his face, and said he totally agreed and that he was going to send them home.

Then we all went back in to watch a movie. Everybody was asking what was going on. Coach told us not to say anything because he was going to address the issue right after the movie was over.

When the movie ended, he came in and started the meeting, which was probably the most emotional one we had during the season. He started by dismissing the four players who had been late. The players hesitated to leave, but Coach Holtz was adamant about it, and they left. Then he explained the situation and said they weren't going to play in the game. He asked if anybody would like to speak on their behalf. There was silence for the most part, but finally one player said he wanted to speak for them.

He basically said we would be making a mistake if we didn't let them play, because they're just human and anybody could make a mistake. He asked if we could live with ourselves if we lost the game and didn't have the best players on the field. He said something to the effect of, "I know a lot of you feel the same way I do about allowing them to play but just aren't going to say anything. However, I want all the guys who feel the same way I do to just raise their hands." Nobody did, and the player sat down.

Frank Stams stood up at the very back of the room, and he was very emotional and vocal. I can't remember exactly what he said, but it was something like, "I don't care what all you guys think. If you're not ready to play this game tomorrow, then I want you to just get the hell out of this room. I don't care if I'm the only one on the field. I'm going to play awfully well tomorrow." Then he sat down and was kind of quiet, you know, and it just sent a charge through the room.

Coach Holtz got a big smile on his face and said, "That's the way it's going to be. I agree totally." Then Ned Bolcar stood up and said he basically thought the same thing. Then Corny Southall stood up and said, "We've come a long way. We're not going to let this stand in our way."

Then Coach wrapped it up, and we said a prayer together as a team, which we do quite often, and that night was probably the closest we had ever come as a team. It was a great feeling.

Then we left the room, and Brooks and Watters were sitting outside and they shook everybody's hand and said good luck in the game. And that was that.

After the movie, I excused the athletes involved and visited with the whole squad about the situation. There were some comments made in that room by some of our players that were very impressive. It was obvious that we were ready to play a football game, and that it didn't matter if we were going to go in there short-handed or at a disadvantage. We were going to play hard. We'd worked hard for this, and it is a shame that we had to have this situation. I have always told our squad we would have at least three crises on a team each year, but that doesn't mean they're bad. A crisis can be great if you react favorably to it, and there is no doubt this was a crisis.

Ned Bolcar, senior linebacker

Coach Holtz will always tell reporters that if something happens to someone, "Someone else will pick up the rifle and keep marching on."

After the meeting, I told Ricky and Tony they could not play in the football game. They weren't surprised, because after our meeting on Thanksgiving I think they knew the consequences. I thought it would be in the best interests of everyone involved to just send them home. We were there to play a football game, and if they weren't going to play and help us, there was no reason for them to be there. We don't take tourists, or people with sunglasses, cameras, and radios on trips. We take people who can help us win. If they weren't going to help us Saturday, there was no reason for them to be there.

Wes Pritchett

When the event first came up, Coach Holtz talked with the coaching staff and then felt it wise to bring in all the seniors. So he called in all the seniors and a couple of the leaders who weren't seniors and explained the situation and asked how we felt and what we thought needed to be done.

I think the decision to send them home was unanimous and one that everybody agreed on. Coach Holtz came in after a team movie and announced what was going to happen. As a result, I think it pulled the team a lot closer, because the guys who were going to have to fill those positions knew they were going to have to pick up the slack that much more.

You know what they say—on this day they jumped a little higher, hit a little harder, ran a little faster. Well, it was really like that. It made everybody realize it was a team concept. Coach Holtz really left the decision up to us. He presented what he was thinking, then he said, "How do you feel?" And he said, "If you feel different, then say so." I mean, this was our whole season. We were playing the number-two team in the country. He really wanted us to say how we felt, and one guy did feel a little differently, but it was a team decision.

We had a great relaxation period, went to bed, and got up ready to play the game.

We got to the stadium a little early, but this was good because it gave everybody a chance to benefit emotionally from the atmosphere. Tickets were at a premium. There was a national television audience, and this was the game of the weekend. This was the time to start getting excited and commence thinking about the magnitude of it all.

We went out and warmed up and you could sense the excitement. I have never seen so many photographers and camera crews since I have been coaching. They were taking pictures of everybody and everything, including themselves. I thought about when I was a youngster and you had one picture taken a year and you really cherished it. Now everybody is taking my picture. I thought, if Sister Mary Hamitt could only see me now . . .

Pete Cordelli, receiver coach

I thought the adversity we had at USC really brought us together because of the Watters and Brooks situation. We had a meeting and there was an attitude of, "We'll win with them. We'll win without them. If you don't believe that, then get out." Tony Rice came up to me and said, "Coach, we're going to win no matter what happens." We'd come so far. When the younger guys saw the veterans saying they would win no matter what, that raised everybody's expectation level. Even for a guy like Tony Rice, who had never played at the Coliseum before.

After the pregame warm-ups we went back to the locker room and I expressed my thoughts. The key word this week has been "checkmate."

We had told our squad that someone would say checkmate, and it had better be us and not our opponent.

When we go to USC, my high school coach Wade Watts is always with me. He's seventy years old now and lives in Laguna Beach. A good friend of mine from Minneapolis, Harvey Mackay, was also there. It's rare that I let any outsiders in the locker room with our squad, but these two individuals have helped me as a person. I probably wouldn't be here if it weren't for Wade Watts, and Harvey Mackay has been as good a friend as you could ever have. Another great friend who couldn't be there was Carl Pohlad. During the off-season I met with Carl in Chicago and he said, "Lou, you won't win the championship unless you stop flinching." He was right. His comments hurt, but it takes a good friend who cares to say these things. We had a four-hour meeting, and I promise you I left that meeting as a better coach.

I did not sleep the night before the game because of the magnitude of the decision we made to send the athletes home. You always worry about being fair to the athletes and to the team. With all the attention being paid to the game, the decision certainly wouldn't be a secret.

I told Dick Rosenthal and Father Beauchamp of the decision we had made, and they supported it. We obviously had to release something to the media, so we put together some brief comments explaining the situation and informed people about a half-hour before the game began.

THE GAME

LOS ANGELES—So much for any late-season questions about Notre Dame's claim to the number-one ranking.

Just when it seemed like Fighting Irish dreams of a national championship would have to be put on hold, all kinds of unusual things happened on the way to a convincing 27–10 victory by top-ranked and unbeaten Notre Dame over second-ranked and previously unbeaten USC.

Ironically, this could have been USC's year. This is the Trojans' 100th anniversary of football, and they were doing it up right with a 10–0 record (that became a 14-game winning streak, longest in the country), a dominating offense averaging 472 yards and a defense leading the nation while only permitting 68 rushing yards per contest. Not to mention the presence of Heisman Trophy candidate Rodney Peete at quarterback. He'd just come off a bout with measles and was good enough to make the cover of *Sports Illustrated*, thanks to the Trojan triumph over UCLA last week.

For Notre Dame to win, the defense would have to slow down Rodney Peete which is normally virtually impossible. They blitzed him and badgered him and put more pressure on him than any USC opponent had all season. Normally, Peete's quickness and scrambling ability made that sort of strategy fruitless. But someone forgot to tell Frank Stams. As he had with Miami's Steve Walsh, Stams found a way to pressure the quarterback more often than anyone had previously before a jam-packed Los Angeles Coliseum. He finished with nine tackles, two and a half sacks of Peete, and a recovered fumble.

"We felt we had to mix it up by blitzing," Holtz said. "All year I've been asked on my call-in talk show why we don't blitz more. Today was the most we've blitzed all year."

Southern Cal is a very talented, well-coached team, and there is just no way to stop their versatile offense. Their defensive statistics also were most impressive. Peete did manage 23 completions in 44 attempts for 225 yards. But Notre Dame made some big plays, picking off two interceptions, one of which completely turned the momentum of the game around. On that same play, which turned into a 64-yard scoring run for Notre Dame by cornerback Stan Smagala, Stams put a tremendous block on Rodney Peete. But Rodney is a great competitor and wasn't intimidated by the hit as some quarterbacks might have been.

Even more amazing was the fact the Irish did all this and managed 27 points, despite only eight first downs and despite playing without their top rusher and top pass receiver. USC's defense held Notre Dame without a first down for the entire second period and the first 14 minutes of the third.

But none of that made any difference:

"We made big mistakes," said USC coach Larry Smith. "We didn't do anything to help ourselves win the game. We moved the chains, but we didn't score."

Maybe USC should have known what was coming after Notre Dame's first play from scrimmage. Backed up to their own two by a Trojan punt, Notre Dame went for broke. The Irish are known as anything but a passing football team, but that didn't stop quarterback Tony Rice from faking perfectly and arching a 55-yard strike to Raghib Ismail on first down. Notre Dame ultimately got no points from that possession, but that initial play set the tone for the afternoon.

"I was tinkering all week with the idea of throwing on our first play," Holtz said. "When we got the ball so deep, I thought it would be a good chance to get out of a hole. Tony made such a good fake on the play, I didn't know if he'd get the ball off in time."

With leading rusher Tony Brooks and leading receiver Ricky Watters out of the game, the Irish had to improvise. Rice is one of the great improvisors in college football, but not the only one. On third and 3 on an option left, Rice kept the football instead of pitching to Mark Green and zipped 65 yards in front of the Notre Dame bench for a 7–0 Irish lead. It marked the longest rush permitted by USC since 1979.

On USC's second play from its 31, Peete was true with a swing pass to Aaron Emanuel, who lost the ball to George Williams. Stams recovered at the USC 19. Four plays later, Mark Green, from nearby Riverside, went in from the two for a 14–0 advantage.

George Streeter picked off one Peete pass and brought it to the USC 22 before Peete tackled him. This opportunity to score was thwarted when Southern Cal forced Rice to fumble on second down. One possession later, USC drove to the Irish 19, only to have Ricky Ervins fumble, and Williams recovered for Notre Dame. The Trojan defense controlled the line of scrimmage in the second period, and the Trojans capitalized on this by going 66 yards in an 11-play drive highlighted by a 26-yard throw from Peete to Erik Affholter. Scott Lockwood's drive from the one made it 14–7 at the 2:24 mark.

Notre Dame again had to punt after three plays, and it looked like the Irish control might be in jeopardy. But on first down from the Notre Dame 49 with 52 seconds left, Peete threw a pass intended for John Jackson. But Jackson had slipped midway through his route, Smagala came up to intercept at full speed and he outran most of the Trojans 64 yards down the sideline to make it 20–7 at halftime. Reggie Ho missed the PAT.

The stunned Trojans had played a half in which they held Notre Dame to the same number of first downs as touchdowns. USC held a 19:33 to 10:27 edge in possession time, but it had paid no dividend.

The Irish were stymied on their first two tries in the third period before USC once again mounted a challenge driving from its own 44. USC started with successful Peete passes to Leroy Holt for 11 yards and Jackson for 16. Consecutive Emanuel runs for 10 and 21 yards gave the home team first and goal at the 4. Emanuel gained one, then on second down was stacked up by Pritchett for a loss of one. This was indeed a great play by Wes. On third down, a false start cost the Trojans five yards, and Quin Rodriguez had to settle for a 26-yard field goal. USC had missed a golden chance to completely wrest the momentum away from the Irish. Notre Dame's offense sensed the momentum switching and responded by driving for a touchdown. Starting from their own 30 with a 13-yard gainer by Rice, the Irish got a couple of huge plays from fullback Anthony Johnson to maintain control. On third and 3 from midfield, Johnson fumbled for 10. Then, on third and 6 from the 36, Johnson nabbed a screen pass and zigzagged through defenders for 23 yards to the 13. Three plays later, Green dove the final yard for his second touchdown and effectively closed the lid on his hometown Trojans, even though 11:55 remained.

Now at the mercy of the Notre Dame defense, Peete enjoyed both success and frustration. Stams and Williams sabotaged the first USC possession with a sack and nine-yard loss. To stop one drive disrupted the second drive by throwing Peete for a loss of eight on first down. The third drive was very impressive as it reached the Notre Dame 10 in the final minute before Streeter knocked down a fourth-down pass for Affholter.

"I think this team is underrated, even though we're number one," said an exhausted Holtz. "I've read articles people have sent me all year saying we were lucky against this team or that team. Our football team is prettier than I am, but that's about it. They don't play pretty all the time, but they sure play together as a team.

"I'm beat right now," he said. "I said to my wife on Tuesday that God works in wonderful ways. He managed to expire my enthusiasm and energy at the same time as our season."

The Irish now have a month to get ready for their Fiesta Bowl matchup with 11–0 West Virginia. Based on their effort against USC, they've earned their rest—and their ranking.

USC moved the ball on its first drive, but we finally forced them to punt, and the ball rolled dead on our two-yard line. We did the unpredictable, violating every tendency Notre Dame has had for three years, by using a play-action pass on the first play of the game from our own two. Our logic was that we could gain 98 yards and the most we could lose was two yards. A good friend, Jay Jordan III—who would make a great coach—said to evaluate a business deal, determine what is the most I can gain and what is the most I can lose. We hit the pass to Rocket Ismail, good for 55 yards. We jumped on top of USC and our defense was outstanding all day. We did score 27 points, but their defense dominated our offense.

We put great pressure on Rodney Peete, and I don't know when I've seen a better all-around effort by a defense than ours put forth. Stan Smagala's interception for a touchdown, George Streeter's great interception, and our defense getting the turnovers enabled us to get on top of them even though we only had one big play offensively ourselves, which was Tony Rice running for the touchdown early.

We came out the second half, and both teams dominated with their defenses. They drove the ball on us, we had a good goal-line stand and forced a field goal that made it 20–10. That's the only time our offense came to life. We drove right back down the field rather methodically and went 78 yards for a touchdown. There was a third-down pass from Rice to Anthony Johnson that was absolutely critical.

We won the game 27–10, and we were awfully happy at that point. To finish the season 11–0 is great. But it's even better when you realize you don't have to come back and do it again next week. I was happy for the players and coaches. Our locker room was bedlam, just like it was after Miami, and I think it's because maybe deep down inside, our players weren't completely positive we could win those games, and that's why the victories meant so much.

Chuck Heater, secondary coach

I think our ability to apply pressure defensively in the second half of the season surprised some people. I don't think USC expected us to pressure them as much as we did. We really researched that. Surprisingly, in that conference, even though the Pac-10 is known for its passing and its man-to-man coverage, we really didn't see other teams try to attack them that way in all the film we looked at.

Secondly, it became a matter of evaluating personnel, and I thought we matched up pretty well against them. So we said, "Hey, this is the thing to do." Barry [Alvarez] and I were looking at the film a couple of months after the season and we said, "I can't believe we did that." We blitzed a lot, even on first down, and we had not done that at all. It was a total surprise to them. But it was just one of those things. The ability to look at the film on Sunday, Monday, Tuesday, implement the plan and then to see it work on Saturday—that's a great feeling as a coach.

Again, I think it's a reflection of our attitude. If you're tight and not confident of winning and you pull back a little bit, you might be in trouble. But we were in the biggest game of our lives and we said, "Just let it go." That doesn't normally happen in a game like that. Usually, you're worried in a big game about getting beat deep on a pass. But we just felt like we had the athletes who could play. The development of that the second half of the year, especially with my kids in the secondary, was key. Then we became more of a dominant team. We had been dominant up front with the running game. Then we became more of a dominant team against the pass the second half.

Our players fell into a great rhythm of pushing continually on game days and at the same time realizing we had to work hard during practice, even though we lacked enthusiasm. All of a sudden there wasn't a tomorrow. We wouldn't have another game for five and a half weeks, and it was great to have the pressure of perfection removed temporarily. To beat USC anytime is a thrill, but to beat one of the five best teams in the country made it feel even better.

I had a chance to visit with Rodney Peete after the game. He's a great quarterback and a classy young man. As a matter of fact, the entire USC organization is class.

As we rode the bus back to the hotel in Newport Beach, I was exhausted, but I'm sure I wasn't alone. I was filled with mixed emotions. I was happy we won, but sorry for Tony Brooks and Ricky Watters. They are fine young men who have made a great contribution to our success. I was hopeful, for their sake, they would be back for the bowl game. I had talked with Tony's mother on the telephone from Los Angeles, but I couldn't get hold of Ricky's father until a few days later. I wish we could have done it without everybody in the country knowing, but that wasn't possible. Hopefully we'll all benefit from this.

Saturday night I had a chance to have dinner with my family at a beautiful country club near our hotel in Newport Beach. It was just my wife, daughter, son, Uncle Lou and his wife, and it was great to have that special time together. This was made possible by a wonderful Notre Dame fan by the name of Joe De Franco.

I got up early Sunday morning to tape my television show by the pool at the Anaheim Marriott. Then we went to the communion breakfast, and it was a beautiful affair. Father Malloy said the mass, and they presented Father Beauchamp with an Honorary Notre Dame Monogram Club jacket, which I know he truly appreciated. The communion breakfast means so much to our alumni in California, and it's always a great affair when you win the football game.

We stopped at Disneyland for a couple of hours, which is when the AP took pictures of me with Pluto and Goofy. I wanted to go on the Magic Carpet Ride, but they only have that at Disney World in Orlando, and the Golden Nugget show was packed, so I just wandered around with my wife, had an ice-cream cone and relaxed.

We flew home and had already made plans to meet with the staff Monday morning and with the players Monday afternoon. As the plane touched down about midnight Sunday, in South Bend, I felt exhausted, but I also felt very, very good. We had gone 11–0 with one to go, and that would be another season in itself.

Jan Blazi, secretary to Lou Holtz

I very seldom get to see him enjoy the victories, because he is always concerned about the next one. He may enjoy wins for a few hours the day and night of the game, but by the next day it's on to the next game. He is not one to sit back and enjoy it. I think he found it very difficult to relax as the season went along, because of the magnitude each game took on as we continued to win. Even after beating Miami, I never saw any feeling of self-satisfaction. It was always a very businesslike atmosphere in the office.

He did lighten up a little after the end of the regular season. We had a month before the Fiesta Bowl, and it seemed he sat back and realized, "We've had a great season and we've got a chance to finish number one." Until that point I don't think he wanted to think about that because there was always another game that week.

29

TONY BROOKS AND RICKY WATTERS: GOOD KIDS, BAD DECISION

THE situation with Ricky Watters and Tony Brooks and their suspension from the USC game drew so much attention that I was just glad the regular season had ended. I hate suspensions because of the national publicity they receive. People immediately draw conclusions that are wrong. I wanted to sit and talk to Ricky and Tony privately. I had every intention of allowing them to play in the Fiesta Bowl, as long as they adhered to the same team rules as everyone else. They had paid the price for their mistake by missing the USC game. That was over now. The punishment should never exceed the crime, and I wanted to make sure it didn't.

The last thing a football coach wants to do is suspend somebody. Anyone who thought I did it for some kind of motivational effect couldn't be more off base. As a coach, you don't need to prove to the public that you are in charge of the team. You don't have to send a message to the public that the team is going to do it our way or else. We do a lot of things within the squad in terms of discipline. You have rules and regulations, and people have to learn to adhere to them. You don't go into coaching to get rid of people. You are in a leadership role to help, advise, guide, counsel, and mold young men to take a positive position in society. People need love and understanding most when they usually deserve it the least, and this was the case with Ricky and Tony.

Steve Belles, senior quarterback
That was something we as a team felt was the right thing to do. We never thought about how it would affect the game. We knew we could make

290

up for them not playing. It was an attitude of discipline that came as much from the players' minds as from Coach Holtz. We all felt the same way, just that it was the right thing to do.

I vividly remember when I was growing up and my dad, who was a bus driver, would leave for a three-day trip. He wouldn't even be down the driveway when I would break a dish drying it or some other stupid thing. My mother would say, "Wait until your dad gets home. I am going to tell him and he's going to give you a whipping." For three days I would dread the thought of my dad coming home. When he came in, I would run and hide because I didn't want to see him. I think you must discipline, but with love and affection. The sooner we met with Ricky and Tony, the better the whole situation would be.

I have a special feeling for Tony Brooks and Ricky Watters. Tony and Ricky are not bad people, they just made a bad decision. We sent them home because I didn't think it was relevant for them to sit in the stands.

I feel like Coach Bear Bryant did. If you can't hug them, pat them, and brag about them, you don't want them on your team. They are on our football team because I can hug them, pat them on the back, and brag about them. They are both wonderful young men with great futures.

Many people tried to compare what happened with Ricky and Tony to the suspension we had at Arkansas before playing Oklahoma in the Orange Bowl after the '77 season. That decision was completely different because it happened twelve days before the game. At Arkansas we could change our gameplan and do a variety of different things to help us win. Secondly, that incident did not bring our football team together. If anything, it served as a divisive force. The longer a situation like that hangs in limbo, the more complicated it becomes. We weren't a good football team due to the suspensions. But once the team knew we trusted one another, were committed to excellence, and loved one another, we became a great team. We won that game 31–6.

I made a vow after the incident at the Orange Bowl never to go through that again. I would not suspend anybody again. I did not decide to suspend Ricky and Tony. They decided to suspend themselves when they chose to miss the Friday night meal. All I did was enforce their decision. The last thing in the world I wanted was their suspension, but unfortunately we had no other option, because I had given them my word in the actions we would take if they were late again. To have done anything else would have been completely contrary to the philosophy of Notre Dame and detrimental to their future.

I don't care if you ostracize the witch in *Snow White*, there are going to be some people who like her. So anytime you take action, you know it's going to be divisive. Many times an athlete who is not involved will side with his teammates and say, "It could have been me," or "I've done the same thing." You have to realize this is not going to bring a team together unless it is an exceptional one with its priorities in the proper perspective. This is the type of team we had at Notre Dame. I don't know if any other team could have supported this decision unanimously. Ecclesiastes 3:13 says there is a time for everything, and I believe that now is the time to heal.

Once we got back from Los Angeles, I said to Tony and Ricky, "Where do we go from here? You have a choice—you can make this a positive situation or a negative one. I think it will end up positive if we all choose to make it one."

After our meeting, when we understood each other, we put our arms around each other and hugged and the matter was over, forever.

Jan Blazi, secretary to Lou Holtz

I think Coach Holtz was amazed at the volume of letters praising him for the decision he made to suspend Ricky Watters and Tony Brooks at the USC game. People seemed to understand they had broken rules, and many people commented about how they felt the morals in college athletics were slipping a little and they hoped this would be a good example.

30

BALANCING THE HIGHS AND LOWS: A SEARCH FOR REALITY

HOW could we even talk about the highs and lows without saying a few things about my family? They are at the center of my attention. My wife Beth is special. We have been married to each other for fifty-six years, twenty-eight apiece. She is not only my wife but also my best friend. She is beautiful and the nicest person I have ever met. She has great common sense and I value her opinion as much as I would Socrates'. We have four beautiful children. Luanne, twenty-six, a graduate of Centenary College, has been married for five years to Terry Altenbaumer, a chemical engineer. They adopted our first grandchild a year ago. Skip, twenty-four, played with and graduated from Notre Dame and is now an assistant football coach at Colorado State, after serving as a graduate assistant at Florida State in '87 and '88. Kevin, twenty-two, just graduated from Notre Dame. Our children graduated from Notre Dame because it is the best school in the world. Having paid for our children to attend the university, we consider it the best money we ever spent. It is difficult to be the child of a football coach at any school, but even more so at Notre Dame. My children have never made anything but supportive comments to me, but I know how difficult their lives have been because of my job. I hope I have made the same sacrifices for my family as they have made for me. One of the great things they do for me is help bring me back to reality when football tends to become larger than life.

Jan Blazi, secretary to Lou Holtz
He is so cool about handling anything that comes up. He smokes a pipe regularly—in fact, he has a desk drawer full of pipes. Once he had

*knocked some ashes into the wastebasket by his desk and the wastebasket
caught on fire. He walked out of his office carrying the basket with the
contents in flames and he just said, "These things happen sometimes." He
walked into the rest room with it, put out the fire, came back, and acted
like nothing had happened. That's typical. He doesn't let anything bother
him at all.*

Chuck Heater, secondary coach

*I thought Lou's performance was masterful. He did a great job of
bringing the team along through the year. He gives such great thought to
what he says to the players and just how he approaches the team. He
draws from many other people in what he says. But the way he brought
them along was really good. He didn't put a lot of pressure on the team,
even though we talked about wanting to be great. He had a way of keeping
the team relaxed no matter what the circumstances. I thought he did a
great job in how he approached it from week to week as we progressed
through the year.*

Wes Pritchett, senior linebacker

*Coach Holtz is good at building you up slowly through the week before a
game. He's not low-key, but he always says, "You can't play the game
until Saturday. Do what the coaches tell you. Believe in the coaching
staff. They won't steer you wrong." And they didn't all year long. That's
always been true since he's been here.*

*He always says that he'll tell you when it's time to get ready. We were
never ready too early for a game. Sometimes guys would get a little fired
up early in the week, and obviously he liked that and enjoyed it. But he
always reminded us that you can't play the game until Saturday. He
always told us to think about football only when you're on the field.
Things like that were really helpful. He always used the example, "If you
keep your fist clenched all week, by the time you play, you won't have any
energy, you're drained."*

Many people questioned why I wasn't more complimentary toward our
football team this season. Our players certainly understand this, because
we discussed it often. It serves no purpose for me to say what a great
football team we are. The only time that's appropriate is when the season
is over. If our team was good, I didn't have to tell them. They would know
themselves. If you have to tell people you are good, no one should or will
listen. I tell our players the same thing I tell the public about our opposition. I speak from the heart, and I have great respect for our opponents.

Consequently our players show respect for the opponents, as well as making necessary preparation during the course of the week.

In addition, if I brag about our team during the course of the season, this puts a tremendous amount of pressure on them, and they don't need that at Notre Dame.

Wes Pritchett

In order to be successful you have to have fun at what you're doing, whether it's business or whatever you're doing. And that's the way Coach Holtz is. He's determined and he pushes us and he's dedicated, but at the same time he's able to throw in a one-liner or crack a joke and keep everybody loose. It just shows that he enjoys what he's doing. He's having fun. That catches on with everybody.

Frank [Stams] and I really enjoyed ourselves last season. We knew it was our last year, and we enjoyed being part of Notre Dame.

I think the offense was a little bit more intense during practice because they have to be a bit more disciplined than defensive guys as far as assignments. So we just always had fun. The coaching staff would laugh along with us, but if they felt it wasn't a time to joke around, they would tell us. If Frank and I felt it was a time to be serious, then we would communicate that to the players. Everybody was working together. We weren't ever fighting ourselves. We really did have fun, which is hard to do during football season for three months. I think that's a key factor.

We won a couple of games and people started putting us in the hall of fame. We had no problem keeping it in perspective, because we weren't a complete team. We still could not throw the football well enough, along with a few other deficiencies. It wasn't until our third game, against Purdue, that we realized it wasn't illegal for our offense to score.

Before the Miami game I felt it was especially important for our players to believe in each other. Miami had dominated us so convincingly in recent years, our players needed to believe they could play with Miami. That's one of the few times I went out of my way to praise them and build them up. They needed to know that I believed they could win and that I was very sincere.

George Kelly, special assistant to the athletic director

He did a tremendous job of maintaining an even keel all year. He was far less demonstrative during the course of the whole season than in previous years. His frustrations left him, and his total belief that we could be a solid team overtook the frustration that had been there—of not reaching the level he had anticipated the second year. We weren't as competent at the end of the '87 season as he wanted. But I think the confidence he developed in this team mellowed him a little bit. That confidence made him far less demonstrative in anything he did, whether it was talking to the squad before a game or at halftime or whatever. He no longer had to appeal to them to play to the best of their ability, because that was something I think he felt they would do without question. He appealed instead to the pride in Notre Dame. He appealed more to that factor than to anything else all season long.

Once we beat Miami, we had to go in the other direction and get back down to earth. Everyone wanted to spend a month celebrating that victory. All the fans wanted to know was, "When do we play USC and who do we play in the bowl game for the national championship?" That's not what our players needed to hear. We had to keep working, improving, becoming a better football team.

Once we became number one, there was another set of pressures to deal with. We needed to understand that being number one wasn't that big a deal. Maybe it was a big deal for the opposition, but it didn't change anything for us. If anything, it made our games more difficult because the other teams got that much more excited about playing Notre Dame.

We needed to understand that we didn't have to defend that ranking every week. All we had to do on Saturday was be better than the other team. It was that simple.

George Kelly

People always are interested in the approach to a Miami game or a USC game, and yet in some ways those are the easiest. There certainly was more riding on those games, and yet if the players can't get excited about Miami or USC, they aren't going to get excited about anything. There really was more of a laid-back attitude those weeks.

The night before the Miami game he really went after the idea that this wasn't the biggest thing in life, this wasn't the most important thing they would do. And that's the last real contact he has with the players, because he does not like to do a lot of things with them on Saturday morning. He allows that time for them to recoup and recall all the things that have happened during the week. He doesn't like to have too many meetings or too much verbalization the morning of the game.

The week of the USC game, he dealt much more with the history and the tradition of the series, instead of talking about it being number one and number two. He downplayed the game itself as much as he could and talked about it only in relation to what it could mean in the long run.

After the USC game we had to deflect all the talk about bowls and the national championship. You should talk about the national championship only after it happens. We weren't playing against West Virginia, we were playing against perfection. We had talked about our goals as far as bowl games back in August, and our players understood that all we could do was try to keep winning. It was the same with the national championship. There was no reason to even think about it until we were 11–0. Even then, that was not the focus of our preparation for the Fiesta Bowl. The last thing our players needed was to spend a month thinking they had to play for a national championship. That wasn't true. All they had to do was prepare to play West Virginia.

Sometimes you have to learn how to deal with failure. This was a year where we had to handle success. If they like being ranked, they should do the things that enable you to stay there. This list doesn't include relaxing and savoring a win.

I told the players a long time ago that they weren't going to hear volumes of praise from me, although we would never allow their self-image to deteriorate. I think they understand that, especially the veterans who have been here for a few years and know what it takes to be successful at Notre Dame. When the season is finished, we all have time to go back and reminisce about it—I guess that's why they make scrapbooks.

I tried to maintain a consistency with this team, just like I did any other season. We had a job to do every week, and we didn't have much time to celebrate from one week to the next. You're never as good as everyone tells you when you win, and you're never as bad as they say when you lose.

Understanding that and being able to deal with it as an athlete is one of the keys to surviving at Notre Dame. What is incredible is that virtually the same things that enable you to enjoy success at Notre Dame will enable you to lead a happy and productive life.

31

FIESTA BOWL: PREPARING IN SOUTH BEND

WE had a team meeting on Tuesday after the USC game, which was our first official act since returning from Los Angeles. The main purpose was to explain to the players exactly what the plans would be for the next five weeks or so. A bowl game is like a whole season in itself, and there are many details that need to be worked out as far as individual players traveling from their homes to the bowl site and back. We wanted to get this taken care of at once so we could proceed with our preparation and with recruiting.

The first thing we did was congratulate Reggie Ho. He was chosen the Hawaiian Athlete of the Year. I jokingly told the squad he beat out two sumo wrestlers and a grass-skirt girl.

The players then voted for the MVP. I wasn't surprised that Tony Rice won it, but I was surprised by the convincing margin. It's obvious that our players appreciate his value to the team, even if there were other people who received more individual recognition during the season.

We also voted for a new award, the Nick Pietrosante Award, in memory of the former Notre Dame player who died of cancer last spring. The award is presented to someone who has displayed the spirit, unselfishness, and team concept that is synonymous with Notre Dame. In addition, the recipient should be a solid person who embraces the value of Notre Dame. This wasn't an easy choice because there were a number of people who fulfilled the criteria for the award. Andy Heck was chosen, and he certainly was a good selection.

Next, we wanted to outline exactly what we would do to get ready to win the Fiesta Bowl. It is imperative to give our players a definite schedule that's as easy as possible, and to follow it. This gives them the security of being informal.

Finals are over on the night of December 16, so we'll start practicing football that night. The following day we'll practice twice, once in pads, once without. Then we'll practice twice a day on December 18 to 20 and scrimmage on the 21st. At five P.M. that day, we'll be finished and the players are free to head home for Christmas.

Everyone has to arrive in Phoenix in time for an afternoon practice on the 26th. On January 2, we will play the game and we will win it. From that point on we will celebrate.

There is always a multitude of information that must be transmitted to our squad. For example, when you play in a bowl, the NCAA is going to test for drugs. The previous year, at the Cotton Bowl, they tested 28 of our players, selected at random. They always test the same number of players from both teams. This is not uncommon in a national championship game. It's important that our players understand they need to clear any medication they're taking with our trainer Jim Russ, including over-the-counter drugs. It would be embarrassing if any player failed the test, but I'm not really concerned because I would be shocked if this happened.

We attempt to do everything we can for a player in a bowl game, but the NCAA puts certain restrictions on the amount of spending money, number of tickets, value of gifts and awards a player can receive. There's a limit of $300 on the items you can receive. The bowl gives everyone a watch and a plaque, which together equals $185.

We'll take 88 players who'll practice every day, and they get four complimentary tickets plus the chance to buy two more at $35 each. We usually give the players a sweater, polo shirt, windbreaker, shorts, T-shirt, and sweats. Those will cease to be of value as the years fade, but the memories of the game will last a lifetime.

The previous year, at the Cotton Bowl, I felt like the attitude was "What am I going to get out of it?" Our 1987 team was far more interested in material things and having a good time than the 1988 team. I think this team realizes Notre Dame is going to go first class but within the rules.

I feel we are going to win the game—period. There will be no thought of doing anything but winning.

For the next three weeks our only priorities would be academics and winter program. The players would report to Meyo Field daily between five and six P.M. and would work one hour in shorts, with an emphasis on quickness, agility, and conditioning. We would do nothing resembling a regular football practice. The players were instructed to lift on their own.

Academics would take precedent over the workout, but I felt confident that a mature individual could balance his schedule to make the most of the workouts.

There's an old saying that goes, "If it's meant to be, it's up to me." In speaking to the team that Tuesday, I congratulated our players on a fine season. I said to them:

"To be 11–0 is a great accomplishment. We've all had forty-eight hours to bask in it. Most people thought it was impossible, but there's no reason for us to think about it any longer because it's behind us now.

"Not many people have ever done what we've done in 1988. No Notre Dame team has ever gone 12–0. No Notre Dame team has played the number-two, number-three, and number-four teams in the polls. You have a chance to go down as one of the best teams in Notre Dame history. However, for this to transpire we must be the best team in Phoenix on January 2. (I felt the Phoenix Cardinals of the NFL would have ended their season by then.)

"West Virginia may be the best team we play. Beano Cook predicted them to win the national championship on ESPN before the season ever started. They were in the top ten in every preseason publication, so don't think they're not an excellent team.

"They average 44 points a game. Their offense is far superior to ours, and I'm not trying to sell you land in Florida. Their offense is a heck of a lot better than ours, and they live on big plays.

"They've got a fullback who's six-three and 240 and is the best we've played by far. They are exceptionally talented up front. I saw one play on film where their offensive line pushed Penn State from the 4 to four yards deep in the end zone.

"Major Harris is elusive. He has a strong arm and has great athletic ability. Everyone tells me he is from Krypton, and if this is true, he must be related to Superman.

"Their defensive secondary is excellent, but it's no better than ours. Their linebackers are strong and physical, but they're no better than ours. Their defensive line doesn't run as well as ours, but it's very good.

"They shut off Pitt and they had Penn State 42–6 at the half. We're playing a legitimate team, and they believe they have a legitimate chance to be number one.

"I was disappointed in our offensive performance against USC. We didn't gain enough yardage in the second and third quarters to bury me, and I'm only five-ten. We can't believe we will win just because we walk on the field in a Notre Dame uniform. I don't believe West Virginia will outhit us or want to win more than we do, but there are certain areas where West Virginia appears to be decisively better. However, we've met every challenge, and I expect we will meet this one.

"There are certain things that are going to be exceptionally important to us as we prepare.

"One is attitude. It must remain positive. Don't fall prey to people who are going to concede you the game. I'd like to play it next week because I think we have fallen into a great rhythm. But we can't play this Saturday. The bowl game is a whole new season, and we will be a totally different team. We can't maintain our continuity for six weeks, so we must build the team all over—especially on offense—or we won't be successful on January 2.

"Second, we have to make a commitment to beating West Virginia. From now until the sixteenth it's a matter of what's important now. Keep your life together, and remember our priorities—our faith, our family, our academics, our team, and then our social life.

"Keep a low profile. If you're any good, people will talk about you. West Virginia is in a great situation because they don't feel they're getting the respect they deserve. But there's no reason for us to talk about how great we are until after we win. Forget the game—it's light-years away from now. Stay on your academics, because that, not football, will determine your success in life.

"Third, concentrate on the winter program. It'll help our agility, our quickness, our togetherness, our discipline, and our attitude.

"Fourth, watch film on West Virginia, when it's possible and compatible with your schedule.

"Fifth, get healthy. If you've got a problem, see Jim Russ.

"Sixth, visualize winning before you go to bed. It will happen. You can mark that down.

"Seventh, you must help us in recruiting. Next week we have thirty of the best high school seniors in the country here for the football banquet. We probably will practice once on Saturday the tenth.

"Everything we've talked about to this point is phase one. We're going to take everything in stages as we go through the next six weeks. Phase one is academics and conditioning.

"Phase two will be from December 16 to 21. That's when we will practice. Hard. We will learn the gameplan and get fundamentally sound again. When we reach this phase, we will not worry about academics, as the semester will be over.

"Phase three will be from December 22 to 26. That's when you enjoy the Christmas spirit. You rest, you relax, you spend time with your family, and you appreciate how many reasons you have to be thankful. Make Christmas better for someone because of your efforts.

"Also, when you go home, the media back in your hometown will be telling you how great you are and what a tremendous year you have had. Don't believe it. Don't worry about your academics or the gameplan for West Virginia. Just enjoy Christmas.

"Phase four is from December 26 to January 1. We will emphasize the things we need to do in order to win the game, and they are perfection and togetherness. We will do virtually everything together as a team.

"Phase five is January 2. This is the time to get ready mentally and emotionally, and not before then.

"Phase six begins the night of January 2. You can celebrate the rest of your life.

"Don't accept all the praise that's coming your direction, but also don't believe the papers when they say how bad we are and that we're not a great team.

"Please remember this—even if both teams play their best, we will win the football game. However, anything less than our best effort for the next six weeks will be an indication that we are not deserving of winning. It's your choice.

"We have not reached our full potential, especially on offense. We will be outstanding, and you can book it. If you are insecure, if you live on praise, if you go into a shell when you're criticized, then you may be in trouble the next few weeks, because we are going to raise our level of excellence another notch. We are not going to sit here and be self-satisfied with anything less than perfection. If this isn't your goal, you obviously have some serious flaws in your philosophy."

One of the players asked about playing basketball at the Rock during the next few weeks. I thought that was unbelievable. I told him, "Sure, go ahead. You have my permission. Then you can tell your grandchildren someday how you were a starter on the 1988 Notre Dame football team but you hurt your ankle at the Rock and you didn't get to play in the Fiesta Bowl. You can also add that they won't remember you at Notre Dame by your real name, but they will recognize you if you tell them your nickname was Wally Pipp."

In the locker room at USC I'd told the captains to decide who should get game balls. We gave them to Father Malloy, Father Beauchamp, Dick Rosenthal, and Father Riehle right there in the locker room, but due to the fact that all our seniors had received one, I thought it best to let the captains decide. The names they came up with were Stan Smagala, Frank Stams, Wes Pritchett, and George Streeter. That said something for our defense.

I think some of the players had seen me quoted about losing weight during the season, so Mark Green presented me with a can of Weight-Gain and everyone had a good laugh.

I kidded the players about how emotional it had gotten on the sideline as the last few seconds wound down at USC. Chuck Heater was standing next to me in tears, and all our coaches were excited. I braced myself to get carried off the field by the players, but everyone just ran past me and onto the field. I decided I wasn't going to wait to be carried off the field any longer, so I followed our last player to the middle of the field.

After the USC game I felt awfully good about what we'd accomplished. I had gone in the office on Monday, even though we hadn't gotten home until one in the morning. On the plane back from USC we spent most of the time working on the organization and logistics of the bowl game.

I'd been to the Fiesta Bowl one other time, when we were at Arkansas, and we tied UCLA 10–10. I felt somewhat familiar with where we were going and what we needed to do to make it a great experience for our players.

I had a brief meeting with the coaches Monday morning and talked about some of the things we would have to accomplish. Our top priority would be the bowl game. It isn't very often you can afford to put recruiting on the back burner at this time of year. While we certainly weren't going to ignore it, we had to recognize that rarely do you go into a bowl game with a chance for a perfect season. We had an obligation to give our players a chance to win the national championship. At that short meeting I told our coaches I wanted to exchange all eleven game films with West Virginia. That's the best way to do it in a game like this. There aren't going to be any secrets about who has done what.

It's very difficult to maintain momentum and continuity from the end of a regular season to the bowl game. We will not be the same team on January 2, nor will West Virginia. We'll either be better or worse, depending on the preparation we make.

I thought the Tuesday meeting went well. I left immediately for Chicago to speak at the *Chicago Sun-Times* football awards banquet. Chicago is very important to us in terms of recruiting, so this is an invitation I could not turn down. In addition, Taylor Bell, who oversees all the high-school coverage for the *Sun-Times*, does a fine job and I have a lot of respect for him. I spent the next five days traveling to various places, doing a variety of things for the university and charity.

Once the game film came in, we assigned each coach a specific film so they would know West Virginia inside out. When I looked at the film of West Virginia, a couple of things were obvious. One, they were very good, and two, they really hadn't been tested. Maybe they were even better than we thought, but we wouldn't know this until they were tested. I pointed out to our staff and our squad that our statistics were nearly as impressive as West Virginia's, and yet we played some of the top teams in the country.

West Virginia did look impressive beating Syracuse 31–9, but Syracuse had seven turnovers in that game. In addition, I did not think West Virginia would be the same football team on grass as they are on artificial turf, where they normally play.

I did an awful lot of traveling for the week or so before we began practicing. I normally dislike traveling, but two of the trips were especially enjoyable. One was to go to Houston on December 17 for the Bear Bryant coaches award presented by the Football Writers Association of America. Having coached against Coach Bryant in the Sugar Bowl, and having known him personally, it was a great honor to receive an award named for him. It was a dual treat because I was informed that I was going to win the Woody Hayes coaches award. That was special, too, since I had coached under Woody. I also went to Washington, D.C., to receive an award from the Washington Touchdown Club, which was particularly delightful.

I was on a couple of the network morning shows, and it seemed like we had a press conference everywhere I went. It was obvious there was a lot of interest in this football game.

I normally have difficulty sleeping on Sunday and Monday because I get worked up about the game coming up and I'm thinking of a million things we need to do to get ready. By Thursday and Friday on a game week, I sleep better because we've made our preparation and I know where we stand. But with a bowl game five weeks away, it was like Sunday or Monday night all the time, and it seemed like I could never get restful sleep. I'm sure our assistant coaches were confronted with the same problem. Your mind is whirling about the gameplan, looking at film, conversations with coaches, and a thousand decisions to make and no deadline to make them. On a gameplan you very seldom make a decision until forced to, because you always are studying film and tendencies. Once you make a decision on the gameplan you can feel a lot of pressure leave.

On December 12 we met as a staff to attempt to finalize a lot of things. I felt good about the gameplan, but like anything else, there will have to be some changes as we go along.

We finished up final exams and our players were fairly optimistic about their grades. For the most part these thoughts were justified.

We started practice on a Saturday morning, December 17, and it was

304

very similar to spring practice. It was fundamentals all over again, and they were very physical practices. We utilized basically the same schedule we employed during two-a-days in August. The players get up at seven, have breakfast, practice, meet, have lunch, take two hours off while the coaches meet, have a kicking-game meeting, practice again, then meet again after dinner. The day ends around ten P.M. with lights out. I don't think it is much different than a Marine bootcamp. One thing for certain, when lights are turned out, they stay out. If they don't go to bed at that time, they are sending us a message that they aren't tired and we need to work them harder.

We only practiced once on December 18 because it was Sunday, but it was a long one. On the nineteenth and twentieth we practiced twice a day again, but unfortunately we had five inches of snow and that made it difficult to go outdoors. I wish we had put the tarp on the field, because it warmed up a little in the afternoon and it would have been nice to get outside. We went out on the twentieth anyway, in order to scrimmage the gameplan.

Merlin Olsen of NBC, who's doing the color commentary on the Fiesta Bowl, was in town to watch us work out and to visit with me and the players.

I emphasized to him that the last thing we wanted to do was make our players spend five weeks carrying around the burden of playing the national championship. You don't win it. You wake up one day and you are the national champion. We're playing West Virginia, and our only goal is to be better than they are for sixty minutes on January 2.

Also, it makes no sense to pick favorites and underdogs in bowl games, as it's a one-game season. If the bowl games were played a week after the regular season ended, it would be different. You are never the same team that ended the season, and that's why you see so many of the supposed underdogs win bowl games.

Merlin asked an interesting question. What did I think Don Nehlen's thoughts were about the match-up? I told him I felt Don Nehlen could answer that better than anyone I knew, but I had given it some thought.

I said, "I think he feels pretty good about this game. He's played and beaten both Pittsburgh and Penn State much more convincingly than we did. He and his players know they dominated both games and we just managed to win.

"He knows he has a quarterback who is as good a runner as ours and is a much more explosive passer. Their running attack has been more productive than ours. Their receivers have been far more effective, especially in making big plays. Their offensive line is bigger and more experienced than ours. Their defense hasn't gotten as much publicity, but I think Don feels it's every bit as good as ours.

"I don't think Don Nehlen will change a thing. I think he feels very good about his chances to win the football game, and he may be right. We'll just have to wait and see."

We scrimmaged, and the weather was unbelievable for the end of December—it was sunny and maybe 50 degrees, so we worked outside on Krause Field. We scrimmaged long and hard, but I had some mixed emotions. Anybody who watched us would not have been impressed, but I felt we were right on schedule. We got a good feeling for what West Virginia would do offensively and defensively. We also got a realistic picture for our defense by having our first offense perform against them. If there is any quarterback who would come close to emulating Major Harris, it would be Tony Rice. We weren't ready to play, but we were still healthy and I was pleased with our progress.

I'm always worried about getting people injured, but we were lucky in that regard. We did lose Rod West in the weight room when he received an abrasion on his knee which ended up with some complications. He had to have it scoped, and wouldn't be able to play against West Virginia. We were lucky because we did not have a single player injured during the course of our practices, despite the fact we worked an awful lot against our top units. As I mentioned, I felt the best way for our defense to get ready for West Virginia and Major Harris was to try to defend Tony Rice, and the best way for our offense to prepare for West Virginia was to work against our number-one defense. It was a good, old, physical spring practice, and we really enjoyed it.

By the morning of the twenty-first, which was going to be our last day, I felt the players knew the gameplan well and we had accomplished phase two. We had gotten better fundamentally and were a better football team than we had been at any point during the season. That was to be expected because they were a young team in many respects, but it is easier said than done.

Our last day of practice before going home for Christmas would be very light. However, we had a lengthy meeting to look at the film and make sure we knew what to do and how to do it.

The staff looked at the film of the scrimmage. It wasn't anything exceptional, but it is always a good scrimmage when there are no serious injuries. One other encouraging thing was that we kept turnovers to a minimum.

One thing for certain, our scout squad has to do a better job. I've never been more disappointed in a scout team than I was during the scrimmage. When the ball is snapped, West Virginia's defense charges at you a hundred miles per hour, and their offensive line is physical and really gets after you every play. This is not the picture we're seeing from the scout team, and that has to change immediately. Maybe the scout squad didn't play hard in the scrimmage because they didn't want to be injured and left at home.

If the coaches don't have something to worry about, they will find something today. I'm concerned because many of our players are driving long distances to get home. That's why instead of practicing right up to five o'clock, we decided to give them some extra time to get on the road. I asked the players to please not drive after midnight or too fast. An extra hour or so isn't going to make a big difference in their Christmas vacation but it could in their future.

We want the players to run and lift while they're home, and then come to Phoenix with a positive mental attitude.

The players went home that afternoon, and that night we had the athletic department Christmas party. Things are very hectic in December when you play in any bowl game, but especially one like this. Still, it's nice to get together and have a chance to see everyone's family. They asked me to speak, and I said that having been to the Fiesta Bowl before and knowing what the Diablos do in terms of hospitality, they should have a great time. I said, "If you don't have a good time at the Fiesta Bowl up to January 2, it's your fault. If you don't have a good time after January 2, it's our fault."

Early on the morning of December 22 we got up and left for Orlando, mainly because Beth's parents are in their seventies, Skip is coaching at Florida State, and we could take Kevin and Liz and have a few days together to celebrate Christmas.

Clemson had arrived there early to get ready for the Citrus Bowl, so I got permission from Danny Ford to stop by to watch them practice. They had an outstanding team. Danny was very nice and he asked me to say a few words to his players. I told them that having coached in the Atlantic Coast Conference, I was well aware of what a fine football tradition Clemson possessed. The one thing that's obvious to coaches around the country is that Clemson has always been a very physical football team. I knew they would play well against Oklahoma, and boy, did they ever.

I played golf with my two sons and my father-in-law, and I must say I played rather well. I watched some film of West Virginia which we brought along. I just wanted the gameplan to sink in. We made very few

307

changes once we had it set. I felt good about where we were and what we had to do.

We all went to mass on Christmas Eve. It doesn't seem to matter how early you get to Holy Family Church on Christmas Eve, it's always jammed and you never get there in time to get a good seat. But it was a beautiful mass. We got up Christmas Day and exchanged gifts. It was a wonderful Christmas, and we spent it as a family. I think our children really appreciate any presents I've picked out because they know I have absolutely no patience when it comes to shopping at this time of year.

It was hard for me to relax, but it also was nice to be in the warm weather. I hope it's like this in Tempe, Arizona. That's our next stop.

32

THE BANQUET AND RECRUITING: THE LULL BEFORE THE STORM

WE didn't play or practice the second week of December, but it's still been as hectic as any week I can remember. That's what happens when you're a game away from a national championship. Everyone wants to meet and discuss something with you, and yet there is nothing more precious than time. Once we lose this time for preparation, we can never get it back. There's no way anyone wants to second-guess themselves on January 3.

I was scheduled to speak at the Heisman Trophy dinner December 9 in New York, but I almost didn't make it when Piedmont canceled my flight out of South Bend even though the weather was beautiful for this time of year. I finally got there on a private plane, but I missed a press conference that NBC had set up for the Fiesta Bowl.

I hadn't been able to attend the Heisman dinner last year, when Tim Brown won, due to a conflict with a University of Notre Dame function, so I promised the people at the Downtown Athletic Club I would speak in 1988. This time I sat next to Dick Enberg, who'll be doing the Fiesta Bowl for NBC, and we had a nice visit. It's flattering that so many people wanted to say hello or get an autograph. Every time I sign one I think about people like Knute Rockne, Frank Leahy, Ara Parseghian. They caused this to happen, not Lou Holtz. I'm just a grateful person from East Liverpool, Ohio, who has had a chance to live his dream.

We had our annual football banquet the next night, with thirty recruits in attendance plus about 2500 other people. This was twice the crowd we normally have, which was possible because we were able to move it into

309

the fieldhouse, rather than holding it on the floor of the basketball arena, as we have traditionally.

It was an evening for celebration, but with the constant reminder that we weren't finished yet.

Phil Motta, president of the Fiesta Bowl, kidded about how much time he had spent in South Bend this fall: "I've established residence here. I can vote now." He is a great guy, and I feel he's like one of the family.

Paul Hornung was the master of ceremonies, and I hope his first remarks had an impact on our younger players. He said, "You men have a rare opportunity. You have a chance to take the mark of excellence with you the rest of your lives."

Tom Gorman won the student/athlete award given by the Notre Dame Club of St. Joseph Valley. He was surprised, but he shouldn't have been. The Pietrosante Award was presented to Andy Heck by Judd Pietrosante, who's a junior at Hillsdale College.

Father Joyce presented the scholarships named in his and Father Hesburgh's honor by the National Football Foundation and Hall of Fame, and he told a cute story after presenting the award to Reggie Ho and Brad Alge.

He talked about how ninety-eight percent of us honestly didn't have any idea we'd be sitting here 11–0, although most of the subway alumni probably did. He talked about receiving a letter in August from a New York taxi driver named Patrick Coyne. The letter said that Coyne's new prediction was that Lou Holtz would lead Notre Dame to a national championship in 1988. Father Joyce had another letter that was to be delivered to me after we won it and read only in a particular setting, in a special convocation with faculty and students present. Father Joyce said he wasn't sure what would happen after the first of the year and that he wasn't trying to be presumptuous, but he wanted me to open the letter now.

I opened the letter, and it read, "Lou, what took you so long?" It was signed, Patrick Coyne, taxi driver number 0432861.

Father Beauchamp said some nice things about having this sort of football success on top of winning the College Football Association Academic Achievement Award for having the highest graduation rate among football teams. I know that has made the people on both sides of the campus especially proud. As Father Beauchamp said, "We have one mission here, that of education. Our coaches are teachers. They educate and train."

He kidded about how nervous he now gets at football games. He said he barely saw any of the second half of the Miami game and talked about the problem he had pacing at USC because of the small booth he was in. He went on to say he realizes the price we have paid for our achievements, which showed what great insight he has into a situation such as ours. Two of our senior captains, Andy Heck and Mark Green, did a nice job putting it all in perspective.

Andy said, "I came to Notre Dame with a lot of hopes and expectations, and 11–0 seemed a long way off in the beginning. But Pete Graham and I vowed if we won the national championship, we'd get tattoos. We'll have to think about that now. I knew there were great people at Notre Dame, but the reason we came was to win a national championship, and now it's in the wings."

Mark said, "Mike Brennan and I were sitting in our hotel room out at USC and I started to think, "How could you leave this place?" Going to Notre Dame isn't a sacrifice. It's a privilege to be part of Notre Dame. I've been here in the bad times and the good, but it doesn't get any better than this."

Lancaster Smith, President of the Notre Dame National Monogram Club, surprised me in his introduction by presenting me with an honorary Monogram jacket. It's such a distinct honor, when you consider the dozens of all-Americans and the seven Heisman Trophy winners who have worn it here. Lank kidded that they voted to do this on September 9, the day before the Michigan game. I hope he wasn't kidding, but I don't know.

It was an awkward time to speak:

"We've come so far, and yet have so far to go. More than anything, it's a pleasure to read the mail and see what our season has meant to so many people.

"It made me think back to my childhood, when the sisters of St. Aloysius instilled the spirit of Notre Dame in me. Those teams in the late 1940s never lost a game, and that always has motivated me.

"I still remember when we were 1–4 that first year in '86. Moose Krause came into my office and told me things would work out. I'm not sure I believed him then. But it was encouraging that Moose believed it.

"The difference with this team has been the love the players have for each other, and the job our assistant coaches have done. We have so many people who have come so far. I had dinner the other night with Tim Brown and Steve Beuerlein, and Tim said to tell Jeff Alm he'd never seen a player improve so much in a year.

"I always single out the seniors at the banquet, because it's their day. They have as much to do with your season as anyone, especially a season like this.

"Reggie Ho was named the Hawaiian Amateur Athlete of the Year this week. What a great honor for someone who had no idea he would ever play football when he came to Notre Dame. He just wanted to come to get an education and become a doctor.

"Pete Graham, I could never express how valuable his contributions have been. Fifteen years from now no one on the team will be any more respected by his teammates.

"Tom Gorman is a Notre Dame man—an overachiever who loves his teammates and university, and they love him.

"When you talk about unselfish people, you start with Flash Gordon. Here's a guy who had every reason to give up about midseason when he didn't get into the game against Miami. But he just keeps asking, 'What can I do to help?'

"Mike Brennan has proven he's a big-time football player. I might have been one of those who said he couldn't play here.

"Steve Belles has to be the only quarterback in the country who plays on every special team.

"Steve Alaniz didn't catch a lot of passes this year, but he started five games for us at split end, and we won them all.

"D'Juan Francisco unselfishly switched to cornerback two years back, and it's obvious the strides he has made.

"Corny Southall is the only current Notre Dame player to score both offensively and defensively in his career. There's no one on this team who has been more positive. There's no one who has put Notre Dame further ahead of his own goals than Corny. Winning meant more to him than individual goals, and that's why we are where we are right now. I'm always partial to those who don't get a lot of recognition, and that's why Corny has been special to me this year.

"George Streeter never got the recognition he deserved. But if we had a most improved award this year, it probably would go to him.

"Frank Stams is just a heck of a competitor. No one even has to say that about him anymore.

"Wes Pritchett really has been a pleasure to watch this year. He's another player who has been underrated. He sets the tempo for us on defense, and he's one of the reasons we have a chance to win on January 2.

"Ned Bolcar put the team first, and that is exactly why we are first. It takes a special person to go 11–0, and Ned is a special person. In my mind he is one of the great ones in Notre Dame history.

"Andy Heck was one of four people who lettered all four years. He's another one you don't have to say any more about.

"Mark Green—I could go on and on about him. He's never said anything but what could he do to help. You can talk about all the accolades in the world, but this guy will be playing football somewhere next fall. I'm just sorry it won't be at Notre Dame.

"Last winter I visited with our three captains and I warned them that there might be some seniors who didn't play—some who had been starters or contributors who wouldn't get on the field as much. They told me not to worry, that the seniors would provide the best leadership I had ever witnessed. That impressed me, but more importantly, they did it."

Just before we closed, the captains surprised me with a plaque that said, "To Coach Holtz, in the tradition of Rockne, for leading us to an unbeaten season in 1988." It was from the 1988 Notre Dame football team.

I was overwhelmed. All I could think to say was, "I want to have another banquet in March, and then I can really say how I feel about you."

This also was our biggest recruiting weekend of the year, because we wouldn't have another one until the middle of January. We only have one weekend that is conducive for prospects to visit our campus in December, due to final exams and the fact our winter semester doesn't start until mid-January. Because of this we had thirty of the top people in this weekend for the banquet, despite being swamped with our Fiesta Bowl preparation.

The thirty players came from twelve different states, and we would end up signing fourteen of them in February 1989. I knew we would have a good recruiting year, but little did I realize we would be so successful this *first* weekend.

We had three quarterbacks in—Rick Mirer and Jake Kelchner, who ended up signing with us, and Bryan Fortay out of New Jersey, who went to Miami.

We had three players from Oklahoma—Tony Brooks's little brother Reggie; Bret Hankins, an offensive lineman from Norman; and Joey Mickey, a tight end who ended up at Oklahoma.

We had three players from California—Todd Norman and Erik Simien, who came to Notre Dame, and Bob Whitfield, a great offensive lineman who ended up at Stanford.

Others who eventually committed to Notre Dame who were here this weekend were Jordy Halter from Michigan; receiver Ray Griggs and kicker Craig Hentrich, from Illinois; linebacker Brian Ratigan, from Iowa; lineman Junior Bryant, from Nebraska; linebacker Shawn Smith, from New Jersey; linebacker Karl McGill, from Florida; and Adrian Jarrell, a great all-around athlete from Georgia. Plus we'd had Chet Lacheta and Randy Scianna in the week before from Chicago, and they both eventually committed to Notre Dame.

Despite the limited time schedule our coaches have to recruit, I feel we will be all right because of Vinny Cerrato. He will continue to recruit every single prospect. Even when we go to Phoenix, Vinny will be visiting or calling every top player once again.

Some people suggested we would have a tough time recruiting after such a successful season, because we were young and had a lot of people coming back. In addition, it is exceptionally rare for the top team in the country to have a productive year recruiting, but I believe if we work hard enough, this will be a good year. We still have a lot of needs, and we will have many freshmen contribute in 1989. Our philosophy is there is always a strong need for a good Notre Dame man.

33

TONY RICE:
THE MVP

Jan Blazi, secretary to Lou Holtz

I remember Coach Holtz emphasizing early on, "Mark this down—Tony Rice is going to be an all-American quarterback." This was back when everyone was saying Tony couldn't pass and he was a horrible quarterback and everyone was putting him down. So I did mark it on my calendar, just to see what would happen.

Tony Rice was elected the most valuable player on this team; it just shows you what can happen when you believe in yourself. He has come so far from the night in Pittsburgh where he started to line up under the guard. Even more incredible, it happened in less than a year.

It's a fact that the quarterback at Notre Dame is so visible that he gets more publicity than he should. They say the toughest jobs in the country are President, head football coach at Notre Dame, mayor of New York, and the quarterback at Notre Dame. With all the publicity the Notre Dame quarterback receives, it is difficult to comprehend that Tony ended up one of the unsung heroes, particularly in view of the fact that we have been very successful.

He didn't make a lot of all-American teams, like some of our other players, but it's obvious the other players appreciate his talents. I don't know where we would be without him, but I like where we are with him. He isn't flashy and doesn't talk a lot, he just goes out and wins.

When we played Miami and USC, all the attention was on Steve Walsh and Rodney Peete, and they deserved it. However, Tony Rice never doubted his ability to perform, and I didn't, either.

315

No one looks at Tony as a great quarterback because he isn't the consistently picture-perfect passer people have come to expect of a quarterback. But Tony throws well enough for us to win, and I think maybe well enough to play on Sundays. There ought to be a special category for quarterbacks where you get credit for having your team win the football game. Tony Rice is pretty darn good in that category. Tony can beat you in so many ways. He can beat you with his head, his arm, his feet, but mainly with his heart.

Ara Parseghian, former Notre Dame head coach

There was a similarity between this team and some of my old Notre Dame teams. I don't think I ever had a thousand-yard rusher—we always strove for balance. Lou has two backs, with a flanker and a split end, and Tony Rice becomes the third back. We used to use it with the wing-T attack with four backs. The key is a quarterback with running ability, and with the maturing of Rice, he fit that mold.

We featured a running quarterback like that during our successful years. I didn't necessarily look to see if our quarterback was the greatest passer in the world—if he happened to be an excellent passer, that was a plus. We looked first of all to see if he was agile, could avoid the rush, could take a broken play and make it into positive yardage—and certainly that's what Rice gave this team. He was the leading rusher, and that speaks for itself. That was a philosophy I embraced all through my coaching.

Tony did not throw the ball especially well last spring, although part of that was because we were breaking in a whole new group of receivers. Then, during the early fall, he threw extremely well in our last few scrimmages. Based on that, I felt he would have a good year throwing the football.

Against Michigan and Michigan State he did not play like he practiced, and this is the only thing that bothered me. Once he gained confidence in himself and knew we believed in him, he went on to become one of the most productive passers in the country in 1988.

I know this—Tony Rice is a winner and competitor. He may change, but I don't think so. He's exceptional in a lot of areas, but his mental toughness may be his greatest asset. I have never been around anyone who is more pleasant, easy to get along with, or loves the game of football more than Tony.

Remember, this is only Tony's second year playing college football. He came out of a high school where he was well coached but hadn't been exposed to the sophisticated defenses he now sees every Saturday. His arm is strong and he does have a good, quick release. He definitely needs to develop a touch on the ball. I don't know how good a quarterback Tony can be if he will throw the ball a lot in the off-season. This is a luxury he hasn't had in the past, but hopefully he will this year.

Tony says in high school you told the receiver where to go and you threw it, and either he caught it or he didn't. You never worried about coverages. If the receiver wasn't open, you just ran it for a first down. Maybe we complicate the game too much. Maybe Tony's way is better. We gave him darts and told him to throw them, as it would help his passing. We're going to have a dart-throwing contest after the season, and he's convinced he'll beat me. There is no doubt he has worked on his release, as it is very good.

The amazing thing about his progress is we never saw Tony Rice as a freshman. He could not play or practice due to Proposition 48, and consequently he never set foot inside our office the entire year. The first time I saw Tony on the football field was in the fall of '87. He was rusty and had a long way to go, but there was something about him that caused the other players to gravitate to him. This I liked.

I wasn't sure he was the second-string quarterback behind Terry Andrysiak, but I was certain he wasn't first team. I just hoped we didn't have to play anyone other than Terry Andrysiak when the game was in doubt. Very seldom has our quarterback been injured in the last seventeen years, so I didn't think we would have to.

Consequently, when Terry went down in the Pittsburgh game and the doctors said he was out for the year, we decided to play Tony. In all honesty, we expected to play three different quarterbacks in the second half against Pittsburgh. Once Tony took charge of the team, he had a comeback that almost pulled the game out for us. From this point on I believed. We just needed to utilize his talents and abilities.

The next week we played at Air Force, and the confidence his teammates already had in him was unbelievable.

This year he has learned to handle all the pressure of being the starting quarterback, and he is learning what it really takes to be a great quarterback. He has to budget his time and get his priorities in order. He needs to mature and be more responsible as a student and as a citizen. He hasn't begun to reach his potential as far as studying film, throwing the football, and things along that line. He doesn't do everything we'd like him to do. He has improved tremendously in certain areas, but he's not consistently what you'd call a total quarterback.

We wanted four things in a quarterback: one, someone who could win; two, lead and be a competitor; three, throw the football; four, move, not run. We don't need a runner, just someone who can move—and then we'll use his talents and abilities.

I don't know if he will be a Heisman candidate in 1989 or not, but he doesn't make many bad plays. He gives us the best chance to win, and that was apparent when he first started to play. I don't know what would have happened if we'd lost him because of an injury this year. We do not push an individual for the Heisman award, and I think it's like the national championship—don't even talk about it until the tenth game.

Another amazing thing about Tony is that he probably knows more people on this campus than anyone else. It's not unusual to have a lot of people know the quarterback at Notre Dame, but it is exceptional when the quarterback knows them.

I've been to his hometown in Woodruff, South Carolina, a couple of times, and they follow Tony. When he started for the first time at Air Force last year, at least two different South Carolina papers sent writers all the way to Colorado Springs to cover his first game.

No matter what Tony does as a football player, our main concern is that he graduates from Notre Dame. We have graduated 98.9 percent of our senior class the last twenty years, and we are proud of that. If Tony plays four years at Notre Dame and doesn't graduate, I will get out of coaching. The reason I say this is because it would mean that Tony didn't understand the true meaning and purpose of Notre Dame. He has assured us he will graduate from Notre Dame.

Pete Cordelli, receiver coach

I think anytime a guy misses eighteen months of football and then has to come back and learn the reads, learn the system, learn how to throw the football all over again—it's going to be a real challenge, as it was for Tony Rice.

A Proposition 48 football player is totally different from a Prop 48 basketball player. In basketball you can get into a pickup game and play and work on defense, work on your shots. You can get into a game and see some quickness and make decisions. I don't know where you can do that in football, especially at quarterback. The decisions he has to make, the reads he has to make, the terminology, the whole communication process that had to take place for him to think like a quarterback—you have to put the mental process with the physical process for it all to be executed.

He got put in at Pittsburgh in '87 when Terry Andrysiak broke his shoulder, and natural athletic ability took over. If you go back and look at some of the things we had called in the passing game, if we complete them, we probably win the game instead of losing 30–22. We missed Braxston Banks, who was wide open on a fullback delay, and that would have put us in position to go ahead at the end. These are all things that come with experience. So maybe Tony Rice was a whole lot better than people had a right to expect in '87, given his experience.

People have expectations based on what's supposed to go with being the Notre Dame quarterback—regardless of where Tony Rice is with his game. In other words, people say, "Don't tell us what's happened before, we want to see you produce." What they saw was a guy maturing and growing mentally, physically, as a person, as a football player. They saw him grow in front of their eyes, just like we did.

In the Michigan game to open the season, if Rocket doesn't drop the deep ball, there's no telling what that does for Tony's confidence. But when we needed it, he still hit Steve Alaniz for a 26-yard gain over the middle.

Against Michigan State we really didn't need to throw the ball that much. But the play that turns the game around and gets us going in terms of momentum is right after the half when we run a slip screen to Mark Green on the right in front of our bench and we make about 45. Steve Alaniz makes a heck of a block right in front of the bench. But Tony completed the pass, and it's like, "Bam," he's in it now. He's got the feeling. I think it was just a matter of hitting a screen pass here, a quick pass there. Now he's got his confidence.

Against Purdue he makes a great throw, Rocket makes a great catch, and we score. Right there, we're hitting the plays.

Stanford game, he threw the ball great, 11 for 14. Then we got to Pittsburgh and he hits Braxston Banks out of the backfield on a third-down play that we have to have. He hits Tony Brooks on a delay-type pattern and puts the ball right where it has to be. With the running game, his athletic ability takes over. Naturally, there are some things he has to read to know what he is doing. But when it came to being the complete quarterback, he grew up in front of everybody's eyes. Every week he got better.

The Miami game, he hits Rocket with the deep ball, hits Ricky on the post corner, hits Derek down the middle. He's making some throws. The interception in the Miami game was poor judgment on his part.

You can go through the rest of the games and see where he matured. The first play of the game at USC, the screen pass to Anthony Johnson on third down—and then in the bowl game I just thought he played great.

It was a culmination of things. We're 11–0 and all he's got to do is go out and play like it's any other game. Don't turn it over. He's just a great guy. The one thing about Tony—he's as fine a competitor as I've ever been around. He's got the same kind of competitive attitude Steve Beuerlein had. Beuerlein could be bleeding, but he's going to fight you tooth and nail to win. Timmy Brown has the same kind of attitude. It's the same with

Magic Johnson. When the game's on the line, who do the Lakers look to? Magic just says, "Give me the ball." Michael Jordan is the guy for the Chicago Bulls.

Every team that's successful has one guy they go to in the clutch. The greatest example is Joe Montana. Two minutes to go in the Super Bowl this year against Cincinnati, and everybody says, "Here he goes again." He says to himself in the huddle, "I thought it was the Dallas game all over. We had to get it done."

Last year for us it was Timmy Brown. The year before it was Beuerlein. So, for three years we've been fortunate to have a bell cow, as Coach Holtz calls them. He's the guy you go to when the going gets tough. You need some help around him. But even those guys in the huddle look at that guy and say, "We know you're going to do it." That's the respect Tony has gained.

When Tony didn't start the season throwing real well, he knew what he had to do to get it done. He knew we were all just going to go out and work on it in practice. It was just a matter of hitting a few of those to gain confidence. If somebody believes strongly enough in something and then has a little success with it, they feel pretty good about themselves. That's exactly what happened this year with Tony. Now he's got to maintain consistency and take it to the next level.

This is what's fun about coaching. Two years ago we started with Tony Rice and he didn't know the system at all. Now he's grown and matured in front of everybody's eyes. He's a great, great competitor.

34

FIESTA BOWL: PREPARING IN TEMPE

SINCE our first practice in Phoenix was scheduled for the afternoon of December 26, I wanted to get there in plenty of time. Consequently we planned to leave Orlando at four o'clock on Christmas afternoon and arrive in Phoenix at six P.M. local time. When we arrived at the Orlando airport, they informed us that our flight to Memphis had been canceled. They rescheduled us on another flight through Denver, but it was late and our connection there was late. We were tired and irritable by the time we arrived at the Phoenix airport at approximately fifteen minutes after midnight their time.

It was so late, there was no one to meet us, and we all had a number of bags, since we were going on to Hawaii for the Hula Bowl following the Fiesta Bowl. We finally ran down a cab, and Beth, Liz, Kevin, and I jumped in. The accommodations at the Sheraton in Scottsdale were excellent, and the people at the hotel were most hospitable. But by this time a flophouse would have looked great.

We had a full week before we played the football game, and it would prove to be a very eventful week. Here's what happened.

December 26

Normally when we go to a bowl game, we leave one whole day for travel, especially at Notre Dame, where you have players coming in from all over the country. We felt it was necessary to try to get in a workout the same afternoon they arrived in Phoenix. We gave them five days off for Christmas because our players hadn't been home since August.

Weather always seems to play havoc with our travel schedule. Bad weather really hit the South Bend and Chicago area hard this morning, apparently just after the charter flight left carrying all our coaches, administrative staff, and families.

Andre Jones got stranded in Chicago for twelve hours and didn't get to Phoenix until four in the morning. But the most terrifying story belonged to Corny Southall. He had an Eastern flight from Rochester which was scheduled to go through Atlanta on its way to Phoenix. But a portion of the fuselage ripped away, leaving a hole a few feet wide, and the plane had to make an emergency landing in Charleston, West Virginia. Fortunately, no one was hurt. Corny's being a Notre Dame football player stranded in West Virginia created a lot of interest. He finally got to the hotel about nine tonight. I think he was just happy to have his feet on the ground again.

Corny Southall, senior free safety

The incident with my plane flight on the way to the Fiesta Bowl made me late for the meeting that night after practice. The players had gone on to the Suns-Lakers game. I ran into Coach Holtz at the hotel after getting in late and he sort of looked at me and smiled. One of the first things he said to me was, "You're not planning on being a pilot when you get out of here, are you?" Then he welcomed me back and asked me if I was prepared for the game.

Corny was interviewed quite a few times about the incident, and he took a little ribbing from the other players about it. The story got better every time Corny told it. Mark Green said, "Pretty soon, you'll be the one who landed the plane."

I was just happy to get on the practice field. We'll be practicing the next few days at Scottsdale Community College. It's located all by itself out on an Indian reservation, and it's perfect for what we need to do. There are two full fields, so the offense and defense can work separately—plus there is one lighted field, which came in handy today, as we practiced later than was initially planned.

We didn't get on the field until about four o'clock. It was already cloudy and the sun was disappearing. The temperature couldn't have been more than 50 degrees, and it really got chilly as the sun went down. This isn't what we expected in terms of weather, but at least it's not much different from what we're used to. In fact, we felt right at home because a big barrel of clouds moved over the field and it actually snowed and rained a little.

We got some things done before the team took off to see the Phoenix Suns play the Los Angeles Lakers. It was a good physical practice, maybe more difficult than the players had imagined, though we worked in headgear and shoulder pads.

We gave our players box lunches to take to the Los Angeles Lakers– Phoenix Suns NBA game, which I told the team would be the first of several activities together. We are not going to play "Can you top this?" This occurs when some players go out and tell what they did that night, and it always appears to be more exciting than it was. The other players feel they aren't getting in on the action, so they go out and do something even more bizarre. This just multiplies as the days pass, and consequently you end up with all kinds of problems. We as a staff are totally committed to seeing that this does not occur this year.

December 27

I went back to the hotel last night and looked at the video of practice to see how much we digressed over the break. I was astounded. The concentration was exceptional. I'm still not happy with the scout squad, but our offense and defense practiced well. I couldn't be more pleased with their attitude.

I honestly feel we'll all be a better football team in the bowl game than we were against USC. If we were a senior-dominated team, I probably wouldn't feel that way. But we play so many young people that we can't help but get better. Tony Rice threw the ball today like he was playing on Sunday. We just haven't done the job with our receivers this year. They haven't made the progress I wanted to see, but they are young.

At the press conference today it was mentioned that each of the last three number-one ranked teams coming into the bowl games had lost, and seven of the last ten. I went back and told the team that was great. The odds are in our favor.

One of those three wins was by Alabama over Arkansas when I coached the Hogs. Bear's team did it by having only one turnover, very few penalties, and a great kicking game. He prepared his team to win the game, and that they did. We thought we had to beat Alabama, and while we played well, it wasn't good enough.

Perhaps Miami got caught up in the same thing a couple of years ago in the Fiesta Bowl. People kept writing how great they were and how badly they would beat Penn State. After a while I think they felt they had to live up to people's expectations and that they wouldn't be doing enough unless they beat Penn State by a convincing margin. Miami experienced eight turnovers and ended up losing, even though Penn State gained around 150 yards. Most of the time the number-one team just beats itself.

I know we're playing a great West Virginia team, but their eleven opponents have combined to win only 49 games, and that includes 10 by Syracuse. They haven't committed many turnovers, and they protect the football, but we've made a living by forcing turnovers.

Dan Devine, who now works at Arizona State with the school's drug-education program, came to practice today, and so did Larry Marmie, the current Arizona State coach. I had sent a letter to Dan a few weeks ago inviting him to come out and be a part of anything our team does in Phoenix. I was sincere, as Dan is a former Notre Dame coach and part of our family.

I asked him to speak after practice today, and he did a fine job: "You're 11–0, and that's something few Notre Dame teams have ever attained against the kind of schedule you've played. January 2 is the frosting on the cake, and I know because I've been there a couple of times. As a former Notre Dame coach, I know what it means. But more than anything, you've made me proud as heck by what you've done this year."

We accomplished what we wanted on the practice field, except we weren't as physical as I would like. I'm sure we will see improvement in this area tomorrow.

The players went to the ballet tonight to see the *Nutcracker Suite*. The scary thing is, they liked it.

December 28

I am really pleased right now with our team. We got here the same day West Virginia did, but we got a day of practice in and I'm not sure they did. I have always felt you should get your work done early for a bowl game, and maybe they have. Our normal routine is to have mass (optional) at eight, brunch at eight-thirty, meetings from ten to noon, and practice around two. As game time approaches we'll try to finish practice a little earlier, give the players more free time during the day, and continue to do things as a team at night. I'm pleased with the players' attitudes. They aren't too tight, and yet their concentration is excellent. They seem to be enjoying the hoopla of a big game.

We were very physical today at practice, even going one against one for a while. I don't think I'll allow them to peak too early, but that is now a concern. Tony Rice threw it great again today, and that's scary.

Dick Enberg came to practice today and wandered around a little in the sunshine. Kari Ross of ESPN did a piece on the Three Amigos—Pritchett, Stams, and Stonebreaker. They are unbelievable in an interview, and it is more entertaining than informative. The media blitz isn't too bad yet, but there will be more reporters arriving every day. I understand the weather in the Midwest is bad. Bill Bilinski and Bill Moor from the *South Bend Tribune* haven't been able to get here yet. Their paper is publishing a diary of the team's activities while in Phoenix. Mark Green is providing the information, but work on the diary can't start until the *Tribune* writers get into town.

Our team is going to attend a concert by the Phoenix Symphony on Saturday night, New Year's Eve. I told them they should learn to appreciate the talents and abilities of other people the same way people appreciate their talents and skills.

NBC had a camera set up at the press-headquarters hotel, the Westcourt at the Buttes. After the normal press conference was over, they asked me to diagram a play that we might use. I drew up an option play that illustrates why we have such rushing balance—since you never know who's going to get the ball. The ultimate ball carrier is determined by the reaction of the defense. It's the kind of play that could determine the outcome of the game, and yet we are not revealing anything significant. I drew our offensive players with tiny O's and the West Virginia defenders in huge capital letters. The camera crew laughed, but they also got the message that West Virginia is much bigger than we are.

The number of media people coming here is unbelievable. I think they've issued about eight hundred credentials, so this is like a Super Bowl. They hold a press conference every day featuring the coaches and selected players. I'm not excited about having to drive twenty-five minutes each way every day to get to press headquarters, but I guess we'll survive.

I'm still concerned about the status of two of our fullbacks—Anthony Johnson, who still hasn't gotten over his ankle problems, and Rodney Culver, who is bothered by a shoulder. But all in all, I like the progress we're making.

We were able to take our video equipment with us and shoot practice every day. That's great for the coaches. Late tonight I was watching a tape of this afternoon's practice when a guy with binoculars, watching our practice from the street, flashed on the screen. Our cameraman had been watching him observe our practices and take notes and had videotaped him.

He was a large person and wore a silver warm-up jacket. We had the shot blown up and made a Polaroid of it. Supposedly our security people had seen him and talked to him. He said he was from Maryland and was a Penn State fan who just wanted to watch our practices. But because they were closed, he decided to watch it from the only vantage point he could see, and that was the street. When he was asked for identification, he said he didn't have any because all he was wearing was his warm-up suit. We let the matter drop because I believe Don Nehlen is an honorable coach and wouldn't do anything of this nature. I'm sure it was just a coincidence.

December 29

I really feel the momentum is swinging our way, and this is important.

There's a big story in *USA Today* this morning about West Virginia's great offensive line. They are awfully good, but there was a comment to the effect that no one could slow them down. We had this article photocopied and put up in the room of every defensive player. Every position analysis that I have seen between the two teams favors the Mountaineers. We're the number-one team, but West Virginia gets the edge everywhere. They say Major Harris is a better quarterback than Tony Rice. They talk about Reggie Rembert's being the best receiver around. Our offensive line doesn't measure up to theirs. We've got good backs, but all you hear about is A. B. Brown. Even as well as our defense has played, people act like West Virginia's defense is as good if not better. All of a sudden we seem to have something to prove. Maybe West Virginia is the better team, but that's why we will play the game.

I can't tell you how much I want to win this game, for a lot of reasons. One of them is so I can point out that only a great team like Notre Dame could beat the number two, three, and four teams in the rankings. As a matter of fact, we will be only the fourth team in NCAA history, and the first since 1945, to win the national championship while defeating four teams that finish in the top ten. Many people still don't believe that Tony Rice is an outstanding quarterback, despite his impressive performances when he's competed against Steve Walsh and Rodney Peete, two of the leading Heisman candidates.

I think we're going to shock West Virginia and the country, and eventually I think this is going to go down as one of the great teams in Notre Dame history.

This game is not a matter of who wants to win the most, because both teams do, but hinges on which team will be relaxed and play with the greatest intensity.

Both teams went out to Rawhide, the western town north of Scottsdale, for a cookout last night. They had the UPI national-championship trophy on display, and a couple of West Virginia players came up to Frank Stams and said, "Get a good look at it. This is the last time you'll see it." This offended Frank and some of our other players. No one meant anything by that comment, and I'm certain that our players said some things that were not appreciated by West Virginia players, although I don't know this for a fact.

We practiced early today, got back to the hotel for lunch, and then the players had the afternoon off. We'll try to do the same thing Saturday.

Tony continued to throw well today. All we need to do is to get him to relax before the game and he'll probably throw great. There is little doubt

Tony is a great runner. Today we pointed out to our team some interesting statistics. Tony has 114 carries for 700 yards. Major Harris has something like 121 carries for 583 yards. They both competed against Pitt and Penn State. In addition to this, Tony has done it against Michigan, Miami, and USC. Major did it against East Carolina and Cincinnati. This analysis was not done to diminish the greatness of Major Harris, as he is outstanding, but to illustrate that he wasn't any more dangerous than Tony Rice.

We had a relaxation period for the defense before dinner tonight. Then we passed out the Fiesta Bowl watches and plaques. I sat around with the players at dinner tonight and we talked about some of the bowl experiences my teams have had. Every one is different. We're still four days away from the game, and I just want everyone to relax and not worry about a thing. One of the most pleasing things is how Tony Brooks and Ricky Watters have conducted themselves. They have been excellent in every area of their life.

December 30

Both teams attended the Fiesta Bowl luncheon today at the Civic Center downtown. There must have been three thousand people there, because it was the biggest luncheon I've ever seen at a bowl game. The building was so large they could have a runway outside the door and have the second-largest airport in the country.

Both coaches and selected players spoke.

"This football team wasn't made by magic," I told the players. "You built it piece by piece. I've never been around better builders than you. You didn't try to do it in one afternoon. You built it day by day."

I thought Mark Green did a beautiful job of speaking for our team at the luncheon. He complimented West Virginia for being there and for all their accomplishments.

I think our players are starting to understand the psychology of a major game. You don't go around saying how great you are. If you have to tell people you're a good football team, no one will listen. Many times a young man will be in a press conference and make a comment that sounds different than it reads.

I told the players a long time ago that it's not in their best interest for me to say they're invincible. It means nothing coming from me. On Tuesday, when the game's over, it's different. Then I can say this is the greatest team in Notre Dame football history if I feel that way.

When we came here West Virginia had the psychological advantage, with nothing to lose, going up against a number-one team that's favored by four or five points.

West Virginia has won five of its last six bowl games because: 1) they are a better team than you think, 2) they are talented, 3) they are well-coached, 4) the opponent doesn't give them the respect they should. We always attempted to put them on the same plane as Notre Dame.

Don Nehlen has impressed me with his comments at the press conference, but I'm not sure if he is pleased with some things his players have said. They've gone out of their way to tell everyone how good they are. Major Harris said he didn't think we could stop their offense because they could do too many different things. They said nobody could get open on their defensive backs, and there wasn't anyone they couldn't block. This all may be true, but if they play us the way they played Syracuse, we will have some receivers open deep. Whether we throw it accurately or catch it is another matter.

The longer the week went on, the closer our team became. They did things together, never complained, were never late for anything all week, and worked hard on the field. We ate most of our meals together, and in our daily staff meetings held at seven A.M. our coaches continually expressed guarded optimism.

Due to the length of the luncheon, we didn't get on the practice field until three-forty, but fortunately we had a light workout planned.

Mel Blount, the former Pittsburgh Steeler defensive back, spoke to the team before practice. He is the personal representative for Pete Rozelle and the National Football League. He owns four Super Bowl rings, and he didn't buy them, so you're prone to listen to what he says.

He said, "I think you know what it takes to win. And you know the eyes of the world will be watching. You'll never have an opportunity like this one again. Believe me, I played in four Super Bowls, so I know what it takes to get here. It takes basic, fundamental football, blocking and tackling and all the basic things. People are proud of you because you did it the right way. No game like this is going to come easy. And you're going to have to get up when you get knocked down. But you've got a great vehicle here to get a great education, and you should understand the kind of example you are for young people today."

I was particularly pleased about his comments concerning fundamentals, because that is what we emphasized.

Our preparation, basically, is now over. We're just fine-tuning things. What's important now is to relax, get our rest and be positive.

Tonight is the USA-USSR wrestling match at Arizona State. Some of the players were starting to focus on the game and asked if they could stay at the hotel and rest. We told the players they could either go to the wrestling match or stay at the hotel and rest or visit with their parents.

My schedule was quite hectic. I had to attend a meeting tonight with the football officials, television executives, and others who run the game.

West Virginia is a fine football team and would have been even more dominating had they not been penalized eighty-eight times, which is an abnormally large number. It is the right of any coach to appeal to the head of the officials who are going to call the game. In this case it was Ken Faulkner of the Southwest Conference. At the suggestion of Ken Hatfield, the head football coach at Arkansas, we sent sample films to the Southwest Conference with an explanation of the concerns we had. Mr. Faulkner is then supposed to view the film you sent with the various officials who will be working the game. I never talked to Mr. Faulkner personally, nor anyone in the Southwest Conference.

I was concerned about how the officials would interpret holding, but I felt we had done everything we could ethically. Perhaps West Virginia did the same thing, I don't know. Once we had sent the film, I never discussed this matter with an official from the Southwest Conference before, during, or after the game.

December 31

Today we again practiced early in order to give the players a free afternoon. We had brunch at eight, kicking game meeting at eight-thirty, team meeting at nine, left at ten-fifteen, practiced at ten-thirty, and were off the field by noon. This enabled the players to have the whole afternoon to themselves. We'll all go to the symphony together tonight. Following the symphony they can stay out until one tonight as long as they're with their families and close friends. It's New Year's Eve and we have two more days until the game, so I don't think this decision will jeopardize our chances for success. There is a thin line between discipline and harassment. Discipline breeds success, and harassment breeds contempt. I felt that to prevent our players from bringing in the New Year with their parents bordered on harassment.

After practice was over, I asked the players how it went. We let them critique their own work, as if they were coaches.

"Coach [George] Williams, how did it go?"

"Great practice, fundamentally sound," he said.

"Coach Stams?"

"It went well today, Coach."

Jan Blazi, secretary to Lou Holtz

I think Coach Holtz is always concerned every week, especially four or five days before the game. He was that way in Phoenix before the Fiesta

329

Bowl. But on Saturday, two days before the game, he came into the office and had a big smile on his face and he said, "I've finally got them where I want them. I've finally got this team at the level I want them, and we're going to win."

On Sunday we will practice carrying the seniors off the field after we win. We'll assign a couple of underclassmen to each senior and we'll make sure that every senior gets carried off the field at Sun Devil Stadium. Since Tim Grunhard and Dean Brown aren't seniors, we'll be okay. I don't know if we could carry those guys.

Yesterday was Barry Alvarez's birthday, and some of his players—Michael Stonebreaker, Wes Pritchett, and Frank Stams—hired an entertainer named Mae East to come to dinner. I had some meetings to attend, so I missed the party. The whole thing really caught Barry by surprise. I understand the players loved every minute of it.

He had gone out to run after practice and went back to his room to shower after really working up a sweat. The players weren't sure if he was going to make it to dinner, so they had one of the managers call and tell him I wanted to see him right away. He was really sweating to start with, and she only made it worse. It was all in fun, and I thought it was great that the players thought so much of Barry that they tried to do something special for his birthday. I had no idea the players were planning this, and they assured me it was in good taste and wouldn't embarrass Notre Dame.

Our veterans are starting to take charge of the situation. As the team got on the buses for the symphony tonight, Wes Pritchett and a couple of others made it plain that after the symphony everybody was coming back to the Sheraton and were spending the rest of the evening there with their parents and close friends. This should be a fun night because so many of the players' families are here by now.

At the symphony the director invited the players up on stage and the audience gave them a standing ovation. While we were on the stage, the symphony played the Notre Dame Victory March. I thought the whole thing was outstanding. Our players enjoyed it thoroughly. They were impressed to watch fifty violinists move their fingers and bows in perfect unison. I said to the players, "You're supposed to be such great athletes, and we can't even get eleven of us to get off on the same count, let alone match the precision of the symphony."

After the symphony my wife and I stopped for a half hour at the New Year's Eve party for the media, then we went back to the Notre Dame party at the Sheraton. By eleven-fifteen I was in my room, and I brought in the New Year by watching the video of practice that day.

January 1

Finally, it's getting close.

We let the players sleep in this morning, had brunch, then a team meeting at one-fifteen before going to practice.

We're not going to do a lot at practice today, but we want to go to Sun Devil Stadium and familiarize ourselves with the layout so we know exactly what we're doing and where we're going tomorrow. We'll practice in sweats. I told the players to bring both pairs of their football shoes and test them out. The field has been used extensively this year by the Cardinals, Sun Devils, and others, so it is only natural that there are some places in the middle of the field where there's not much grass. Some players may feel more comfortable or get better traction in a cleated shoe, while a skilled player may feel that a turf shoe is better suited for his needs. In any event, it's the player's choice, and today is the time to make that decision.

We'd talked about practicing carrying the seniors off, but there were so many news media people at practice that I decided not to because this would send the wrong message. I thought we might have the place to ourselves, and if this were the case, we could get everyone in a positive frame of mind by practicing what to do after we win. Our workout was short, casual, loose, and disorganized. This is the one day our motto is "hang loose." The weather was beautiful and it's supposed to be better tomorrow. No one has spent any time sitting by the pool, but it's been pretty comfortable for football.

In my daily address to the squad I covered some miscellaneous items and then went over the schedule. We'll come back after practice today and have a kicking game meeting at four-thirty, individual meetings at five, dinner at six, then Captain Video. The movie tonight is *Patton*, which may be my all-time favorite.

Tomorrow we get up, have mass at ten, pregame meal at ten-thirty, and leave at twelve-fifteen.

"This game is no different than any other," I told the players. "It's no more important than Michigan or Michigan State or Purdue or Air Force or Miami or any of them.

"Why? Had we not played our own football game every week, we would not be here. We got here by doing what we needed to do on a week-by-week basis.

"This is not any different. It's not larger than life. We don't have to play over our heads. We will win—you can put your mind at ease about that.

"We're a better football team today than at any point during the season. I was worried about that the week after the USC game because I didn't know if we'd come back and make the improvement we needed to make.

But we have done that. There's no reason we shouldn't play better in this game than we've played all year.

"Our defense was excellent during the season, and yet we've gotten better.

"Our kicking game is now much better than it was. Jim Sexton, I've never seen you punt as well as you have out here.

"I believe we execute better on offense than I've seen all year.

"What we have to do tomorrow is very simple."

I then went over the keys to victory. I felt like Lee Marvin in the movie *The Dirty Dozen*, where you keep reiterating certain things you have to do to win.

"One, people have talked about Notre Dame not being real physical. Tomorrow we are going to put that to rest once and for all.

"Two, we must be fundamentally sound. We're playing against a good quarterback, but we've played plenty of good quarterbacks, including people who could run, like Dee Dowis of Air Force. We're not going to be shocked just because Major Harris is a good player. We've played against good players all year.

"They talk about West Virginia's offensive line, but we've played against several great offensive lines this year.

"Three, West Virginia doesn't make many mental errors, and yet I don't think I've seen a Notre Dame team better prepared than you are.

"Four, we will not flinch. You will not talk to the West Virginia players. You just butt 'em in the mouth and pull your teammates to their feet.

"Five, I don't know if West Virginia really and truly expects to win. I know they want to win. But deep down inside, I don't know if they truly believe they will win. They may, I don't know for sure. But I do know for a fact that we believe we will win and we expect to win.

"Six, there's nothing more important than togetherness. You've got to care about one another every minute we're on that field tomorrow.

"You should savor this game. Enjoy it, give it your best for sixty minutes at six-second intervals. That's all a football game is.

"We should enjoy everything we do. Don't worry about anything, relax and be ready at the right time."

35

FIESTA BOWL:
MEET THE PRESS

ANY time you play in a bowl game, you receive a tremendous amount of media coverage the month leading up to the game. It is usually on national television, so you receive national attention.

It's amazing how much interest there is in the game that decides the national championship. I don't think there's a major newspaper in the country that doesn't have at least one person here.

Before most bowl games they have two or three press conferences for the coaches and players. At this game we have a daily press conference, and I don't mean for just ten or fifteen minutes. I would venture to say I am spending three hours a day with the media or traveling to meet the media.

As I said before, the press headquarters are located at the Westcourt at the Buttes, which is about twenty-five minutes from our headquarters at the Sheraton. The team hotels, press hotels, and press headquarters all change from year to year. Last year the press stayed right across the street from the Sheraton. That really would have simplified my life. They even talked about a helicopter to go to the Westcourt and back, but I vetoed it because that's not me, and it's not Notre Dame. We'll get there in a car like everyone else. There is no doubt that it is easier with all the media in one location. It would be a zoo if they were scattered.

We had some fun with the media, and I don't think there are any questions that weren't asked during our week in Phoenix. Here's a sample of how it went:

Q. In the event of a tie, would you be for a sudden death?

333

A. I have always been for a sudden death.

In nineteen years of coaching, I have been involved in five ties. Two of them have been in bowl games. We tied UCLA out here in the Fiesta Bowl in '78, and we tied Houston in the Bluebonnet Bowl in 1974 when I was at North Carolina State. I am sure the NCAA has their reasons for not playing off a tie, but I would prefer it. With the two-point conversion, there really shouldn't be a tie unless there is a series of unusual events. If somebody scores late, it normally isn't going to end up a tie. I know West Virginia will go for a win and Notre Dame will go for a win.

Q. Don Nehlen has been saying all week that this is the biggest game he has ever coached in, the biggest game West Virginia has ever played in. Is this the biggest game that you have ever coached in?

A. No, I don't think it is any bigger than any other. I really don't. I want to tell you something. I was with William & Mary, and winning was very important. This one is important also. Maybe this game has greater significance nationally. Maybe this game has more people reading about it. Maybe this is a game that you remember longer, but no, this is just another football game. You put all your time and your effort into it and you do everything you possibly can, and if we win the football game, I won't be any different than if we do not win the football game. You can't be a miracle worker. You do the best you can and you go from there. Don't make it out to be bigger than life. This is the biggest game today. There will be a bigger one tomorrow. The biggest game is when you are fighting for your job. That's a big game.

Q. If Notre Dame wins this game, it is assumed, based on the polls, that you will be the national champion. What if West Virginia wins this game and Miami wins? Where do you stand on that? Is West Virginia national champion?

A. Well, as I said before, I was born in the state of West Virginia and have great respect for that state, and they have an outstanding football team. But nobody has ever asked me who was number one before, and if we don't win, I don't care who is number one. I really don't get a chance to say who is number one. Other people make that decision.

Q. Don Nehlen is in a position that maybe you can relate to, having been a coach at William & Mary, at North Carolina State, at Arkansas.

It's the idea of playing in a game of this magnitude, and the perception that he's the little guy. You have been the little guy, and now suddenly here you are, in the minds of guys like me, the fat cat. Is it a little different this time around in a game of this magnitude, not having suspensions, not being the underdog, that kind of thing?

A. No, it isn't any different to me because I don't think there is a favorite in a bowl game. That is why the number-one team has lost eight out of the last eleven games. I pick up the paper and all I read about is the great offensive line at West Virginia. You can look at it statistically, and you look at comparative scores, and there is no favorite. All we are talking about is that in people's minds Notre Dame should beat West Virginia. However, there isn't a single individual in here that can give me a fact, a figure, or a reason why Notre Dame should win. Whether you are comparing maturity, strength, or statistics, this game is even.

So as far as our football team is concerned, we are just going to go out and play the best game we possibly can. We may not win this football game, but I will tell you this—if we don't win this football game, it will be for only one reason and one reason only. We weren't good enough. It won't be because we aren't ready emotionally. It won't be because we aren't ready physically. It won't be because we haven't adequately prepared, and it sure won't be because our players didn't practice hard.

Q. Your players say you do magic tricks for them once in a while. Can you talk a little bit about that?

A. I get requests to do magic tricks from time to time. Let me tell you how the magic came about, because I have really tried to stay away from it. I have not used it with our football squad extensively. But we had a talent show on our football team, and the talent show was just that. I'm not talking about getting up on Freshman Night and singing your high school fight song. We have talented people in a lot of areas other than football. Two years ago we had a concert pianist up there. We had singers. So the players came to me when I said we were going to have a talent show and asked if I would start off by doing some magic. So I did about four or five magic tricks for them to loosen them up and make an idiot of myself. I did this so they would not feel real conspicuous when they got up. I was absolutely amazed at the talent they possessed. When Wesley Pritchett got up and recited Shakespeare, I was absolutely flabbergasted.

I used to think I was a fair amateur magician, but I don't have the time to practice it or do anything else along that line. The newspaper trick has sort of become synonymous with me. If you go somewhere and speak and you don't do it, you get a lot of people coming up afterward and saying, "Good Lord, I was telling my wife about this trick and you didn't do it." It's sort of like Bob Hope singing "Thanks for the Memories." I am embarrassed to do this, but it is just something that people sort of expect. I don't do magic to fool people. If I do any magic, it is strictly to entertain people. You go in a home recruiting somebody, and they've got this little five-year-old child who keeps sticking his lollipop in your ear. You take a coin and show it to him and get his attention and tell him, "I am going to turn you into a rabbit if your brother doesn't come to Notre Dame."

Some of the players I have coached have taken up magic strictly as a hobby. That's how it started with me, when my little daughter Luanne was small, she was fooling around and I was trying to watch a game. I was babysitting, so I did a couple of little tricks. I told the children I would put on a magic show for their friends if they would clean up the garage. We would charge admission. I was going to teach them about the free enterprise system. So I learned a couple more tricks. I went out to the garage, and they charged a quarter and had about fourteen children there and about thirty adults. I made an idiot of myself. Well, every Christmas, every birthday, everybody in the neighborhood brought me a magic book. That is where it all got started. I decided to try and improve my magic, and did so until I became a head coach at Arkansas, but the time demands are too much to do both.

Q. A couple of times during the season you made known your feelings that you did not feel that Notre Dame was the number-one ball club or number-three ball club or whatever you happened to be at the time. Also, on a couple of occasions you expressed some degree of surprise at what you had achieved. When did it really occur to you during the season that this team was a little more special than you thought it was going to be?

A. We went into this season and we had good expectations. But to say that your team is just going to go out there and dominate your opponent is a mistake. Our execution is not very good, and I think maybe that's the reason West Virginia is so confident. They talk about how nobody can stop them, and maybe we can't because we have not executed very well this season, although we have improved recently. We are very young. We don't have continuity on offense and we can't throw the football. We just aren't consistent and our execution from the perspective of a football coach is not what we desire. This is not the type of team where I would take our offensive film and show it to a clinic unless I were talking about defense. We just don't execute as well as what we need to really be a machine.

What I did not estimate accurately was the competitiveness of the team, the leadership of the team, or the togetherness of the team. This football team has exceeded my expectations in those areas. We rely on the intangibles an awful lot. I think back to the '68 Ohio State football team with Kern, Tatum, Brockington, Zalena, and Stillwagon. You knew when you went out there that you were fixing to whack somebody. Even then, as good as that football team was, we just didn't dominate everybody, and we haven't done that this year. I still will not stand up here and say we are a great football team. We are really not. We feel very blessed to be here, and I am greatly concerned about how well we will play in this football game. I think we will play well, but I don't know if it will be good enough or not.

Q. I hate to keep picking on you about this business of you continually knocking down your ball club. I think you have realized it is a better ball club than you say it is. You say you wouldn't take offensive films of this club to a clinic. The fact remains that in the Miami game, when Miami scored the two touchdowns just before the half to tie the score, Notre Dame needed to make a long drive to reassert command. Your team took the second-half kickoff and went 80 yards, as I recall, for a touchdown. When USC closed up at 20–10 and your team needed the long march, which you hadn't had in the second half at that point, Notre Dame took the ball and went 80 yards for a touchdown. Now, obviously, this team is capable of doing something on offense against good ball clubs.

A. There is no doubt about that, and I won't deny it. Please don't labor under the misconception that I think we are an absolutely horrendous football team. You have to understand that you are not addressing Barry Switzer. I have not coached the number-one team fifty-two weeks during my career. This is a new experience for me. I told the football players, "Don't look to me for guidance about this sucker." Being a perfectionist, I try to look and say, "We should be far more consistent. We have done some good things, but we aren't very consistent as a football team." Perfect ten is the standard I use.

What I did say was this football team was exceptionally competitive. They are very close. On the other hand, there have been times when we have not moved the football with consistency. As well as our

337

defense played against USC, we did not keep USC's offense on the sideline, as we had planned to do in that game. We felt the best thing we could do was put Rodney Peete on the bench. Yet we went eight or nine series and never made a first down. So what I am looking at is, "How consistent are we?"

Now, I could give you a million excuses why we aren't more consistent, but not a single reason. We have not been able to have the same offensive line two weeks in a row, and with Tim Ryan getting hurt, we really had to rebuild that sucker about three different times. We have had to move personnel from tackle to tight end and vice versa. Mike Brennan started out as an offensive tight end and ended up as an offensive tackle. Now, maybe he is going to start this football game as an offensive guard. We've had to rebuild the offensive line. That is the thing about West Virginia, they have been able to play the same offensive linemen most of the year, and we will all acknowledge that they are bigger and stronger and more mature than us. We have people who haven't played much before. In addition, we haven't been very consistent at the wide receiver spots, and we have had to play five different fullbacks almost an equal amount of time this year for a variety of different reasons.

The last thing I want you to do is to get the impression that we are not very good and the only reason we win is because of coaching or because we are pulling rabbits out of the hat. This is not true at all. We have a good football team. I think the players have done very well, considering the adversity we have faced. We are very one-dimensional in many areas, and this causes me to say, "Are we invincible?" and I am here to tell you we sure aren't invincible.

Q. Since a game of this significance is a new experience for you, is there any concern that a situation could somehow arise that you had not anticipated, that your inexperience in this kind of situation could affect the outcome of the game?

A. I don't think it would be inexperience on our coaching staff that could affect the outcome of the game. When you go through the whole course of a season and come to a game like this, I don't think there is anything that could occur that we aren't adequately prepared for, whether it be two-minute play or two-point defense, two-point offense, taking a safety, kicking off after a safety, executing an outside kick or receiving on outside kick. I just don't believe that there is anything that can possibly come up that we have not practiced, and I would be shocked if something came up that West Virginia wasn't adequately prepared for. I think when you get to this stage in the season, you are prepared for everything. The main question is, how well are we going to play after a six-week layoff? Boy, that is one thing that really concerns me greatly. What is going to happen after a long, long layoff? This is always like an opening game of the season, and that is just how we have approached it.

Q. Neither team has been behind very much this year. Is that a concern to you, that your team has not had to play catch-up? If you have to, can you do it?

A. I am concerned that we have not had to play catch-up this year. It's the same thing that concerned me in the past games we have played. What happens if we fall behind? How do you play a low-scoring game, the type that we like to play? I won't know how we will react until we do fall behind and until we do have to play catch-up. We certainly don't plan on that happening, but if we do, that would be the worst scenario we could possibly write for Notre Dame as I see it. I think teams have scored something like eighteen times against us, and fifteen of those times we've answered by getting on the board after receiving the ensuing kickoff. I just don't think if we fall behind by three touchdowns that we can throw the ball all over the lot, because we are not a very good passing football team by any stretch of the imagination. On the other hand, West Virginia does have many weapons available to them, so playing catch-up for them should not be a problem.

Q. Have you ever gone into a game with a certain amount of swagger or uncharacteristic optimism?

A. Wake Forest, 1974, at North Carolina State, and we lost. Every week it is a different world. So many different things during the course of a football game, and you are always concerned about the unknown and unforeseen. You can look at statistics. You can look at common opponents. You can look at a variety of things. You can look at experiences. You can look at strength. You can look at versatility. I just am always rather pessimistic as we approach a football game. Yet I don't want you to interpret this to mean that we don't believe we can win, because that is not the way we approach a game. I think the individual who isn't concerned with potential problems just isn't very smart. We want to leave as few things to chance as possible.

I don't know if you've ever played golf. I've gone out there and played many tough golf courses. I went out to California and played Pebble Beach. The first time I played it, I didn't think it was a real tough course until I found where all the trouble was. Like on number

8, you have a blind second shot. I hit a great three-wood on the green and then walked up and saw that huge crevice and thought if that three-wood hadn't carried that crevice, I would have been in all kinds of trouble. The next time I didn't hit the three-wood very well and ended up in the crevice. I think, as you go through life, you've got to be aware of where the problems are and concentrate on what you have to do to adequately prepare your football team for those situations.

Q. Games of this magnitude tend to be played somewhat conservatively. How would you anticipate this game being played, and how would you approach it?

A. We are going to approach this football game like we have every other one. You go into a ball game saying, "This is the way we would like to play it," but you don't know. You take the field with a gameplan in mind, but if they score the first three times they have the ball and you punt the first three times, I think you better go to Plan B. Because of West Virginia's versatility, this is not the type of game where we can afford to bring one facet of our game or even two. We better bring our entire arsenal. I promise you this, we'll play them for sixty minutes, and if we have to go to Plan B, we'll go to Plan B. But if Plan B was better than Plan A, we would have used it first, so don't think that we are saving an ace in the hole. When we go to Plan C, we are getting into real trouble, but we also have a Plan D.

36

FIESTA BOWL:
THE GAME

I got up very early the morning of the game and turned on ESPN. I ,ouldn't believe they were showing *Wake Up the Echoes*. I wished I had shown it to our team. I was ready to play right then.

We had our mass and pregame meal and went to the stadium. On our arrival there, I told Father Jim Riehle, our team chaplain, that after we won the game, I wanted to come back and have a mass of thanksgiving for our team. I really felt that we would win, but deep down inside I may have been trying to convince myself we would. I'm very negative when we start preparing to play an opponent, and as the game draws closer, I become exceptionally positive. Why? I don't know.

Derek Brown, freshman tight end
When we went to the Fiesta Bowl, I liked what Coach Holtz said about dominating the whole football game. He said he wanted to dominate the game so much that whenever the opposing team gets a first down, he wants them to start playing their fight song and tearing down the goal posts.

Our players were very calm about the game and the atmosphere that permeated the stadium. I can't say the same thing about our fans, as they appeared delirious to me. It seemed like a fourteen-dollar cab ride to the far end of the field, where we were to warm up, so we walked. It seemed odd to me when the West Virginia players stopped and looked at us as we came on the field. I thought maybe we hadn't worn our headgear or something.

341

I didn't say much to the team before the game, other than to remind them that this was just another game. We all knew there were certain things we had to do well in order to win. I felt it was important we not put any more pressure on ourselves than we already had, so I gave a very placid talk and then we went out to play.

Wes Pritchett, senior linebacker

Coach Holtz just reminded us of everything he does before a game—the seven areas he always stresses. He told us that we were the best-prepared team and to bring Notre Dame another national championship. It was very emotional. The guys were anxious to play the game—that's why you come to Notre Dame and play college football in the first place. It wasn't real rah-rah, because Coach Holtz is always intense before a game.

We won the toss and elected to defer, as we had all year long. We may be the only team to play in a bowl game that didn't wear the bowl logo on its uniforms. The reason we didn't wear the bowl logo was that our approach to the game had been, "It's just another game," and, "Let's play for the spirit of Notre Dame." We didn't even order new jerseys for the game. We wore the same ones we'd been wearing at home all year. Our jerseys have an interlocking N.D. on the sleeve, a number on the front and back, no names, and we wear black Adidas shoes. People ask me why we wear black shoes, and I said, "I didn't think the players would like brown ones." People complained because we don't have names on our jerseys, and I said, "You should feel lucky we have numbers on them." It has the N.D. and that says it all.

It was obvious after kicking off, holding them after three downs, driving down and getting a field goal, holding them again and then scoring a touchdown just six minutes into the game, that we had shocked West Virginia because they hadn't been behind this entire year. However, the game was far from over, because West Virginia was an explosive offensive team.

THE GAME

TEMPE—Combining a knock-'em-in-the-dirt style of defense with a timely passing game set up by the pounding Irish running attack, Notre Dame did it all in putting the finishing touches on its first national championship since 1977.

The Irish got on the scoreboard early, contained the talented West Virginia star quarterback Major Harris, and methodically dismantled the only other unbeaten team left in the country. The result in this Fiesta Bowl battle of perfect records—the 13th in bowl history—left Notre

Dame with a 34–21 victory that actually was more convincing than the score indicated.

This was supposed to be a battle between Notre Dame's smothering defense and a West Virginia offense that lived by the big play in averaging 42 points and 483 yards per game. It was supposed to be a showcase for a Mountaineer offensive line loaded with fifth-year seniors. But it was Notre Dame's day. On another occasion the results may have been different. But not on January 2, 1989.

Michael Stonebreaker and Jeff Alm tackled Harris, smashing his left shoulder into the Sun Devil Stadium turf on the third play of the game, leaving the West Virginia quarterback forced to operate under a handicap for the remainder of the afternoon. A Mountaineer team that had never trailed at halftime all year found itself staring at a 16–0 deficit before ever managing a first down of its own. The Irish established immediate superiority over both lines of scrimmage and maintained it all day.

"They were more physical than we were," said West Virginia coach Don Nehlen. "It was obvious from where I was standing that they were beating us both offensively and defensively up front."

With Harris' effectiveness—and, thus, West Virginia's—reduced from the start, it was Irish quarterback Tony Rice who played like a Heisman Trophy contender. Shrugging off the nagging doubts about his passing ability, Rice first went about establishing Notre Dame's relentless ground game as Notre Dame rushed on 16 of its first 17 plays.

It appeared that every time West Virginia was poised to stop the Irish option, Rice took advantage of single coverage in the secondary by throwing for big yardage. He attempted only 11 passes, completing seven, but averaged more than 30 yards per catch on his way to the offensive MVP award.

"I did say Tony's passing had been improving in practice this week," Notre Dame's Lou Holtz said with a grin.

In the end, it was just another day at the office for the Irish, who played in their standard blue jerseys with no bowl logo, to downplay the national-title hype. They finished their 12–0 slate with wins over Miami, USC, and West Virginia, all of whom were otherwise unbeaten.

"This is a great team because nobody proved otherwise," said Holtz.

It took Notre Dame hardly any time at all to prove that to 74,911 fans in attendance. Sending West Virginia's offense to the sideline after three downs and a punt, Rice got the Irish offense started by scampering for 31 yards around left end. This was the key play that set up a 45-yard Billy Hackett field goal just 4:35 into the game.

After the ensuing kickoff, West Virginia ran three plays that netted only six yards, and consequently Notre Dame got the ball back again at their own 39. Rice connected on a pass to Derek Brown for 23 yards, but otherwise stayed on the ground, which resulted in a touchdown and a 10–0 lead. This touchdown was bitterly contested by the Mountaineer defense, and it took a great effort by Anthony Johnson on the fourth down to score.

West Virginia went two more possessions without gaining first-down yardage, and the Irish capitalized again. On third and 11 at his own 48, Rice again found Brown wide open over the middle—and Notre Dame's rookie tight end sprinted to the Mountaineers' five. Rodney Culver scored on the next play to make it 16–0, 5:19 into the second quarter as Reggie Ho missed the PAT.

The Mountaineers finally got on the scoreboard on a 29-yard Charlie Baumann field goal, but two of the first three first downs on the 52-yard drive came via Irish penalties. The Irish came right back with an impressive drive as Rice hit Johnson for 19 yards, then zipped one to Raghib Ismail for 29 yards and six points for a commanding 23–3 advantage. Only a 36-yard pass play with four seconds left from Harris to Reggie Rembert put West Virginia in position for a 31-yard field goal to close the half with a 23–6 lead.

Early in the second half Notre Dame matched those three points when Pat Terrell intercepted Harris on West Virginia's initial possession in the third period. This time it was Reggie Ho who kicked a 32-yard field goal. The key play that put the ball in position for Reggie's kick was a pass from Tony Rice to Mark Green for 35 yards.

Next came the only opportunity the Mountaineers had to get back in the game. After Harris had led his team 74 yards for a touchdown to make it 26–13, Willie Edwards intercepted a Rice pass to give West Virginia the ball back at the Irish 26. Notre Dame's defense proved equal to the challenge.

On first down, Flash Gordon hemmed in Harris on the option for a loss of two.

On second down, Stan Smagala made a spectacular deflection in the end zone of a Harris pass.

On the third down, Frank Stams—who earned defensive MVP honors—and Arnold Ale stormed Harris for a loss of 12, knocking West Virginia completely out of field-goal range. The Mountaineers had to punt, and Notre Dame promptly drove for another touchdown.

"That was disaster," said Nehlen. "Had we put something on the board we would have been in business."

"We weren't going to flinch," Holtz said. "The attitude of the defense was to go out there and put the fire out."

Starting at their own 20, the Irish needed only seven plays to go 80 yards. Rice's picture-perfect aerial for 57 yards to Watters gained most of that. His three-yard shot-put throw to Frank Jacobs made it 34–13 not quite two minutes into the final period.

West Virginia came back with one final touchdown, but it came in the final two minutes with the game long since decided—and it came by benefit of a couple of penalties against Notre Dame, one of which brought Holtz onto the field to set his team straight.

Rice's 213 passing yards marked a career best, as the Irish rolled up 455 total yards. Notre Dame's junior quarterback also led all rushers with 75 yards. Harris finished with 13 completions of 26 attempts for 166 yards, but the Irish limited the Mountaineer ground game to 108 yards, 49 of them by A. B. Brown.

Holtz admitted that maybe he had underestimated this Notre Dame team.

Today, even he couldn't do that.

Tony Rice had a spectacular day, which was absolutely vital if we were to win. Judging from the defensive scheme West Virginia employed against us, I don't think there's any way West Virginia expected us to throw as effectively as we did. I wasn't surprised with our ability to throw the ball, because I felt all week long that Tony was vastly improved in that area. Bob Shaw, West Virginia's defensive coordinator, put together an excellent gameplan. If we could not throw the ball successfully, we would have had a bad experience.

We'd heard so much all week about the West Virginia defense's ability to dominate a game, but I thought our defense really set the tone for the game by stopping them on their first four possessions. Four series in a row they went three plays and out, and by that time we were ahead 16–0, which surprised me.

We continued to try and run the ball, without consistent success. However, in taking this approach, West Virginia was forced to employ a running defense, which made them vulnerable to the play-action pass for most of the game. Against an eight-man front Tony made some great throws, and we had some great catches for big yardage. Had we thrown the ball more frequently, we may not have had success, as I'm sure they would have adjusted their secondary to cope with it.

I was really proud of our defense all year, but particularly in the third quarter. After West Virginia scored to make it 26–13, Tony threw an interception on the second play and West Virginia had it first and 10 at our 26. The momentum was going their way rapidly. We nailed Major Harris on first down for a loss of 2, Stan Smagala knocked away a pass into the end zone on second down, and on third down, Frank Stams and

Arnold Ale sacked Harris for a 12-yard loss. This series completely eliminated a field goal attempt, and West Virginia was forced to punt. The Notre Dame defense had come to the rescue again. They had saved us more times than Roy Rogers and Trigger had rescued the heroine. Our offense then simulated the Canadian Royal Mounted Police by getting their man every time, and we immediately drove 80 yards for a touchdown. The big play was a long pass to Ricky Watters down to the Mountaineer 5. For all intents and purposes the game was now over and we were national champions.

Chuck Heater, secondary coach

In the Fiesta Bowl, the big play was a concern. Major Harris was the key to their offense. He would make five or six big plays in a game and maybe three or four would result in touchdowns. That was by himself and against good football teams.

We felt going into the game that we really had to take him out of it and keep him from making those big plays—and yet he still made a couple. When he scrambled, we had to make him pull up. When we went man coverage against them, we were doing it to pressure him. We had a plan for him. But looking at film, people didn't always do everything they could have done to take him out of it.

Our plan was not to let him beat us in the option. We had an extra man on him all the time. They will say they didn't option it as much because Major got hurt. But the options they ran, we knocked them in the head pretty good. We weren't going to let him do that to us.

But the game came down to plays like the great one Stan Smagala made in the end zone to deflect the pass. It was a play typical of what Harris had done all year—he scrambles toward our bench, stands up and throws the ball in the back of the end zone. In every other game that throw is a completion, and all of a sudden it's a close game again. But in a critical situation Smagala makes a great football play—he gets his head turned around, misses the ball with one hand and gets it with the other. That's the way West Virginia had been winning all year long. For the most part we controlled Harris. And he was the key, no question.

I don't think West Virginia would have scored as much as they did if we'd eliminated the penalties. Near the end, we were called for personal fouls on about five consecutive plays. I finally went out on the field to find out what was going wrong. I asked the referee if our players were talking to West Virginia. He said no. I said, "Are they using profanity?" He said no. I said, "Are they fighting with West Virginia?" He said no. I said, "Well, then, what's happening?" He said our players were making caustic comments about the caliber of officiating.

Our players were very frustrated, saying the officials should receive only half of their fee because they only watched one team in the game rather than honoring their commitment to watch both. It is a fact that we were penalized eleven times for 102 yards and West Virginia three for 38 yards—which disappointed me because this is an area I thought we would have an advantage in, predicated on the number of penalties West Virginia received during the year.

When I went out on the field at the end of the game, there were so many flags on the ground I couldn't tell the color of the grass. I asked Mr. Shepard, the referee, who the last penalty was on, as we had five in a row. He said, "You, for coming on the field." I said, "No, the one before mine." He told me, and I walked over to our defensive huddle and noticed we only had ten men present. I asked where the player was who had just gotten the penalty for talking to the officials, and the players said, "When he saw you coming on the field, he went off."

I then talked to our squad about the following things. It didn't take me long to express myself, as I was upset and disappointed. Our players are not allowed to talk to the officials except to say "Yes, sir" and "No, sir." The officials have a difficult job and they are going to make mistakes, but if you think they are doing it intentionally, you better get out of the game because you don't deserve the privilege of playing.

In addition, if the officials made a mistake, and I'm not saying they did, they still didn't make as many as the coaches and players did. I would rather lose with class than win with controversy, even if the game determined the national championship. Our players are also not allowed to use profanity. We are only allotted so many words of profanity per team, and I will use our entire quota. Incidentally, our quota is ten words per year. The only reasons someone uses profanity are to (1) please their parents (2) make their girlfriend proud (3) show they come from a God-fearing home (4) show they have a great vocabulary and (5) show they have great self-control.

In addition, our players aren't allowed to talk to their opponents. We are there to play and not debate. We aren't trying to bargain for the win, nor are we trying to talk them into surrendering. We only have a short period of time between plays, and we should spend that time as profitably as we can, and that should be communicating with your teammates. If you talk to your opponent rather than your teammates, you are in essence saying I like my opponent better than my teammates.

347

I then went to the sideline to look up the missing player.

It was my pleasure to coach A. B. Brown, the running back from West Virginia, in the Hula Bowl the following week. I asked him if our players had been talking on the field. He said no, that all everyone did was try to play the game. So, naturally, this bothered me, because it was not the way I wanted a season and a game like this to end.

Having visited with our players, the officials, and the West Virginia players, I can offer a thousand reasons why these incidents happened—but not a single excuse. No Notre Dame player should ever conduct himself in a manner that exhibits anything less than the highest standards that have become synonymous with this university. However, there were extenuating and mitigating circumstances.

The conduct of our players off the field this entire season was exemplary. We received a number of compliments from people we came in contact with, including the staff at the Sheraton in Scottsdale. When our players attended the Phoenix Symphony and the *Nutcracker Suite*, I thought they were awfully impressive.

During the entire season we seldom received a report that our athletes were violating training rules. And to my knowledge, the football team of 130 players went the entire fall semester with very few players being summoned to the office of student affairs for any disciplinary problem. They were a joy to coach, and for eleven games and fifty-eight minutes I was exceptionally proud of their performances and their conduct both on and off the field.

Frank Stams, senior defensive end

Everybody asks me about the West Virginia game—what happened the last two minutes when Coach Holtz came running on the field. I say, "I don't know. When I saw Coach Holtz come running onto the field, that's when I came running off."

I felt we were a better football team than West Virginia on that day. Perhaps another day the outcome might have been different. I don't know if that was a typical West Virginia performance or not, but I'm sure they feel it wasn't. They say Major Harris was injured early in the game and that certainly handicapped his performance.

I felt West Virginia was a good football team, definitely one of the top five in the country. One thing was certain, Notre Dame was number one, and the question of who should be national champion if we had lost is now moot. If I were forced to pick a champion had West Virginia won, my pick would have been Miami. Why? Because we play them next year and I sure don't want them mad when we do.

Mark Green, senior tailback

The biggest thing this season was to stay loose. Coach Holtz told us, "It's just another game until it's over, then it's something big." Now that it's over, you can say it was for the national championship.

In the locker room after the game they passed out newspapers that said, "Irish Win!" with the team picture in color. That was nice and it was a great feeling, but there wasn't a great deal of excitement, because our players expected to win. However, the fact that the Fiesta Bowl had them printed up and our football players could see it in print made a very favorable impression upon our players, coaches, and certainly myself.

Chuck Heater

The Fiesta Bowl was very different. If you had been using a barometer to gauge the emotionalism, you might have wondered because it was very quiet before the game. You might have wondered if we were ready to play.

After the game it wasn't as much of a rah-rah thing because I think we expected to win. On the down side, if we had lost the game, I think you really would have seen a lot of emotion. But Lou had us believing, after looking at the film, that we would win.

You looked at Miami and USC on film and you felt like you were just rolling the dice. With West Virginia we really felt we would win. Controlling Major Harris was a big if, but we thought if we could do that, we'd have an awfully good shot at winning the football game. We just expected it.

A week or two before the game, after we finished practice, Lou would pretend to interview some of the players and ask them things as if we had won the game. It was a mental thing. He'd say, "Okay, Wes Pritchett, you beat West Virginia by three touchdowns. When did you think you had the game?" He had everyone drilled that we would win. He would bring Barry Alvarez up after practice and say, "Barry, you shut 'em down today. How'd you control Major Harris?" It was the whole mental thing of saying we were going to do it. It wasn't like the locker room after the Miami or USC games, but it was because winning was not a surprise to us.

To say our locker room was quite crowded is the greatest understatement since General Custer said they look like friendly Indians. I haven't seen that many people I didn't know in our locker room since I played and had amnesia after the game. Nevertheless, I admonished our football team for our lack of class at the end of the game. I was upset and I think my sentiments showed.

349

We said our prayer and shortly thereafter the phone rang in the coaches' locker room. I think George Kelly answered it. He said, "It's the President." I was talking to Father Malloy at the time so I said, "I'm talking to the President."

It turned out to be the White House calling. I said, "I live in a white house, too." I thought it was President Reagan calling, but it turned out to be Vice President-elect Quayle. He said some nice things about our team, and then I said, "This is a new experience for me, but does this mean our players get to come to the White House?" This is probably the first time a team invited itself to the White House. I later received phone calls from both President Reagan and President-elect Bush. As I said previously, both these outstanding men had addressed our football team in the last ten months.

After getting off the phone I felt I needed to say something to the squad. We gathered around and I stood on a stool so they could see me, but I do this also so I can see them and verify the fact that I had their complete, undivided attention.

My initial comments were very similar to the ones I made to the players when I went on the field at the end of the game, only in more detail and with less emotion. After I felt I had made my point, I shifted the direction of my conversation.

I told them I was proud of them and that they were the greatest team I've seen. I asked them if it was worth the effort. They replied with a loud yes. I went on to tell them I didn't know how other national championship teams at Notre Dame performed over an entire season, but I couldn't imagine any exceeded their achievements. I proceeded to tell them that everything I've ever believed and loved about Notre Dame was embodied in our 1988 team—the trust, commitment, and love they displayed has rarely been duplicated.

I then said, "You've joined the Notre Dame greats now. You've won more games than any team in history at Notre Dame. You beat the number two, three, and four teams. If it weren't for you, Miami, West Virginia, and USC all would be unbeaten. We were only the fourth team in the history of the NCAA, and the first one in forty-five years, to win the national championship and defeat four teams that finished in the top ten in the final poll. To the seniors, juniors, sophomores, and freshmen, I say thank you. You'll find the trip to the top has been great. Staying there is a whole different matter, but we'll talk about that later. We'll be all right if you believe in the Notre Dame spirit. Take the lessons we have learned this year and apply them in your future endeavors and make certain you are a positive force in our society."

350

Next I asked Father Malloy, Father Beauchamp, and Dick Rosenthal if they had anything they wanted to say to the squad. Here's what they said:

Father Malloy: "I recall very vividly being in the locker room last year after the Miami game and after the bowl game against Texas A&M. I thought to myself at that time that you can have a great season and still feel a sense of disappointment at the end, as you did. I was just as proud of you last year as this year. Only things fell into place this year. I hope you all realize how proud we are of you—that you've entered into a great tradition. Yet none of you did it alone, you did it as a team. You're a part of the legends now. Congratulations to you. Relish it and enjoy it."

Father Beauchamp: "One thing I want to repeat that Monk said and that's how proud we are of all of you. I think I relaxed about a minute and a half ago. One thing that goes with a national championship is a lot of pride. But I think you and people around the country can be especially proud because you won the national championship as students, not just as athletes. You know the commitment you've made in the classroom as well as on the football field."

Dick Rosenthal: "I think we all owe Lou and his staff a vote of thanks for everything they've done. Lou said first you'd get good, then you'd get great, then you'd be number one, and that's exactly where you are right now."

We gave game balls to everybody on offense and defense who started or played key roles. On offense I singled out Tony Brooks and Ricky Watters. They'd been through a lot since the USC game, but I thought they'd handled it with class and I told them so in front of the squad.

I did the same thing with Tony Rice. The players believed in him before I did.

At the press conference, I felt I could open up and say some things I hadn't said earlier in the week.

"This was a football team that played today the way it has all year, doing the things it had to do to win. We got a lot of big plays. Tony Rice threw the ball very well, and we made a lot of clutch catches in critical situations. Our defense finished up the season as they started last spring, by being the foundation of our team.

"I really feel I've underestimated this team in a lot of areas. Even today we couldn't fall into a rhythm on offense, but we found a way to score 34 points and gain 455 yards. This football team had done everything we've asked of them. They went 12–0. I don't know how you rate or evaluate a football team, but this one has to go down as being worthy of wearing the championship crown they won. Somebody asked me earlier in the week if I thought if we won, would it go down as a poor national-championship team. I replied that I would have to evaluate that when the season was over. The one thing this team does over and over is find a way to win. We have some liabilities, but all teams do.

"I wasn't downplaying our football team or playing games with you. Honestly, in my heart, I was scared to death of West Virginia, although I thought we would win. I just look at how well our opponent is capable of playing against us, and I felt they were capable of beating anyone.

"Other than penalties, this team played exceptionally well against West Virginia. For me to say before today that this was an excellent team and that we deserved to be number one would have been putting a lot of undue pressure on our team, and they did not need that.

"I told the players a long time ago that we could end up being an awfully good team. But if we were, I wouldn't have to say it. If they were waiting for me to get up in front of the television cameras to say we were good, then they were in trouble, because that isn't the way we do it. When you go 12–0, I will then get up and say so. Is this a great football team? I would have to say yes, because nobody proved it wasn't. It's like a racehorse. They did everything we asked them to do, and that was win with class, and they did it on a consistent basis.

"The one thing we weren't going to do was flinch. We weren't going to worry if something went against us. Carl Pohlad gave me this advice last winter and it has proven to be invaluable to us. When Tony threw the interception, our attitude on the sideline was, this is a total team. The offense made a mistake and now it's up to the eraser defense to go in there and eradicate the mistake. That's exactly what they did. Then our offense justified the expense to bring them out here by immediately driving down the field to score.

"West Virginia's conventional defense had been so effective against all opponents, that we worked awfully hard on taking advantage of their strengths, one of which was quick run support by their secondary. That is why some of our play-action passes were open.

"We felt we had to keep Major Harris contained and not allow him to improvise. We thought we had to disrupt his rhythm and stop their power running game, and this we did.

"We wanted to do everything we could to make this just like a regular game in the minds of our players. That's why we didn't wear the Fiesta Bowl logo on the uniforms. We deferred when we won the toss, because we've been doing that all year.

"We felt it was important to set the tempo early in the game, and we do that best when our defense is on the field. Our team was aware that West Virginia had never been behind this entire year. That is rather incredible. We obviously need to lead at the end of the game, and the sooner this happened, the better it would be for us. Our coaches have done a great job all year, but please do not think this was a coaching victory. West Virginia has great coaches and they were every bit as prepared as we were.

"I think West Virginia is an excellent football team. I don't think there's any question that playing on grass hurt them. Major Harris is an excellent quarterback, and I'm sorry to hear he got hurt early in the game. We were not aware of that because they do not send West Virginia injury reports to our sideline.

"I think Knute Rockne would be proud of this team because it exemplifies what the Notre Dame spirit is all about. They subjugated their personal welfare for the welfare of the team and they played together. They cared about each other, and I can't say anything that would compliment this group more than that. There may be more talented teams and there may be better-coached teams, but there can't be a team that typifies the Notre Dame spirit better than this one.

"This is the happiest time of my professional life. There are two experiences in my life that I look on as the most depressed times in my life. Whenever I get down and get depressed, I think back to those two times and ask if it's as bad now as it was on those two occasions. From now on, when I'm happy, I'll always compare it to right now. I dreamt about winning a national championship, but I have to be honest with you. I didn't think there was any way in this world I'd ever be a part of something like this as a head coach. You think, man, that's for other people, that's for movie stars. I humbly say God watches out for stupid people, and there is no doubt he guided us this season."

Chuck Heater

I was truly a fortunate individual to walk into a national-championship situation. I know I'm not going to be back at Ohio State once Earle Bruce leaves and John Cooper takes over—and yet I end up with a job that's even better than Ohio State, which I thought would be difficult to do. There were question marks here. We'd lost three in a row the previous year. We'd lost Timmy Brown. People were predicting 6–5 and 7–4. But it was a tremendous thing for me.

Winning the national championship means, for one brief moment, you can say you were the best. That's great. You know you're in a very privileged group, even with all the teams Notre Dame has had that have won the whole thing. You get respect amongst your peers for what you've accomplished. Sometimes the process of getting to the top is the real substance of it all. Once you get there, it's great. But you think about the struggle, the run to get there. It'll be neat twenty years from now to come back and see all the guys, because any national championship team has a unique chemistry, with some significant individuals that make up the team. We'll always have a common ground from this time on out.

Prior to our departure from the locker room, I asked the squad to go back to our meeting room at the Sheraton so we could have a mass of thanksgiving. This was the first thing we did and was one of the most precious moments we shared together all year. I gave the homily, which was very short. Father Riehle said the mass and was assisted, as he had been all year, by Monsignor Anthony Gomes from Fall River, Massachusetts. The mass was not very long, but most meaningful. Those in attendance were limited to our team, coaches, and administrators.

Afterward I went back to my room and watched the end of the Auburn–Florida State game in the Sugar Bowl. We had great interest in it because my son Skip was a graduate assistant for Bobby Bowden at Florida State. After Florida State won, I went to the lobby and did a live interview with one of the South Bend stations and a taped interview with CNN, in which they presented us the national championship trophy. That really and truly was a great feeling. To be part of a national championship anywhere would kindle a great sense of accomplishment, but to be part of one at Notre Dame is special.

Chuck Heater
The difficulty with having a season like we did is that you don't really get a chance during the year to sit back and enjoy and appreciate what is happening. You don't do that until it's all over, after the Fiesta Bowl. There's always another game to play. For any coach, you can enjoy it on Saturday night, then on Sunday you've got to move on. After the Fiesta Bowl, we could finally relax and say, "Hey, we got there."

Even at this thrilling time I was plagued by a lingering headache. I thought that it was a result of the pressures I felt. At a formal dinner hosted by the Fiesta Bowl four nights before the game, they showed a video on each of the head coaches. They asked me to preview the video earlier that day, and I felt uncomfortable with it because I thought it portrayed me as something other than a simple father, husband, teacher, and coach. I didn't want them to run it, but I knew how much work they put into it. To do anything other than approve it would have been unfair to the bowl people. Coming out of the television truck where we viewed it that Thursday with Bruce Skinner and John Junker from the Fiesta Bowl, I banged my head. Little did I realize at the time, but that's how I ended up with a deep gash on my head and a four-day headache.

Later that night Skip called and said he had accepted a job at Colorado

State as a full-time assistant with Earle Bruce. I had coached with Earle at Ohio State. He's an outstanding coach, and I was so happy for Skip. To win the national championship and have our son get a full-time coaching job in the same day meant that God was really smiling on us. I stopped by the party that Notre Dame had in the hotel for the players, staff, and families, but it was pure bedlam so I left it shortly. I went to my room and tried to call the Beckmans, the Faccendas, and the Hickeys, all good friends of ours, but couldn't locate anyone. Consequently, our championship day ended very quietly.

Chris Zorich, sophomore defensive tackle
Everyone says, "That's Lou Holtz—oh, my God." He's a very personable man. At the championship celebration the mayor of South Bend was up on the stage and Coach was sitting down with little kids signing autographs.

Words can't express my sincere appreciation to the Fiesta Bowl, executive director, officers, board members, volunteers, and the Tempe Diablos, the host school. Phoenix is a great city, and the entire area could not have been nicer. The Fiesta Bowl is a great bowl in every sense of the word. This didn't surprise me, but the fact they understood a coach's problems when chasing a national championship did.

I have always been impressed by the friendliness of all bowl representatives over the years. Chuck Rohe and the entire Citrus Bowl organization is outstanding, and I hope we can get there in the near future if we are good enough. Notre Dame has never played in this classic. Maybe the reason I don't get as involved in the bowl selection as I used to is because all the bowls are outstanding. I would love to go back to the Cotton with Jim Brock, or the Orange Bowl or the Sugar Bowl, and the list goes on.

In reality, we can only go to one bowl a year, provided we are good enough, and it is a tough decision to make. One thing is certain, Father Beauchamp and Dick Rosenthal made the proper decision this year, because no one could have done it better than the Fiesta Bowl.

37

FIESTA BOWL: THE DAY AFTER

I stayed up packing all night after the game. Over the next four weeks I would go everywhere except to bed. Despite staying up all night, it was a happy feeling. Beth, Liz, Kevin, and I are flying to Hawaii at noon today for the Hula Bowl this weekend. I'm the head coach of the East. Bill Mallory of Indiana will coach the defense, while Galen Hall of Florida and I handle the offense. We are supposed to practice tomorrow, and I have no idea how. At least we get to take Wes Pritchett, Frank Stams, George Streeter, and Flash Gordon with us. There is no doubt we will have a great time at the Hula Bowl, because we always do.

I went to the lobby about five-thirty this morning to do a live interview on *CBS Morning News* with Harry Smith. I was glad I did it, because they asked me what happened at the end of the game and I was able to explain that there was no taunting, profanity, or fighting directed at the West Virginia players. Our players were frustrated and said some things they should not have. I couldn't justify it. We were in the wrong, and that's exactly what I said.

I reflect back on the fact that we assigned all the players to carry off the seniors, and I thought that worked out well. That's a moment every one of those seniors will remember. This may have been one of the smarter things we have done.

A daughter of a high school classmate attends West Virginia, and she sent me a hat that said, "West Virginia, '88 National Champions." I had kept it in my room all week because I didn't want to be negative. I finally gave it away just before we departed Phoenix. Someone will have a keepsake from the game.

Ralph Anastasio, my first-grade buddy from Follansbee who played at West Virginia, sent me a telegram, hoping we'd be number one if West Virginia couldn't be. That was awfully nice.

After the interview I sat in the lobby with Chuck Heater and a couple of our players. I think there were a lot of people who hadn't gone to bed, not just me.

Chuck and I flipped through the newspapers while we waited for the restaurant to open, and we talked about some of the things that happened yesterday and the entire year. We discussed how we both were impressed with Major Harris. He threw the ball better than we expected. We also agreed we were better as a team than we had been at any time during the year, and that Tony Rice is still the most dangerous quarterback our defense faced this year.

George Kelly, special assistant to the athletic director

When we got into December, he really hit an evening-off point. He let the players know during the practice sessions immediately after finals that this [the Fiesta Bowl preparation] was very, very important, without taking advantage of them physically. I think a lot of coaches make mistakes by going back to work in their bowl preparation and trying to be too physical just to get their point across. He didn't do it in that fashion. He got it across verbally. The practices we had during that month—eight or nine, total, before we went to Phoenix—were lengthy. They were not real physical, but they were very constructive. They were all pointed in one direction—to how we best could defeat West Virginia. It was real workmanship. It wasn't boring, it wasn't laborious. He kept it light, and he approached the practices down in Phoenix the same way.

Riding back and forth with him to practice every day in Phoenix, I know he felt very, very strongly that we would play very efficiently on offense. That didn't surprise me, because right from the beginning of our preparation for the Fiesta Bowl, after looking at film of West Virginia, he felt we could do well offensively. I think he had some greater concerns about West Virginia's ability to throw the long ball. The stress was really on the big play, and that's what he tried to take away. I think we did that successfully. He didn't want them to be able to get back into the game with one or two plays after we'd worked extremely hard to establish an advantage. I don't think he had thought that much about the big plays on our side of the ball. Those things just happened. But he was extremely confident riding back and forth each day, as he would continually see something new fall into place, on either offense or defense.

I just had not been around him at any time in the previous two seasons where he had the total confidence that he exhibited during the entire

357

season. He just felt so confident about everything we were doing. It wasn't that we were doing anything drastically new. There were wrinkles from week to week to take advantage of weaknesses that were seen on the part of our opponents. But we did make a lot of changes during the year that were hardly visible to the unknowing eye. The formations didn't change too much, but the schemes did. I thought he did a great job in handling that.

The execution in the West Virginia game was the big point. He thought there were things we could do offensively against them, and we were able to do those things. Lou still made ninety percent of the play calls, but he was in constant contact with the coaches in the press box—and there were some very timely, fine calls made from above in some long-yardage situations which really helped us.

Chuck made a good point—we beat the best team in the Midwest (Michigan), the best team in the South (Miami), the best team in the West (USC), and the best team in the East (West Virginia). That's four wins over teams that might have been number one if it hadn't been for Notre Dame. Those were the best teams from all across the country, and we beat all of them. Chuck gave me the perfect way to open the press conference later that morning.

Tony Yelovich, offensive line coach

The whole thing went so fast, you didn't feel it. You didn't have time to reflect on the past, and there was no opportunity for any foresight. The whole focus was on what was at hand, what was in front of you. It was total concentration and intensity. The further we went, the more intense we became. We never had a chance to relax. We took it one at a time and everything blended in. It was no accident what happened.

It's amazing how many people are in the lobby. I don't know if they rent their rooms in the lobby, but in any event, I signed a lot of autographs. Any time I sign one, I realize how fortunate I am that my name is not Samuel Skestosenorich from Massachusetts Institute of Technology.

Marc deManigold came through on his way to the airport. He's a freshman who never got in a game this year, but he's going to be a good one.

"Go home and lift weights. You're the future of this team," I told him.

Marc said he was going to Derek Brown's home for a few days.

I said, "Tell Derek that we fulfilled our promise." When we recruited him, the last thing he said before he committed to attend Notre Dame was, "Coach, you've got to promise me we'll win at least one national championship." I told him at that time he determined this far more extensively than I did.

It's almost impossible to describe how I feel today. I don't think our winning the national championship has hit me yet, and it probably won't for a week or so. However, I feel like the most fortunate man in the world. We were lucky this year, but then again, Dariell Royal said it best in 1964: "Luck is when preparation meets opportunity." We were lucky to get so close to the top and reach it on our first attempt. There are no more games, no more practices, no more mountains to climb this year. There is no doubt we coaches will continue to work long hours in recruiting and it is critical we have a good year in this area. We will enjoy this 1988 season until January 15, when we meet to start it all over again. They tell me the pressure next year will be greater, but I don't know how this can be true.

Jan Blazi, secretary to Lou Holtz

More so than the first two seasons, I think that Coach Holtz had a bit more confidence overall this year. Despite all the questions coming into the year, I think he was more confident with the players, but around the office he was increasingly tense each week during the year. I could see it with each game. I think that's what winning does here at Notre Dame. I often commented that if we had lost a game, it would have relieved some tension. It was not the kind of thing he talked about, and yet you could sense how important winning was as we continued to have success.

He started out the season by telling me, "Jan, this year we're going to be good. But next year, we're going to win the national championship." So, as optimistic as he always is, I think it may have been a little bit of a surprise to him that things fell into place as well as they did this year.

In any event, I'm going to enjoy this feeling for two weeks maximum. We'll be in Hawaii this week, then Nashville next week for the NCAA coaches convention.

The game may have ended, but there was one more press conference the morning after the game. I said a prayer prior to the press conference. I prayed I could express myself without being obnoxious.

Here is a sampling of the topics covered.

Q. Can you talk a little about Tony Rice?
A. Tony Rice competed against three of the top five Heisman candidates this year—Rodney Peete, Steve Walsh, and Major Harris—and he just finds a way to win. I visited him this morning before I came over here and told him he was not going to be in the background anymore.

He was going to be the hunted, rather than the hunter. There will be a lot more pressure on him. Now we are going to find out how well we all handle success. It is going to be very difficult for us to bounce back. I would be shocked if we have a good year next year. Our players and coaches are really going to have to respond to that challenge. But I plan on being shocked next year.

Q. A lot of coaches with conference affiliations say it is easier for an independent team to win the national championship. Do you agree?

A. I do think in some respects it is easier to win the national championship when you're an independent, because it's easier to adjust your schedule according to how good your team is. It is a fact that virtually all conferences have three or four teams that are experiencing a poor year. It is also true that if one team improves in a conference, somebody else is going to regress because they basically recruit the same players. Teams generally will get emotionally prepared when they play within the conference. Even if a team did poorly in the nonconference games, they will look at the conference games with enthusiasm. When I was at Ohio State, Woody Hayes called nonconference games exhibition games. He didn't really prepare for them or worry about them. He was concerned about the Big Ten. It is true that you can sometimes win the conference title with two losses. You virtually always go into your ninth game, at minimum, with a chance to win the conference and go to the bowl. It is a fact that playing in a conference can be much more emotionally draining because the teams know each other exceptionally well and there are certain rivalries that exist. When I was at Arkansas, we would always play Texas and Houston back to back. Those two teams were always in the top ten. Then we would end up the season playing Baylor, Texas A&M, and SMU in a row. When you are in a conference, you can't balance your schedule.

Q. What were your feelings after Willie Edwards intercepted the ball for West Virginia in the third period? Was there a big shift in momentum?

A. One of the key things in handling this situation was a phrase we use all the time. We say that we cannot flinch. I use that for myself more than the players. I never want to get upset and lose my patience, and I have done this in the past and it always has a negative effect on our team. So, no matter what happens, we feel somebody will eradicate the mistake. It is this situation that creates heroes. Tony Rice came off the field and said, "Sorry, Coach, but I just didn't see the defender." I said, "That wasn't your fault. That was my fault. That was a poorly designed play." However, our defense just said, "This is what we have to do," and they did it.

What we have attempted to convince our players is that what looks like a bad situation can become a positive situation and break the game open. For example, give the other team an opportunity, then go in there and shut them off. You may completely demoralize them. We gave West Virginia an opportunity to get back in the game, then we went in there and they ended up punting. They started on our 26-yard line, and not only did they not score, but also they had to punt it back to us. That changed the momentum of the game. We picked up a first down, then we hit the pass to Ricky Watters to the 5-yard line, then came the lob pass to Frank Jacobs. Basically, the game was over at that point. What could have been a disaster for us turned into a victory celebration primarily because we refused to flinch.

Q. You have just won a national championship with six seniors in the starting lineup, the lowest number of seniors on a national championship team in over ten years. Can you talk about the feasibility of winning it again with having so many returning players in key positions?

A. Starting out the 1989 season we have a chance to be a pretty good football team. We do graduate six seniors, which is more than Michigan, Miami, USC, Penn State, or Pittsburgh lose. In addition, next year we play Michigan, Miami, and Penn State on the road. Out of a total of six away games, we play four of our first five games on the road. It is much more difficult to remain on top than it is to get there. But, once again, I'm a novice. You are not talking to Barry Switzer or Jimmy Johnson. This is a first for me. I don't think you can say we are going to be an outstanding football team simply because we won this year and have a lot of the same names returning. I wish to remind you we may not have the same players returning even though the same names are. I think we have a chance to be good, but it is going to depend upon the chemistry and the leadership of our seniors. We will be a good football team, if the intangibles we possessed this year are apparent in 1989.

We have some questions. Are the players going to be willing to work like this year's team did? One thing about this year's team that was really great was that from day one they said, "Hey, tell us what we have to do." They never questioned anything. I said if we ever became a good offensive football team, you could circle August 29 as the day it happened. Why? Because we went out there and had the most brutal offensive practice you have ever seen, and yet the players never complained or questioned our motives. This attitude permeated the entire football team and is a major reason why I'm standing here today as coach of the national champions.

Q. All of us who are around coaches, we hear them talk about how teams have to be disciplined, have to have fundamentals, have to be physical. We hear it from every coach on any level. Why is it such a relative minority are able to put that theory into practice?

A. Well, Larry Marmie, the Arizona State coach, came out and watched us practice one day. He saw the equivalent of a typical Tuesday practice during the season. Larry said to me, "I've never seen a football team work as hard as hard on fundamentals as you do." We had a fundamental practice every day we were in pads this entire year. That's what I learned from Woody Hayes—basic, sound fundamentals. That is why Coach Hayes has never had an assistant who did not succeed as a head coach. Check them out—Bo Schembechler, Bill Mallory, Earle Bruce, Dave McClain, George Chaump, Ara Parseghian, Doyt Perry, Bill Hess, Rudy Hubbard, Gene Slaughter, and the list goes on.

It's just like when I was growing up. A guy I knew who played the piano was playing chopsticks, then all of a sudden he starts playing Beethoven and says, "I don't want to play chopsticks." But you've got to learn to play chopsticks. It is basic fundamentals. You can't get bored watching your team run the same play over and over.

When did Tony Rice become a much better passer? When we narrowed down the passing game. Instead of running nine hundred patterns once—and believe me, we could have taken our playbook to the pros—we ran one pattern nine hundred times. We decided we wouldn't try to do as many things, but the things we did do, we would do fundamentally very well.

Q. You said just after the USC game that you had lost eight pounds during the regular season. Have you lost any more since, and if so, what weight are you now?

A. I haven't lost any more since the USC game. What is really amazing is that I probably even gained a little bit of it back. I am allergic to food preservatives, and I have trouble with low blood sugar when I don't eat enough on weekends. It happened for the first time when we played in the Gator Bowl back in 1981. My pupils dilated, my vision got fuzzy, and I got spots in front of my eyes. A strawberry milkshake will prevent this. So now before every football game, I drink a minimum of two strawberry milkshakes, sometimes three or four. I tried to have a milkshake almost every day since the regular season ended, and my weight has come back up gradually. I am trying to lose enough weight so our players can carry me off the field. But I told them if this ever happened, I didn't want the receivers doing it.

Q. You make the point that your team has beaten the best team in the West, the best team in the South, the two best teams in the Big Ten, and the best team in the East. Because of that, you are probably uniquely qualified to say who the second, third, and fourth teams are behind you. Can you rate those teams that you have played?

A. I thought Miami and Michigan were both outstanding teams. I thought USC was an excellent team. I thought USC and Michigan were very, very close, and Miami might have been a notch ahead of them, but not much. I thought those three teams were as fine as any three teams I have seen in any given year. I am not talking about just this year. I think in any other year that any of those three teams could have won the national championship. What was really crazy this year was that the top four teams—Miami, USC, Michigan, and Notre Dame—played one another so many times. We played all three, Miami played two, Michigan played all three, and USC played two. Whenever you have a round robin and you go by win-loss record, somebody isn't going to finish real high. I also believe Florida State and West Virginia were among the top six teams.

Q. You told the story of going into athletic director Willis Casey's office after having some success at North Carolina State and being told that you had done what you were hired to do. Ultimately, in the minds of the people that follow Notre Dame football, have you done what you were hired to do, and do you think you might get a raise out of this?

A. I definitely do not expect a raise. You don't come to Notre Dame to coach for money, but I think everybody would tell you that. No Notre Dame coach has had a pauper's funeral. I left a great job in a great state when I decided to leave the University of Minnesota. I was excited about coming here, but I was sorry to leave the Gophers. I think we have done what we were hired to do at the University of Notre Dame, and I am proud of it. We wanted to say that our athletes graduate, to say that we have the best football team we could have within the parameters as set forth by the university. We have never compromised those values that have made Notre Dame great, nor have we asked the players to compromise them. We have some areas we need to improve upon, but we have played with the Notre Dame spirit, and I think our players are student/athletes in every sense of the word. Winning the national championship was never mandated by the administration or board of trustees.

Did I ever dream about winning the national championship? Yes, you dream about it, but I never really thought it would happen to me. However, we take greater pride in winning the College Football Association's academic achievement award this year by graduating a hundred percent of our seniors.

This year I had a bet with Dr. Hofman that he would lose a freshman student before we lost a football game. Obviously I won this bet because we didn't lose a game. But what angered me was I didn't win the bet until the week of Thanksgiving, when a young lady got sick and had to drop out of school.

These are the things Notre Dame is proud of, not football teams, and that is the way it should be.

38

FINAL THOUGHTS:
A CHAMPIONSHIP SEASON

As we flew to Hawaii for the Hula Bowl, I wrote an article that would appear in *Time* magazine. In addition, I attempted to evaluate our football program. I approached it the same way we had the year before. How can we get better? What are the problems? What assets do we have that we can accentuate?

I realize it will be much more difficult next year, if that's possible. We play basically the same schedule we did this year, except now we must play Michigan, Penn State, Miami, Penn State, Air Force, and Stanford on the road. That will really be difficult. The preseason prognosticators for next year will place Michigan, USC, and Miami in the top five, as all of them return virtually everyone on their team.

I don't think we could have enjoyed success at Notre Dame this year without a strong faith in God. I said the rosary every day, not for victories, but for guidance and direction. In my heart I firmly believe this season was a miracle.

Our athletes were led by some great coaches. Barry Alvarez is a great leader, a positive person who did an unbelievable job.

Chuck Heater wasn't sure what he wanted to do after the coaching change at Ohio State a year ago, and fortunately for us he ended up at Notre Dame, because I don't believe we could have won a national championship without him. I knew John Palermo would do a great job after having him on our staff at Minnesota, but nobody in the country did a better job with the defensive line than John did. George Stewart is one of the most respected coaches I've been around. He is a disciplinarian and yet has great compassion for the players. He is the type of coach all players like to play for.

Jim Strong is an unbelievable worker—intense and dedicated, one of the great, young head-coaching prospects in the country. He is a great coach. Joe Moore is an outstanding coach and motivator. He is a class act in every respect and a great teacher. Tony Yelovich is as tireless a worker as I've been around. His contribution to our success cannot be minimized. Pete Cordelli is a wonderful person and coach. He has an excellent football mind and has done a great job for us. He will be a head coach in the near future, also.

George Kelly has been absolutely invaluable to me as a person and a friend. He takes much of the pressure off me by very thoroughly handling so many administrative details. And he really and truly epitomizes a Notre Dame man. Jim Russ, our head trainer, and our team doctors have done an unbelievable job of establishing a positive environment in the training room, which has enabled us to experience few injuries. Vinny Cerrato does an amazing job with recruiting. He'll be the reason Notre Dame keeps winning. I don't know of anyone as talented and gifted as Vinny. The many unsung heroes within the athletic department, including our graduate assistant coaches—Mike Bossory, Jay Hayes, Tim Scannell, Brian White, Jerry Partridge, and Larry Tomich; associate athletic director Joe O'Brien, who handles all our road trips; Brian Boulac and Missy Conboy, our assistant athletic directors who work so closely with our athletes day to day; associate athletic directors Roger Valdiserri, John Heisler, and Jim Daves in sports information; Gene O'Neill and Brother John Campbell in the equipment area; Mike Bobinski and Bubba Cunningham in marketing and tickets; Mike DeCicco and Kate Halischak and everyone else who helps our athletes in the academic area; Mike Danch and his staff in the Joyce Athletic and Convocation Center; Lefty Smith, who runs the Loftus Center; Benny Benninghoff and his staff at the Stadium; Bruce Harlan and his photography staff; Steve Horvath, Chuck Linster, Tim Collins, and Terry Beyer, who handle all our film and tape needs; Mike Green, Shawn Patrick, Peter Witty, and all the other student managers and trainers; Pete Battista, who handles our coaches' phones, and so many others whose contributions are invaluable to our operation.

There may be no one more efficient in the athletic department than my secretary, Jan Blazi. Katie Stanley, Julie Martin, Mary Carmola, and Kay Catanzarite are the greatest secretaries you could hope for.

Another good friend, who was always helpful whenever I had a problem or needed advice, was Phil Faccenda, the university's legal officer.

The one individual who was involved with us on a daily basis was Dick Rosenthal. He is a talented individual whose advice I constantly pursued.

He is a winner and a competitor, but most important of all he loves Notre Dame and he loves people.

We had so many players make so many memorable contributions this year. Wes Pritchett was vastly underrated. He's a great leader and a great person to be around. Frank Stams made all-American in his first year as a starter at defensive end. Notre Dame has never won a national championship without having an all-American defensive end. Andre Jones has great potential and made a great contribution as a sophomore. Flash Gordon won the starting job, lost it completely, then won it back again and played very well in the bowl game. Scott Kowalkowski is so very intense—he's a young man of the future. Arnold Ale played as well as any freshman we have had. Devon McDonald, Kevin McShane, and Kurt Zackrison were invaluable.

Chris Zorich was a young man we felt would make a big difference in our team, and he did. Jeff Alm was vastly improved, maybe as big a surprise as we had on the football team. George Williams, like Chris and Jeff, is an outstanding player. Bryan Flannery's contribution was to be totally unselfish and play anywhere we needed him, and he not only did this, but he played well. Bob Dahl has a chance to be an outstanding player. Steve Roddy, as a senior, just wanted to know how he could help and contribute. And he did. Mike Crounse, Bernard Mannelly, George Marshall, Mike Callan, and Marc deManigold all enabled us to be a good football team. Mirko Jurkovic was outstanding.

Mike Stonebreaker is maybe one of the better linebackers in the country. Ned Bolcar is a great winner and competitor. Donn Grimm is an underrated football player but as consistent as any linebacker. Mike Smalls, Troy Ridgley, Scott Bufton, and Joe Farrell gained the respect of our team.

In the secondary, Stan Smagala is a young man who has exceeded all our expectations. He's one of the better defensive backs I've seen. With his athletic ability, Todd Lyght could end up being one of the best in the country. He sure has made some great plays for us. Corny Southall is one of my favorite people of all time. He's a winner. He's a competitor. He's unselfish. I don't think we could have won it without him. Patrick Terrell turned into an outstanding free safety. When I think about greatness, Pat Terrell comes to my mind. George Streeter was as improved as anyone on this team. He made an invaluable contribution both on and off the field. D'Juan Francisco was a running back when we came here. Once we moved him to the secondary, he really blossomed. He is exceptionally talented and solidified our secondary. Antwon Lark, Doug DiOrio, Bobby Satterfield, George Poorman, David Jandric, Rick Purcell, Jerry Bodine, Marc Dobbins, and others helped us win.

As odd as it seems, Tony Rice was completely underrated. They talk about the *Sports Illustrated* jinx, but he made the cover three times in one season and kept playing great. Every time we played against a great quarterback—and we played against three of the top five vote getters in the Heisman voting—Tony emerged victorious. Kent Graham, Steve Belles, Peter Graham, and Mike Miadich combined to give us a very close-knit group of quarterbacks.

Anthony Johnson was one of the best fullbacks I've been around, and this was on one ankle. Rodney Culver shocked all of us with the contribution he made, and it will be greater in the future. Braxston Banks spent the summer in China studying, and thank goodness we recruited him. Tony Brooks is a talented young man who is a winner. His future is unlimited. Mark Green was definitely one of the leaders on our team. He was absolutely outstanding in every area. There is no way we can replace the intangible qualities he exhibited on a consistent basis. Ryan Mihalko is a good fullback we have come to appreciate. Ken Spears, Rusty Setzer, Tank McNamara, Joe Jarosz, and Mike Gatti all made us a better team.

Rocket Ismail came in as a freshman and established himself as a big-play receiver. Steve Alaniz hadn't played much until this year, but played a lot and well. Ricky Watters has as much talent as anyone we have. He made a lot of big plays and we couldn't have won it without him. He could be an all-American receiver, but we will move him back to tailback. Pat Eilers is very unselfish and willing to help any way he can. All great teams need a Pat Eilers on it. Derek Brown became a starter as a freshman and will be a great one. Frank Jacobs was a starter until he hurt his foot, but he played well all year and scored against West Virginia. Notre Dame has had some great tight ends in the past, but I don't know if we have ever had two as good as Derek and Frank. Rod West played awfully well, particularly in running situations. Aaron Robb, Rod Smith, James Dillard, Tony Smith, Brad Alge, Pat Fallon, Jeff Baker, and others were people we could count on.

How can you minimize the contributions of Andy Heck—maybe as good an offensive lineman as there was in the country this year? He moved to tackle from tight end and looked like he'd been there forever. Dean Brown is going to be excellent. I didn't think he could play as well as he did this year. Tim Ryan played very well for us, and exceeded my expectations. Next year this will be harder to do as I expect him to be a great one. Mike Brennan moved from tight end to tackle to guard and always played well. We counted on Tim Grunhard to be one of the leaders of the offensive line, and despite a bad ankle, he did this. He handled the snaps on the kicking teams and did so flawlessly. Tim must become a great player if Notre

Dame is going to be competitive next year. Winston Sandri, Joe Allen, Marty Lippincott, and Justin Hall were just some of the unsung heroes who made our offensive line such a pleasant surprise. Mike Heldt played exceptionally well all year. I didn't realize how well until I reflected back on the season. Gene McGuire developed into a solid center even though he was a freshman. Jim Kinsherf, Dave Prinzivalli, Brian Shannon, Mickey Anderson, Chuck Killian, Ted Healy, and Lindsay Knapp all gave us a chance to win.

Jim Sexton improved so much as a punter, and Reggie Ho made many important field goals for us. Billy Hackett got us off to a good start with the longest field goal of his career in the West Virginia game and did a respectable job with his kickoffs. Sean Connor is a talented punter who did a good job and was a positive addition to our team.

When we began this past season, I thought we could win the national championship but we had a tough schedule and were awfully young. We didn't have many seniors and we'd had some staff changes. We were like the bumblebee that theoretically shouldn't be able to fly. I am just glad our players and coaches didn't realize we couldn't win.

It didn't happen because of the head coach. It happened because of the Lady on the Dome, faith in God, and a group of young men who truly believed. When you talk about the spirit of Notre Dame, you've got to talk about this football team. It was a miracle, and I do believe in miracles.

39

EPILOGUE:
THE BEST AND WORST OF TIMES

I woke up early on the morning of January 18 in order to fly with our football team to Washington, D.C., to visit the White House and President Ronald Reagan. I've been involved in plenty of football games over the years that have produced all kinds of amazing, emotional finishes. But never in my life has a football game produced the emotional extremes that I and the team experienced today.

It took a while to work out the details and get the date settled, but we finally decided that we would go to the White House to be honored by President Reagan on the eighteenth, just two days before President-elect Bush would be inaugurated. The White House people had wanted us to come the week before, but that was impossible because our players were still spread all across the country, since the spring semester hadn't started. January 18 was the first day of classes for the new semester and was the first time we could possibly get the whole team together for a trip like this.

President Reagan, according to his staff people, wanted to be there when the Notre Dame team was honored. He had played the part of George Gipp in the 1940 movie *Knute Rockne—All American*. So he is like a member of the Notre Dame family. We were fortunate to be able to work out the details, since he only had a few days remaining in office. President Reagan had met many members of our football team personally when he visited our campus last March at the Knute Rockne stamp dedication.

We took everyone who won a monogram this season, so we ended up with sixty-five players plus the coaching staff and administration people, along with Father Malloy and Father Beauchamp. Most of our coaches were on the road recruiting, so they met us in Washington. The rest of us got on the buses at the Joyce Center at eight that morning and headed for the airport. A great guy named Jay Jordan enabled us to take a Sun Country charter directly to Washington National Airport. The weather was absolutely perfect. We had breakfast on the flight and everyone was in a great mood. It was a day everyone had been looking forward to since the Fiesta Bowl victory.

When we arrived in Washington, the buses took us on a quick tour of the area around the Capitol. It was buzzing with activity because the inauguration was just two days away. There were workmen everywhere building scaffolding or putting up bleachers. You could feel the electricity in the air.

We parked in front of the Rayburn Office Building, where we were met by Rep. John Hiler from the third district in Indiana, and Rep. Ron Mazzoli, a Notre Dame graduate who is in the House of Representatives from the state of Kentucky. They immediately took our entire group to the Capitol building. We went into the House of Representatives and sat down. Rep. Hiler and Rep. Mazzoli took turns explaining a little about the workings of the House. It was very interesting to get a first-hand look at how our government operates and the decision-making process that determines the direction of our country.

We didn't complete the tour of the Capitol because we were a little behind schedule, so we walked back to the Rayburn Building, where they had lunch planned. We were joined by several congressmen who were Notre Dame graduates, as well as Nordy Hoffmann, who played football for Rockne and had been the Sergeant-at-Arms of the Senate. Dan Coats, who had just been named to replace Dan Quayle as Indiana's senator, also was there. There were a few brief speeches, including one by Father Malloy, who hails from Washington and played on a great high-school basketball team. I believe John Thompson was one of Father Malloy's teammates. Father Malloy went on to earn a letter in basketball at Notre Dame. He still plays basketball with students on a regular basis and more than holds his own. Jack Hiler talked about coming to both the Michigan and Miami games in South Bend, but missing the best part because his crack staff had him scheduled to leave at half time. The hospitality and the reception we received were great.

After lunch, we got back on the buses and headed to the White House for the ceremony, which was scheduled to begin at two o'clock. We arrived in plenty of time, which was fortunate because we all had to go through security individually. We waited in one of the rooms just off the Rose Garden, and eventually Chris McCarrick of the President's staff explained to us exactly what the procedures would be. She assured us that the President would shake everyone's hand before the ceremony began. I think that was awfully impressive for our players, because it really lent a personal touch to the whole affair. I know the White House had been concerned about how many people we were bringing with us, but having everyone shake hands with the President made sure that no one would feel they were going to be left out because they were at the end of the line.

We drafted Mark Green to hold the bags we were going to present to the President along with the autographed football and sweaters and shirts. We had Wes Pritchett and Frank Stams hold the wooden case that held George Gipp's letter sweater, which also was going to be presented to Reagan. The staff people wanted to make sure we didn't try to give the heavy case to him because he was still recovering from hand surgery.

We were listening to the instructions when President-elect Bush and Vice President-elect Quayle came into the room. They hadn't wanted to interfere with the official ceremonies, but they said they just wanted to add their congratulations and pass along their best wishes. Father Malloy, Father Beauchamp, Dick Rosenthal, and I got to visit with them for a few minutes. They made their visit with us very special by just talking and joking with the players and the rest of the group. Things have really changed since President Bush visited with our team in November. We were now national champions and he was now going to be the new President. With Vice President-elect Quayle hailing from Indiana and President-elect Bush having addressed our squad two months ago, we really felt we were among friends. I hope they felt the same way.

Shortly after the departure of George Bush, they brought Father Malloy, Father Beauchamp, Dick Rosenthal, Dan Quayle, and myself into the Oval Office to meet the President. It was a fun visit, as the President talked about some of his football experiences, which I enjoyed. President Reagan is a great storyteller. Then, at two o'clock, we all walked out into the Rose Garden, where the team and everyone else was waiting. The weather was beautiful, so we were able to hold the reception outside. I was amazed at the number of people in attendance, not to mention the reporters and television cameras.

President Reagan went down the entire row, shaking hands with everyone in our group. He got to the very end, and our last player introduced himself by saying, "Tim Grunhard, right guard." The President said, "The only reason I could ever play, I was telling Coach Holtz, was that he designed that system of right guards coming out to run interference." Tim grinned and said, "We'll go over it afterward," and everyone laughed and the ceremony began.

The staff people had told us we would enjoy the President's remarks. They were right:

"I thank you all very much. Vice President-elect Dan Quayle, Reverend Edward Malloy, Coach Lou Holtz, members of Congress that are here, and distinguished guests, players, coaches, and the Irish at heart—welcome to the White House.

"My life has been full of rich and wonderful experiences. Standing near the top of the list is my long and honored association with the University of Notre Dame and its legendary hero, Knute Rockne. So, I want you to know, the INF treaty and George Bush's election were important. But having the Fighting Irish win the national championship is in a class by itself.

"Lou, what you've achieved in only three years is inspiring. Maybe you could coach Congress on the deficit. With Notre Dame going undefeated this season, they might listen to you.

"You know, Coach Rockne believed there are no shortcuts to success. Practice and hard work combined with respect for your opponent is the path one must take to achieve the greatest glory. As Rockne himself once wrote, 'Sportsmanship means fair play. It means having a little respect for the other fellow's point of view. It means a real application of the golden rule.' You young fellows here today are living proof of the truth of Rockne's ideals. All of you, coaches and players, have made sacrifices and borne many a burden. And you did it all for one goal—to be the very best.

"As I mentioned when I was on your campus last year, Knute liked spirit in his ballplayers. Once when he was working with his four backfield stars who became known as the Four Horsemen, one of them, a fellow named Jim Crowley, just couldn't get it right. You know, I never tell ethnic jokes, unless they're about the Irish. But maybe today I can be permitted some leeway. Rockne, who by the way was Norwegian, was commonly called 'the Swede.' He finally got exasperated after Crowley muffed a play and hollered, 'What's dumber than a dumb Irishman?' Without missing a beat, Crowley said, 'A smart Swede.'

"Well, at this year's Fiesta Bowl, you showed us what you're made of, and reached the goal of being the very best. The West Virginia Mountaineers didn't luck into playing you for the national championship. Just like you, they fought hard all season and earned the right to play for the title of being number one. Just like the Fighting Irish, they're a talented, well-coached team and they deserve a salute. Their record should make them proud. Speaking of pride, I noted that Coach Holtz thought Rockne would be proud of this team, and I'm sure he would be. Right now, I can't help but think that somewhere, far away, there's a fellow with a big grin and a whole lot of pride in his school, and he might be thinking to himself that maybe you won another one for the Gipper.

"Congratulations and God bless you all."

Next up was Father Malloy: "Mr. President, we are extremely proud of this team and of its fine coaching staff, headed by Lou Holtz. You have honored our campus twice during your term of office as President, once as commencement speaker and honorary degree recipient—which obviously makes you a Notre Damer—and more recently for the Knute Rockne stamp commemoration. We thought it would be fitting at this time in which you have honored the university and its winning football team, to make a small presentation to you. Since I'm a little puny, I've asked two of our seniors and leaders this year to bring over a particular plaque that I'd like to read the inscription for. It reads, 'Monogram sweater awarded to George Gipp, halfback of the Fighting Irish, 1917–1920, presented to Ronald Reagan by the University of Notre Dame, January, 1989.'"

The President noted that it was a great sacrifice by the university, but that no one would treasure it more than he would.

Finally, I added a few remarks: "Mr. President, it's indeed a thrill for us to be here as the number-one team in the country. We're exceptionally proud of this feat. We're also proud of the fact that in addition to being the number-one team, we've won the award for graduating the entire class of football players that came in five years ago. We also realize that to reach a position such as this, you have to be very lucky and very fortunate. We're also aware of the fact that many other teams could have been standing here instead of us had it not been for the many fortunate things that happened to us. It's a great thrill to be number one. But it's also a great thrill and a dream for any American to be able to come to the White House to meet the President. I know I speak on behalf of our football team when I say we are deeply gratified and feel blessed to be here. It's been a great honor for us, but it's also a great honor to come here representing the University of Notre Dame family. We have just a small gift from our three captains, Mark Green, Andy Heck, and Ned Bolcar. We know you're going to be packing up, Mr. President. So we brought something you can pack things in—it says Notre Dame, it says Ronald Reagan, and it says The Gipper. We brought you a sweater that says national champions, which signifies a great accomplishment for us. When we consider the accomplishments you've made in the Oval Office, this may seem very small. But we wanted to share our greatest accomplishment with you, Mr. President. Thank you."

At that point we gave him an autographed football. The President said,

"Right guards stick together," and he threw it to Grunhard, who made a rather linemanlike catch.

I thought the whole day was kind of magical. Many of our players were seeing Washington and the Capitol and the White House for the first time, and I know it was a thrill for them.

President Reagan himself epitomizes a dream in many respects. He was an actor who became one of the most popular Presidents we've ever had. I think we were in awe of everything today.

Somebody said it was a good thing we won the national championship a year ahead of schedule, as some people had suggested, since this was President Reagan's last year in office. I said, Yes, but wouldn't it be great to come back here next year and see President George Bush?

After a few interviews we left the White House and headed back to the buses. The team stopped at the Smithsonian Air and Space Museum before they went home, but Beth and I stayed behind because we were going to stay overnight in Washington and participate in the television salute to President George Bush. From there we were to fly to Palm Springs and attend a dinner honoring former President Gerald Ford. I have known him for several years and we have played golf together five or six times. He is an astute person whom I admire very much.

At every place I've been in coaching, I've had my home number listed in the phone book because I always felt that if a parent of one of my players really needed to get hold of me, they should be able to do so without any problem. As I said earlier, you end up getting some strange phone calls at unusual hours of the morning, but I still think it's the right thing to do. However, when the telephone rang at three A.M. in our hotel room in Washington, I couldn't imagine who it could be or why they were calling.

It was Father Dave Tyson, the university's vice president for student affairs. He was calling from the hospital in Niles, Michigan, to tell me that Bob Satterfield had died. I couldn't believe it. He explained all the details that were known, said there wasn't much that could be done at that point but that they had felt it important that I be notified.

I hung up the telephone in shock. I don't know of anyone on our football team who more typifies what Notre Dame is all about than Bob Satterfield. He may not have been a familiar name to a lot of the fans, but we all knew who he was. He paid his own way to come to Notre Dame, all the way from California, and walked on the football team as a defensive back. He was a good athlete who played in some games, did anything we asked to assist the team, and invariably exhibited a pleasant personality and a winner's attitude. We had awarded a scholarship to Bobby just prior to the start of the season. This was our way of saying thank you for what he had done for our program and for being Bobby Satterfield.

Bobby Satterfield was listed as alternate defensive back on our second team, but he helped make our team very competitive by the way he worked in practice every day. I don't think anyone will forget the hit he put on Tony Brooks in the scrimmage we had just before we went home for Christmas this year. It was as loud as anything you'll hear on Saturday or Sunday. He got up with that typical, big smile on his face and received high-fives from his teammates. I was also impressed that Tony Brooks jumped up immediately, patted Bobby, and went back to the offensive huddle.

Father Tyson had said that he had been able to reach Bob's father, who'd be flying to South Bend the next day. Beth and I immediately made plans to return to South Bend ourselves, but first I called Mr. Satterfield in California and spoke with him.

The captains called a team meeting for four o'clock that day to inform our players what had happened. We also needed each other for support.

I don't think anyone could have shown more strength in dealing with this tragedy than Mark Green. His mother had died when he was a freshman, and I know it had been an awfully difficult time for him. Yet, somehow, he stood so strong in this time of need. In fact, the first thing I had to do as a head coach at Notre Dame was inform Mark that his mother had passed away.

It was a somber meeting. Everyone talked in hushed tones, and no one seemed to know exactly what to say to each other. What an unbelievable turn of events. Yesterday everyone had been in such a good mood knowing it was a day that we all would remember the rest of our lives. Then, suddenly, we were faced with a tragedy that would require all the courage we had to cope with it.

Mark tried to explain exactly what had happened, how he and Flash Gordon had thought that either someone had hit Bob or he was just kidding around, until they finally realized that he had really collapsed and wasn't getting up. Bob had had no history of heart problems or anything else that might have indicated something like this might occur. He'd had a seizure and eventually cardiac arrest, and there wasn't much the paramedics could do once they arrived.

Many of the players expressed their feelings about the situation with Bobby. It was obvious that our team has very strong religious beliefs. The comments by our players were sincere, emotional, compassionate, and appropriate. There was one request made of me during the meeting. George Streeter, who was visibly shaken, asked me to make certain Mr. Satterfield knew the team desired to have a memorial service for Bobby.

Then Dr. Jim Moriarity, one of our university physicians, who had been called to the hospital along with our trainer, Jim Russ, explained exactly what had happened during the autopsy that morning. Nobody on our team was in better condition or took greater pride in how he lived than Bob Satterfield. Dr. Moriarity could not explain why Bobby died, but he could explain what he did not die from. There was a complete absence of any drugs or alcohol.

I've been involved in plenty of team meetings, but never anything like this. Father Riehle said a prayer, and I tried to say something that would help all of us deal with what had happened, but I felt woefully inadequate.

I tried to emphasize to the squad how much more difficult it is for those of us left behind. I explained that many times I've been in airports and witnessed parents putting their child on an airplane. The child is having the time of his life, but the parents are worried, sad, and crying about their child leaving. Then, when the plane arrives at the other end, the grandparents are laughing and smiling and everything is wonderful. That's how it is when something happens like this. There's no reason for any of us to worry about Bob Satterfield right now. He's going to be fine. It's his father, his brother, his stepfather, friends, and teammates who need our support. They're the ones who are going to have a difficult time trying to understand why these things happen. It's just God's way of doing things.

It's sadly ironic that this would happen hours after we'd been at the White House. Just when we think we're on top of the world, invincible, everything is put in perspective again. However, if you have a strong faith in God, He will give you the strength to continue your life with a positive attitude.

That night a prayer service was held in Fisher Hall, Bob's dormitory, and it was packed. Bobby's friends stood up and talked about Bob and what he had meant to them. The funeral mass the next day at Sacred Heart was the same way. Mark Green did one of the readings. George Streeter read a poem, and Bob's former roommate read a eulogy that assistant coach Jim Strong had written.

Despite the fact that it was a cold, snowy afternoon, dozens of people stood outside the church as the snow flew. They watched in silence as the players stood in a huddle around the casket, trying to draw strength from each other. I searched for something to say that would ease the pain we all felt, but it was beyond my capabilities.

We constantly talk about trust, love, and commitment in our football program, but I often wonder whether we are successful in getting our athletes to accept them as gospel. Sometimes it takes events of this magnitude to realize that trust, commitment, and love really are the cornerstone of our team.

I told the players two things they should never be embarrassed to do—to let someone see them cry at a time of sadness and to tell someone you love them. We sat and talked about how much Bob meant to us. But why do we only say these things after he's gone? Why couldn't we say them when he was with us? That's the saddest part, that someone has to leave us before we're moved to explain how much we appreciated him.

A couple of months from now we'll all receive our national-championship rings. They'll bring back all kinds of memories about a season and a team that none of us will forget. But something tells me that when we put on that ring, we'll read the three inscribed words—trust, commitment, and love—and when we read those words, we will think of all our teammates.

How do you say thank you?

How do you say thanks to so many people responsible for some of the good things that happened to us this year? The assistant coaches, the players, Dick Rosenthal and the administration, the fans, the band, the cheerleaders, Father Hesburgh, Father Joyce, Father Malloy, Father Beauchamp—they all had a part. We could pass out accolades forever and still not touch everybody who played a prominent role.

It isn't very often in your life that you get to stand up and say, "We are the very best at what we chose to do." That's why a national championship carries special significance. It's not because of what you achieve. It's because we can say, out of everybody in the entire country, we were the very best in 1988.

I was part of a national championship team when I was an assistant coach at Ohio State in 1968. But this one soothes the pain I felt the last time Notre Dame won a national championship. In 1977 I was at Arkansas and our record was identical to Notre Dame's. We beat Oklahoma 31–6 in the Orange Bowl that year. Notre Dame was voted number one, but now I see why. I truly am deeply indebted to the people who enabled me to come to the University of Notre Dame.

When we look back years from now, it won't be the fact we won the national championship, it'll be the trip—the journey to get there. And yet it all happened so quickly that it seems like just yesterday we were in that meeting in August for the first time.

The years will fade. As the players come back for their reunions, their accomplishments will grow and their speed will get better. I just hope they remember some things I'd like them to.

Why are we here? We're here because of attitude. There's no other reason. It was the self-confidence that was ultra-important.

If I thank the seniors profusely for the next twenty years, I could not thank them enough for their great leadership. I remember the meeting we had when I said this was not a very strong senior class athletically. But that didn't keep them from contributing. Andy Heck and the rest of the seniors had a meeting in my office and said, "Coach, we're going to provide you with the greatest leadership you've ever seen."

I don't think you can talk about the seniors without giving Gerry Faust all the credit in the world. He brought those seniors here, and they were exceptional. Their attitude toward work and adversity was tremendous.

Most important, we're here because of the spirit of Notre Dame. As George Connor, the great all-American, said, "Maybe there is and maybe there isn't, but when you put on a Notre Dame uniform, you feel it—and you play for it." Whether it was the Holy Spirit or the Notre Dame spirit, it was on this football team.

Football is a team sport in the true sense of the word. You take a bucket of water and fill it up to the brim. You put your hand in and pull it out—and the hole you leave in the water will be just how much you'll be missed. People come and people go—that's life. But there's one thing you cannot lose—that's a love and a belief and a faith in Notre Dame.

I loved this team, not because of the accolades they earned or the trophies they won, but because they refused to be mediocre. When John F. Kennedy was asked in 1960 if he would accept the United States nomination to be Vice-President, he said, "No. Once you accept second place when first is available, you have a tendency to do it the rest of your life."

This football team refused to be second. They refused to be discouraged. They refused to lose. They loved one another and cared about one another, and that's why they were celebrating the night of January 2.

We had certain slogans this year, like "Count on me," and "First we'll be best, then we'll be first." But the one thing we always said was, "We are N.D." Notre Dame is no average school. Notre Dame is not comprised of average people. Notre Dame wants to be outstanding in all fields of endeavor.

I had heard all the reasons it was difficult to win at Notre Dame—the high academic standards, the difficult schedule, the lack of an athletic dormitory. But Notre Dame is the easiest place in the world to win, because of the discipline and the love and the family atmosphere and the intelligence and the commitment to excellence that all carry over onto the football field.

I want to tell you one thing. God answers prayers. Believe me, God

379

answers prayers. I was at St. Aloysius, playing for the sisters of Notre Dame under my uncle Lou, who was my first coach. I was a very poor athlete.

I was an altar boy, and I prayed every single day for God to make me bigger and quicker and faster. I would have given anything to have the talent and ability that our players at Notre Dame have. I prayed every day, and I kept asking myself, "Why doesn't God answer prayers?" He did not make me a very good athlete and He did not put me at a place like Notre Dame to play football.

But God answers prayers, because He directed my life and allowed me to be in a profession where I can enjoy the thrill and the excitement of working with people on and off the football field—and not just for one or two years.

I've had the thrill that goes beyond compare. I've had the thrill of being at the University of Notre Dame. So don't tell me that God doesn't answer prayers. He has more than amply answered all those prayers that I didn't think He had. He can take me tomorrow, because He has been more than good to me.